NATURE A
IN PLATC

Plato's *Timaeus* is one of the most influential and challenging works of ancient philosophy to have come down to us. Sarah Broadie's rich and compelling study proposes new interpretations of its major elements, including the separate Demiurge, the cosmic 'beginning', the 'second mixing', the Receptacle, and the Atlantis story. Broadie shows how Plato deploys the mythic themes of the *Timaeus* to convey fundamental philosophical insights, and examines the profoundly differing methods of interpretation which have been brought to bear on the work. Her book is for everyone interested in Ancient Greek philosophy, cosmology, and mythology, whether classicists, philosophers, historians of ideas, or historians of science. It offers new findings to scholars familiar with the material, but it is also a clear and reliable resource for anyone coming to it for the first time.

SARAH BROADIE is Professor of Moral Philosophy and Wardlaw Professor at the University of St Andrews. She is the author of *Ethics with Aristotle* (1991), and (with Christopher Rowe) of *Aristotle's Nicomachean Ethics* (2002); also (as Sarah Waterlow) of *Passage and Possibility: A Study of Aristotle's Modal Concepts* (1984), and *Nature, Change, and Agency in Aristotle's Physics: A Philosophical Study* (1984).

For Ted Stahl, a dear friend of many years and many conversations — from Sarah Broadie

NATURE AND DIVINITY
IN PLATO'S *TIMAEUS*

SARAH BROADIE

CAMBRIDGE
UNIVERSITY PRESS

CAMBRIDGE
UNIVERSITY PRESS

University Printing House, Cambridge CB2 8BS, United Kingdom

Published in the United States of America by Cambridge University Press, New York

Cambridge University Press is part of the University of Cambridge.

It furthers the University's mission by disseminating knowledge in the pursuit of education, learning and research at the highest international levels of excellence.

www.cambridge.org
Information on this title: www.cambridge.org/9781107686199

© Sarah Broadie 2012

This publication is in copyright. Subject to statutory exception and to the provisions of relevant collective licensing agreements, no reproduction of any part may take place without the written permission of Cambridge University Press.

First published 2012
First paperback edition 2014

A catalogue record for this publication is available from the British Library

Library of Congress Cataloguing in Publication data
Broadie, Sarah.
Nature and divinity in Plato's Timaeus / Sarah Broadie.
p. cm.
Includes bibliographical references and index.
ISBN 978-1-107-01206-6
1. Plato. Timaeus. I. Title.
B387.B76 2012
113–dc23
2011023916

ISBN 978-1-107-01206-6 Hardback
ISBN 978-1-107-68619-9 Paperback

Cambridge University Press has no responsibility for the persistence or accuracy of URLs for external or third-party internet websites referred to in this publication, and does not guarantee that any content on such websites is, or will remain, accurate or appropriate.

To
John Waterlow, Judith Waterlow, and Richard Gray
in loving memory

Contents

Acknowledgements		*page* viii
	What lies ahead	1
1	The separateness of the Demiurge	7
2	Paradigms and epistemic possibilities	27
3	The metaphysics of the paradigm	60
4	Immortal intellect under mortal conditions	84
5	The *Timaeus–Critias* complex	115
6	The genesis of the four elements	173
7	Divine and natural causation	243
	In conclusion	278
Appendix on 'parts of the paradigm'		284
References		286
General index		293
Index locorum		296

Acknowledgements

Some of the ideas for this book took root when I was invited to give the Nellie Wallace lectures at the University of Oxford in 2003. I warmly thank the Oxford Faculty of Philosophy for the invitation and for the hospitality I enjoyed while I was there.

Several scholars have helped improve the work by their encouragement and criticism. My greatest debts are to Myles Burnyeat, Christopher Rowe, and an anonymous reader for the Press for their extensive comments on an earlier version. I am also grateful to Christopher Gill for his comments on a version of Chapter 5. These critics have forced me to address a variety of faults and inadequacies. I am conscious that many remain, and I even know what some of those are. For instance, one might reasonably wish that I had dealt more fully with the wealth of relevant scholarship. But so be it for now: this book has already more than once in the writing threatened to become a web of Penelope. I must ask readers to forgive its intricacy, complexity, and no doubt at times a certain heaviness. I have tried as best I could to simplify and lighten the arguments and presentations; but the topics of the *Timaeus–Critias* are not ones that exactly lend themselves to lightness and simplicity.

For parts of this book I have reworked material from the following publications:

- (2001) 'Theodicy and Pseudo-history in the *Timaeus*', *Oxford Studies in Ancient Philosophy* 21, 1–28 (Chapter 5)
- (2004) 'Plato's Intelligible World?', *Proceedings of the Aristotelian Society, Supplementary Volume* 78, 65–79 (Chapters 1 and 3)
- (2007) 'Why no Platonistic Ideas of Artefacts?', in *Maieusis: Essays in Ancient Philosophy in Honour of Myles Burnyeat*, ed. D. Scott, Oxford, 232–53 (Chapter 7)
- (2008) 'Theological Sidelights from Plato's *Timaeus*', *Proceedings of the Aristotelian Society, Supplementary Volume* 82, 1–17 (Chapters 1 and 4)

- (2010) 'Divine and Natural Causation in the *Timaeus*: The Case of Mortal Animals', *La Scienza e le Cause a partire dalla* Metafisica *di Aristotele*, a cura di F. Fronterotta, Bibliopolis (C. N. R., Istituto per il Lessico Intellettuale Europeo e Storia delle Idee), 73–92 (Chapter 7)
- (Forthcoming) 'Fifth-century Bugbears in the *Timaeus*', in *Presocratics and Plato: A Festschrift in Honor of Charles Kahn*, ed. A. Hermann, V. Karismanis, and R. Patterson, Las Vegas (Chapters 4 and 6)

What lies ahead

To introduce the *Timaeus* briefly, I cannot do better than quote an excellent summary by R. B. Rutherford:[1]

The *Timaeus* falls into three main parts, the first two of which are continuous. The first is an introductory exchange in which Socrates greets three friends – Timaeus, Critias and Hermocrates – and recalls how they met the previous day and considered in theoretical terms the social and economic structure of an ideal society: there are clear reminiscences of the *Republic*, but it is also obvious that much that was essential to that society is ignored. Socrates expresses the desire to see this ideal state in action, and the second part of the dialogue consists of a speech by Critias in which he declares that such a society can in fact be exemplified in early Athenian history, known from records of a forgotten age which were found by his ancestor Solon in Egypt. He whets the appetite of the company with the beginnings of his narrative, which will narrate the great war between Athens and the lost island of Atlantis; this topic, however, is deferred to the *Critias*, already anticipated as the second work of a trilogy. Today, Timaeus, represented as a Pythagorean[2] from Italian Locri, will give an exposition of something older and perhaps more magnificent – an account of the creation of the universe. Timaeus' speech occupies the third and by far the longest part of the work, and can be further subdivided into sections. In brief, it describes the shape and structure of the cosmos, narrates in 'mythical' form the deliberate designing of it and all that it contains by a divine 'demiurge' (craftsman), and proceeds to describe in some detail its motion, its elements, the stars and planets (conceived as divine), and the living creatures, above all man, which have been created to inhabit the earth, placed at its centre.[3]

And:

The main speech in the *Timaeus* embraces an extraordinary range of subject matter and style, ranging from macrocosm to microcosm, from the cosmically great to the clinically minute: an example of the former might be the passage describing Time

---

[1] For a survey of scholarly questions about the *Timaeus*, together with close summaries of each of the sections and a useful analytical table of contents, see Zeyl, 2000, xiii–xcv.
[2] I should warn that this book will not be discussing, as such, any Pythagorean aspect of Timaeus.
[3] Rutherford, 1995, 286.

I

as the likeness or mirror-image of Eternity (37c–8c), of the latter the bizarrely technical discussion of the process of taste (e.g. 65b–6c). In this speech Plato draws on many fields which were evolving their own specialised vocabularies: mathematical astronomy, medicine, music, metallurgy to name but a few.[4]

Plato through the character Timaeus presents our rich, complex, and fascinating universe as having an origin beyond itself.[5] We are to think of the physical cosmos as made by a divine incorporeal intelligence in accordance with an eternal, incorporeal, intelligible paradigm. Although the cosmos is Timaeus's focus and his object of study, we are never allowed to lose sight of what for him is the foundational fact about it, namely its trans-natural origin. Within this framework he offers an explanation not only of how the world-order came to be and what that order consists in, but also of how we humans can reasonably hope to speculate about cosmological questions. He gives an account, too, of the existential position of human beings. He shows how they are (of course) embedded in the physical world, but also how there is more to human rational selves than that. He therefore has to show how these come to be in the physical world.

It is remarkable, in fact, how minute changes in the surface texture of Timaeus's discourse shift the reader between extra- and intra-mundane perspectives on the cosmos. To see this, first consider the many passages where the enquiry is said to be about 'the All'. Timaeus at the start is identified with such an enquiry, when the character Critias profiles him as the one among them most versed in astronomy, and most dedicated to knowing about the nature of the All (*peri phuseôs tou pantos*; 27a3–5). Timaeus himself shortly afterwards describes his task as 'producing accounts [*logous*] concerning the All' (*tou pantos*; 27c4). He will use the phrase 'the All' several times in his progress through his cosmological agenda.[6] So the investigation is to be of the physical universe considered as a whole. Such an enquiry supposes a seemingly conceivable standpoint from which the whole of the natural world could be considered: thus a standpoint located nowhere in particular within the natural world, and

---

[4] Rutherford, 1995, 293. See also 294–6 for an admirably clear and succinct account of the importance of the *Timaeus* for the history of ideas.
[5] Scholars today refuse, rightly, to take it for granted that any character in any of the dialogues speaks for Plato himself; see, e.g., Cooper, 1997, xxi. This applies to Timaeus too. (Indeed Taylor, 1928, 10–11, 17–19, maintained that Timaeus, far from representing the mid-fourth-century Plato, represents a fusion of Pythagoras and Empedocles from a hundred years before. For rebuttal of Taylor, see Cornford, 1935, vi–ix.) While I agree that it makes sense to consider the possibility that Timaeus does not represent Plato, there seems to be no good reason either for holding that this is so or for remaining undecided.
[6] E.g. at 30b5; 47a3; 48b8; 53a7–b1; 90e2; 92c4.

therefore perhaps in some sense positioned beyond it. (The assumption of such an extra-mundane *standpoint* does not, of course, carry with it commitment to an extra-mundane *origin* for the natural world or anything within it: the standpoint is assumed in any enquiry into nature as a whole, whether the inquirer supposes that nature does or does not exhaust reality or has no view on the question.)

But now consider the fact that Timaeus sometimes refers to the physical realm demonstratively, as '*this* All' (28c4; 29d7; 41a5).[7] This seems perfectly natural: but does it make sense, given that referring to something as 'this so and so' often implies having picked it out from other, more distant, objects of the kind, which in principle one might have picked out instead? How could there be more than one *All*, or more than one to which *we* could refer definitely?[8] But any such logical worry is irrelevant, for Timaeus's 'this' has a different force. It calls attention to the fact that the All of which Timaeus speaks does indeed environ him and his interlocutors in the dialogue-world – and also, of course, Plato and Plato's audience and readership. The referent is not simply the natural realm, but the natural realm as (*inter alia*) habitat for us who are authors and audiences of discourses about it.

Thus even while invoking the standpoint already mentioned, the one not locatable anywhere within the world, Plato does not let the audience lose sight of their own intra-mundanity. I think that the use of 'this All' and similar locutions throughout the discourse is meant to keep us constantly in touch with two connected thoughts. One is that it is a central fact *about us* that we who are inevitably bound at any given time to a given place and a given point in our personal and cultural history, and who encounter what is beyond ourselves first and most obviously through limited sense-perception, are also capable in imagination of assuming the extra-mundane standpoint that considers nature as a whole and in abstraction from all particularities of human history. Only by assuming such a standpoint can we engage in natural philosophy, and our capacity for natural philosophy is a capacity for developing the most important part of us. The second thought is that it is a central, indeed fundamental, fact *about the one and only cosmos* that it has in it beings like us. The physical realm as such would

---

[7] Cf. 41c3; 30c8; 92c6; 8–9. 41c3 is exceptional because it occurs in the Demiurge's speech to the other gods; thus it means 'this All that I am engaged in bringing into being'.

[8] As some of the passages just listed suggest, 'this All' may be equivalent to 'this cosmos'. Up to 31a3 it is still an open question whether *this* cosmos (i.e. orderly system) is the only one. Timaeus argues for its uniqueness at 31a3–b3. At 55c7–d6 he flatly dismisses the Democritean theory that there are infinitely many, but says that it is worth considering (although he rejects it) the suggestion that there is a small definite plurality of cosmoi, namely, five.

be horribly incomplete (not that this would ever have been possible on Timaean assumptions, as we shall see) if it did not include mortal animals able to think comprehensively about the physical realm, and about the fact that this realm includes them thinking comprehensively about it and themselves together.

Throughout this book I shall both rely on and seek to elaborate the two thoughts just articulated. At its most general, the object of the enterprise is simply to sharpen understanding of the *Timaeus*. More specifically, the focus will move between the great cornerstones of Timaean cosmology: the beginning of the world-order, with the Demiurge and the eternal paradigm from which he worked; the construction of the cosmos (body and soul) as an immortal god; the construction and destiny of rational souls in mortals; the Receptacle and the pre-cosmic condition of matter. I shall also discuss the cosmology's epistemic status, its place in the whole *Timaeus–Critias* complex, and its relationship to Platonic metaphysics. One of my main contentions will be that, its metaphysical underpinnings notwithstanding, the *Timaeus* ought to be read primarily as a cosmology and not as an introduction to Platonic metaphysics. The fundamental difference between these approaches has not, I think, always been fully understood. The discussion of the eternal paradigm in Chapter 3 is intended to clarify the difference, and Chapter 6 shows how the difference affects our understanding of the Receptacle.

The aim throughout is to identify certain major philosophical concerns that shape Plato's fashioning of the Timaean system. Quite often this will involve working out the implications of his *not* having adopted some feature or assumption of the actual account. Applying this method is not a matter of portraying Plato as psychologically deliberating between unsettled options: it is a matter of making conceptual comparisons between his actual positions and alternatives not chosen. But whereas it is mostly pointless and irrelevant to try to tap into Plato's personal psychology, it is not pointless and irrelevant to bear in mind his historical time and place in trying to reconstruct the problematic that underlies one or another portion or aspect of the *Timaeus*.

This last remark has to do with the fact that in the eyes of various interpreters, ancient and modern, one or another of the well-known Timaean cornerstones sticks out as a philosophically offensive anomaly. The most notorious case is Timaeus's depiction of the proto-historical origin of this world. Another is his depiction of the divine world-making principle as wholly separate from the world and from corporeal matter. Influential interpreters over the ages have thought it desirable or necessary to chisel away at these elements, rounding them off, smoothing them down, or making them disappear by merging them with something else that is in the picture. It is thought that Plato could not have meant the supposedly anomalous motifs to be taken at face value: he places them in the account only for the sake of presentation, not as part of what is being seriously presented. The present study will argue *per contra* that both the proto-historical beginning and the separate Demiurge are essential to the content of the account: no less so than undisputed king-pins like the cosmic soul and the Receptacle. In each case the argument will be that subtracting the allegedly awkward element endangers the whole system. The separateness of the divine world-maker is, I shall argue, bound up with Plato's need to forge for cosmology a conception of the human person that breaks with certain implications of some of the fifth-century cosmologies. The proto-historical beginning is necessary, I shall argue, for realising a vision of the universe as both the product of a transcendent divine origin and a genuinely natural domain working in accordance with its own processes and mechanisms. There may in principle be another way to avoid sacrificing this vision, but (so I shall contend) this other way, even if genuinely viable, was not imaginably available to even the greatest mind of Plato's time.

The *Timaeus* has been many things to many thinkers over the centuries: there has been the *Timaeus* of Plotinus and that of Proclus, and so on for many others. And with respect to its more metaphysical, less empirical, aspects, philosophers down the ages have mined the *Timaeus* for perennial truth as if the source of the dialogue were an intellect beyond history – rather than an Athenian individual who lived from 428/7 to 348/7 BCE. This book is intended to be about the *Timaeus* composed by that individual philosopher.[9] Thus 'Plato's' in my title is not superfluous, although the intention behind it may of course be over-ambitious.

In what lies ahead no conclusions have been allowed to hinge on potential evidence from dialogues other than the *Timaeus–Critias*.[10] This is partly because adequate evaluation of any such evidence would have led me beyond a reasonable limit. It also seemed no bad project in itself to see how far one can get examining the *Timaeus–Critias* solely from within, so to speak. Thus I have not attempted to establish any features of the Timaean account by inference from trends of Plato's thought appearing in other dialogues or other late dialogues. Such inferences require decisions on

---

[9] This point will also be relevant to the interpretations of Critias's story: see Chapter 5.
[10] I have, however, occasionally pointed to passages in other dialogues for the sake of comparison, usually contrastive, with features of the *Timaeus–Critias* that can be verified independently.

difficult and often indeed scarcely decidable questions such as whether a given pattern or habit of thought is in fact discernible elsewhere to the exclusion of contrary patterns, or whether some pattern found in one dialogue can be assumed to carry over to another. So, for example, the question of the separateness or not of the Timaean world-making intelligence will not be allowed to depend on parallels either way in the *Phaedrus*, *Phaedo*, *Philebus*, *Statesman*, or *Laws*, but will be discussed entirely with reference to implications for the Timaean account.

CHAPTER I

The separateness of the Demiurge

I.I WORLD-MAKING: MATERIALS, USER, AND PRODUCT

In this opening chapter I want to look at how Plato puts in place one of the metaphysical elements behind the cosmology. In a very deliberate way he gets the reader of the *Timaeus* to see our natural world, this orderly cosmos,[1] as distinct and metaphysically *separate* from its origin. I shall particularly focus on the separateness, in Plato's presentation, of the world-making god from the cosmos he constructs.[2]

Some have thought that this separateness is one of those aspects of the account that Plato would not (or could not) have meant philosophical readers to take seriously – or, as is often said, 'literally'.[3] This is the inference of interpreters who, for one or another reason, begin by assuming that the rational view for Plato to have held would be one on which the divine world-making principle is not separate. The same conclusion would be drawn if the image of a separate Demiurge were simply to strike one as too childish to be meant seriously by a great philosopher. My approach, however, takes the opposite course. It starts by accepting at face value the account Plato has given, and then attempts to understand why he wanted a Demiurge separate from the world.

---

[1] Throughout this book I use 'world' and 'cosmos' so as to imply a single physical order or system. Thus the as yet disorderly materials in their pre-cosmic state do not constitute a *world* in this sense. Again in this sense, it is a logically open question whether all that is physically actual makes up a world. I use 'physical universe' and 'physical realm' to denote all that is physically actual. Not bare analysis of the word '*kosmos*' but considerations of perfection lead Timaeus to the conclusion that *this* cosmos contains the totality of the corporeal materials, and therefore is the unique cosmos, not one of many as the atomists held (32c5–33b1; cf. 31a2–b3).

[2] The other element 'separate' from the world is, of course, the intelligible cosmic paradigm, which I discuss in Chapters 2 and 3. I shall have little to say on whether the paradigm is or is not separate from the Demiurge.

[3] E.g. Archer-Hind, 1888, 38–40; Cornford, 1935, 38; 197. Carone, 2005, ch. 2, has a vigorous and thoughtful defence of the view. For some arguments to the contrary, see Robinson, 1993.

The separateness of the Demiurge

As we have seen, Timaeus refers to his mighty subject as 'the All' and 'this All'. These designations prepare us for the thought that if the order of nature around us is to be accounted for at all, it must be accounted for as a whole. That it cannot be accounted for at all is an option which Plato in the *Timaeus* never considers. Another possibility, that it is self-explanatory and self-supporting, he vigorously dismisses. He maintains that whatever can be perceived by sight and touch, including in this category even this entire cosmos,[4] is not ultimate; strictly, objects of sense cannot be said to be but at most to have become, or to occur in a condition of becoming; but that entails that they have been caused (28b6–c3). Thus we begin to be led towards the doctrine of a trans-natural origin for the world.

The lead comes from the platitudinous principle that a cause is prior to and different from the things which it is invoked to explain, together with the assumption that what has to be explained is the entire order of nature in which we live. Still, something more than these premises is needed to bring us to the high Platonic metaphysics (as traditionally understood) according to which the cause of the world is separate or absolutely incorporeal. Something is needed to fend off the suggestion that the present order of nature originated by evolving out of a primitive, formless, ancestral condition that differed from what we have today by being, for example, hazy and indeterminate, or by being massed together without arrangement at any level of largeness or smallness, or by consisting of a vast indiscriminate scatter of minute things. The task of cosmology is to explain the order of nature; but an original state of things along one of the lines just sketched is sufficiently different in character from the *explanandum* to satisfy the platitudinous principle. Hence, for all that has been said, such an original state of things may have been the source from which the cosmos arose.

Plato blocks off this entire direction of explanation by setting aside the possibility that any such primitive materials or matter-like things could by themselves have evolved into the order that exists today. He does this by displaying how, at the beginning of things, 'everything that was visible' was in disorderly motion until the Demiurge 'took it over [*paralabôn*] and led it from disorder to order' (30a2–6; cf. 68e3). In other words, left to themselves the visibles would have continued moving without rhyme or reason. Their change into an ordered condition depended on the formative

---

[4] Plato need not be accused here of the fallacy of inferring from parts to the whole. Arguably, it is built into the notions of seeing and touching that we see/touch by seeing/touching a proper part of the object; this is reflected in the fact that the grammatical objects of the Greek *aisthanesthai* ('perceive') and *haptesthai* ('touch') are in the genitive.

1.1 World-making: materials, user, and product

intervention of a principle of a completely different type, namely divine Intelligence.[5]

This doctrine rests on Plato's fundamental tenet that this cosmos is as good, beautiful, and orderly as any empirical entity could be. The tenet is not the conclusion of an argument: it is something the denial of which divine law (*themis*) forbids us even to express (29a4). (Thus Plato could not attempt to establish it by a *reductio* proof.) Clearly this axiom is, to put it mildly, a necessary truth. Consequently, the cause that brought this cosmos into being must be of a sort that could from the beginning have been *reliably* counted upon to produce what is as good and beautiful as possible. No matter what the circumstances of the cause and its causative activity – vary these mentally as you wish – the cause will track whatever is the best and most beautiful effect.[6] Thus the cause must be such as to produce what is good and beautiful for its own sake: not as an accidental by-product, nor as a means to some quite different kind of purpose that conceivably could have been reached by-passing the beautiful and good.

It is, of course, an additional assumption that the corporeal materials of the cosmos – whether they are thought of as still present and constituting it, or as superseded because of having turned into it – were not themselves invested with world-making intelligence. On Timaeus's account, they cannot begin to be relied on by themselves to come up with a supremely good and beautiful universe, or on their own to behave as if they appreciated the value of such an entity by producing it for its own sake. For instance, at 46d4 he says that since they are inanimate, they are incapable of reason and intelligence.

Thus the scheme assumes and conveys a stark contrast and separation between the intelligent formative cause and the materials. It thereby conveys an equally stark contrast and separation between the empirical cosmos, and the formative cause. For we have three functionally related factors: *cause*, *product*, and *materials*, the cause being maker of the product and user of the materials. Notice how the presence in this picture of *materials used by a separate user* safeguards the separateness of maker and product. For suppose the cause were not a user of separate materials, but instead gave rise to the product by itself or from itself or immediately. In that case it would be natural and reasonable to say one of two things: either the cause-entity *has evolved into* what we were calling the product, so that in fact there is a single

---

[5] On whether to take this proto-historical change literally, see Ch. 7; also the preliminary discussion in this chapter, section 1.3.
[6] Cf. Johansen, 2004, 69–79, on the themes of this and the next paragraph.

continuous entity of which these two are successive stages; or the cause-entity *constitutes* the product. Thus in one of two ways there is a relation between cause and product that approximates identity, in the case where the cause is such as to cause without using separate materials. By contrast, when the cause is such as uses separate materials from which to make the product, the presence of those materials in the product establishes the product too as plainly separate from the cause. The matter which the cause 'takes over' and uses has the attribute of *being sharply distinct from the cause*; and this attribute of the matter (unlike the primal unorderedness) is inherited by the product.[7]

We should consider this picture in relation to the Greek philosophical background. In that culture it was possible to speculate – people had speculated – that the present natural order is due to one or another intelligent material principle that has evolved into it or that constitutes it.[8] Now, if in this same culture there also arises (for whatever reason) a very different kind of theory, one that sees the natural order as separate from its cause, this would still have something important in common with the types of theory just sketched. For the idea of the material principle is essential to the new sort of theory too. But now it becomes the idea of matter *used* by something distinct. And so the new theory is inevitably triadic, since as well as (A) the using cause and (B) the result or product, there must also be (C) the matter used. Given that C turns into B, the separateness of A from C ensures the separateness of A from B. And: given that C turns into B, the separateness of A from C is, I think, also necessary for the separateness of A from B. Make A the cause identical with the matter C, or make A an aspect of C, and it will be impossible not to see B as a continuation of or as consisting of AC, hence as not separate from AC and A.

But let us now contrast this triadic picture of *user*, *used*, and *product*, with a very different conception of the divine origination of the world: the idea of creation *ex nihilo*, which has its roots in the two creation-stories in the book of Genesis.[9] Creation *ex nihilo* involves just two things, the world and its divine creator. It is worth asking: what is it about this conception that makes coherently thinkable its simple dyadic contrast between creator and world? Here the creator *both* radically differs from the world and anything worldly *and* produces a world without mediation of matter sharply distinct from

---

[7] This paragraph does not, of course, pretend to sketch a complete taxonomy of ancient Greek cosmogonic schemata.
[8] E.g. Heraclitus and Diogenes of Apollonia (constitution); Empedocles (evolution).
[9] Genesis chs. 1–2.

himself. Whether or not we believe in such a creator, we are thoroughly used to the idea. Through familiarity, its combination of features – the radical difference of world and creator, and the absence of a distinct matter used – can seem metaphysically quite unsurprising. Isn't it obvious that an agent who creates *ex nihilo* is utterly unlike the world or anything worldly – and utterly unlike them precisely *because* he creates *ex nihilo*? Well, what is obvious is that well-worn intuitions shaped by the Abrahamic theological tradition leave us without need to posit for the creator a distinct material whose use by him marks his distinctness from the world he makes. The picture is not one that has to include a distinct *matter used* in order to block off any suggestion of the world's being all but identical with the divine principle – either as its continuation in a later stage, or as constituted from it. But how can that be, if, as I have argued, in Plato's model the separateness of God[10] and the world crucially depends on its *not* being the case that God gives rise to the world *ex nihilo*? What exactly is it that enables creation-theology in the Abrahamic tradition to present a complete dyadic account involving only the world and a god who is radically distinct? In the light of Plato's account, we should, in my view, regard it as genuinely puzzling that Abrahamic theology manages to assert simultaneously (1) that God and world are radically distinct, and (2) that God gives rise to the world *ex nihilo*. For from the perspective of our analysis of the Platonic account, proposition (2) no longer appears as a support or explanation for proposition (1). On the contrary: from that perspective, proposition (2) seems to destabilise proposition (1). For from that perspective proposition (2) seems to move the mind towards the thought that God gave rise to the world by becoming it, and then – if the latter seems monstrous – towards the yet more radical thought that God is identical with the world, which therefore shares God's eternity. In this way there opens up room for wondering how the Abrahamic tradition can *afford* proposition (2) given that it is committed to proposition (1).

The answer, I think, lies in the fact that Abrahamic theism assumes not only that God, the cause of the world, is holy and to be worshipped, but also that the world is *not* holy and to be worshipped, but is a place, rather, of worship*ers*. The world was created to be *pro-fane* in the etymological sense, i.e. it exists outside the space of the divine. This contrast is strong enough by itself to support a sense of the radical distinctness of God and world. (In itself, in my view, this basic contrast would remain in place whether we suppose that the god of this contrast created using distinct matter or that he

---

[10] Throughout, the initial letter is in upper case if the word is being used as a proper name.

created *ex nihilo*. Neither supposition either strengthens or weakens the contrast between the divine and the pro-fane as such, even though in developed Abrahamic theology total creative self-sufficiency is a criterion for what is to count as divine.)

So the Abrahamic perspective takes it for granted that whereas the cause of the world is divine and holy, the world itself, however truly seen by its creator to be 'very good' (Genesis 1:31), is not a holy being nor a divine one. It is this that establishes the utter distinctness of cause and product in terms just of the two of them, without interposition of the barrier concept of *matter used*. In this way the Abrahamic perspective can afford *creatio ex nihilo*. The possibilities we saw in the Greek context for cause–product assimilation if *matter used* is absent from the account, are automatically eliminated when holiness separates cause from product. For it is surely essential to holiness that what is holy cannot of itself evolve into what is not holy, or freely function as stuff or matter of what is not holy. Within the world, after all, except under the constraint of some kind of emergency, it is desecration knowingly to use some holy object as material for a secular object. It follows that for a holy being to turn itself into one that was not holy would be self-desecration, and hence impossible.

1.2 THE COSMIC GOD

In the last section I compared Plato's triadic account of the coming to be of the world with two kinds of dyadic account. The first comparison was with earlier Greek theories in which a primal material principle evolves into or constitutes the world. The second comparison was with the Abrahamic schema that recognises only a transcendent incorporeal principle and a corporeal world. Plato's account resembles those earlier Greek theories in making corporeal matter a *principle* of this finished cosmos. It resembles the Abrahamic schema in maintaining a sharp distinction between the cosmos and its divine maker. I argued that for Plato this distinctness depends on the prior distinctness of the world-maker from the material principle in its pre-cosmic condition. I then suggested that in the Abrahamic schema what upholds the distinctness of world and maker is that the maker is divine and holy, while the world is not.

We now have to face what from the Abrahamic point of view is the most outlandish tenet of Plato's account: the divinity of the cosmos itself. Yes: for Plato in the *Timaeus*, the empirical, corporeal, cosmos, exists in the domain of sense-perceptible becoming as distinct from intelligible being (27d5–28a6; b2–c2), and is a made thing framed as a 'likeness' of an eternal paradigm (28c5–29a5; cf. 28a6–b2); and yet it is literally itself a god (34a8; b8–9; 92a5–9). It shares this appellation not only with various other created deities dwelling or functioning within it, but also with the god who made it from matter. For Timaeus argues that since this cosmos is supremely excellent, it must have intelligence (*nous*), and therefore it must have soul[11] – it must be a perfect living creature living a perfect life. This means that although, of course, it has a body – a perfect body – the cosmos is immortal and completely independent of any physical environment. It is because of this combination of attributes, beginning from intelligence, that the cosmos has the status of a god.

We should take careful note of this divinity when we consider the world-maker's famous motive for carrying out his work:

He was good, and in the good there never occurs any grudgingness [*phthonos*] about anything whatsoever. Being devoid of this motive, he formed the desire that everything should become as close in nature to himself as possible. (29e1–3)

The Demiurge desired not merely the out-flowing of his goodness through creation of good beings other than himself – a desire often attributed to the god of the Abrahamic tradition[12] – but his total ungrudgingness took him so far as to bring into being yet another *god*, and a universal one at that.[13] In fact, it is this cosmic god rather than the Demiurge that figures as an object of worship in the text. Timaeus concludes the cosmology in hymnic language:

This cosmos, visible living being containing <whatever is> visible, sense-perceptible god that images the intelligible – greatest and best, fairest and most perfect, this cosmic system [*ouranos*] has come to be, one and unique of its kind. (92c6–9)

---

[11] This inference from having intelligence to having soul (30b1–5; cf. 46d4–7) has given rise to much debate. The Demiurge is obviously an intelligent principle; but the *Timaeus* seems to imply (a) that all souls are produced by divine demiurgy. It might also be taken to imply (b) that soul is necessarily immanent in a formed body (cf. 30b4–5; also 42b3–5, where even purified human rational souls retain a link to the corporeal by rejoining their respective stars). But every formed body is the work of divine demiurgy, and the Demiurge is causally prior to all his works; hence (a) together with (b) entails that he is without soul. Does that contradict the inference from having intelligence to having soul? Menn, 1995, 10–24, has argued, in my view convincingly, that the inference applies only to what *has* intelligence, whereas the Demiurge by contrast *is* the world-making intelligence. See also Hackforth, 1936, and Mohr, 2005, 189–95. For some arguments to the contrary, see Carone, 2005, 42–6.
[12] Cf. Taylor, 1928, 78, *ad* 29e1–2, quoting from Dante's *Paradiso*, on which Cornford, 1935, 34, comments: 'The reader must be warned against importations from later theology.'
[13] Cf. Baltzly, 2010, 201; citing the 'ungrudgingness' motif, he challenges the orthodox theist to answer the question 'Why do *you* suppose that [the] creator [god] creates a world that is *not* itself a god?' without falling into *petitio principii* about the uncreated status of gods.

Timaeus then specifically prays to the cosmic god (*Critias* 106a1–b6). By contrast, neither here nor anywhere else does Timaeus single out the world-maker to address in prayer.[14]

Timaeus's concluding prayer is for the parts of the cosmological account that make sense to be preserved, and for any other parts to be forgiven and corrected. It is the cosmic god to whom Timaeus prays because it is *his* nature that Timaeus has attempted to spell out (even though it is the maker-god's achievement).[15] And even more telling, perhaps, is what Timaeus says at the end of the cosmology about care of the soul. We must feed and strengthen our rational element in order to win happiness, and we win happiness to the extent to which that element of ours grows to be like the divine. But the divinity whose likeness we are to seek to realise in ourselves is not the maker of the universe: it is the created cosmic god. Our own reason is akin to the cosmic soul, and the *latter's* intelligent activity, evinced in the regular motions of the heavens, is the model to which human reason should aim to approximate. The path towards this salvation consists not in focusing our meditation on the maker of the world, but in contemplating the harmonies and revolutions of the stars visually and through astronomical study. *This* contemplation is what brings our own kindred intellectual activity more into line with its proper exemplar (90a2–d7; 46e7–47c4).[16] Thus in a way the cosmos itself is put forward as principal god in the *Timaeus*, or at any rate as principal god for us. This is so not because the cosmos is presented as somehow also identical with the higher principle that made the cosmos (for this is not at all how it is presented), but because it is proposed as our pre-eminent object of worship and religious contemplation.[17,18]

---

[14] At 27c6–d1 Timaeus invokes 'gods and goddesses' for help. At 48d4–e1 he invokes an unspecified god as saviour. Cornford, 1935, 35: 'Neither in the *Timaeus* nor anywhere else is it suggested that the Demiurge should be an object of worship: he is not a religious figure.'

[15] See also *Timaeus* 28b2–4: 'Now as to the whole heaven (*ouranos*) – let that be our name for it, or "cosmos", or whatever other name is most acceptable to it . . .'. Taylor, 1928, 66: 'it is a point of ritual piety to call a god by the name "acceptable to him"'. Taylor quotes Aeschylus, *Agamemnon* 160–2: *Zeus, hostis pot'estin, ei tod' au|tô(i) philon keklemenô(i),|touto nin prosennepô* ('Zeus, whoever he is, if he is pleased to be called by this <name> then by this name I address him'), and Plato, *Philebus* 12c1.

[16] See Sedley's examination (1999) of *homoiôsis theô(i)* in Plato, with some discussion also of Aristotle. Carone, 2005, ch. 3, especially sections 1.2 and III, has an excellent discussion of the *Timaeus* material. Carone, 1997, 344, refers to the religious function of astronomy in the *Timaeus*.

[17] However, the cosmos enjoys this status only because it is the perfect product of a supremely wise and good maker, and we, its worshippers, must understand this fact about it, since on this rests our assumption that the cosmos is indeed divine. Nevertheless, Timaeus's speech is primarily a hymn to the creation not the creator (*pace* Rutherford, 1995, 286).

[18] It is interesting to chart variations on the linked themes of assimilation to God and divine freedom from *phthonos* in the *Timaeus*, the *Epinomis* of Philip of Opus, and Aristotle, *Metaphysics* 1.2. At *Timaeus* 29e1–3, the Demiurge makes the cosmos because he ungrudgingly 'wanted everything to

1.2 The cosmic god

No doubt Plato, like Parmenides and others before him, and Aristotle and others after him, would have regarded it as inconceivable that anything should come or be brought into being from absolutely nothing at all. To this familiar consideration the argument of the previous section enables us to add a conjecture less familiar: perhaps Plato in particular had to insist on the pre-cosmic reality not only of a divine world-maker but also of materials sharply distinct from him – a distinctness, as we saw, passed on to the product – precisely *because* Plato's world is a divine and holy being whose distinctness from the intelligence that accounts for it could not otherwise be upheld!

All this may leave us scratching our heads. For we must by now be wondering why it should be so important for Plato, if indeed he really means it, to maintain a divine world-making principle that is wholly other than the cosmos itself. It looks easy to make sense of this as long as we think of the Demiurge more or less on the model of the god of the Bible (except that the former but not the latter does his making from something already there) and, as part of that picture, think of the cosmos as not a god. But once it is allowed that the cosmos itself is divine and imbued with its own divine intelligence, why should this not suffice to explain the order of the world? Why attribute world-making to *another* divine intelligence, that of the separate Demiurge? In the account in the text, the separate Demiurge is shown making the cosmic god: he makes its body and he also (indeed first, we are told) makes its intellectual soul (31b4–34b3; 34b3–36d7). But why does Plato not simply posit that very soul as the ultimate world-making principle? After all, in the story as Plato tells it, the cosmos once made lives its own life of intellection and circular movement (36e3–5). It lives from itself, and so from then on it is the source of its own existence (even though we are told that the Demiurge could dissolve it if, *per impossibile*, he wanted

---

become as much like himself as possible' (this may be taken as evidence that the intelligible paradigm is 'in' the demiurgic intelligence). In a remarkable passage, *Epinomis* 988a5–b7, Philip transfers the lack of *phthonos* to the *ouranos*, the astronomical god, and *we* are now the beneficiaries. The *ouranos* knows that we learn and improve through studying it; it would therefore be seriously lacking in self-knowledge if it did not know itself to be our teacher; hence it must rejoice ungrudgingly when through it we improve! Philip is not explicit about our becoming more like the *ouranos*, but the idea may be implied in the teacher-pupil conceit: in Aristotle, *teacher–pupil* is a standard illustration of *agent–patient*, and the agent acts by 'conferring the form' (*Physics* III, 202a32 and b2–3, with 202a9–12; *On Generation and Corruption* 1.7). At *Metaphysics* 1, 982b32–983b10, Aristotle declares that since divine *phthonos* is impossible, we have no reason not to aspire to *sophia* even though *sophia* is the most divine sort of cognition because (a) it is the sort that God would have, and (b) it is the study of first causes (982b9–10), and God is a first cause. Here for the first time, it seems, the god which humans may seek to emulate is explicitly a first cause. The same picture is suggested by *Metaphysics* XII, 1072b13–26. On the human relevance of 'God is without *phthonos*', see also *Nicomachean Ethics* X, 1177b31–4; cf. 1178b7–32 and 1179a22–30.

16   *The separateness of the Demiurge*

to; 41a7–b6). So surely in a way it is the very nature of the cosmic soul to function as 'world-maker'.

The separate Demiurge seems to be redundant. So why does Plato posit this figure? Or is it something that we are not meant to take seriously? Is the supposedly separate Demiurge not really separate after all – is he nothing other than the cosmic soul presented in a certain way?[19]

1.3 AN IMMANENT DEMIURGE?

The worry that a separate Demiurge would be a redundant principle stems from the desire for theoretical economy. So let us begin by considering whether Plato could have adopted a much more obviously economical account. I shall briefly consider a materialistic picture in which the corporeal elements of Plato's world are themselves alive, and intelligent in the way expected of the cosmic soul of a cosmos as perfect as possible. Could Plato have reasonably chosen such a picture for his cosmology, instead of his actual picture in which the corporeal elements are inanimate?

Surely not, if an immanent intelligence is supposed to arise as an emergent property from some kind of physical order amongst the elements or portions of them.[20] For Plato, I think, would see the existence of that very order as itself the work of intelligence; and an intelligent principle that produces this order, whether by mixing the elements in proportions or in some other way, cannot be the same as the intelligence that results.

Let us then assume an intelligence that is somehow grounded in the corporeal elements, but not in a way that presupposes any prior order in them. Then this intelligence may be cast as responsible for all the ordering from the beginning. But there is a major cosmological difficulty. It is the nature of the corporeal elements to be here and there in space, and repetitively so. Different portions of each are together in different places. Even if intelligence is immanent in them, nothing in this situation can guarantee the existence of a single cosmic intelligence having the totality of the elements within its charge. There could be as indefinitely many intelligences as there were local collocations of the elements, and each could be a source of order to some extent. But the perfection of Plato's universe requires a single source of cosmic order. This is because the perfect cosmos must include all corporeal matter within it. If there were other cosmoi besides this one, or if there were matter outside this cosmos, there could be

---

[19] On the supposed redundancy, see Archer-Hind, 1888, 38–9; Carone, 2005, 49.
[20] Cf. the *harmonia* model of soul, *Phaedo* 85e3 ff.

collisions. Our cosmos could be damaged; the activity of its intellect could be thrown off course (as easily happens to our intellects when our bodies are acted on by external bodies, 43b6–c5); it could be shaken apart. A blessedly active immortal cosmos must be physically unique (32c5–33b1; 34b2; 5–8). Therefore it must also be psychically unique, with all its corporeal matter subject to a single soul. The materials alone could not possibly guarantee this uniqueness and total control.[21]

Let us then move to a different model, one in which corporeal materials are not the source or basis of the cosmic soul, but in which a single all-embracing cosmic soul is the source of order throughout the totality of the materials. The cosmic soul forms these to be the body of the cosmic god, and maintains them in that formation, one that is suitable to its own continued function as animator of this body. Although the cosmic soul is not dependent on the materials in the sense of arising somehow from them, it is wholly immanent in the cosmic body, if only because the animating and ordering functions attributed to it all make reference to the body. According to such a picture, either the cosmic soul has itself been constructed by some different principle – the separate Demiurge of the actual Timaean presentation – or not. In the spirit of economy, let us try the second alternative.

On this alternative, nothing in the cosmos is prior to the cosmic soul. We can suppose that this intelligent soul, like the separate Demiurge of the actual story, is guided by an eternal intelligible paradigm in carrying out its function,[22] and that it disposes everything in the realm of becoming to be as excellent as possible. Thus this picture safeguards certain essentials of the actual Timaean account. But are the divergences unimportant?

Let us approach this question by examining one apparently rather striking divergence; we may then be able to see whether it is important. The difference I have in mind is this. In the story in the text the cosmic soul and the separate Demiurge are not merely distinct beings: they are different types of cause. In the story in the text the cosmic soul has the one function of animating the cosmos. Because of its soul the cosmos – the cosmic animal – engages in intellectual activity expressed in the visible circulations of the heavenly bodies. These visible movements manifest the invisible

---

[21] This problem arises for any theory that sanctions a plurality of cosmoi, e.g. the cosmology of Anaxagoras on Sedley's interpretation (Sedley, 2007, 8–26). Plato may have seen the famous 'unmixedness' of Anaxagoras's Intelligence as providing the solution of the problem (which may have passed unnoticed by Anaxagoras). If Intelligence is 'mixed with no thing, but it alone is by itself' (B12, Sedley's translation in Sedley, 2007, 11), it can be a unique centre of control over everything besides itself. See also Menn, 1995, 28, on the unity of action of cosmic Intelligence.

[22] Cf. Carone, 2005, 46–51.

intellectual rotations of the cosmic soul in the circle of the Same and the divided circle of the Different. These twin systems of intellectual activity are engaged in by the same one soul, composed of the same incorporeal ingredients mixed in the same way, marked out in the same series of proportions. The mixture constitutes a sort of psychic whole cloth which the Demiurge (in the textual story) divides into the complementary circles of Same and Different within which is contained the cosmic body (34b10 ff.). Notwithstanding this complexity, the cosmic soul is plainly a single principle responsible for the life of the single, though complex, cosmic animal. This soul stands to the cosmic body in what is necessarily a one–one relation: the relation of *animating*. The effect of this soul is necessarily single: it is the living activity worked out through this one cosmic body. By contrast, the separate Demiurge in Timaeus's account is a source of many effects. The Demiurge produces the cosmic soul and the cosmic body; he creates the visible celestial gods in vast numbers; along with them he creates demiurgic gods to whom he assigns the task of fashioning the bodies of mortal animals, while he himself has created the rational souls of these animals. The ancillary demiurges are, as it were, extensions of him, and it is clear that their creations are plural. Their first creation is the human being, which necessarily makes its way in families and societies (cf. 87a7–b6). And these families and societies are made up of individual rational animals living their own lives. Thus in the story presented by the text, the cosmic soul is a one–one cause, the Demiurge a one–many cause. A cause of the one–many type is 'separate' from any given one of its effects because it is the actual or possible cause of different effects, either in addition to or instead of some given actual effect.[23]

This difference between the cosmic soul and the Demiurge shows up in Plato's language when it is explained that the Demiurge would not have made other cosmoi in addition to this one (30c2–31b3). This cosmos must have been made in the closest possible accordance with a fully comprehensive intelligible paradigm, for else this cosmos would not be superlatively excellent. Such a paradigm 'contains all the intelligible living beings within itself' (30c7–8), i.e. it includes intelligible paradigms for every sort of living being. This comprehensiveness of the paradigm entails its uniqueness.[24] Consequently, this cosmos has been fashioned so as to contain all the

---

[23] The most obvious example of one–many causality in Plato is that of a Form in relation to the particulars called after it. The one–many causality of the Demiurge is also indicated when he is called 'father': 28c3–4; 37c7; 41a7. The cosmic soul is never called 'father' of anything. Note that Plato never suggests that the same soul could (at the same time) control several distinct bodies.

[24] On the details see Chapter 3, n. 19.

1.3 An immanent Demiurge?

other kinds of perceptible animals, and so as to be unique.[25] Plato has Timaeus say:

> So in order that this <cosmos> should be like the all-perfect Living Being [i.e. the paradigm] in uniqueness, the maker made neither two cosmoi nor an indefinite number: instead, this heaven, alone of its kind that has come to be, is and will be one. (31a8–b3)

It would be absurd to state that the soul of this cosmos took care to form just this cosmic body so that there would be only one cosmos, instead of also forming other bodies as well so that there would be two or indefinitely many such systems, as if these were coherent options – even if ones that a wise and good agent would be bound to reject. The soul of this cosmos is so immediately related to this cosmos and this cosmic body – it animates the latter – that it makes no sense to consider whether it might also be related in this way to others.

However, this shows only what we already know in a general way: that Plato speaks as if there is a Demiurge over and above the cosmic soul. The crucial question is whether we lose anything important by discarding the separate Demiurge (and the language that goes with it) as no more than a presentational tactic. Let us see how we fare if we assume that the cosmic soul alone is responsible for the perfection of the cosmos.

The cosmos would have been incomplete without mortal rational animals (39e7 ff.; 41b7–c2). They are constituted from immortal rational souls created (in the actual story) by the Demiurge; on to them are joined mortal bodies fashioned by the demiurgic ancillaries. It is clearly very important to the *Timaeus* that these rational mortals are morally independent individuals, themselves responsible for their choices and their choices' moral effects on the soul.[26] In this Plato stands by the doctrine of the myth of Er (42d2–e4; cf. *Republic* x, 617d6–e5). But it is also important to him that the rational souls of mortals are closely akin to the cosmic soul. This kinship is bound up with the Timaean theory that the rational soul in us is helped to function as it should by our study of the celestial revolutions. This study, which begins with visual observation, brings the rational soul in us into closer synch with the soul of the world, disengaging it from the disturbances that come from

---

[25] The argument assumes that the Demiurge would not make numerically different cosmoi of the same comprehensive kind. In fact, this is not excluded until 32c6–33b1, where we are told that the Demiurge made this cosmos out of all the fire, water, earth, and air that existed, so that it would be fully complete and unique, and because any materials left outside might attack it with disease, ageing, and dissolution.

[26] The point is emphasised by Carone (2005), 60.

implantation in a mortal body subject to biological needs and impacts from the environment (46e6–47c4; 90a2–d7). The *Timaeus* story combines our cosmic kinship with our distinct moral autonomy by showing the separate Demiurge fashioning a vast number of individual rational souls from a version of the same kind of incorporeal material that he previously used for making the cosmic soul. This material (the result of the Demiurge's 'later mixing', 41d4–7) is *another* version of the same kind; it is not numerically the same material, nor any part of it. A theory that eliminated the separate Demiurge separately constructing the plurality of rational souls of humans would not be well-placed to proclaim our kinship with the cosmic soul while at the same time proclaiming our autonomy as individuals.

Let me explain this last remark by raising a question. If there is no separate Demiurge, and if the cosmic soul's function is to animate body, how is the resulting account to be presented in a way that clearly and firmly rules out the possibility that *our* bodies are animated by the cosmic soul, and *our* rational minds are localised expressions of it? It is not as if Plato could take it for granted that a cosmologically interested audience of his time would be free of any cultural predisposition to entertain a pantheism in which an intelligent world soul governs absolutely everything.[27] Had Plato been in a position to take that for granted in his audience, he could perhaps have written for Timaeus a speech that simply featured the great world-at-large-animating soul but carried no explicit message ring-fencing the individuality of *our* rational selves. And that might possibly have been a speech that featured no separate Demiurge. Plato, however, was in no such position. In the actual world in which the *Timaeus–Critias* was written and first presented, the following sort of view was in the background:

> And in my opinion, that which possesses intelligence is what people call 'air', and all humans are governed by it and it rules all things. For in my opinion this very thing is God, and it reaches everything and arranges all things and is in everything. (Diogenes of Apollonia, B5, tr. McKirahan)[28]

---

[27] As might indeed have been the case for an audience brought up in an Abrahamic religion.
[28] It is true that there was an interval of seventy years or more between the time when Diogenes is supposed to have been active and the time when Plato probably composed the *Timaeus–Critias*. But during this period nothing much happened in cosmology that could have created in the *Timaeus–Critias* audience a tacit but definite understanding that a divine cosmic soul need not, and had better not, be an all-governing pantheistic soul. The atheistic atomism of Leucippus and Democritus was not a forum in which clarification of this issue could even have got off the ground. Xenophon (*Memorabilia* 1. 4. 8) attributes to Socrates an argument to the effect that the mind of each human individual is, in David Sedley's words, a 'tiny fragment' of the mind responsible for the large-scale order of the universe (Sedley 2007, 218). This passage and its context show no trace of philosophical concern with possible negative implications for our distinct autonomy. (See Chapter 4, section 4.4,

1.3 An immanent Demiurge?

With such a view in the offing, a Timaean speech without the separate Demiurge would have left the gates of Timaean cosmology open to an all-controlling pantheism.[29]

How exactly does that follow? Well, according to Timaeus, (1) the immortal rational souls of mortals are not absolutely original existences: they were brought into being by a god. (2) They are a genuine plurality of distinct individualised entities, and therefore (3) bringing them to be was the bringing to be of such a plurality. (4) These souls, although destined for mortal bodies, are each of kindred nature to the cosmic soul whose body is immortal. (5) That which brought the rational souls of mortals into being is, given that fact about it, a one–many cause (from 3); but (6) the cosmic soul is not that kind of cause. Hence (7) the god that brought our rational souls into being is other than the cosmic soul (from 5 and 6). Now, (8) the affinity between the cosmic soul and reason in mortals must have an explanation. The explanation cannot be that the cosmic soul *made*, i.e. fashioned, crafted, the individualised rational principles in mortals (this would contradict 6). Nor can it be that these principles are portions of the cosmic soul (this would contradict 2). Hence the explanation of the affinity must be that (9) our rational souls and the cosmic one have the same source or cause. Therefore (10) the cause of the cosmic soul is a god other than the cosmic soul itself (by 7).[30]

In sum, the figure of the separate Demiurge does important philosophical work. Take it away, and one or another substantial piece of the system has to be denied.

I shall return to the topic of the distinct rational souls of mortals in Chapter 4. Meanwhile, let us go back to the contrast between the one–many causality of the separate Demiurge and the one–one causality of the cosmic soul. Would it make sense for the sake of theoretical economy to combine these two types of causality in one being? (To do so would subvert the argument just given, for it would permit the denial of proposition 6.)

---

for discussion of the *Philebus* version of this argument.) Anaxagoras's 'unmixed' cosmic Intelligence (*nous*) likewise fails to safeguard our distinct autonomy if, as Sedley has argued, 'the reference [in Anaxagoras] of the word *nous* ranges, without clear demarcation, over both intelligence as a power resident in each of us, whose properties we therefore know at first hand, and the great cosmic intelligence which created the world. The ambiguity is permissible because Anaxagoras almost certainly holds that the great cosmic intelligence, having created the world, apportioned at least some of itself into individual living beings, ourselves included' (Sedley, 2007, 11). At 24 Sedley speaks of Anaxagoras as regarding human beings 'as, among all living creatures, *the best vehicles for nous itself to occupy*' (emphasis added). See also Menn, 1995, 26 ff., on *nous* as a mass-noun in Anaxagoras.

[29] More accurately: it would have entailed a disjunction of uncongenial positions, of which pantheism might well seem the least unpalatable.

[30] If the notion of self-causation is incoherent, there is no need to argue that if the cosmic soul has a cause this cause is other than it; but as applied to a soul the notion may not be incoherent.

The combined entity would be one that both animates the single cosmic god and produces directly or indirectly the multiplicity of mortal rational creatures. But I do not think that such a two-sided notion makes sense. All that the theory says about each side is that it is a cause of certain effects. Since each causes by a different kind of causality, they are distinct principles according to the theory, and each is necessary.[31] To insist despite this that the two must nevertheless be identical makes sense only if one is responding to a demand for something other than *cosmological* economy. It might be a more purely theological demand, a requirement of divine unity to the point of monotheistic uniqueness. We can understand how this consideration may have moved certain past interpreters to inject it into their understanding of the *Timaeus*. But *we* have no such reason as theirs to read the *Timaeus* in this fashion. Some modern interpreters may indeed believe *in propriis personis* that a unique god is responsible for the universe; but they carry no intellectual or religious burden of assuming that Plato must have been a fully satisfactory authority on theology and metaphysics. Plato is at ease about a plurality of gods and of divine cosmic principles, because what matters to him is that whatever is divine be in harmony with whatever is divine.[32] This is not hard to achieve when the different divinities are assigned clearly distinct complementary functions and no interest in anything besides fulfilling those functions. We may even think it an advantage of Timaean polytheism that it can, without fuss, provide examples of the divine attributes of out-going beneficence (the Demiurge) and all-perfect self-sufficiency (the cosmic god) – attributes which monotheistic theology has to work hard to unite in one being. (Each of the Timaean attributes comes with its own distinctive kind of wisdom. See the account of the cosmic god's unceasing intelligent life at 36e2–37c3.)

To round off this defence of the separateness of the Demiurge, let me note a linkage between this motif and the oldest question of *Timaeus* interpretation: that of the cosmic beginning. The debate is almost as ancient as the *Timaeus* itself. Perhaps quite soon after Plato brought out

---

[31] Cf. Gerson, 1990, 70. In discussing the fashioning of mortals, Timaeus sometimes conflates the ancillary demiurges with '*the* god' (e.g. 71a3–b1; 73b8 ff.; 74d6 ff.; 75b7–d2 ff.). This should not encourage one to infer to the further conflation of the demiurgic kind of cause with the cosmic soul. Demiurgy makes pluralities: immortal souls in the case of the supreme one, mortal bodies in the case of the ancillaries. There is no obvious analogy between demiurgy in general and the function of the cosmic soul. See Chapter 4, section 4.7.

[32] Cf. *Republic* II, 378b8–e3, where Socrates anathematises stories about gods fighting and plotting against each other. These were staples of literature, sculpture, and painting, and people were exposed to them from earliest youth. See also *Euthyphro* 6b7–c7. On the theology of the *Timaeus*, see Broadie, 2008.

1.3 An immanent Demiurge?

the dialogue, and possibly while he was still alive and active, philosophers close to him in one way or another were divided, and knew themselves to be divided, over whether he seriously meant to depict the cosmos as having a proto-historical beginning.[33] Now, this question is logically connected with whether Plato seriously meant the separateness of the Demiurge. A negative answer to the latter entails (if we assume that Plato is consistent) a negative answer to the former. For, as we shall see in a moment, if there is no separate Demiurge but only the cosmic soul, the cosmos must be everlasting in both temporal directions (sempiternal). This means that by arguing, as I have done, that there is good reason to accept that Plato is serious about the separate Demiurge, one keeps open the possibility that he is serious about the proto-historical beginning. In Chapter 7 I shall argue that Plato *is* serious about the beginning. Consequently, the main thesis of the present chapter is an important preliminary to Chapter 7.[34]

It is obvious without argument that the separate Demiurge is consistent with a beginning of the cosmos. What about a separate Demiurge and a sempiternal cosmos? Some interpreters take it that these two are inconsistent.[35] This is certainly true if one understands 'separate Demiurge' as meaning an agent who enters an idle work-place, sets about working, finishes his task, and then steps away (cf. 42e5–6). But it is not so clearly true if one understands 'separate' in the more abstract way which I have explained, i.e. as marking the causality of a one-many cause. If the cause of this cosmos has the competence to cause more than one, or to cause another instead of this – even though his goodness ensures that such choices do not occur – then, even if this cosmos is sempiternal, in a sense the cause is beyond it. It is beyond in that its competence extends to cosmic possibilities other than this cosmos. (We distinguish between the type of cause that the Demiurge is – i.e. world-making and therefore one-many – and the goodness that governs his particular exercise of this causality. The Demiurge *qua* cause of a certain type might have produced one or another cosmos other than the most perfect one; *qua* best possible cause of that type he is certain to have produced only the most perfect.)

---

[33] For references, see Chapter 7, n. 2.
[34] It will be clear from these remarks that I do not regard the fact that Timaeus calls the cosmology an *eikôs muthos* (29d2) as a licence to treat major elements in the presentation as diverging from the philosophy being presented.
[35] Dillon, 2003a, 81: 'we must recognize, I think, that if the account of a creation of an ordered world from a previously existing disorderly substratum is deconstructed, then the creator-god himself, the so-called Demiurge, goes up in smoke as well'. That was my understanding in Broadie, 2007, 236–7. For the contrary view, see Menn, 1995, 61.

Let us take it that the separate Demiurge is consistent both with a proto-historically begun cosmos and with a beginningless one. By contrast, if we reject the separate Demiurge and retain only the cosmic soul, we rule out a proto-historical beginning. For such a soul – essentially an animating principle – cannot be thought to have existed separately from body before 'taking over' the matter that would be its body. If, on the other hand, the cosmic soul was never not immanent in a body, a proto-historical origination would only be possible in one of two ways. On one alternative, the cosmos, complete in all its details of body and soul, simply sprang into existence from nothing antecedent. I take it that no one is going to entertain this as an interpretation of the *Timaeus*. On the second alternative, the cosmic soul first has a primitive and unformed body which it proceeds to develop into the perfect cosmic body, and so the complete cosmos begins. But surely the soul in the primitive unformed body would be an unformed and primitive soul. It would have to develop itself as well as developing its body, with no help or protection from anything else. And how do we know that it is not still developing and getting better? If this is allowed to be an epistemic possibility, we lose the axiom that our cosmos is as good, beautiful, and orderly as any empirical entity could be. Thus it follows from Timaean principles that if the cosmic soul (perhaps guided by the intelligible paradigm) is the cause of the cosmos to the exclusion of any separate Demiurge, then the cosmos must have been existent from everlasting.

1.4 SUMMARY

I have looked at the idea of the separate Demiurge from several angles. Section 1.1 had two purposes. The first was to show how, in the story as we have it in the text, the separateness of the Demiurge from the cosmos he makes is secured by the fact that he makes it from pre-existent materials. The fact, taken as given, that the cause was separate from the unordered materials is reflected, through a sort of logical transmission, in its separateness from the finished product. This triadic situation was contrasted with a dyadic picture involving only the cause and the product. I argued that, given the ancient Greek context, a dyadic picture would have entailed that cause is not separate from product: either they would have appeared as earlier and later stages of a single entity, or as constituent and what it constitutes. The second aim was to compare the Timaean situation with Abrahamic creation-theology according to which there is God and a created world not made from anything, and yet it is perfectly clear that God is transcendent and in that sense separate. What is the factor that safeguards the separateness in this

1.4 Summary

account, given the difference from the Greek one? I answered that the exclusive divinity and sanctity of the Abrahamic God as contrasted with the worldliness of the world is sufficient to enforce the separateness without further ado.

This answer led us to another difference, broached in section 1.2: Timaeus's cosmos is itself a god, and is to be worshipped as such. That the cosmos is divine follows from what has to be true of it in order for it to satisfy the axiom that this cosmos is as excellent as any such thing could be. Section 1.2 developed the question why, given that the cosmos is divine, it or rather its soul should not be regarded by Plato as the ultimate principle of cosmology. As long as we look upon the separate Demiurge rather on the model of the biblical creator, it may seem perfectly natural that a divine origin means a separate divine maker. But this understanding fails to take account of the biblically unspeakable Timaean portrayal of the physical world as itself a god. Once this aspect of the account comes into full view, it is equally natural (especially from a perspective imbued with monotheism) to ask whether Plato's account really needs both its gods. Isn't the cosmic soul by itself enough? If it is, then perhaps Plato does not mean readers of the *Timaeus* to take the separate Demiurge seriously.

In section 1.3 I approached this question by considering two models having greater theoretical economy. The first was one in which the intelligent cosmic soul is closely based on the corporeal materials as they occur here and there in space. This was inadequate because any world-making intelligence grounded in that way in corporeal materials cannot be supposed to be necessarily the only one of its kind and capable of reliably controlling all the corporeal matter in existence. It follows that this model cannot guarantee that our cosmos fits Timaeus's fundamental demand that it be as perfect as possible.

The discussion of this model shows that we do not have to think of Plato, anyway in the *Timaeus*, as eschewing this sort of materialism about cosmic intelligence because it is simply repugnant to his cast of mind, or because the assumption that corporeal matter is inanimate is somehow built into his way of thinking. These things may have been true of Plato as a matter of psychological fact. But it may instead be true that he was willing to give serious consideration to various earlier theories in which matter, or some force that operates in matter, is intelligent and works purposefully to form the cosmos and its parts.[36] Since such willingness is at least a possibility, it is

---

[36] E.g. the theories of Empedocles and Diogenes of Apollonia. David Sedley has argued in convincing detail against the 'widespread perception that the Presocratics were materialists who did not think teleologically' (Sedley, 2007, 1).

interesting to see that Plato possessed, whether or not he used it in his actual thinking, a cosmological *reason* for rejecting any simple form of teleological materialism: namely, that this sort of theory cannot bear the weight of the assumption that this cosmos is superlatively excellent.

The second economical model discussed in section 1.3 was one in which it is simply postulated that the cosmos is unique and the cosmic soul is in control of all corporeal matter. I examined this by comparing the types of causality exemplified by the Demiurge and the cosmic soul in the text: one–many and one–one respectively. I argued next that the picture of the Demiurge fashioning first the cosmic soul, and in a distinct act fashioning the rational souls of mortals, enables Plato in a clear way to exhibit in combination the two essential aspects of the rational souls of mortals: their kinship to the cosmic soul and their individual responsibility. I then argued that the distinct types of causality indicate distinct cosmic principles, each cosmologically necessary for Plato's universe; and I claimed that any impulse to unite them in a single being probably stems from a purely theological assumption which we have no reason to think that Plato shared.

Finally, I argued that the question of the separate Demiurge and the famous question of the proto-historical beginning (in each case, 'Did Plato really mean it?') are related in such a way that a negative answer to the first compels a negative answer to the second. In Chapter 7 I shall be arguing for a positive answer to the second question. This present chapter's defence of a positive answer to the first one is therefore a necessary preliminary.

One can also draw a sort of inductive conclusion: if we uncover good specific reasons for taking one disputed part A of Timaeus's story as 'really meant', we have some ground for believing that there are good specific reasons for drawing the same conclusion about some other disputed part B. It may, of course, turn out that we fail to find such reasons for regarding B as 'really meant'; but the experience with A should make us less likely to fail through not looking strenuously enough.

CHAPTER 2

Paradigms and epistemic possibilities

2.1 'WHICH OF THE TWO PARADIGMS?' – DEFENDING THE QUESTION

I turn now to that most notoriously Platonic of Plato's metaphysical entities, the intelligible paradigm with reference to which the cosmos was made. The discussion in the last chapter of the 'separateness' of the demiurgic principle was about its distinctness from the cosmos and cosmic soul, not about its distinctness from the cosmic paradigm. This latter question, with concomitant proposals that the paradigm is an aspect of the Demiurge, or demiurgic efficacy an aspect of the paradigm, is also not the topic of this chapter. Whatever ontological mergers might be suggested between Demiurge and paradigm, the function of the paradigm is clearly different from that of the Demiurge: and the *function* of the paradigm-object is our present concern.

The topic of paradigms occurs first in complete generality. The cosmology is prefaced with an exordium (27d5–29d3) which (a) introduces three general considerations, (b) applies them to the cosmos in particular, and (c) draws a conclusion about the kind of discourse that is to follow.[1] The three general considerations are: the distinction between being and becoming, which is introduced along with a corresponding distinction of cognitive states; the principle that whatever comes to be has a cause (which it is taken for granted is a purposeful agent); and the principle that a craftsman's use of a changeless, as distinct from a generated, paradigm is sufficient and necessary for a beautiful product:

Whenever the craftsman[2] keeps in view what is always changeless, and using a thing of that kind as his paradigm reproduces in his work its form and meaning,

---

[1] See Runia, 1997, on the historical antecedents of this exordium.
[2] Archer-Hind, 1888, 87, says 'the Artificer' in his translation here, but the capital letter obscures the generality of what is being said.

everything that he completes in this way is, of necessity, beautiful. But whenever <the craftsman has in view> something that has come to be, using a paradigm that has been generated, beautiful his work is not. (28a6–b2)

What is the basis of this general principle? It can only be the human practice of making things. But in applying the principle a few lines later to the particular case of our cosmos, Plato seems to exaggerate the parallel with human making in a ludicrous way:

Now the maker and father of this All is hard to find; and <even> if we found him, representing him in speech to everyone would be impossible. And so we must go back to this question about it: which of the two paradigms (*poteron tôn paradeigmatôn*) guided its maker when he fashioned it – the one that does not change and stays the same, or the one that has come to be? Well, if this cosmos is beautiful and its craftsman good, then clearly he had the eternal paradigm in view, whereas if . . . what is irreligious for anyone even to put into words, then he <had in view> one that has come to be. So it is evident to all that <he had in view> the eternal one. For the cosmos is the most beautiful among the things that have come to be, and he is the best among causes. This, then, is how it has come to be: it has been crafted in accordance with that which is changeless and grasped by wisdom in a rational account. (28c3–29b1)

For all the intended sublimity, this passage seems spoilt by a ridiculous implication: that the divine craftsman had, as human ones often do, a choice between two ways of proceeding, a worse and a better: model your product, which of course will be changeable and perceptible, on another such object of the same metaphysical kind;[3] or model it in accordance with an intelligible paradigm. But how could a cosmos-like perceptible object *be there* for the world-maker to pass over it in his choice of paradigm?[4] Surely the reason he uses an intelligible paradigm ought to be that for him, unlike human makers, no perceptible one would have been available. Of course, if sheer unavailability of the inferior alternative were the reason he adopted the superior one, his doing so would not manifest his prior goodness as clearly as the better choice would if choice were possible! But to pretend, in effect, that the inferior alternative was possible just so as to be able to congratulate the Demiurge on his 'preference' for the superior one, seems absurd. It is

---

[3] That is, a perceptible object. The discussion does not depend on whether that object is another world like ours or whether it stands to our world as the wooden couch to its picture (*Republic* x, 596e5–597e5).

[4] The definite article at 28c6, *poteron tôn paradeigmatôn*, repeated at 29a1–3, may have existential nuance: both models exist. (Some MSS also have *to* at 29a4.) Alternatively, the reference is to kinds of model: the question at 28c6 can be translated: 'a model of which of two kinds did the maker use?' with the answer at 29a1–3 referring also to kinds. But this is still absurd on the face of it. If no instance of the second kind is available, the above question seems without foundation.

2.1 'Which of the two paradigms?' – defending the question

not as if there will be a shortage of other opportunities for displaying the power of the principle that the world-maker is the best of causes.

However, perhaps Plato is rather heavy-handedly stressing that what makes making excellent, whether divine or human, is guidance by an intelligible paradigm. Thus the passage may be meant more to remind us how to be superior makers ourselves than to spell out the superior nature of divine making.[5]

Also, and more relevantly for the present context, Plato is indicating how we are to do cosmology by getting us to assimilate the world-maker to a human agent guided by a plan. The affinity is brought out by showing the world-maker rightly choosing an intelligible paradigm 'instead of' a merely perceptible one: the consequence being that we are to try to understand the cosmos in the same way as we try to understand the intelligent works of our fellow humans when we are not in a position to hear their first-hand explanation of what they have produced and why. The world-maker is not so infinitely superior as to make it nonsensical for us to try to reconstruct the process of world-making from inside, entering into the divine demiurgic point of view on the basis of our own intellectual experience as makers.

That it is *possible* to do cosmology in this way is not to be taken for granted. I have just implied that it would not be possible if the world-maker is so great as to be beyond any sort of human comprehension. And, as we are about to see, it would also not be possible if the world-maker had opted for the absurd alternative of using a generated paradigm. Plato, I think, mentions that alternative precisely in order to underline the not-to-be-taken-for-granted goodness of the situation we humans are in: we are in a world of which we *can* hope to have some degree of science.

But before explaining this more fully (in the next section), I want to look harder at whether the supposition that the world-maker might have used a generated paradigm is in fact as absurd as all that, given its very early place in Timaeus's discourse. Of course it appears absurd in the light of assumptions and results that only come up later: for instance, the bald statement that before the making of this world began, the realm of the perceptible was in discordant and disorderly motion (30a3–5); the conclusion that this is the one and only cosmos (31a2–b3); and the conclusion that it contains within itself all the matter that exists (32c5–b1). These propositions rule it out that before this world was made there could already have been a physical object ordered enough to function as cosmic paradigm to a not very enlightened

---

[5] Thus Broadie, 2001, 21–6.

world-maker. But we are not entitled to read the 'Which of the two paradigms?' question as if the discourse already has those propositions on board. In fact, Timaeus is going to derive the uniqueness of our cosmos from the premiss that it was made in accordance with a perfect intelligible model (30c7–31a1); hence when he lays down that premiss the uniqueness question is still open.[6] Moreover, the conclusion that our cosmos contains all existing matter cannot be drawn until Timaeus has laid down the axiom that this cosmos and its maker are superlatively excellent (this being the premiss for omni-containment), and this comes only *after* (immediately after) he has asked 'Which of the two paradigms did the maker of this cosmos use?'

Even so, someone might retort: 'Isn't this all the same an absurd question, given that already at 27a4, c4, and 28c4 Timaeus has spoken of our cosmos as "the All" and "this All"? For the phrases surely refer to the totality of everything physical; hence the notion of a generated paradigm used in making this cosmos is already nonsensical when it appears at 28c5 ff.' In reply: if those phrases were meant completely strictly they could only refer to absolutely everything there is, including eternal, intelligible, reality; but that understanding makes it nonsense to speak *simpliciter*, as Timaeus does, of the 'maker' of this All (27 c4), and of its 'coming to be' (29c5).[7] So: given that the actual reference is not determined in all strictness, it is not clear why we should identify it with the totality of the physical rather than with something possibly narrower – namely, the entirety of this cosmos, the one that we are in.

It might seem that the two paradigms question as applied to our cosmos cannot be taken seriously because the idea of a generated paradigm implies an infinite regress. A generated paradigm would have to have been made, and made according to a paradigm. So, the objection goes, a changeless paradigm should be postulated straightaway, i.e. for our cosmos, or we trigger the regress. However, an *infinite* regress (which let us grant would be absurd) is triggered only if it is irrational to take the first step and not the second, the second and not the third, and so on. Otherwise, all that can be concluded is that every series of generated paradigms must end after one or more steps in a changeless one. This weaker claim allows for the possibility that *our* cosmos was modelled on something generated. For example, it would not be logically incoherent to halt the regress after two or three steps if one reversed Timaeus's actual reasoning: that is to say, if one started from

---

[6] In fact even after settling it at 31a2–b3, Timaeus revisits it at 55c7–d6.
[7] Cf. Burnyeat, 2005, 12, n. 12.

the premiss (which he says would be unholy to express; 29a3–4) that our cosmos is an inferior thing, and then explained this by supposing it the work of a shoddy world-maker whose mistake was to use a no better than generated paradigm. This would leave one free to suppose that the generated paradigm used for making this cosmos is, or is descended from, a cosmos decently made in light of an intelligible one.

2.2 THE POSSIBILITY OF HUMAN NATURAL SCIENCE

Why have I been arguing that the two paradigms question about this cosmos should not be dismissed as an odd ineptitude? Because only if both alternatives are initially presentable will Plato's reader really sit up and take notice when the generated paradigm is shown off the field. It is momentous that *this world was made in accordance with a changeless paradigm*. Plato lets the fact come at us by shouldering aside its alternative. We are meant to dwell on the difference it makes that this world was modelled in accordance with the changeless. The fact itself, for readers who are already Platonists, can never have been in doubt or have run the slightest risk of not being the case; but framing the question gets us to look harder at the significance of the actual dispensation by for a moment rhetorically threatening us with what would have been so instead.[8] This is a vital development in the exordium to the cosmology. For that counterfactual situation is one in which we – if we were still part of it – *should have had no hope of getting anywhere with cosmological speculation*. From the point of view of anyone interested in cosmology who is not already convinced of Platonism, a glance at the counterfactual situation generates a lively sense of the epistemic promise that Platonism holds.[9]

To explain: we are in a perceptible world, and our senses tell us almost nothing about its nature or its properties as a whole. Now suppose we are given to understand that our world was made in accordance with a paradigm. Consequently, we gather, it is a *likeness* (*eikôn*) of that paradigm (29b2).[10] Our only hope of finding out about our world as a whole lies in inference from what we can tell about the paradigm to which it corresponds.

---

[8] On the assumption that this world had a paradigm-using cause at all; cf. Johansen, 2004, 69 ff.
[9] On not taking for granted the intelligibility of the cosmos, see Lloyd, 1975, 142–3.
[10] Here I simply accept the inference from 'It was made in accordance with a paradigm' to 'It is a likeness of that paradigm'. The inference depends on taking 'likeness' in a broad sense, so that for X to be the likeness of some paradigm it is sufficient that X has been made so as to match the paradigm's specifications, and not necessary that X is an image of it in any familiar sense of 'image'. In Chapter 3 the notion of the cosmos as a likeness in the way in which an image is a likeness of its original will come under pressure, but the problems there do not affect the present discussion.

Now suppose that the paradigm was a generated thing. How can we confidently say anything about it? It might have already perished. If it exists, then since it is physical it is presumably perceptible (cf. 28b7–8). But 'perceptible' here would have negative rather than positive import, meaning not that the object is humanly perceptible, but that it falls into the class of things that beings like us cannot find out about except through sense-perception. But none of *us* can find out about a generated cosmic model in that way! *Ex hypothesi* it is not part of our world, and sense-perception depends on physical action of objects on percipient subjects within the same cosmos (43b7–c7; 45b7–d6; 64a2–68d7 *passim*). It follows that any creatures who *were* in a position to perceive a generated cosmic model would be living in it just as we live in our cosmos, and their perceptions would tell them no more about their cosmos as a whole, nor therefore about any other one made in its likeness, than ours tell us of ours.

On the supposition that this cosmos was made in accordance with a generated and perceptible paradigm, we might conclude that the paradigm must at least be made of earth and fire and any other elements whose existence is necessarily implied by the existence of these. For it might seem reasonable to us, as it does to Timaeus, to explain the tangibility and visibility of things as due to the presence in them of earth and fire (cf. 31b4 ff.). But just from this knowledge about the model we cannot infer new information about our cosmos: that it is made of earth and fire etc. we already know. A generated cosmic paradigm would be *hidden* from us, and so therefore would the nature and properties of our cosmos as a whole. We would lack not merely knowledge of these things, but also any basis for reasonable (*eikos*) speculation.

This line of thought can be extended. Suspend for a moment the presupposition that whatever is perceptible by sense has come about through the agency of a cause that employs a model, and consider the hypothesis that our perceptible world is not made in accordance with any sort of model. So in terms of the contrast between originals and their likenesses, our world is an original.[11] For Plato this would mean that it is opaque to the human intellect. For he proceeds entirely on this double

---

[11] It does not follow that it is in no sense caused, but this does not affect the point about intelligibility, given Plato's assumptions. Timaeus's words: 'Whereas [*men*] finding the maker and father of this All would be a task indeed, and having found him to tell of him to everyone would be impossible – even so [*de*], we must return to this question about the world: after which of the two paradigms did the builder frame it . . .?' rather suggest that if the intelligible paradigm dropped out of the account, the notion of an agency behind the world would not automatically drop out, but would be the notion of something whose nature was inaccessible to us.

2.2 The possibility of human natural science

assumption: (a) what enables this perceptible world to be also in a way intelligible to us, is a relation it bears to another entity, one that is more intelligible to us and non-perceptible; and (b) that relation is what he calls 'being made in the likeness of'. Only on this basis can we make sense of this world.

Some of Plato's associates, encouraged by central passages of the *Republic*, may have come to the conclusion that there can be nothing worthy of the name of science of the physical world.[12] (Some may have been disappointed, others may have welcomed the licence to concentrate full time on mathematics or practical philosophy.) That conclusion beckons if it is assumed that because sense-perceptible things are not themselves eternal and purely intelligible, but are only imitations of eternal intelligibles, they are completely shut out from intelligibility. Now, on the contrary, Timaeus exhibits our perceptible world as rationally comprehensible after all precisely *because* it has been brought into being as the 'likeness' (*eikôn*) of an eternal Form accessible only to intellect. Thus, in the crashing emphasis of *gegonen* at 28b7 we should hear triumph for the possibility of natural science:

> Now as to the whole heaven [*ouranos*] – let that be our name for it, or 'cosmos', or whatever other name is most acceptable to it at any point – we must first ask about it the question which, it is agreed, must be asked at the beginning of enquiry about anything: did it always exist, without any origin of its becoming, or has it come to be [*gegonen*], having originated from some origin? It has come to be! For [and then Timaeus supports what he has just asserted] . . . (28b2–7)

That our perceptible world has come to be[13] is part of the precondition for its being a system that we can hope to understand. We can hope this because and only because the world has come to be as the likeness (*eikôn*) of something purely intelligible. In this way Plato explains how human beings living round the Mediterranean like 'ants or frogs round a swamp' (*Phaedo* 109a9–b3) can aspire to an account of the whole cosmos.

The sort of account of it at which we are to aim is marked off by him as an *eikôs muthos* (29d2; cf. *eikotes logoi*, 29c2).[14] The verbal echoing is not just play. The account sought is *eikôs*, reasonable or likely;[15] that is, it is

---

[12] V, 475e3–480a13; VI, 506c6–VII, 517c5.
[13] The wording can be interpreted proto-historically or as referring to metaphysical dependence.
[14] Important recent studies of *eikôs muthos* in the *Timaeus* include Johansen, 2004, 48–68; Burnyeat's seminal paper, 2005; Betegh, 2010; Mourelatos, 2010.
[15] Following many others, I use 'likely' to catch the verbal linkage between *eikôs* and *eikôn*. 'Reasonable' above is a corrective gloss on 'likely', being intended to deflect the impulse to understand 'likely' as an easy synonym of 'probable'; see Burnyeat, 2005. *Eikôs* has both positive and 'restrictive' aspects (Betegh's word); i.e. it can express approval in one context and depreciation in another. Because of

reasonable and likely as distinct from baseless speculation – and this is precisely because the realm which the account will reveal to us is *not* a metaphysically self-standing thing but an *eikôn*, a likeness, of something else – of something intelligible. In Timaeus's words:

> Again, these things being so [i.e. this cosmos is generated; its maker is the best of causes; hence it was made according to a changeless and intelligible paradigm], our world is necessarily a likeness [*eikôn*] of something. Now in any matter it is most important to begin at the natural beginning. Accordingly [i.e. this is our beginning], we should make the following distinction concerning a likeness [*eikôn*] and its model, to wit: accounts of things are akin to the things which they reveal. So: accounts of that which is permanent and stable and manifest to reason are themselves permanent and unchangeable – to the extent that it is possible and fitting for accounts [*logoi*] to be irrefutable and invincible [*anikêtois*],[16] there ought to be[17] no falling short of this; whereas accounts of that which is made to be like [*apeikasthentos*] that other and so is itself a likeness [*eikonos*] will themselves be likely [*eikotas*], and will stand to those other accounts in the following proportion [*ana logon*]: as being is to becoming, so truth is to assurance [*pistis*].[18] If, therefore, Socrates, in many respects concerning many things, regarding gods and the generation of the universe, we find ourselves unable to furnish accounts which are entirely and in every way in agreement with each other and made completely precise, do not be surprised. But if we can offer accounts which are no less likely [*eikotas*] than anyone else's [*mêdenos*],[19] we ought to be satisfied, remembering that I the speaker and you the judges have human nature. Consequently, about these

---

this, we have to ask (I quote from Bryan, forthcoming, ch. 3): 'Is Timaeus pleading with his audience to show leniency in their judgements because, through circumstances beyond his control, he is limited to *mere* likelihood? Or is he championing his account as possessing the *merit* of being "likely"?' The right answer, of course, is 'Both'. Burnyeat, 2005, acknowledges the restrictive use in the exordium, but only after making a strong case for giving the positive side its due. Before Burnyeat, *Timaeus* scholars have tended to harp on the restrictive force. E.g. Taylor, 1928, 59–60; 73–4; 440–1, explains *eikôs* by referring to the provisional, approximate, and tentative character of physical theories as compared with 'the finality and exactitude' of pure mathematics. Cornford, 1935, 28–30, takes issue with Taylor's specific interpretation, but he too leans in the negative direction, commenting: 'no account of [the visible world] can be more than a likely story' (28). In fact (as noted by Robinson, 1986, 14, and Burnyeat, 2005, 143), Cornford mistranslates *eikotas* at 29c2 as if the word by itself meant '*no more than* likely'. *Post* Burnyeat, Mourelatos and Betegh re-emphasise the provisional (Mourelatos) and restrictive (Betegh) status that Timaeus accords to cosmological theories. The account I give in this chapter, largely written independently of Betegh and Mourelatos, attends to both sides of the coin. Bryan (forthcoming) articulates clearly the need to show how 'the link between *eikôn* and *eikôs* can be anything more than a philosophically insignificant pun', and to do so in a way that properly reflects the positive as well as negative force of *eikôs*. Interpretations that derive the (merely) *eikos* status of cosmology from the *changeability* of its subject-matter fall down, as Bryan points out, because they bypass the fact that the physical world is an *eikôn*.

[16] MSS F and Y have *akinêtois*, but Cicero's translation supports *anikêtois*. Mourelatos, 2010, comments interestingly on the modal pleonasm of this sentence.

[17] Reading *dei* at 29b8.   [18] Burnyeat (see n. 20) has 'conviction'.

[19] Or: 'any other [sc. account]'. On reasons for taking *mêdenos* as masculine, see Burnyeat, 2005, 148, n. 13; for more discussion see Betegh, 2010, 220, and Mourelatos, 2010, 227–8 and 238–47. Mourelatos, who accepts the 'personal construe', adduces the idea of equipollence of theories, with

2.2 The possibility of human natural science

things [sc. gods and the genesis of the universe] it is fitting to accept the likely story [*ton eikota muthon*] and seek nothing further. (29b1–d3)[20]

The difference between irrefutable *logoi* and *eikotes logoi* mirrors the difference between a purely intelligible and stable object, and the generated *eikôn* which is this cosmos. How exactly are we to understand these contrasts and correspondences?

As Myles Burnyeat has emphasised, Timaeus's 'likely' presents the epistemic standard which cosmological *logoi* should aim to meet, just as 'irrefutable' is the standard for *logoi* about eternal, intelligible, things.[21] Hence calling a cosmological *logos* 'likely' is rating it highly – *as* a cosmological *logos*. On the other hand, likely accounts, *eikotes logoi*, are as a class epistemically inferior to irrefutable *logoi*: hence Timaeus's *captatio benevolentiae* in the second half of the passage just quoted.

Clearly, the inferiority of the *eikotes logoi* as a class is somehow bound up with the fact that their subject-matter, this cosmos, is not a pure intelligible but the sensible, generated, image or *eikôn* of one. So the verbal echoing reflects an explanatory link: the metaphysical inferiority of the subject-matter translates into the epistemic inferiority of the discourse about it: the *logoi* at best are *eikotes*, because their subject is – not an intelligible, but – merely the *eikôn* of one. But this negativity is only one side of the coin. The negative side is salient when we compare the subject-matter of our cosmology with that of *logoi* for which irrefutability is the standard. But, as I have argued, Plato also invites the reader, even if glancingly, to compare this cosmos with what would have come to be if the maker had not been excellent and had chosen for his model a generated thing. Had that been so, efforts to cosmologise about the result could not have hoped to produce *eikotes logoi*: they would have wandered at random, wholly beholden to opinion based on unreasoning sense-perception (cf. 28a2–3; c1). As things are, there *is* a standard of excellence to which cosmological *logoi* in *this* world can, hence, ought to, aspire: the standard of the *eikos*.[22] This standard is available to us because our world is indeed an *eikôn*: an *eikôn* of something eternal and intelligible. The metaphysical superiority of the paradigm

---

particular reference to Xenophanes, Democritus, and Epicurus. Scholars see here an allusion to Parmenides, B8, 60–1: *ton soi egô diakosmon eoikota panta phatizô | hôs ou mê pote tis se brotôn gnomê(i) parelassê(i)* ('This order of things I declare to you to be likely in its entirety, in such a way that never shall any mortal outstrip you in judgment', tr. Coxon with one change). For the point of the allusion, see n. 34.

[20] This translation is closely based on Burnyeat, 2005, except that he eschews 'likely' for *eikôs*, leaving this word (as well as the phrase *eikota muthon*) untranslated.

[21] Burnyeat, 2005.   [22] This is the neuter form; *eikôs* (used with *logos* and *muthos*) is the masculine.

actually used, as compared with the other conceivable paradigm, translates into the epistemic respectability of the corresponding *logoi* at their best.

This is how Timaeus started the exordium:

> What is that which always is and has no becoming, and what is that which is becoming and never is? Well, the one of these can be grasped through thinking joined with reason [*noêsei meta logou perilêpton*], for that one is always the same; whereas the other is object of opinion joined with unreasoning sense-perception [*met' aisthêseôs alogou doxaston*], for <this other> is in process of coming to be and perishing, and never really is. (27d6–28a4)[23]

It was only after this that Timaeus introduced in general terms the idea of a maker-cause, and contrasted making with reference to an eternal paradigm and making with reference to a generated one. He then applied these generalities to the case of this cosmos, showing first that it falls into the category of the generated. We know this because:

> it is visible and tangible and has body, and all such things are sense-perceptible; but sense-perceptible things, being objects grasped by opinion joined with sense-perception [*ta d'aisthêta doxê(i) perilêpta met' aisthêseôs*] come to be and are generated, as was shown. (28b7–c2)

The phrase '*sense-perceptible* things, being objects grasped by opinion *joined with sense-perception*' is strangely pleonastic. What is the point of this? It must be that Plato means to echo the phrase he used at 28a2–3: 'object of opinion *joined with unreasoning sense-perception*'. But in the echo, 'sense-perception' is no longer qualified as 'unreasoning'.[24] This verbal repetition-plus-omission surely conveys that it is no longer appropriate to call sense-perception 'unreasoning'. Why so? Because Timaeus has begun to speak about this cosmos, which he is about to explain was modelled on an *intelligible* paradigm. When opinion partnered with sense-perception has *this* cosmos for its object, the partner is not radically irrational. It was called 'unreasoning' in the earlier passage because (as I see it) the redeeming theme of maker and intelligible paradigm had not yet been introduced. By verbal arrangements Plato shows, not says: were it not for the eternal paradigm, cognitive responses to the cosmos would be incurably devoid of reason; given that paradigm, they can and should aspire to something better. Given it, we can achieve *logoi* about the cosmos which are *eikotes* and carry

---

[23] Omitting *aei* at 28a1; see Whittaker, 1969 and 1973; Robinson, 1986, 14–15.
[24] Cf. 52a7, *doxê(i) met' aisthêseôs perilêpton*; 'unreasoning' is missing here too, and *aisthêton* at line 5 creates the same pleonasm as at 28c1.

2.2 The possibility of human natural science

assurance (*pistis*), i.e. reasonable credibility,[25] and which (therefore) exhibit a ratio (*ana logon*, 29C2) to the irrefutable *logoi*. The formula 'as being is to becoming, so truth is to assurance' (c3) indicates that ratio.[26] By contrast, opinion allied with wholly *irrational* sense-perception would be too far removed from 'truth' to stand in a ratio to it.

Putting all this together, we can say that the ontological inferiority of the cosmos to any eternal, intelligible, object accounts for both (1) the negative and (2) the positive sides of the fact that cosmological *logoi* are *eikotes* at best. (1) They are no better than *eikotes* because their subject-matter is not a pure intelligible, but only an *eikôn* of one. This point divides into two. (1a) The comparison is with human sciences that study pure intelligibles. Cosmology is an inexact discipline in the way in which description of the chalk marks constituting a geometrical diagram would be at best inexact by comparison with the geometrical proof to which it is an aid. Moreover, (1b) since cosmology is ultimately a conjecture as to the content of the divine paradigm, it is epistemically inferior to the Demiurge's first-hand knowledge (which is at the same time knowledge of the paradigm and of the physical cosmos).[27] On the other hand (2), if our sense-perceptible cosmos were on the same ontological level as its paradigm (or if it were simply an original existent), this could only be because the paradigm (if there were one) would be another generated thing – in which case *logoi* concerning this cosmos could never be more than foolish opinions.

As a defence of the human possibility of rational cosmology, this approach assumes that the cosmic paradigm is to some extent accessible to us; in other words, that the world-maker (to whom, of course, the paradigm must be without qualification accessible) is an intellect not alien to the human one.[28] The crucial assumption is that we have a correct sense of the maker's values. If our own views on the nature of the finest world are

---

[25] Burnyeat notes (2005, 153–4): 'by Plato's day *pistis* was in use as the orator's word for the kind of "proof" or "argument" one hears in court or assembly'; cf. Johansen, 2004, 52, n. 5, on *to eikos* as the desideratum in forensic arguments. See also Mourelatos, 2010, on forensic language in the exordium.

[26] It does so indirectly by stating the converse proportion, i.e. the one in which 'truth' stands to *pistis*, the state of mind associated with *to eikos*. (On truth as a state of mind see Burnyeat, 2005, 152, n. 22.) The original proportion-statement (*tous de tou pros men ekeino* [sc. the intelligible paradigm] *apeikasthentos, ontos de eikonos, eikotas ana logon te ekeinôn* [sc. the irrefutable *logoi*] *ontas*, 29C1–2) presents accounts corresponding to the *eikôn* as caught up into the orbit of rationality by being *ana logon* to accounts corresponding to eternals, whose rationality goes without saying.

[27] More in section 2.5 on the difference between (1a) and (1b).

[28] Thus Plato rejects Xenophanes's dictum that 'there is one god greatest amongst gods and men, in no way similar to mortals either in body or in thought (*noêma*)' (B23). But his reason for rejecting it would not be simply that the god is to some extent similar to mortals in thought; it would partly be that human *nous*, our power of thought, is not mortal.

shaped by standards peculiar to us, our attempts at hermeneutic cosmology are useless. As things are (so the Timaean vision goes), this cosmos is the maker's because he made it; it is ours because we live inside it; and these mutually exclusive possessor-perspectives come together because of shared understanding of what is good, orderly, and beautiful.

An element of reassurance on these preliminary fundamentals has been built into the detail of the cosmology itself. According to Timaeus's account, the main features of the cosmos as a whole and the human condition are *déjà vus* by Timaeus, his friends, and all of us. It is part of Timaeus's story that just after the Demiurge creates the rational souls that will be first embodied as humans, he reveals to them the nature of the cosmos and the primary features of human life within it (41d4–42d4).[29] Thus the whole cosmology, according to itself, rehearses and builds on a schematic lesson already given to rational souls before they descended to human bodies. Our maker implanted the seeds of human cosmological science along with the seeds of human self-knowledge. From our first inception we have received some resources for understanding both the greatness of the whole and the struggles facing us as parts of it.

2.3 HOW THE COSMOLOGY SHOULD BE JUDGED

With human makers, even if we could know exactly what they intend to make (and this is possible because I myself might be the maker, and also because I can often find out from other makers by asking them), we do not thereby know how the product will turn out, because of possible hindrances in the making. But with the world-maker (this becomes apparent in the course of Timaeus's exposition) we need not worry that his product might have fallen significantly short of his intention. Here, then, the sole reason we have for caution about the character of the product is that we may not read his intention aright.[30] Adopting the starting point stated above and then applying our best intelligence means we shall be on the right wavelength for producing a good cosmology. Even so, nothing guarantees that our reading of what the world was meant to be will ever completely match the actual intention (nor, if we did achieve a perfect fit, could anything tell us for sure that we had done so). We can never claim to have the last word. Thus Timaeus prepares his listeners for the fact that his current best practice in cosmological hermeneutics cannot be expected to yield irrefutable results. That is, cosmological results can in principle be refuted without

[29] This passage will be discussed in Chapter 4, section 4.5.   [30] Cf. Sedley, 2007, 110–11.

2.3 How the cosmology should be judged

revoking the starting point. But this, he explains, is not automatically a defect. Yes, there certainly is (according to him) a kind of account that falls short of the excellence required of it if, its starting point being fixed, a result is offered that is vulnerable to refutation; however, the discourse about to be presented is *not* of that kind. On the contrary, the possibility of refutation is inherent in the distinct genre to which the cosmology belongs. But it is not as if, on the level of cosmology, anything goes. This genre comes with its own by no means undemanding standard by which instances are to be judged: this is the standard of the *eikos*, the likely or reasonable.[31]

Towards the end of the exordium Timaeus says:

If, therefore, Socrates, in many respects concerning many things, regarding gods and the generation of the universe, we find ourselves unable to furnish accounts which are entirely and in every way in agreement with each other[32] and made completely precise, do not be surprised. But if we can offer accounts which are no less likely [*eikotas*] than another's, we ought to be satisfied, remembering that I the speaker and you the judges have human nature. Consequently, about these things [sc. gods and the generation of the universe] it is fitting to accept the likely story [*ton eikôta muthon*] and seek nothing further. (29c4–d3)

This is a request that the standard applied be the appropriate one for the subject-matter. It would be met by a cosmology whose fullness and rationality reflect the completeness and rational order of the universe, and whose reverent delight in its subject-matter reflects the maker's joy over the world he has made (cf. 37c6–d1). On the other hand, whereas the god-made world, itself a god, is as excellent as any generated thing could be, the Timaean cosmology, also a generated thing, is essentially susceptible of improvement. Timaeus's final speech in the *Timaeus–Critias* is a prayer to the cosmic god to help the human cosmologist correct errors and thereby progress towards scientific knowledge (*epistêmê*) of the cosmos:

to the god who has come to be – once upon a time long ago in reality [*ergô(i)*], and in discourse [*logois*] only just now[33] – I pray that for whatever we have said that was said with due measure he will grant us preservation, and that if we unintentionally

---

[31] That the standard is not undemanding is clear from the characterisation of Timaeus himself as an expert on astronomy and physics (27a2–5), and also from the extraordinary quality of almost every section of his monologue.

[32] Burnyeat, 2005, 155, suggests that the possible inconsistency is between implications of the individual portions or chapters of Timaeus's discourse (on the cosmic body, on the cosmic soul, on the celestial system etc.), rather than within a portion. Internal inconsistency would ruin a portion's chance of counting as *eikôs*. This suggests that the *eikos*-standard is to be applied to the portions one by one, on which see section 2.4.

[33] On the translation see Chapter 7, n. 1. Timaeus unequivocally speaks of a beginning of the world 'long ago'. Whether we should take it that *Plato* means this is another question, on which see Chapter 7.

said anything out of tune he will impose the fitting penalty. But the correct penalty is to bring back into tune the one who sounds a wrong note. So in order in future [*to loipon*] to be correct in the way we give accounts of the coming to be of gods, we pray that he will grant us a remedy that is the most perfect and best of remedies – scientific expertise [*epistêmên*]; and with that prayer I hand over to Critias as agreed. (*Critias* 106a3–b7)

The petition that the cosmic god *himself* will preserve what is right in Timaeus's account of him, and correct what is wrong, not only carries the vague and common religious thought that if we turn in the proper way towards the invoked divinity, this higher power will confirm our achievements and help repair our losses: it also suggests that only from continued study of the cosmos itself, i.e. from continued efforts to practise natural science, can confirmation and correction come. The prayer also plainly implies that such a sequel is to be pursued. In sum, the right sequel would be to maintain awareness of the possible inadequacy of any cosmological account, while setting about to do better in terms of that same genre. Moreover (although this only emerges in the course of the cosmology itself), anyone who counters a Timaean theory by producing a superior one, thereby refuting the other, is a *friend*.[34] (One gains by being refuted.) When Timaeus starts to construct from triangles the regular polyhedra that give the shapes of the physical particles, he says this about the particular triangle he takes as basic for fire, water, and air:

If anyone can say that he has selected a more excellent one for the construction of these, that person gets the better of us [*kratei*] as a friend, not an enemy. Of the many triangles, then, let us pass over the others and posit as most excellent a single kind: that which doubled constitutes the isosceles triangle. The reason for this requires a rather long discussion; but if anyone tests this theory and finds that it is not so, the prize is his with our friendship. (54a4–b2)[35]

The message that the study of nature is a *corrigible* and therefore a progressive enterprise may seem to us unnecessary because so obvious; but Plato presumably could not assume that everyone he hoped to reach via the *Timaeus* would automatically view the work in that light. It is, I suppose, imaginable that some in his audience may have been predisposed to look upon Timaeus's monologue as more *muthos* than *logos*, i.e. more as a story,

---

[34] Compare the lines of Parmenides (see n. 19), echoed at the end of Timaeus's exordium. Here the goddess reveals to the youth an *eikôs* cosmology *such that no other mortal will outstrip him*. 'Outstrip' implies rivalry, and failure for those outstripped. Timaeus by contrast is open to the possibility of refutation even at the hands of a mortal, and he even welcomes it. On the contrast, see Mourelatos, 2010, 238–41.
[35] Reading *mê* at b2.

2.3 How the cosmology should be judged

indeed a work of art, to be delighted in for its own sake and told again and again, and not also as a set of theoretical proposals calling for critical examination. For example, some might think that its main purpose is to establish an enlightened theogony, one of divine harmony and co-operation, in place of the childish, often nightmarish, stories of Hesiodic tradition. Thus for them the Timaean cosmology fills a gap that is left if rulers bowdlerise as demanded in *Republic* II. One is not off-track in being reminded of that demand. Timaeus, Critias, and Hermocrates are entertaining Socrates in return for his regaling them yesterday with a discourse about an ideal polity that in many ways calls to mind the city of the *Republic*. If, as Plato says, man is the most god-revering of animals (*Timaeus* 42a1; cf. *Laws* x, 902b5–6), then man must have stories about gods, and it may well have seemed that the *Republic* ideal was highly impractical in gutting traditional myths while suggesting rather little by way of replacement.[36]

Now, it might be felt that *as a story about the genesis of the gods* (29c4–5; 34a8–b9; 39e10 ff.; 40d3–5; 41a6–7; 92c4–9) Timaeus's account is beyond improvement. So from that point of view (one that might leave us somewhat baffled by its wealth of patient detail about down-to-earth things) the correct way to respond would be to treasure the account as it is and plant it in everyone's minds by the simple expedient of reciting it again and again like the poems of Homer and Hesiod, or indeed reproduce it minus the drier details of sublunary physics and mortal physiology. But if that were its general reception, it would have little chance of being subjected to the strenuous critical examination which a work that is a venture into natural science – even if this is not all that it is – needs for the sake of its own improvement.

This discussion has not yet foregrounded the important fact that Timaeus's cosmology prefaces a story, told by the character Critias, in which a virtuous Greek *polis* confronted and defeated a mighty alien aggressor. This is the story of ancient Athens and Atlantis.[37] Such a positioning of the cosmology might have seemed like further encouragement to treat it as first and foremost a noble and edifying story. What do I mean by treating something as a story? The crucial point for now is not the question of fact versus fiction, but that stories exist to be told and told again in the same form. For a story to be successful as a story the audience must enter into it; they are not meant to stand back, look at it critically, and judge it by what they may know from the world outside the story. One might well

---

[36] Cf. Johansen, 2004, 67–8. [37] Discussed in Chapter 5.

say that if they do this the story-telling has failed as such. Clearly this holds as much for stories based on fact as it does for fictional ones. Take the Athens–Atlantis story: within the dialogue-world it is accepted by the characters as true;[38] but in that world it seems to exist merely in order to be told and retold and faithfully received.[39] The evidence for the story (which mainly consists in an elaborate explanation of why there is so little evidence for it) comes as part of the story itself – it is part of what Critias recounts. The Socrates-character is shown simply accepting the truth of what is told (26e4–5). He makes not the slightest gesture towards checking it against possible facts or likelihoods, even facts and likelihoods confined to the dialogue-world.

Still, that sort of scrutiny, the scrutiny of a historian, would be totally out of keeping with the Socrates-character of the *Timaeus–Critias*: it does not fall within his competence. Now, this 'lack of competence to criticise' is part of the dramatic framework in which is presented not only Critias's story, but also Timaeus's cosmology along with its strictures on how to judge the cosmological proposals. The dramatic framework is such that *within the dialogue-world* no probing question or critical judgement can be levelled against those proposals by any of the other characters. When Timaeus has delivered his account, Socrates simply expresses admiration (*Critias* 108b3–5), just as at the beginning he looks forward to the long version of Critias's story with simple acceptance (*Timaeus* 27a2–b8). This all grows from the fact that these two discourses are parts of a great feast of *logoi* which the other characters have arranged for Socrates (17a2–3; b2–4; 20b7–c3; 27a2–3; b7–8). Gracious acceptance is, of course, the proper response in that situation.

But the Socrates-character's gracious acceptance means something more than good manners. In the real world, good manners might well be all that inhibits a person from posing critical questions about the content of an elaborate performance put on to please him or her. But the cardboard persons of the dialogue-world – Socrates, Timaeus, Critias, and Hermocrates – stand for different intellectual genres.[40] (At least this is so for Socrates, Timaeus, and Critias. We do not know about Hermocrates since he never gets his turn.[41]) It is not within the competence of any of these genres – ethical and political theory (Socrates), cosmology (Timaeus),

---

[38] However, Plato's real-world audience would immediately have recognised it as a fiction: see Chapter 5, section 5.3.
[39] See Chapter 5, section 5.8.   [40] More on this in Chapter 5, section 5.2.
[41] Hermocrates is billed to speak after Critias (*Critias* 108a5–b3), and the latter's story breaks off just as the main action in it starts to get under way (121c5).

2.3 How the cosmology should be judged

and historiography (Critias) – to take up a critical stance towards anything said under the heading of any of the others. So: within the dialogue-world where there are only Socrates, Critias, and Hermocrates to receive Timaeus's cosmology, the recipients listen as unchallengingly and submissively as we in the real world drink in a fascinating story – *not* scrutinising it as a set of inherently refutable scientific proposals.[42] But the real world of Plato and his associates is absolutely not the dialogue-world. In the real world Plato surely intended and expected the cosmology to be probed and tested as cosmology, i.e. to be engaged with as serious science by people thinking from inside this kind of discipline.[43]

So in having Timaeus at the outset pointedly contrast his own sort of account with the sort that is expected to be irrefutable and invincible, Plato, I suggest, is not only asking that the cosmology not be judged by the more demanding standard that would be inappropriate for this *genre*: he is also laying it down that no one is epistemically entitled to dismiss or reject any part of it except by refutation or defeat in accordance with its own standard, the standard of the *eikos*.[44] Once this happens, if it does, then the cosmology, or the relevant part of it, will no longer be 'no less likely or reasonable than another's' (29c7–8), and its proponents and admirers will have lost their right to be satisfied with it. However, until this happens, they do have that right, and may claim it legitimately even while acknowledging that the possibility of refutation cannot be excluded.

Putting together the considerations of this section so far, we can see Plato marking off the right reception of Timaean cosmology from two opposite directions. The work is not to be set on a pedestal to bask in uncritical appreciation; but on the other hand, the correctly critical spirit will not refuse to welcome and take it seriously on the sheer ground that it may one day be refuted. This dual attitude is clearly the right one to adopt towards a venture into natural science.

While some in the audience round Plato may have mainly welcomed Timaeus's *logos* as an edifying story of the gods and their works, others may

---

[42] At *Critias* 108b4 Socrates speaks of himself as a theatre-audience of Timaeus's monologue and of Critias's monologue to come. Thus he praises the cosmology *as a performance*. At *Critias* 106b8–108a4, Critias complains that it will be harder for him to produce a fault-free account than it was for Timaeus, because his own subject-matter is down-to-earth and open to everyone's inspection. But this is not an objection to any cosmological specifics.
[43] As was to happen through criticism and reworking by Aristotle, the early Academy, and the Stoics. Sedley, 2002, and Johansen, 2009, are useful recent studies.
[44] Cf. Mourelatos, 2010, 244. Having the *epistemic right of rejection* is to be distinguished from being *at personal liberty to turn aside from* this whole type of enterprise, e.g. through being engrossed by other studies; on which see the 'postscript' to this section.

have been predisposed to scorn all cosmology for its lack of mathematical rigour. From this point of view nothing counts as science except the irrefutable. Plato's attitude by contrast is that a cosmological proposal only deserves to be sent packing if shown to be unsatisfactory by the standard relevant to cosmological proposals; that demonstrating the unsatisfactoriness is essentially a matter of engaging hands-on with the proposal and framing a better one; and that wholesale *a priori* dismissal of cosmology is not a reasonable stance. In connection with this last point, and by way of postscript to this section, consider an extraordinary passage which comes almost exactly halfway through the cosmology. Timaeus is in the middle of a disquisition on the different kinds of 'water', i.e. fusibles and liquids, when he breaks off to say:

Explaining the other substances in this category would not be an elaborate task for one who aims for the genre of likely narrations [*tên tôn eikotôn muthôn idean*]. Whenever someone for the sake of relaxation [*anapauseôs heneka*] has laid aside discussions [*logoi*] of eternal things and looks at the likely [*eikotas*] <discussions> of coming-to-be, thereby obtaining a pleasure not to be regretted, he adds to his life a moderate and sensible pastime [*metrion paidian kai phronimon*]. (59c5–d2)

The message of this passage is not that thinkers should resort to cosmology merely as a pastime for breaks from the study of eternal things, as if eternal things were the only serious objects of study.[45] Rather, the passage acknowledges that there are thinkers who see their main work as the study of eternal things, and of them it says that when they take a break, which of course they must at times, they would find good recreation in cosmology.[46] Thus it recognises the presence of colleagues whose vocation is for the study of, for example, mathematics, or the Form of the Good, or the One and the Indefinite Dyad; but it does not say that these are the only respectable intellectual vocations.

This is relevant to our main discussion because it brings out the difference between two attitudes which could easily have been confused: one, a personal bent for concentrating on 'eternal things'; the other, an ideological rejection of cosmology as unworthy of a serious intellectual's attention. (Some of Plato's associates may have felt that worthwhile philosophy focuses only on the most honourable subject-matter: being as distinct from becoming. Some may have regarded the conflicting claims of existing cosmologies, impotent to reach the definitive resolution that mathematical questions can achieve, with the queasiness evinced by Hume, Kant, and many others in the modern period, in face of the conflicts of traditional

---

[45] This is what Taylor's comment *ad* 59d2, 1928, 418, rather suggests.
[46] Cf. Johansen, 2004, 64. The study of eternal things is hard work in part because the goal is supposed to be irrefutability, which can only be shown by watertight demonstration.

metaphysics.[47]) In the *Timaeus* Plato plainly disassociates himself from the second attitude through the methodology of the *eikos*; whereas in the passage just quoted the first attitude receives a rather conspicuous friendly wave. The second attitude, with its potential for dictating to others a teaching and research agenda dismissive of cosmology wholesale, has been shown the door, while the first, in those who have it, is gently acknowledged and left on the ground.

The repeated mention of the *eikos* in the passage last quoted, along with the allusion to respite and diversion, harks back to the conclusion of the exordium, which links the *eikos* with the *humanly* attainable:

> if we can offer accounts which are no less likely [*eikotas*] than another's, we ought to be satisfied, remembering that I the speaker and you the judges have human nature. (29c7–d1)

The contrast momentarily implied here is with God, who enjoys perfect understanding of the nature of the cosmos. In that light we see 59c5–d2 as a reminder to those who concentrate on eternal things that their irrefutable grasp of their material may be godlike but is not divine: this is because their human understanding is gained only through activity that tires.[48] These thinkers are not so sublime that they have the right to look down on the study of *genesis* wholesale and without trial. Nor is the study of *genesis* so low that pleasure in it is 'regrettable', as would be pleasure in a time-wasting activity.

2.4 THE TONE OF CONFIDENCE

We must try to make sense of the almost completely unfaltering self-assurance of Timaeus's presentation in the body of the cosmology.[49] It is true that along the way he places explicit reminders that his goal is the

---

[47] In the background is the Socrates of the *Phaedo*, who despite his interest in the workings of nature turned away from perceptible things to *logoi* for fear of being 'blinded' by the former (*Phaedo* 96a–99e). Also: Critias's complaint that his task is harder than Timaeus's (see n. 42) may be insinuating the sneer that in cosmology 'anything goes': a perception probably shared by intellectuals of very different stripes, e.g. some professional mathematicians as well as 'humanists' such as the Critias-character. A real-life 'humanist' example was Plato's contemporary, the influential rhetorician Isocrates, who dismissed the speculations of e.g. the atomists, Empedocles, and Alcmaeon, as 'intellectual extravagances [*perittologias*], no better than those conjurors' tricks [*thaumatopoiiais*] which, even though useless, gather round them audiences of mindless people' (*Antidosis*, 268–9). On intellectual interests associated with the Critias-character, see Chapter 5, n. 41.

[48] A further lesson for any prideful pure mathematicians and dialecticians comes in the passage that grounds our basic grasp of number in visual awareness of *cosmic* phenomena: day and night, months and years, etc. (47a4–b2).

[49] There is a shade of tentativeness at 65b7–c1 (cf. 3): 'We must try to say, if we somehow can', where he begins the discussion of the senses.

in-principle refutable *eikôs logos*. But surely these reminders would sit better with a more tentative, less roundly declarative, approach? They are certainly meant to catch attention, tending as they do to occur at important junctures of the exposition.[50] But, we may say, that is all very well: *de facto*, as one tunnels on into the prose of each section, the force of the most recent such reminder, if I am typical, tends to wear off. At pit stops we are duly fed reminders, but then we are propelled along the laps between by an extremely confident voice telling us *what is so*, and *what we must think*. Thus placing 'this is the likely account' in front of a long block of highly detailed declarations is not, rhetorically, an effective way of reinforcing a stance of scientific caution. Would it not have been more effective, if that were the aim, to use a diction softened into modesty by frequent interjections of 'perhaps', 'may be', 'I suppose', 'I wonder whether', and the like? Even if, as the fragmentary evidence may suggest, a good many earlier cosmologies were presented with remarkable assurance,[51] this still leaves us free to wonder why Plato would have echoed any such stylistic tradition; he had the rhetorical command to mitigate it, and the methodological reflectiveness to move him towards some degree of mitigation.

If, as surely we should, we take it that Plato adopts the tone of confidence in full awareness and for a deliberate reason rather than from a somewhat mechanical adherence to some pattern existing in earlier natural philosophers, we can draw the conclusion that he plants the track with those conspicuous reminders that the standard to be expected of this discourse is, after all, that of the *eikos*, precisely to try to counteract the impression, created by the tone, that the case is closed and that doubts and queries will be futile. The tone of confidence and the signalling of the *eikos* are not

---

[50] E.g. 30b7, the intellectual nature of the cosmos itself; 44c7–d1, the beginning of the construction of mortals; 48d1–2 and d6, the beginning of the entire account of the 'effects of Necessity'; 53d5–6, the beginning of the geometry of the particles; 56a1–b6, the assigning of shapes to fire, air, earth, and water particles; 56c8–d1, where he begins to show how the particles recombine; 57d5–7, where he reveals the huge variety of types of the four elements, having just explained how this is possible (because the elementary triangles come in different sizes, 57c8–d5); 67d1 and 68d2, where he begins and ends the account of colours; 72d7–8, where he rounds off the account of soul in mortals; 90e8, where he starts the account of females and lower animals.

[51] Here is Lloyd, 1991, on earlier cosmological confidence (which he is contrasting with the Timaean *eikos*): 'Plato distances himself from the dogmatism of the Presocratic philosophers, from the unrestrained speculation about how the world was in the beginning, about the physical elements and their modes of mixture and combination, from the unqualified assertions on these subjects in such as Empedocles and Anaxagoras' (350). Also: '[Plato's] reluctance to claim any more than a certain probability is readily understandable, indeed laudable, when we reflect on the excessive dogmatism shown in this general area of inquiry not only by most of Plato's predecessors but also by most of his successors' (345).

2.4 The tone of confidence

unassimilated bedfellows, but two aspects of a single approach: the first needs the second in order to disclaim a possible implication of the first.

If that is correct, the question that arises is why Plato should have chosen the tone that requires the disclaimer. We can see at once one thing that would have been lost by having Timaeus pepper the monologue with 'perhaps', 'I suppose', etc.: Timaeus would not now be telling a good *story* (*muthos*). A story works by gripping us, and being gripped entails being moved along in a sure-footed way. Reminders to be cautious and open-minded, and to hang back from fully committing one's imagination, would ruin the narrative dynamic.[52] Plato must mean the monologue to have, among other attributes, the declarative quality that a story has. I shall suggest presently that one reason for this is that he is launching Platonic cosmology as a genre.

Meanwhile, however, there is an important point to be developed about the epistemic status of each of Timaeus's *specific* theories. The first thing to note in this connection is that the methodology spells out the goal of the *eikos* by an injunction to be satisfied with 'accounts [note the plural] which are no less likely [*eikotas*] than anyone else's'[53] (29c7–8). Plato's reference here includes accounts which people have actually proposed. Plato knows what these are, and it is not at all surprising that he should be highly confident that his own accounts (via Timaeus) are at least as likely or reasonable as those of any known thinker to date. Those results that flow more or less immediately from the axiom that this cosmos is as beautiful and excellent as any generated thing could be, would have for him a very high epistemic status.[54] (That starting point could in fact rank as 'irrefutable and invincible' from the Timaean perspective: this is because there is no conceivable rival to stand up and challenge it, since even to put the alternative into words is ruled out of court by divine Law [*themis*; 29a3–4].) As for results that are answerable more closely to the observable phenomena, Plato may well be on objectively solid ground in judging that his are as good as anyone's. They are explained and argued for with impressive fertility, connectedness, and detail. What is more, at the great hinge of the cosmology, when Timaeus turns from the works of Intelligence to the domain of

---

[52] Cornford: 'Plato chooses to describe the universe, not by taking it to pieces in an analysis, but by constructing it and making it grow under our eyes' (1935), 31. As for not ruining a narrative dynamic: consider modern historians who when they engage in narrative exercise their epistemic responsibilities concerning evidence, opposing views, etc., in footnotes, a device not available to Plato.

[53] Or: 'than any other'; see n. 19. The difference does not affect the present argument.

[54] On varying levels or degrees of the *eikos* in the *Timaeus* see Johansen, 2004, 60–4; Mourelatos, 2010, 236–7, discusses variation in the standard for refutation; see also Bryan, forthcoming, ch. 4.

48   *Paradigms and epistemic possibilities*

Necessity and announces a second beginning (48a7–b3; d4–e1), he goes further and says:

> keeping to what was laid down at the beginning, i.e. to what can be achieved by likely accounts [*tên tôn eikotôn logôn dunamin*], I shall try to give an account [*legein*] of things individually and collectively [*peri hekastôn kai sumpantôn*][55] that is no less likely than anyone <else's> but more so [*mallon de*], and as before < I shall try to give it> from the beginning. (48d1–4)[56]

Is Timaeus here raising the standard for satisfaction from 'as likely as anyone else's' to 'likelier than anyone else's'? I think not, since such a change of epistemic policy would require a fuller announcement, with explanation attached, than is given here by the rather casual *mallon de*.[57] Instead, we are being told that we can now expect accounts which, as a matter of fact, are likelier than anyone else's. That means that we should be more than merely satisfied with the accounts we are about to get, not that the standard for satisfaction has been raised. Again, Plato may well have solid grounds for the confidence shown at 48d1–4 that the accounts to follow are more illuminating than anyone else's of the same *individual* phenomena, and more skilful in exploiting basic principles to explain the *collectivity* of the phenomena.

Now for the main point about the epistemic status of the specific theories. Since Plato has Timaeus speak of *eikotes logoi* and *eikotes muthoi* in the plural, the methodology allows for an epistemic flexibility which I think has not been fully appreciated by interpreters.[58] Let us suppose that Plato finds and expects others to find that some parts of the discourse carry more assurance (*pistis*) than others. In that case, he regards some parts as more *eikota*, likely, than others, because it was laid down in the exordium

---

[55] Zeyl's translation, 2000.
[56] The MSS *kai emprosthen* at d3 is untranslatable. I have accepted Cornford's emendation <*hê(i)*> *kai emprosthen* as giving a better sense than Taylor's *kai tôn emprosthen* (Taylor, 1928), accepted by Zeyl. The main question is whether Timaeus is saying of what is about to come (a) that it will be more *eikos* than anyone else's account of the same topic, or (b) that it will be more *eikos* than what he himself has offered so far. See Mourelatos, 2010, 241–4. I favour (a) because, if (see the next paragraph) Timaeus's sole method so far, the method which he reaffirms at 48d1–4, has been to compare his sections one by one with external theories on the same topic, then it does not recognise 'intra-mural' comparison (Mourelatos's phrase) between some and others of his own sections. Indeed, Timaeus himself offers *no* official basis for intra-mural comparisons, although Plato can hardly prevent his readers from making them.
[57] Mourelatos, 2010, 242: 'It is hardly credible that we have this sort of *volte face*.' But he does not consider the possibility that alternative (a) refers to a *de facto* rise in quality rather than a *de iure* one.
[58] The argument of this paragraph builds on Burnyeat's reading of the plural *logoi* at 29c6 and *muthôn* at 59c6 (see also *tôn eikotôn logôn* at 48d2) as referring not to distinct propositions, but to the different sections of discourse that constitute the Timaean cosmology (Burnyeat, 2005, 153–5; cf. 148, n. 14). Users of Cornford's translation should be warned that at all three of the passages just referred to it renders Plato's plurals by the singular 'account'.

2.4 The tone of confidence

that the state of being assured (*pistis*) is the cognitive correlate of *ta eikota* (29b3–c3). He himself may have recognised that at times the account is essentially flying by the seat of its pants. Although the whole thing is a work of the imagination, we may distinctly feel in some places more than others that the conclusions are hostage to discoveries of new phenomena and to shifts whereby different phenomena become salient, and that the reasoning relies on analogies that have no independent credentials. There is no reason why Plato and those whom he hopes to reach with the *Timaeus* would not have been aware of this too. We, if we were giving such an account to our peers, would mark those descents to a shakier epistemic level with cautionary touches like 'This is a possible model'; 'One might look at it in this way', and so on. Timaeus does not do that. He presents himself as *satisfied* with just about every part of the cosmology. But it does not follow that Plato is dishonest or pig-headed in this. He has good reason to be confident that every part is satisfactory, or in some cases more than satisfactory, for the condition of satisfactoriness was that the accounts be *no less likely than another's*. The plural 'accounts' refers to the well-marked sections on distinct subject-matters of which the whole cosmology is composed. That indicates that comparison with rival theories is to be carried out subject-matter by subject-matter.[59] It follows that Timaeus's different sections can each be as *eikôs* as the corresponding sections in other thinkers' accounts, and in some cases more so, even though among themselves some of Timaeus's different sections are more dubious than others. They can vary in their level of plausibility, some being blatantly conjectural, or flamboyantly held together by imagination, and others epistemically better founded (we would sooner bet on the correctness of some than of others), even though they equally meet (at least) the standard of being no less *eikotes* than their counterparts in other people's theories. It also follows that Timaean sections *Q*, *R*, and *S* can be more *eikotes* than their counterparts in other people's theories while at the same time being epistemically shakier than Timaean sections *F*, *G*, and *H*; and this can be so even when *F*, *G*, and *H* themselves are only as *eikotes* as, not more so than, *their* counterparts in other people's theories. Thus even sections where Plato particularly seems to be 'making it up as he goes along' may count as better than satisfactory if it is clear that other theorists have weaker proposals on the same questions or have nothing to say. The tone of confidence tracks the accolade 'satisfactory'

---

[59] On a topic where there is no existing theory in the field, presumably Timaeus's account automatically meets the standard of the *eikos*, at least as long as it contains no glaring factual mistake or contradiction.

spelt out in the way which Plato, through Timaeus, has explained. Regardless of variation in what we might call the 'intrinsic' epistemic quality of different parts of the cosmology, the tone of confidence is almost uniformly strong: justifiably so, because it reflects not what *we* might mean by epistemic reliability, but *his* standard of satisfactoriness.

So the tone of confidence about specific results is not unwarranted given the methodological framework. The framework lays it down (1) that each set of results is to be explicitly or implicitly prefaced by 'It is *eikos* that – ', and (2) that this condition is fulfilled in any given case if and only if the results stand up to comparison with anyone else's on the same topic. This framework is surely an energetic invitation to make those comparisons.[60] (Remember that the design of the dialogue-world rules it out that Socrates, Critias, and Hermocrates would be spurred to respond to the invitation. It is not an invitation to them. But to suppose that it is therefore not an invitation to anyone would be to assume that the Timaean cosmology is only meant to exist as a piece of the dialogue-world, like the view from the window of St Jerome's study in the painting by Antonello.[61]) Timaeus's monologue not only demonstrates Plato's own efforts at cosmology, but is also meant to focus further critical discussions through which cosmology will develop.[62] The monologue mentions no predecessors by name, and it is conceivable that in the dialogue-world the Milesians, Pythagoras, Heraclitus, Parmenides, Empedocles, Anaxagoras, Alcmaeon, the Hippocratics, the atomists, Diogenes, Philolaus, Archytas, Eudoxus, *et al.* of real history (important sources, many of them, of ingredients in Timaeus's discourse) are not even supposed to have existed.[63] But Plato must have meant to promote detailed real-world discussions assessing Timaean views against earlier views and rival contemporary theories.

I have argued that it is reasonable for Plato to regard the various sections of the cosmology as epistemically satisfactory by the standard which he has set. Thus the tone of confidence maintained in each section is reasonable.

---

[60] Brisson 2006, writing about the *Timaeus* cosmology, says '... competitive debate, or *agôn*, seems ultimately to have furnished the framework in which sciences of nature were developed in ancient Greece' (229); cf. Lloyd, 1968, 81–4. The observation is apt, but must be taken in conjunction with 54a4–b2, on which see the discussion in section 2.3 with note 35.

[61] See Chapter 5, section 5.9, on transferability to the real world of elements in the Timaean and Critian discourses.

[62] Cf. 38e2–3, where details of astronomy are deferred for future discussion *kata scholên*; this may mean 'at leisure', but at this period it can also mean 'in a scholarly discussion'; cf. *Laws* VII, 820c8–9; Aristotle, *Politics* VII, 1323b39.

[63] See Chapter 5, sections 5.3 and 5.4, on some undecidable questions about who and what exists in the background in the dialogue-world.

2.4 The tone of confidence

But that same tone also has the whole enterprise in its scope. On this level, the tone (I suggest) is meant to launch the entire genre of Platonic cosmology. One of the most noticeable things about this genre as exemplified in the *Timaeus* is that it covers a vast range of subject-matters. The goodness of the cosmos entails its unity, and its unity entails that a scientific account must be possible about every important aspect and ingredient.[64] How better to demonstrate that no aspect of this world is beyond reach of science than by actually providing a reasoned, interesting, and coherently connected account of each one? But to make that comprehensive point Plato does not need to hold many of these particular theories otherwise than lightly (although we cannot know that he was not wedded to them). For now, they at least hold the ring. To offer some of them with the tentativeness that would perhaps be appropriate in the context of an *already established* enterprise of Platonic cosmology might well put the current, actual, launch at risk. To convey consciousness – say by an apologetic tone – that many of the specific views are desperately speculative could trigger wholesale doubts about the generic enterprise, especially in an Academic ethos, one that set such high value on rigour and exactness.

In law courts and assembly, where the *eikos* is meant to decide every issue, one is expected to put one's own case stoutly. The aim is to make it seem more plausible to others by appearing confident in it oneself. However, if I am right, Plato has a different motive for his cosmological tone of confidence: it is not to sell a particular theory but to transmit confidence in the generic enterprise. Timaeus is being sent forth, with as it were the blessing of the Socrates-figure, to colonise, set up camp in, every part of the field of nature: but only through further engagement and criticism will the colonies take root and develop. And the further engagement and criticism will only be forthcoming if people believe that it is worthwhile. No doubt there is an agonistic ring to the Timaean tone of confidence. A *position* that stands there boldly and asserts itself with eloquence is calling for challengers to come forward and test it; whereas offering conjectures or hypotheses as 'only conjectures and hypotheses' could seem like pleading for non-confrontation – a request to be excused the pressure of serious criticism.

---

[64] Mourelatos, 1991 speaks of the 'encyclopedia of the sciences in the *Timaeus*' (26). Compare the extremely sketchy attitude of the youthful and inexperienced Socrates at *Parmenides* 130c1–d5: Socrates is uncertain whether there are Forms of man, fire, and water, certain that there are not Forms of hair, mud, and dirt. Timaeus explicitly mentions Forms in connection with fire and water (50c4–52a7) and the intelligible paradigm in connection with man (see 39e3–40a2 with 41a7 ff.). He also discourses scientifically on hair (76b1–d3) and on varieties and mixtures of earth (60b6–61c2).

Finally, there is also the religious dimension. Timaeus's account is of a god which a god has made. So presenting the cosmology is, amongst other things, an act of religious celebration of maker and work together. But celebration, like story-telling, does not sit well with cautious expression. For this reason too Timaeus comes out with all flags flying.

Here, I have not approached head-on the endlessly discussed question of what Plato means to convey by calling the cosmology a *muthos*. I have focused instead on the apparent disparity between the avowed standard of the *eikos*, and the confident tone. Such a tone is appropriate, for reasons I have suggested, for a set of proposals meant to launch a research programme of a type that not everyone already believes in. A confident tone is also what one uses to tell an ordinary *muthos* or story. This common feature, as well as the theogonic subject-matter,[65] may be why Timaeus speaks of his *logos* not merely as *eikôs*, but as an *eikôs muthos*.

2.5 TWO FURTHER QUESTIONS

Some questions remain about the epistemology of the exordium. Timaeus aligns the ontological contrast between eternal model and its likeness with a contrast between the corresponding *logoi*: those that deliver an account of what is changeless should themselves be impossible to uproot through refutation, whereas those that are about the likeness should be *eikotes*. The subjects of the first contrast differ as being from becoming; and the *eikotes logoi* in the second one are cosmological. This organisation strongly suggests that the 'being' subject-matter in the first contrast is the paradigm of this cosmos. It also suggests that the *eikotes logoi* in the second contrast are, as such, in principle refutable. How exactly are we to understand these suggestions?

(1) Let us begin with the refutability of cosmological *eikotes logoi*. Now, Timaeus takes up a number of positions that are clearly not negotiable.[66] This is true of the metaphysics, epistemology, and methodology of the exordium, 27d5–29d3.[67] It must also be true of the dichotomy that launches the 'second beginning' between the works of demiurgic Intelligence (*nous*),

---

[65] Cf. Burnyeat, 2005, 144–5.
[66] See the appeals to necessity at 28a4–5 and c2–3 ('Everything that comes to be necessarily comes to be through the agency of some cause'); 28a6–8 ('What a craftsman makes looking to the intelligible is necessarily brought to completion as something fair'); 29b1 ('This cosmos must be an *eikôn* of something'); also *dihoristeon* at 29b4 framing the epistemology; *lektea* at 46e3 on the two kinds of cause; *dêlôteon* at 48e4 on introducing the third kind (although similar gerundives and *dei legein* etc. are also often applied to more negotiable parts of the account).
[67] Cf. Berti, 1997, 127.

2.5 Two further questions

and 'the effects of Necessity' (47e3). That Intelligence is a principle distinct from the materials of the world follows from the premiss that the materials, being lifeless, lack intelligence (46d4–7), and this too is not negotiable. So too for the tenet that Intelligence is successful in 'persuading' Necessity to fall in with its direction (48a2–5), and the closely linked tenet that whereas Intelligence is the principal cause, the materials are auxiliary causes (*sunaitia*) (46c7–e7). Then there is the Receptacle, which enters into the genesis of the materials: it too is part of the non-negotiable framework. It takes its place as a third sort of thing alongside intelligible being and its generated counterpart as distinguished in the exordium (48a2–52d4). Finally, there is the 'unchallengeable'[68] axiom that this cosmos is the most perfect physical system that benevolent divine intelligence could have made.

But these positions are either directly about the created cosmos or belong to cosmology because they are about its method and epistemic standard.[69] Insofar as they refer to the cosmos they are of a piece with all that Timaeus puts forward as being in principle refutable. But if they are not negotiable, they are obviously not refutable. Does this imply that these non-negotiables are not *eikotes logoi* even though they belong in, or with, the cosmology of the created cosmos? If it does, then that careful alignment of distinctions in the exordium is incoherent.

However, the supposed implication only follows if we assume that the *logoi* which are to be judged by one or the other epistemic standard are individual sentences or propositions. Instead, as Burnyeat has argued,[70] they are blocks of discourse. (In the last section we used this idea to develop the point that different sections of the cosmology may be equally satisfactory on Timaean terms even though some may be far more speculative than others.) Now, the cosmological blocks of discourse are built up from non-negotiable starting points or within a non-negotiable framework. But we are not meant to assess the starting points by themselves or the resulting propositions by themselves. A block as a whole is refutable in principle if a better account could, in principle, be generated within the same basic

---

[68] Burnyeat's word, 2005, 163.
[69] The assumption that it belongs to a given discipline (rather than a distinct meta-discipline) to reflect on its own methods is ubiquitous in Aristotle. In order to save the methodology of the *eikos* from itself being ranked as *eikos* and therefore refutable, we could clarify its own status as meta-cosmological and restrict its application to cosmological proposals only. But there is no obvious step of this kind for saving the non-negotiability of the other great elements listed above.
[70] See the previous section. The argument is: since (1) the words *muthos* and *logos* (or their plurals) are several times used by Timaeus to refer to the same linguistic entities, and (2) an individual *muthos* (story) must be a complex of several propositions, the same must hold for an individual *logos* in the sense relevant here. A mathematical proof would be a *logos* in this sense.

framework. So a whole block is *eikôs* at best even when its fundamental principles are beyond question.

It helps if we distinguish between the *irrefutable* and the *non-refutable*, treating the former as a sub-class of the latter. Irrefutable (*anelenctoi*) *logoi* are ones that are admitted to the corpus of a science, e.g. mathematics, because testing (*elenchos*) has shown them immune to refutation (where irrefutability is the standard for admission to that science). Quite different are the framework principles of the respective sciences. Such a principle is not subject to testing either for admission to the science to which it pertains or for admission to some other science; hence it is neither refutable nor irrefutable, but is non-refutable because never a candidate for possible refutation.

(2) I turn now to a problem to do with the subject-matter of the *logoi* concerning the changeless, the ones that fall short unless they are irrefutable (29b3–c3). The passage pulls us in different directions. On the one hand, as I have noted, it strongly suggests that this subject-matter is the eternal paradigm of the cosmos. On the other hand, it also strongly suggests that the irrefutability in question is the norm relevant to certain human disciplines such as mathematics. For Timaeus is pleading that his *logoi* not be judged by the more rigorous standard we apply to our studies of changeless things. Thus the exordium (a) contrasts the refutable *logoi* of human cosmology with the (ideally) non-refutable *logoi* that encapsulate existing or possible human studies of changeless things, and it also (b) contrasts the former with a non-refutable, divine, *logos* of the cosmic paradigm;[71] and it proceeds without registering that these are distinct contrasts. The charitable, and I think correct, interpretation is that Plato is simply assimilating the

---

[71] I diverge from Burnyeat, 2005, in ascribing to the Demiurge a non-refutable (hence better than *eikôs*) *logos* of the paradigm. Burnyeat argues that human cosmology is at best an *eikôs logos* because we develop it through reconstructing the Demiurge's practical reasoning, and '[p]ractical reasoning is seldom, if ever, deductively valid' (159). The thought seems to be that human cosmology is *eikôs* at best because it reflects the inevitable *logical imperfection* of the Demiurge's practical reasoning. But I doubt whether this feature means that the demiurgic reasonings or conclusions are *eikotes* at best. The exordium surely excludes the divine *logos* from being *refutable*. By 'divine *logos*' I mean not merely its content, but the account as held by the Demiurge. Who or what could refute *this*? So: whether the divine *logos* is rightly called *eikôs* depends on whether *eikôs* entails 'refutable'. The exordium leaves this open. (The converse entailment, i.e. running from 'refutable' to '*eikôs* at best', is what does the work.) In any case, not being logically valid is not sufficient for refutability: an agent is normally the authority on his plans and reasons regardless of whether the reasons entail the practical conclusion. Hence even if we decided that 'is not logically valid' does entail 'is *eikôs* at best', we could understand the latter as not entailing refutability, and the divine *logos* could count as *eikôs*. The exordium does not, however, feature the notions of logical validity and invalidity (only the coarser ones of refutability and non-refutability), and absent the notion of logical invalidity there seems no way to prise being *eikôs* at best apart from being refutable. I conclude that the practicality of the Demiurge's *logos* does not render it *eikôs* at best. Nor is it what explains why human cosmology has that status. The latter is due to the fact that our *logos* of the cosmos is *not* the practical one of the god who made it.

2.5 Two further questions

two contrasts (a) and (b), not identifying them. He is in effect saying: human beings cannot aspire to an account of the cosmos that meets the standard we rightly apply when we do e.g. mathematics; for our account of the cosmos is as good, but only as good, as our best account of the cosmic paradigm; and God alone has a non-refutable account of that.[72]

But what if Plato means to identify the contrasts? That would entail identifying the subject-matter of human mathematics (and the like) with the cosmic paradigm. This is difficult, to say the least. Such an identity would imply: either human beings have no possible access to any non-refutable *logoi* about eternal things (since eternal things are entirely comprised in the cosmic paradigm, and only God is capable of a non-refutable grasp of that), or humans can in fact attain to a non-refutable grasp of the paradigm. To spell out the first alternative: the epistemic quality of human mathematical understanding even at best would be no better than that of our grasp at best of the paradigm, and hence of the nature of the cosmos itself. Thus human grasp of Timaean cosmology would no longer be epistemically inferior to some other kind of human discipline; for us refutability would be 'fashioned over all things', to echo Xenophanes. What about the second alternative? If we interpret it as straightforwardly saying that human beings are capable of a non-refutable grasp of the cosmic paradigm as such (i.e. it belongs immediately to their grasp of it that they recognise the object to be the cosmic paradigm), the proposition is absurd, since it entails that we can know the paradigm as the Demiurge of the cosmos knows it. The only remotely plausible interpretation of the second alternative would be as saying something like this: human studies of mathematics and the metaphysical foundations of mathematics (domains where, it is already agreed, irrefutability is the standard for success, and where it is uncontroversial that we can attain this standard) are addressing what is in fact the cosmic paradigm, whether or not typical practitioners are aware of this. In other words, the content of that paradigm turns out to be (or, alternatively, to be reducible to) nothing other than one or more branches of abstract mathematics or mathematically oriented metaphysics. Something like this assumption must have helped to inspire the heavily mathematicised metaphysics and physics of Plato's successors in the Academy, Speusippus and Xenocrates.[73] It is of some interest to find in the *Timaeus* a passage that might seem to support the assumption.[74]

---

[72] This thought also surfaces at 72d4–8.
[73] On whom see Dillon, 2003, chs. 2 and 3. See Aristotle's complaint, *Metaphysics* 1, 992a32–b1: 'Mathematics has come to be the whole of philosophy for modern thinkers, though they say that it should be studied for the sake of other things [i.e. physics]' (tr. Ross, in Barnes, 1984).
[74] For some more discussion, see Chapter 3, section 3.2.

Such a theory faces considerable, perhaps in some cases insurmountable, difficulties. There is a question about how statements of abstract mathematics can adequately describe objects in the world of becoming. There are questions about the status and justification of the theory itself. There is the problem of how physicists are to set about describing and explaining specific physical kinds in the mathematicised terms of the theory. Clearly this task will be most difficult and dubious for topics such as human anatomy where we already have considerable working knowledge and functional understanding of a mostly unmathematical kind. How, in obedience to the theory, are we to convert this into some kind of mathematical language while still preserving a grasp of the original subject-matter? And how would doing this teach us any more than we can otherwise find out about the physical nature of these and related phenomena?[75]

2.6 SUMMARY

This chapter has been about Timaeus's exordium, which lays down the *eikôn* status of this cosmos and the *eikotes logoi* (or *eikotes muthoi*) of cosmology. The first task was to understand the connection between these ideas. The ground was laid in section 2.1, which focused on Timaeus's question: 'Which of the two paradigms did the maker of this world refer to, changeless or generated?' The main aim there was to show that although the question is surprising, it is not in any way logically out of order. This makes way for supposing the surprise to be intentional, and for wondering about its purpose. In section 2.2, I maintained that it is a device for making us jump to attention to the full import of Timaeus's answer. From the moment paradigms are first mentioned (28a6), it is totally predictable that Timaeus is going to say that our world was made in accordance with an intelligible paradigm. Such a statement will easily sound like a Platonic truism, as Plato with the *Republic* in the background must have been well aware. But truism or not, it is for Plato a truth of immense richness, so he needs a way of presenting it that will halt us in our tracks so that we dwell on it rather than looking straight ahead to the next thing. What if the model *had* been a generated one? (What if this perceptible universe *had not been made according to any model at all*?) Plato's answer: there could have been no discipline of cosmology: for reference to the intelligible paradigm is what guides the actual practice by which we frame reasonable (*eikotes*) answers to cosmological questions. Forced for a

---

[75] There is an obvious parallel in contemporary discussions of reductive materialist theories of mind.

moment to gaze at the alternative we begin to take stock of the sheer fact of the availability to us of theories of the cosmos that deserve to be ranked as *eikotes* – as distinct from idle suggestions not governed by any criterion for assessing the quality of questions and answers.

We have such a criterion in our understanding of what a maker aiming to make the most excellent possible world would have aimed at. But since this understanding is necessarily conjectural, cosmological *logoi* are inherently corrigible. Section 2.3 began an examination of this theme. There I suggested that proper reception of the cosmology can be charted by reference to an over-demanding attitude and one that is not demanding enough. The first is dismissive because cosmology does not aim to be beyond refutation. The second is hospitable but welcomes Timaean cosmology just as an ethically pure and splendidly wrought story about the generation of gods. To regard it as *only* a story, even while accepting that this story is not a fiction, is to fail to understand that it has been put forward not only to show glorious and edifying things, but also to be itself developed and improved through scientific criticism. Such a critical attitude is not compatible with simply taking it in and recounting it as we do stories, just as it is incompatible with judging it purely as a work of art or as an aid to religious contemplation. Plato means the Timaean monologue to belong with the sciences, not (or certainly not just) with the humanities.[76]

I further argued in section 2.3 that it would be a mistake to assume that the depicted uncritical receptiveness of Socrates, Critias, and Hermocrates is any sort of template for the real-world reception Plato surely hoped for. As figures representing other genres of discipline they can smile a welcome to this Platonic example of cosmology, but the work of responding with scientifically critical seriousness has to be left to people in the real world.

In section 2.4, on Timaeus's tone of confidence, I suggested that there are several strands in what is going on. Why the reiterated declarations that the path being pursued is the path of the *eikos*? Partly, I think, to register that each stage of the cosmology is indeed living up to the general standard set for it; but partly also to counteract any impression that the present proposals are meant as the final word. Such an impression might well be conveyed by the almost unwavering tone of confidence with which Timaeus presents his material. So why adopt a tone that then needs to be counteracted? Well, as I pointed out, Plato is probably entitled to be confident throughout that his

---

[76] Burnyeat, 2005, 156, 160, 162, speaks excellently of how the Timaean method invites its audience to become connoisseurs of the cosmos as a beautifully rational work of art – not the same as becoming connoisseurs of the Timaean *cosmology* as a beautifully rational work of art.

cosmological *logoi* meet the standard of the *eikos* even though some are surely more speculative than others. This is because he glossed the *eikos*-standard with: 'no less *eikôs* than anyone else's'. If we understand the plural *logoi* as referring to the different sections of the cosmology, distinguished by subject-matter, we see that the comparison would be subject-matter by subject-matter with the findings of other thinkers. On that system, the Timaean sections could certainly all meet the standard even though comparison with each other may reveal that some are distinctly shakier than others. Since such intra-cosmological comparison is not in view, there is no reason or opportunity for Plato to have Timaeus discuss any variation in epistemic quality between the sections. It is not clear whether Plato is aware of such variation but is silent about it, or whether it has no salience for him.

Still in section 2.4, I suggested that the confident declaration that each *logos* meets the standard can be construed as an invitation to real-world recipients to check the assertions by detailed comparisons with known views of other thinkers, and also as a challenge to do better. We do not know enough about the intellectual ethos to be able to rule out the possibility that remarks like 'This is of course only a speculation' would have been interpreted as requests for the gentle tolerance that lets everyone go on holding whatever opinion they hold. Socrates in earlier dialogues is shown demolishing the bar to progress that consists in regarding oneself as already possessed of the answer. There the questions were about excellence and happiness, on which everyone is full of assumptions firm enough to act from. No doubt in cosmology Plato saw the opposite mind-set as a great bar to progress: the one that says 'No one can be wise about these things – and anyway having views about them is not what matters in life.'

Also in section 2.4 I suggested that the tone of confidence is meant to transmit confidence in the generic enterprise of Platonic cosmology. Although maintaining such confidence depends on making specific proposals that are visibly as reasonable as anyone else's so far, the point now is that this is a worthwhile *kind* of discipline that deserves to be carried forward. Obviously, it will only be carried forward if others are infected by the same spirit. In this spirit Plato need be doing little more than having a brave go at filling in with some picture or other every one of the vast range of areas which the principles of the work, and his own genius for organisation and analysis, have shown that cosmology should cover. Finally in section 2.4, I touched on the fact that as well as everything else that it is, the Timaean monologue is a theogony and a celebration of the cosmic god and of all the demiurgic handiwork. For this an unfaltering tone is appropriate. From this perspective, the references to the *eikos* cease to be salient:

2.6 Summary

we enjoy the wonderful intellectual spectacle of our universe, concentrating on the perfect thing that is shown and forgetting for a while the corrigibility of the showing.

Taking the phrase *eikotes logoi* as a genuinely plural reference to the sections has so far figured as alternative to understanding it to refer to the mass of the discourse as a whole. But in the first part of section 2.5 the rejected alternative was itself a genuinely plural reference, this time to individual propositions. On that basis it became possible to see how the Timaean *logoi*, the sections, can be *eikotes*, hence refutable, even though each depends on (and they often overtly include) various non-negotiable, hence non-refutable, propositions.

Section 2.5 also looked at the way in which the exordium makes human cosmology the subject of two distinct contrasts: one with human studies of eternal things, the other with the Demiurge's *logos* of the paradigm. The exordium does not clearly mark the difference. But I doubt whether Plato here intends to affirm the tempting but problematic view that these contrasts somehow amount to the same.[77]

---

[77] Some of the lines of thought worked out in this chapter point in very much the same direction as Dorothea Frede's in her 1996 paper, although her perspective is different.

CHAPTER 3

The metaphysics of the paradigm

3.1 COSMOLOGY OR METAPHYSICS?

Consider the ambiguous phrase 'intelligible world'. In the context of Platonism it could allude to the assumption that this sense-perceptible universe may also become to some extent intelligible to us since it was made according to a rational and benevolent plan which we may reasonably attempt to reconstruct. Alternatively, the phrase may refer to an object accessible only by intellect, an object which constitutes the eternal original of which this universe is a merely temporal copy. The eternal original is called a 'world' (or 'cosmos') because the world-hood of the sensible world, which is to say its physical order and complexity-in-unity, is inherited from corresponding features of the intelligible model. A question worth pondering – even though we may have no doubt of the answer – is: which of these two 'intelligible worlds' is Timaeus's monologue principally *about*? Is the account first and foremost about the physical cosmos and its contents, an attempt to make more sense of this subject-matter than previous cosmologies had done – but an attempt that depends for its specific shape on an underpinning in trans-natural metaphysics? Or is the account primarily about that intelligible entity in accordance with which the physical cosmos was made – does it treat the physical cosmos as the taking-off point for an investigation of *that* intelligible entity? To understand Timaeus's monologue in this second way is to look upon it as a gateway through which to enter into the study of the metaphysics of the incorporeal, this being the primary object of interest.

I distinguish between these two approaches for the sake of philosophical clarification and analysis. Thus the aim is not to provide a clear-cut contrast by which to classify historical interpretations of the *Timaeus*. For Plotinus, Porphyry, and Proclus the world of nature is the launching pad for the soul's ascent to the intelligibles and beyond, and these philosophers were surely more occupied with the metaphysical problem of how the intelligible

3.1 *Cosmology or metaphysics?*

manages to be reflected in the sensible and in matter, than with constructing a picture of the physical world by conjecturing the contents of its paradigm. One might therefore infer that they read the *Timaeus* accordingly; and broadly and impressionistically this may be plausible. But Plotinus and Porphyry are not in the business of giving an extended commentary on the *Timaeus*, and Proclus, who is, understands his task in a way that certainly accepts the cosmology as such even though for him there is a great deal more to it than just that; and he seems to have no uneasiness in combining these different perspectives.[1]

The modern consensus is that the *Timaeus* offers first and foremost a cosmology,[2] and I think that this is correct. If we look at the text as a whole and accept it at face value, the following features stand out. (1) The monologue is announced in advance as a cosmology, an account of the coming to be of the universe we are in, not an account of anything else as well (27a5–6). (2) The monologue is indeed announced as the portal to something beyond itself, but what follows it is not an ascent to the domain of pure intelligibles, but downward immersion in the particularities of human history (actually, pseudo-history) (27a7–b6; cf. 23c3 ff.). (3) Timaeus's exuberantly detailed scientific explanations of a very wide range of empirical phenomena go far beyond whatever could be needed for the 'gateway to metaphysics' approach. (4) At one place Plato indicates that although he recognises recondite principles of reality, they cannot be made clear through an account like this one (48c2–d1[3]): which suggests that the Timaean monologue is not intended as *entrée* to a full-blooded examination of metaphysics for its own sake, and therefore must be intended as something else, namely a cosmology. (The claim here is that an interest in fundamental metaphysics for its own sake does not inform the *Timaeus*, not that Plato had no such interest. We only have to think of the *anhupothetos*

---

[1] See the preface to his *Timaeus* commentary (Diehl, 1904), especially 1, 1A; 4A; 4F on the target (*skopos*) of the dialogue and 1, 5A on its relation to the *Parmenides*. He says: 'This whole dialogue, throughout its entire length, has physical inquiry (*phusiologia*) as its aim' (1, 1A4–6, tr. Tarrant). For Proclus even the Athens-Atlantis story is a contribution to *phusiologia*. Following Iamblichus, he treats it as an allegory covering the whole of metaphysical and physical reality starting with the One and the Dyad and Unlimited (1, 24D–F; cf. 40C). This tells us something about what counts as physical enquiry for Proclus.

[2] However, Arthur Platt (quoted by Lloyd, 1968, 79) wrote: 'Plato, being first and foremost a metaphysician with a sort of religious system, would not have us study anything but metaphysics and a sort of mystic religion' (Platt, 1927). By contrast, Bury said in 1929: 'In truth, there is but little of metaphysics in the *Timaeus*; it is mainly occupied with the attempt to give a "probable" account of matters which belong to the sciences of physics and physiology' (Bury, 1929, 13).

[3] The passage is quoted and discussed in section 3.3.2 below.

archê tou pantos of *Republic* VI, 511b3–c2; cf. 510b4–9, and the One and the Indefinite Dyad[4] of his unwritten doctrines.)

Despite this indisputable evidence that Timaeus's speech is a cosmology rather than an introduction to incorporeal metaphysics, it is not (I think) a waste of time to describe and compare these contrasting ways of receiving the discourse. Even modern interpreters may on occasion operate on the assumption that some passage of the *Timaeus* is principally metaphysics rather than cosmology, and on that basis make an exegetical decision that might have gone a different way if Plato Physicus had been uppermost in their minds.[5] Clarity about the difference between the approaches I am distinguishing surely helps the interpreter. Moreover, the difference is philosophically interesting in its own right. In grasping it one grasps what is perhaps the central ambiguity of the tradition called 'Platonism', one that can be traced back to the *Timaeus* itself. For the text offers contrary clues, of which some (the majority) authorise reading the monologue as cosmology with metaphysical underpinnings, while others (fewer but striking) authorise reading it as metaphysics approached through cosmology. The ambiguity is present because Plato's distinction of eternal paradigm and object generated in accordance with it can be developed in two radically divergent ways.

According to one way, the eternal paradigm of the cosmos is an original of which the Demiurge makes a copy or representation or reproduction in a different medium.[6] According to the other, the paradigm is a recipe which he follows. The information that the chocolate cake about to be served has been made in accordance with a certain recipe does not leave us expecting the cake to be a copy, likeness, image, representation, reproduction, imitation, or semblance of a recipe. By contrast, the image, stamped on a tea-towel, of half a page of Mrs Beaton *is* a reproduction of an original – in this case, of a page in a recipe book. I shall argue in the rest of this chapter that thinking of the cosmic paradigm as the *recipe* for the cosmos leads to engagement with cosmology as such, whereas thinking of it as the *original* of the cosmos leads to treating the cosmology as merely a gateway to metaphysics. We shall see that this second notion of the paradigm lurks in the curious question which Timaeus poses in the exordium: did the Demiurge refer to an eternal paradigm or a generated one when he fashioned this

---

[4] Which perhaps also surface in the *Philebus*.
[5] The major contemporary example is the ontological interpretation of the Receptacle discussed in Chapter 6, sections 6.5 ff.
[6] Cf. Johansen, 2004, 56–60.

world (28c5–29a2)? We have seen (Chapter 2, section 2.2) how Timaeus's asking this question brings it to the fore that the natural world is accessible to human understanding precisely because it is derivative from an eternal paradigm. Thus in one way the question about the paradigms is an auspicious start to an account that aims to be *about* the natural world. Yet, as I shall argue, that very question's rhetorical and perhaps even logical structure begs for a 'cosmology as gateway to metaphysics' interpretation. This interpretation encourages the idea that we are or should be enquiring about the eternal cosmic paradigm for its own sake; and it tends to generate a hyper-realist outlook on this object. 'Hyper-realism' (as I name it) concerning the eternal paradigm will be sketched in contrast with the perspective afforded by the other approach. This latter perspective is more modest and economical, but nonetheless it deserves to be called both 'realist' and 'Platonic'.

3.2 WAYS WITH PARADIGMS

First, we may think of the famous likeness between a Platonic Form and its this-worldly correlate (or correlates) in terms of representation: this is encouraged by Plato's frequent statements that this-worldly objects are imitations of Forms. It is also encouraged by the imagery whereby he presents the this-worldly object as a shadow, reflection, or dreamed appearance of the Form. Now, our first-order experience of representations, given that we take ourselves to be dealing with representations, whether in words or in some other medium, is dominated by interest in the things the representations are of (or that we take them to be of). Thus in dreaming we are typically taken up with what the dream is about. We often look at shadows and reflections, e.g. of ourselves in the mirror, just in order to obtain information about the original objects whose shadows or reflections they are. No doubt it is partly because of the intensity of our interest in the originals that it sometimes seems as if the originals themselves are actually there, standing or happening in front of us or around us, when in fact they are in no such place and may even be non-existent, and all that is physically present to us is the representing medium. We are prone to a double mistake. We may, without realising, 'project' properties of the representing medium on to the represented original, so that the original seems to us to be, for example, 'here', when only the medium is 'here'. And we may fall under the illusion that what is in fact an image borne by the representing medium is the one and only real thing: i.e. that we are dealing not with an original and its representation but with a single non-derivative entity.

Now, it is plain that the *transparency* of the medium, the fact that it does *not*, in our basic interaction with it, draw attention to itself, facilitates these mistakes.[7] Suppose, however, that we manage to avoid or to correct these mistakes. In that case, we are free of the illusion that the objects represented are here with us, and of the illusion that what is in fact the image of the object is all there is. We shall now be correctly 'reading' what goes on among the objects as going on in whatever space or domain *they* are in, whether far from us or in a different world from us. But the medium will still be transparent, if it is a good one. Thus, now that we are reading correctly we are still taking no notice of the medium as such, and we are surely giving much less attention than before to the representations in it as such, since we are now sure-footedly using them as signs of the things we are interested in.

The point of this discussion is to bring out the fact that if the sensible world is essentially a representation of an intelligible original, then the right attitude towards the sensible world and things within it is not to be interested in them at all for themselves, as the cosmologist most certainly is, but to do one's best to 'look through' them at what they represent. There is something of a tension between such an attitude to the cosmos and the attitude which Timaeus's words seem meant to encourage: that we admire and love this cosmos for its beauty, and venerate it as a god. It might be said that Timaeus also encourages us to love and venerate this cosmos as an expression of the genius and benevolence of its author. But such an attitude towards the cosmos, even if it is also an attitude towards its maker as such, is nonetheless focused upon the cosmos itself. It does not try to treat the cosmos as a virtually unnoticed written page mediating readers' access to the real objects of attention, i.e. the persons in the story; or as a church fresco whose purpose is attained if through it congregants behold the angels and devils of the next world.

The existence of a causal relation (or our assumption that such a relation exists) between one set of items and another leaves it open which side is or should be the primary object of attention. Thus the fact that Timaeus assumes a causal relation between an intelligible object, the Demiurge's paradigm, and the sensible cosmos[8] does not preclude regarding the latter as a mere representation through which to access the former, but it certainly does not dictate this direction of interest. A medical technician reading blips

---

[7] If the medium is a bad one, e.g. foggy or noisy, what is supposed to be represented may hardly appear in it; in which case, if we notice anything at all we notice just some bit of the medium, and perhaps take that to be the one and only reality.
[8] By 'causal relation' here I mean no more than that the Demiurge is guided by the paradigm.

on a screen is interested in them only as representing the patient's heartbeat. By contrast, as was argued in Chapter 2, the Platonic cosmologist conjectures the contents of the good world-maker's eternal paradigm in order to achieve a reasonable account of major features of the physical world. The cosmologist as such is not primarily trying to find out about the paradigm, but about the cosmos. He or she does not 'use' the cosmos as a medium by which to penetrate to truths *about the paradigm*, but refers to the paradigm as an aid for research *about the cosmos*.

We can, however, ask whether this specifically cosmological direction of interest is in fact the direction that most determines Plato's thinking in the *Timaeus*. It is obvious that the causal relation between heartbeats and blips on the medical screen is meant to be used to monitor the heartbeats *via* the blips, because it was in order to monitor heartbeats that we created the technology that embodies that causal relation. But in the case of the sensible cosmos and its intelligible paradigm, is it in fact so clear in the text which way the direction of our interest is meant to go? Was the physical world, according to the *Timaeus*, created primarily for its own sake as a splendid god, and also as a place to be lived in, coped with, wondered at, and with luck and inspiration scientifically explored, by mortal rational creatures: or are we instead to treat it primarily as a sensible sign-system through which we try to make out the nature of the eternal? To affirm the latter is to imply that even if the Platonism of the *Timaeus* can be used by us as a heuristic for cosmology, its primary or central purpose is to get us moving towards a science whose subject-matter is a Platonic Form or domain of such Forms.

This latter way of receiving the *Timaeus* corresponds to the idea that this world was made as a representation of the eternal paradigm – made 'in its image'. In the last section I contrasted this with the idea that the paradigm stands to the cosmos as a recipe, prescription, design, or plan stands to a product made in accordance with it. Let us now turn to thinking about the function of a recipe or design. The primary reason for following a design when making something is not in order to create a representation of the design, or to communicate the design by means of the representation, but in order to be more effective in making the product.[9] True, someone else might be able to infer the design from the product; but there is a great deal else that a product is typically intended for than to take our minds back to the recipe for it. For example, a shuttle is made as a tool for weaving. And if it is made according to a template, this is not so that it should reveal the

---

[9] A secondary case occurs when one operates in accordance with a recipe in order to demonstrate or test the recipe.

template in a veiled form, but so that it will be a better shuttle than one haphazardly made. On this line of thought, the intelligent cause of the cosmos looks to an intelligible pattern in order to raise the chances of producing the most perfect possible physical system: that he guides production by the pattern is not for the sake of *the pattern* (in order, say, to show it forth), but for the sake of the product – so that this should be excellent of its kind.

Here are some lines that can be taken in either of the two ways.

Now the maker and father of this All is hard to find; and <even> if we found him, representing him in speech to everyone would be impossible. And so we must go back to this question about it: which of the two paradigms guided its maker when he fashioned it – the one that does not change and stays the same, or the one that has come to be? (28c3–29a2)

It seems that Timaeus turns to the question of the paradigm because *by himself* the maker and father is hard to find and impossible to describe to everyone. Once we note his link with the intelligible paradigm we have located him as, and can describe him as, 'the maker of this cosmos', spelling this out with whatever we can infer about the content of the paradigm. Now, is Timaeus's primary interest in the god responsible for this cosmos, or is it in this cosmos? Does he start by hoping to find the maker-god and then he discovers at least this much about the god: that the god made a physical world in accordance with an intelligible paradigm? Or is Timaeus primarily trying to say something about this cosmos (his stated task being to explain its genesis, 27a3–6), and because of that he moves to the maker-god (and thence to the paradigm)? With human individuals we sometimes set about determining who they are, and even what they are like, by identifying their parents. Such an enquiry need not involve independent interest in the parent-figures themselves. Is that what is going on here? Is it in order to explain the cosmos that Timaeus tries to pinpoint its father or something about its father, or is it this fathering being and his paradigm that Timaeus really wants to know better?

I now return to Timaeus's question about the two paradigms. I shall argue that this question has the potential to shunt us towards a 'gateway to metaphysics' interpretation of the Timaean cosmology.

Timaeus introduced the notion of eternal paradigms by laying down the generalisation that good craftsmen look to these rather than to generated ones (28a6–b2). He then applied the disjunction 'Looking to an eternal or a generated one?' to the particular case of the maker of this world. In both generalisation and application the two kinds of paradigms are presented in a

3.2 Ways with paradigms

symmetrical way. This symmetry in a way is natural, because the generalisation leads up to the application, and (1) the application is effected by demanding *a choice between two answers to the same question*. As the objects presented by the respective answers, the two paradigms are logically and rhetorically symmetrical, so to speak. Each functions as (2) *a method for producing the same result*. Simply as methods they are on a par. One is superior, but this can only be judged by putting them logically side by side. Furthermore, (3) *the reader apprehends both in the same way*. The reader simply *thinks* of each. (The reader is not the world-maker actually choosing between perceptible and intelligible cosmic paradigms; nor is the reader currently getting ready to make a human artefact and choosing between an actually perceived existing example and an intelligible source of guidance.) One might consequently imagine, and Plato's language encourages it, that the paradigms *involved in the methods* are a matching pair of objects: alternative versions, eternal and generated, of what is essentially the same type of thing. Just as the artificer who works from a sense-perceptible paradigm works by copying it, perhaps in a different material, so it may seem that the artificer who chooses the better method works by *copying* his intelligible paradigm in a different medium. But this is a confusion, and one that makes it seem that Timaeus offers first and foremost a cosmological gateway to trans-natural metaphysics rather than a metaphysical gateway to cosmology.

It will take some time to explain the confusion and why it is a confusion. Let us begin by considering what it means for a human maker to 'look to an eternal paradigm rather than to one that has merely come to be'. Plato treats it as self-evident that a good maker looks to an eternal paradigm. Consequently, we should interpret this principle so that it is common sense. Translated into commonsense terms, the principle is: rather than trying directly to copy or reproduce a thing that already exists in the world, whether a shuttle someone has made or an existing political constitution, intelligent shuttle- or constitution-makers begin by turning back within themselves to first principles,[10] working out what such a thing essentially is and what it is for. Alternatively, they should accept the instructions of someone else who has gone back to the first principles of the matter. It is common sense that productive work is better guided by an intellectually sought for, intellectually worked out, answer, than by looking at an

---

[10] This is meant in a relaxed sense, i.e. as returning to first principles of the relevant subject matter. Someone designing a gun goes back to first principles of ballistics and metallurgy, but not to first principles of sub-nuclear physics.

unanalysed pre-existing object of the kind.[11] The maker who merely tries to copy or reproduce may labour over superficial characteristics of the model-object as if they were the essential ones, and may ignorantly reproduce characteristics that were appropriate for the context in which the first object was meant to function, but not for the context of the new one. The merely reproductive maker might copy what is actually a broken shuttle[12] or an unjust constitution through ignorance of what shuttles and constitutions really are.[13]

We are now about to notice an important *a*symmetry between the paradigm that has come to be, and what, on the commonsense interpretation, we are equating with the eternal paradigm. The eternal paradigm is an answer to a 'What is . . . ?' question. It is a quiddity. It is eternal because the right answer is necessarily always the same, or so the Platonist assumes. So the maker who makes the right choice of guide will be guided by a quiddity (more or less perfectly grasped by him or her). Now it surely makes no sense to try to think of the answer to a 'What is . . . ?' question as having any role other than, or as making any impact otherwise than as, the answer to its question. Let us recognise as a distinct class of 'What is . . . ?' questions those whose answers are sought in order to provide guidance for *bringing something into being*; and correspondingly we recognise a distinct class of (let us call them) practical quiddities. The point then is that it makes no sense to think of a practical quiddity as having any role except, primarily, to guide the maker or practitioner, and, secondarily, to assess or criticise someone else's attempt to make a thing of the kind in question. The asymmetry with the non-eternal case is this: the non-eternal (generated, usually perceptible

---

[11] These remarks, I hope, are enough for the present purpose, but a general account of the use of existing examples should be more nuanced. Often it is impossible, and often unnecessary, to give 'an intellectually worked out' answer to a 'What is –?' question, if this means a verbally articulated definition. People may grasp intuitively what to aim at by being shown a sample or a demonstration, so that their successful production of new instances is not 'mindless copying' but expresses mastery of a principle. But they have to trust others to provide a good sample or an accurate demonstration.

[12] Cf. *Cratylus* 389b1–3.

[13] The point is nicely illustrated in Aristotle's polemical response at *Nicomachean Ethics* x, 1181a12–b2, to the claim of Isocrates (*Antidosis* 82–3, from which Aristotle quotes at 1181a16–17) that setting up a system of laws is *easy* because it only involves collecting (and then reproducing in one's own community) the laws most respected in other states. After emphasising the importance of relevant experience (which is not easily come by) for picking out the best laws, Aristotle culminates with our Platonic principle: 'The laws are like the products [*erga*] of political expertise; how then could someone become a legislative expert, or discern what are the best of them, *from* them?' (1181a23–b2, tr. Rowe). Someone may say: the Platonic principle must be something more arcane than the above piece of common sense, for why would Plato make such a fuss over a truism? But often in Plato the fuss is more over getting people to *apply* the principle when it comes to setting up such things as political institutions. In the *Timaeus*, as I argued in Chapter 2, section 2.2, the fuss is because, as applied to world-making, the truism gives us cosmology.

and physical) object used as a paradigm has a life of its own outside this context. It contributes to weaving if it is a shuttle, it constrains social activity in various ways if it is a political constitution. It makes no sense to try to think of a particular shuttle's being nothing but a physical paradigm for making shuttles or for explaining to someone what a shuttle is or for criticising someone's botched attempt at a shuttle. Even a colour-card sample can be used otherwise than as a sample: samples can be arranged into attractive patterns, and tunes could be played using different tuning-fork sounds. And certainly a shuttle, and objects of most kinds, must have a great many other things true of them before it is true that they can be paradigms of their kinds.

I have been focusing on empirical paradigms that are in fact examples – exemplary instances – of the kind of object someone is aiming to make. But, of course, the word *paradeigma* does not mean 'example': it has the more general meaning of 'pattern', and what we call a pattern for something may be a plan, design, or instruction for bringing it into being.[14] However, *pointing to a good example* of F is such a central and frequent way of setting up guidance for producing an F that it is easily assumed that a *paradeigma* is essentially an example. When philosophers think of people pointing at or looking to some empirical object as the *paradeigma* of something, F, they are very likely presupposing that the object is an exemplary case of F. Hence for now in considering the use of empirical objects as paradigms I shall continue to focus on objects used as examples of the kinds they are meant to explain.

So empirical paradigm-objects are themselves instances of the kinds they illustrate: instances put to a certain use. And we use empirical objects as paradigms by trying to *copy* or *reproduce* them, i.e. by trying to make some sort of *likeness* of them. However, as we have seen, they contribute to the world in other ways antecedently to our using them as paradigms. But now suppose an illusion of *symmetry* to be at work, generated by Timaeus's evenly constructed question: 'Which of the two paradigms?' The illusion is that *eternal* paradigms are like non-eternal ones, the difference (admittedly momentous) consisting *only* in the difference between eternal and non-eternal, and the associated difference between intelligible and sensible! Since non-eternal, empirical, paradigms are instances of the kinds they

---

[14] At *Protagoras* 326c8 (although some scholars have questioned the MSS reading) there is an unself-conscious example of a *paradeigma* that is not an example: (Protagoras speaking): 'The city compels them [sc. young adults] both to learn the laws and to live according to them <as if> according to a *paradeigma*.' The law is not itself an exemplary instance of civic behaviour, but the basic answer to the question 'What is a good citizen?'

help explain, one would now picture an eternal paradigm as a sort of instance too of the kind with respect to which it gives guidance (a 'perfect particular'). This point is a notorious implication of certain formulations of Platonism, and it was made the basis of a *reductio ad absurdum* of such formulations by Plato himself in the *Parmenides* (132c12–133a4; cf. 132a1–b2). That argument is meant to show how a certain way of conceiving of Platonic Forms generates, for any multiply instantiated characteristic F, an infinite regress of Forms of F. I shall return to this briefly in section 3.3.1. For now, however, the main point is this: thinking about a Form as an eternal and intelligible, *rather than* perishable and sensible, paradigm easily leads to two false steps. (1) One step takes us into the mind-set of assuming that the way to make something in accordance with an eternal paradigm is to *copy* or *reproduce* it. For this is how we operate when making something in accordance with an empirical paradigm. (2) The other false step gets us to a place where the Form appears as an eternal object which, as it were, does a great deal more than simply function as a paradigm.[15] For this is how it is with empirical objects taken as paradigms. But to look at the Form in this way is, in effect, to be committed to thinking of it as enjoying a rich and in a sense concrete life of its own: a life not merely additional to its playing its role of paradigm, but metaphysically prior. If it is in this fashion that we imagine Plato's world-maker's intelligible paradigm, i.e. not as a quiddity – what is expressed in an intelligent answer to the question 'What would be a supremely excellent physical system?' – but as an eternal object that exemplifies the kind in question,[16] then we are all set to say that the paradigm, like the cosmos made in accordance with it, is a living being – only a supernal one, 'the Intelligible Animal'; and it becomes attractive to think of its life as busily and multi-directionally unfolding and being enjoyed (even though strictly in eternity) in an incorporeal domain that stretches in other directions (just as a physical shuttle exists in various contexts before someone uses it as an example of shuttles) – a domain where chains of intelligibles rise tier upon tier beyond the rather humble level at which the Intelligible Animal – almost accidentally, it can begin to seem – serves as paradigm for

---

[15] Philoponus brought to the fore a related question: is it essential to an intelligible Form to be a paradigm, i.e. to be reproduced in a copy? Proclus assumed this to be so in Argument 2 of *On the Eternity of the World* (Lang and Macro, 2001, 39–42); Philoponus countered in his *On the Eternity of the World, against Proclus*, Rabe, 1899, 24.2–26.9.

[16] Why should any maker need both quiddity and eternal example? And if he doesn't, the dispensable one seems to be the latter, because perhaps he can grasp the quiddity without considering any eternal example (e.g. by analysing sensible examples), whereas it seems that he must have already brought the quiddity into play if he fully understands what the eternal example is an example of. This kind of criticism goes back to Aristotle's *Metaphysics*.

3.2 Ways with paradigms

the empirical world.[17] I do not think Plato in the *Timaeus* coolly intended to pitch us into all this, but there are notable passages where his language pulls in this direction. But before turning to them, let me introduce the term 'thick' in this connection. To conceive of an intelligible paradigm as an object essentially endowed with important properties and relations over and above any function it has of guiding human thought or practice is to treat it as a 'thick' intelligible.[18]

Quite often in the *Timaeus* Plato allows himself language that implies thickness for the cosmic paradigm. For example, the seductive collocation of *apeikazesthai* (to be made like, or in the likeness of), *eikôn*, and *eikôs* at 29c1–2 presents the physical cosmos not merely as made *in accordance with* the divine intelligible plan, but made so as to be a *likeness* or *image of* it. That

---

[17] Cf. the ontology of Proclus, on which see the summaries and diagrams of Festugière, 1966–8, vol. 1, 177–9; Opsomer, 2000; Brisson, 1998a, 68–9. (Brisson writes: 'Bien sûr, ce développement ressemble à la production d'une machine affolée'; but at the same time he expresses the view that of all the systems rooted in Plato, the Neoplatonism that culminates in Proclus is the one most faithful to those roots.) Still, Proclus himself emphasises that the aim of the *Timaeus* is physical enquiry (see n. 1). In Tarrant, 2007, Baltzly and Tarrant write: 'To be sure, Proclus thinks that the *Timaeus* communicates many truths about the various levels of hyper-cosmic gods, as well as those within the cosmos. It is, in this sense, a theological work. But it is also a work of physiology or natural science, and at many points Proclus is keen to show that (what he takes to be) Plato's view is defensible as a contribution to Greek science and mathematics' (19). Proclus might have allowed that the theology he attributes to Plato is far more complex than is necessary for the study of the cosmos, but no doubt he would have defended it on the basis of other Platonic material as interpreted from his point of view. Siorvanes, 1996, writes: '... for Proclus, physical theory is an integral part of his whole metaphysics and epistemology'. He continues: '[Neo-] Platonists were positive, *as Plato himself was, that science* [i.e. natural science] *leads to comprehension of the eternal, transcendent reality*', (206, emphasis added). This seems to me to be the 'gateway to metaphysics' interpretation. This type of approach to intelligibles seems to have become established in some quarters very early, if we go by Aristotle's remark about the philosophers 'called "Pythagoreans"': 'The causes and principles which they mention are ... sufficient to act as steps even up to the higher realms of reality, and are more suited to these than to theories about nature' (*Metaphysics* 1, 990a5–8, tr. Ross in Barnes, 1984).

[18] By 'thick' here I mean what people sometimes informally mean by 'concrete'. 'Concrete', however, has two unwanted connotations. (1) In the Aristotelian context it means a matter–form composite. (2) In contemporary philosophy 'concrete' is used by contrast with 'abstract', but since it is frequently assumed that everything concrete is physical or supervenient on the physical, 'concrete' is often heard as having that implication; hence the word is unsuitable for application to incorporeal entities. I touch on the 'concreteness' of intelligibles in Broadie, 2009, 136–8; there the point is explained by means of a contrast between 'inventory of reality' and 'necessary postulate' approaches to Platonic Forms. Instead of using 'thick' one could speak of the paradigm as having 'wide ontological role'. This is analogous to Crispin Wright's phrase 'wide cosmological role'. One of Wright's markers of the realism of discourse featuring a concept *C* is that the corresponding property has 'wide cosmological role' ('cosmological' because instantiations of the property have consequences in the physical world independently of our responses); Wright, 1992, 196–9. For an intelligible to have 'wide ontological role' (from the point of view of a given intellectual enterprise) is for it to be embedded in an incorporeal realm that extends in directions irrelevant to that enterprise. (The present discussion is about paradigms as used for practical purposes, but some of the points are probably relevant to the case of defining a thing for theoretical purposes.)

use of *eikôn* of course recalls the wealth of occasions in the *Republic* and elsewhere on which Plato glories in the language of images, copies, imitations, reflections, and shadows to indicate the relation of participating empirical particulars to their Form. And it is this current that carries him along in the famous passage where Timaeus argues that this cosmos must be all-comprehensive and therefore unique (30c2–31b3). The cosmos has those attributes, we are told, because the Demiurge made it as a likeness of the perfect Intelligible Animal, and the latter is the all-comprehensive and therefore unique intelligible of its kind.[19]

Then there is the even more famous passage that explains why this cosmos was made to be chronological, i.e. why it is configured with ever-recurring regular visible rotations (37d1–38c3). The reason was so that the life of this cosmos would resemble as closely as possible the strictly eternal life (*aiôn*[20]) of the Intelligible Animal of which it is a likeness (37d6). Time

---

[19] (i) On likeness: *homoios* and cognates are used five times in 30c2–31b1, and *eoikos* once.
(ii) On the uniqueness of the Form (or kind) Intelligible Animal: it is unique *as an animal-kind*, i.e. is sole occupant of its level in the taxonomic tree of animals. Horse-kind is unique (truistically) in the sense of there being only one such Form, but not in the above sense since it is co-ordinate with elephant-kind, etc.
(iii) The Intelligible Animal's comprehensiveness can be understood in either of two ways which Plato seems to combine: (a) The Intelligible Animal is the kind that contains all the other animal-kinds as species; thus it is the highest animal-genus. (b) The Intelligible Animal is the animal-kind of which the following is true: a particular animal of that kind is such that particular animals of all other kinds are essentially proper parts of it. (An animal is essentially a proper part of something if and only if it belongs to an intra-mundane species of animal, i.e. one whose members depend on an environment.) A physical cosmos made in accordance with the Intelligible Animal understood as in (b) will necessarily be comprehensive in the sense of being inhabited by animals from the gamut of animal-kinds. However, some further condition must be added to ensure that this physical cosmos is numerically unique. E.g. we can strengthen (b) to (b*): The Intelligible Animal is an animal-kind of which the following is true: a particular animal of that kind is such that *all* particular animals of all other kinds are proper parts of it. So given (b*), and given that this cosmos is a physical instance of the Intelligible Animal, it follows that there is no animal outside this cosmos. Therefore there is no animal that is an independent cosmos outside this cosmos. Therefore this is the only cosmos. (The reasoning assumes that nothing not an animal would amount to a cosmos.) Plato could simply have said, interpreting 'comprehensive' in terms of (b*): 'Our cosmos is comprehensive and unique because it was made in accordance with (*kata* + accusative) a recipe for the best cosmos, and this was a recipe for making a comprehensive and therefore unique animal.' Instead he says: 'Our cosmos is comprehensive and unique because it was made so as to *resemble* a unique and comprehensive paradigm.' On the relationships between these two explanations, see Patterson, 1981.

[20] The word *aiôn* originally meant 'natural life-span', and is first commandeered here to denote the *is* without *was* and *will be* of eternity (cf. 37e3–38a5). Since living things provide our most obvious examples of natural life-spans, the word strongly suggests that Plato at this moment is thinking of the paradigm as itself a living being. If that is what the paradigm is, then, as I have argued, there must be a great deal more to it than its role as paradigm for this cosmos.

3.2 Ways with paradigms

(*chronos*), which circles according to number, imitates eternal life (*aiôna mimoumenou*, 38a7). There are 'likeness' words at 37c8; d2; 5; 7; 38a7; 38b8.[21]

Plato's emphasis on the status of the cosmos (or some feature of it) as a *likeness* of the paradigm (or some attribute of it) conveys that this is how the enquirer should view the cosmos. He or she must never forget that it is a copy, not an original. However, something like this point can be expressed in terms not of copies and originals, but in terms of recipes, plans, designs, or practical quiddities, and objects made in accordance with their specifications: the enquirer must never forget that the cosmos was made in accordance with a practical quiddity. Either message drums in Platonistic awareness of the derivative status of the cosmos, so it may seem that the two messages amount to the same. But Platonistic awareness of the derivative status of the cosmos can become the starting point for two different types of intellectual journey. In one, the enquirer uses the datum that our cosmos has an eternal, intelligible, reality in its background as the basis for arriving at reasonable theories about our cosmos. In the second, the enquirer regards the cosmos as a point of departure (or even a barrier to be surmounted) for finding out more about the eternal object in the background. To the extent that one makes the second kind of journey, one lays aside interest in cosmology or in the physical world as such. One will probably then find many metaphysical questions to address whose answers make no difference to cosmology.[22]

It is beyond doubt that Plato at times presents the relation of this cosmos to the paradigm in terms which, on careful analysis, point towards the more purely metaphysical of the journeys just distinguished. Even so, the weight of the four considerations marshalled in section 3.1 in favour of understanding Timaeus's discourse as cosmology (albeit with metaphysical and theological underpinnings) is not, in my view, diminished. Here is another consideration. On the more purely metaphysical reading, one would rather expect Timaeus to direct his religiosity not only at the physical cosmos but also at the intelligible paradigm. But no such thing happens. This suggests that Plato himself did not see clearly the detailed implications of his language about likenesses. If he had intended them, surely he would not have missed the opportunity to call the paradigm a god.[23] As well as the

---

[21] See also the references to copies and likenesses of eternal things in the Receptacle-passage: 50c5; d1; 51a1–2 (with Cornford's conjecture, *ta tôn noêtôn aei te ontôn* at a1); 52a5; c2–3.

[22] Perhaps the same thinker can approach the *Timaeus* cosmology in both ways, although not at the same time. However, an ontology of incorporeals that fits one of those ways will be either too sparse or too lavish for the other.

[23] At 92c7 understand *zô(i)ou* with *tou noêtou*, following Taylor, 1928, and Cornford, 1935. At 37c6–7 this cosmos is said to be *tôn theôn aidiôn gegonos agalma*, 'brought into being as an *agalma* of the everlasting gods'. According to Cornford, 1935, 99–102, an *agalma* is a cult-object in which the god comes to be

world-maker's joy at the birth of the divine physical cosmos (37c6–7), would Timaeus not have depicted his joy in the intelligible god of which it is the image?[24]

3.3 SOME QUESTIONS ARISING

3.3.1 *Thick intelligibles and the Third Man argument*

It may be thought that if Plato's Forms are conceptualised in a way that saves them from the regress ('Third Man') arguments of the *Parmenides*, then they cannot coherently be conceptualised as 'thick' in the sense explained in section 3.2. The regress paradoxes seem to be generated by the idea that Forms are perfect particulars (the 'Two Worlds' view), and this ushers in the notion of them as thick entities with a teeming life of their own. Hence one might think that a successful demolition of the regresses would make the 'thick' conception untenable. If that is so, and especially if Plato has shrugged off the Third Man by the time he writes the *Timaeus*,[25] it becomes questionable whether the 'thick' interpretation of Forms is relevant at all to that dialogue, even if some of his language there does suggest it. Since the 'thick' interpretation is a topic of this chapter, being linked to the question whether Timaeus presents a metaphysically supported cosmology or a cosmological avenue to metaphysics, something must be said here about thick intelligibles and the Third Man.

So let us ask: does conceiving of Forms in a way that blocks off Third Man regresses preclude conceiving of them as thick entities? In my view, the answer is No.

The regresses arise from supposing that just as the resemblance of sensible *f*s to each other follows from their common participation in a distinct Form *F* that is *F* (self-predication), so the resemblance of the Form to the sensible *f*s must be due to its and their common participation in a further Form *F* that is *F*; and so on. Just as the shared *F*-ness of the sensible *f*s is not

---

present; Cornford's gloss here is 'shrine'. An *agalma* may consist in a statue of the god, but '[the word] contains no implication of likeness and is not a synonym of *eikôn*', 99. The gods in question must be the visible heavenly bodies which the Demiurge has still to make.

[24] The idea, absent from the *Timaeus* (cf. Frede, 1996, 42), of joy in the splendour of the intelligible original is not foreign to Plato. Elsewhere in the dialogues certain Forms appear as presences which the philosophical initiate longs to approach, behold, and commune with (*Symposium* 210a1–212a5; *Phaedrus* 249e4–250c8).

[25] Most scholars today regard the *Timaeus* as the later dialogue (for the contrary view in recent scholarship see Robinson, 1992, 2004; Wright, 2000b).

self-explanatory, but derives from a distinct Form in which they participate, so the F-ness shared by this Form and the sensibles must likewise derive from something else. There are different ways of preventing the regress from starting. One can point out that the reason for the Form's resemblance to the sensibles is the same as the reason why the latter resemble each other: namely, each of them was made in the likeness of the Form; hence there is no need for explanation in terms of another Form. Alternatively, one can maintain that the Form is not F in the same sense or way as the many sensibles (but in a sense or a way that is related and analogous), and therefore it should not be grouped as an F thing alongside them to create a new plurality demanding another Form to account for their common F-ness. Each of these solutions blocks off a proliferation of Forms of F, thus safeguarding the uniqueness of the F-Form as such. But neither solution rules it out that the unique F-Form is embedded in an ontology vastly over-stocked (as most of us would think) with *other* intelligibles. Unchecked Third Man regresses are pernicious for Platonism because they imply the absurdity of explaining the shared F-ness of the sensible fs by reference to *any* intelligible object. But the over-stocked ontology of intelligibles is objectionable for a different reason, namely because it invokes *too much* intelligible machinery to explain the F-ness of the sensibles; and checking the Third Man regresses leaves that problem untouched. In sum, a philosopher might side-step Third Man regresses while continuing to view the F-Form as a thick intelligible, i.e. as carrying on its back a great deal more baggage than whatever is needed for it to be the quiddity of F.[26]

3.3.2 Mathematical entities, and metaphysical first principles

As we have seen, interpreting Timaean cosmology as a gateway to the metaphysics of the incorporeal is bound up with a theoretical interest in the metaphysics for its own sake. This is by contrast with the attitude that refers to the intelligible paradigm not for its own sake but for the sake of understanding this cosmos. Some may find it incredible that such opposite attitudes could fail to be distinguished, so that even Plato himself in the *Timaeus* veers between them (or so it seems from his choice of expressions), while some of his followers have been so impressed by the metaphysics that they hardly noticed that, according to the sweep of the evidence, this is metaphysics strictly in the service of cosmology. But a reason for failing to

---

[26] See, e.g., Proclus's discussions of the regress arguments in his commentary on the *Parmenides*, Steel, 2008, IV, 888.29–890.11; 911.27–913.11.

distinguish is not far to seek. There *is* an incorporeal domain for which a theoretical interest in the territory for its own sake is unproblematically legitimate: the domain of pure mathematics. In geometry, moreover, we standardly use sensible representations as a means to investigate intelligible structures and relationships. In the *Republic* Plato speaks of this practice as follows:

> although they use the figures that are seen, and make their statements about them, their thoughts are not about *them* but about those beings which these ones resemble [*eoike*]. Their statements focus on the square itself, and the diagonal itself: not on the diagonal which they draw. And so on with the other cases. *These very figures which they mould and draw (of which shadows and reflections in water are likenesses [*eikones*]) they now use as likenesses, and seek thereby to see* those *very figures that cannot be seen except by thought*. (*Republic* VI, 510d5–511a1)

This exactly hits off the 'gateway to metaphysics' approach to the cosmos. The approach is wrong if one purports to be doing cosmology, but right for pure mathematics done with perceptible diagrams.

Add to this the fact that some of the objects and relationships studied by the pure mathematician play a vital part in Timaean cosmology, just as some of them do in the plans of human architects and engineers. Number-theory and geometry can be, and are, '*applied*'. Examples in the cosmology are: the continuous proportion with four terms that explains why there must be four corporeal elements and how they coexist in indissoluble harmony (31b4–32c4); the sequences of ratios used to mark out the intervals in the cosmic soul (35b4–36b5); the assignment of certain regular polyhedra to be the shapes of the four kinds of elemental particles (55d6–56b6); and the selection of specific triangles for constructing those polyhedra (53c4–55c4).[27] It is incidental to these mathematical entities as such that they are

---

[27] The regular polyhedra can also be geometrically constructed from triangles excluded by Plato. Timaeus chooses the triangles he does because these and not the others make possible (a) inter-transformation of the elements, and (b) a variety of sizes of particles of each shape while keeping them all minute. Both (a) and (b) are necessary for a good cosmology. See Cornford, 1935, 214–15 and 231–9; also Harte, 2002, 236–44. Harte also presents Artmann and Schäfer's alternative explanation of the choice of triangles, one that echoes the proportion of the elemental masses at 31b4–32c4; Harte, 2002, 244–7 and 227–35. She describes Artmann and Schäfer as concentrating on the *mathematical* properties of the triangles; however, a choice intended to mirror the unifying proportion of the elemental masses is dictated by the application to physics, not by pure mathematics: it follows from the goodness of the cosmos that the masses coexist in the friendship that due proportion secures (32c2). In general: pure geometry allows for but cannot dictate the physics-friendly choice of triangles, and it explains what a given choice of triangles makes possible; whereas the *eikôs logos/muthos* must identify the choice actually exemplified in the cosmos. This is why Timaeus says that his account of the construction of the particles will feature both the *eikos* and (mathematical) necessity (53d4–6); cf. Cornford, 1935, 212, n. 3. At 53c1–3 Timaeus introduces the theory as involving 'an unfamiliar account

paradigmatic for world-making. At the same time, their purely mathematical nature relates them essentially to other mathematical entities which play no part in world-making. Thus the cosmically appropriate mathematical entities are multiply relevant intelligibles, since they have a life beyond cosmology, and (one might well think) antecedent to cosmology. Conversely, insofar as mathematical entities are cosmically appropriate, their life outside cosmology is a logically incidental fact about them.

Tracing those mathematical relations *qua* mathematical, e.g. in the search for underlying connections of greater generality, is the work of enquirers who should aim for irrefutable *logoi* (29b5–c1). Timaeus lacks terms like 'incidental' and 'mathematical *qua* mathematical', but his contrast between the epistemic standards of the irrefutable and the *eikos* takes care of the point well enough. The mathematical structures which, according to the *eikôs logos*, were applied in divine world-making are the same as some of those studied in pure mathematics.[28] But the identity (as far as it goes) of the subject-matter should not obscure the difference of the disciplines since this is independently marked by the difference in their epistemic standards. Even so, the situation is sufficiently complicated for it to be perhaps understandable if some interpreters have inferred that features of the perceptible cosmos stand to the mathematical structures applied in designing them as the sensible diagrams drawn by pure geometers stand to the geometrical objects. From this it is no great stretch to a philosophical vision of this cosmos as a sort of perceptible diagram by which the Demiurge teaches us about its intelligible Form.

The complication I have just mentioned is, so to speak, nobody's fault, because it is built into the way things are; i.e. the complication is a matter of the real connections and differences between (a) taking mathematical things as objects of study in their own right, and (b) employing them in further sorts of intellectual enterprise such as construction of an artefact by someone, and (c) the attempt by others to understand the artefact by hypothesising what the constructor was aiming for. However, add to this complexity the fact that some of the signals Plato sent in earlier writings either ignore or blur crucial distinctions. The fundamental contrast between sensibles and

---

[*aêthei logô(i)*]'. Taylor, 1928, 359–60, takes this to refer to the geometry of the regular polyhedra. But this branch of geometry was familiar in the Academy by the time the *Timaeus* was brought out, and Timaeus expects his listeners to have learnt it. I think the reference is, rather, to Timaeus's insistence on certain triangles, not others, for constructing the solids. From the purely geometrical perspective, his selection is *outré* because it is arbitrary.

[28] If, as I am arguing, the *Timaeus* is clear about the difference between pure (or abstract) and applied geometry, this has a bearing on whether the exordium equates the content of the cosmic paradigm with the object of some kind of mathematical study (see Chapter 2, section 2.5).

intelligibles, with the associated drama of 'turning from the sensible to the intelligible' (*Republic* VI, 508c4–d10; 509d4–6; VII, 514a1–520d4; 522e5–525c6; 532a1–d1; cf. *Theaetetus* 175b9–d7), promotes a picture in which each side of the contrast constitutes a single (even if internally divisible) 'realm' or 'domain'. This may foster the impression that when we 'turn to the intelligible' it is for some single general intellectual purpose. Thus the difference between turning to intelligibles as objects of theoretical study, and as guides for practical action and production, may fall out of sight. For example, in the *Republic* the studies that prepare philosophers for government must also be so absorbing for their own sake that any pleasure or dignity to be got from ruling pales in interest by comparison (VII, 519c8–520d4).

Again, while it is tempting to look at two kinds of imperfection together – the imperfection of a geometer's diagram as compared with the circle it represents, and the imperfection of many human artefacts as compared with the demands of their ideal design – doing so easily results in the notion that the ideal objects in the two cases are objects for thinking in the same way. After all, the geometer's ink-drawn circle and the wheel produced by a wagon-maker are both accessed by us through sense-perception, and they may be functionally interchangeable: the wagon-wheel can be used to illustrate a point of geometry, just as a wooden circle made for classroom purposes could be taken over to serve as the rim of a wheel. Easy, perhaps, to move from such facts to the thought that since only one ideal circle is involved there is just one way for enlightened intellects to deal with the ideal circle.

Furthermore, in the early Academy there were intellectual pressures towards a grand unifying vision. We can make this out dimly from fragments of information preserved in Aristotle and from hints in some of Plato's dialogues. Some, including perhaps Plato himself at some stage, held that all Forms of natural objects, or perhaps the cosmic paradigm in all its aspects, turn out to consist in mathematical entities. Thus to some it must have seemed that physics could be reduced to a mathematical discipline, or at least the parts of physics that deal with natural *formations* as distinct from the material realisation. There was also the hope of running everything back to more fundamental metaphysical principles, the One and the Indefinite Dyad, whether by generating numbers from these, and from numbers lines, from lines surfaces, from surfaces geometric solids, and from them physical bodies in motion, or in some other way. Such theories do not necessitate the other-worldly focus that sees the physical cosmos as a windowpane on to intelligible realities, no more a subject of enquiry in its own right than the

3.4 Types of Platonic realism

geometer's drawings; but one can imagine how they might have helped to strengthen that focus.

Plato himself, however, makes clear that he does not adopt it at least in the *Timaeus*, when he has Timaeus say concerning the pre-cosmic nature of the four physical elements:

> The task now is to survey the nature of fire and water and air and earth <as it was> before the coming to be of the cosmos – their nature itself and their properties as they were before then. For no one has ever yet revealed their genesis; instead, we talk as if our listeners know what fire and what each of them is; we posit them as principles [*archas*], the A, B, C [*stoicheia*] of the All [*tou pantos*], whereas even a person of meagre intelligence would not in likelihood [*eikotôs*] find their likeness [*eikasthênai*] even amongst the forms of mere syllable. But for now let the matter rest thus, at least as far as *we* are concerned: the principle – or principles, or however one sees fit <to speak of them> – *of all things* [*tên . . . peri hapantôn eite archên eite archas eite hopê(i) dokei*] is not a matter for the present discourse, solely because of the difficulty of making clear the views <in question> while keeping to the present mode of exposition. Therefore: just as *you* must not suppose that I ought to state them, so *I* could not persuade myself that I should be right to attempt taking on such a major task. (48b3–d1)[29]

Timaeus then proceeds to the 'second beginning' (48d3–e3; cf. a7–b3; e1), where he introduces the Receptacle. The passage just quoted sets a clear boundary between cosmology and enquiry into metaphysical first principles of everything. This can only be because Plato, when writing it, thought that the metaphysical first principles are not germane to cosmology: cosmology is done correctly and completely (according to its own standard of the *eikos*, which Timaeus speaks of again at 48d2–3) without running back into them. But in that case, Plato at the time could not have thought that the point of finding out about the nature of the cosmos is to penetrate through this veil to anterior reaches of incorporeal metaphysics.

3.4 TYPES OF PLATONIC REALISM

I have been contrasting reference to the cosmic paradigm as a means of understanding the physical cosmos, the object of primary concern in the *Timaeus*, with reference to the paradigm as itself the object of primary concern. This second approach has these characteristics: first, it involves

---

[29] See also 53d4–7, about the construction of the particles of fire, water, etc., from triangles: 'So this is the principle of fire and the other bodies that we posit as we move on in the account that combines likelihood with necessity; but as for the principles at a yet higher level, these are known by God and by any man that is his friend.'

turning away from the cosmos and treating cosmology not as a science in its own right but as a *praeparatio* for a science of the incorporeal as such. Second, it involves treating the cosmic paradigm as a thick intelligible, which is to say: focusing on, as distinct from prescinding from, aspects of this intelligible object that go beyond what is needed for it to function as a practical quiddity governing construction of the cosmos. The two characteristics reinforce each other, for once a Platonist turns away from studying the cosmos in its own right there is nothing for him or her to do with the undeniably Platonic cosmic paradigm except use it as a starting point for penetrating further into the territory of the intelligibles as such; and the more interesting that sort of expedition seems to be, the less motive there is for doing cosmology.

Platonists are all in some sense realists about Platonic Forms like the cosmic paradigm of the *Timaeus*. Let us call 'hyper-realists' those for whom the paradigm is a thick intelligible, an object of a science of incorporeals as such, or analogous to a mathematical structure which can be applied in making something physical but which it makes sense to study for its own sake because of its wider mathematical connections. It has been the gist of this chapter that Timaean cosmology does not require hyper-realism about the paradigm.[30] The question now arises: what then *are* the metaphysical commitments of Timaean cosmology? Well, it is committed to the reality of production-guiding quiddities. Accepting these as real does not depend on imagining them as the 'front-ends' of thick intelligibles, in the way a flower is the front-end of a plant with a root-system. For now, we need only say that production-guiding quiddities are as real as they need to be in order to function as such. Since the most important one is the quiddity of the natural cosmos, such quiddities cannot in general be ontologically founded in the thoughts or practices of human beings considered as parts of corporeal nature. If they are founded in the thoughts and practices of rational beings, and rational beings include the world-maker, their foundation is firmly situated somewhere beyond corporeal nature, no less than if they somehow exist independently of all rational minds but are nonetheless 'there' for rational minds to access. There is enough in this Platonism to keep contemporary naturalists comfortably scandalised.

It may be felt that this more moderate Platonic realism renders the quiddities too 'thin': how can they make a difference (in guiding thought

---

[30] The same holds for the Forms of fire, water etc. which are introduced near the 'second beginning', 48e2 ff. This is a distinct point because the discussion of them does not mention the Demiurge and his paradigm. The general claim that the Forms are eternal quiddities seems to be the position (minus this terminology) of Frede, 1996, 52.

3.4 Types of Platonic realism

and action) unless they exist, and how can they exist unless they are founded on an antecedent intelligible reality? Perhaps a Platonic answer that avoids hyper-realism would go as follows: it agrees (1) that the quiddities must have a foundation beyond themselves, and (2) that thickness must indeed pertain to them; but it says that the foundation and the thickness lie in opposite directions. Thus: (1) the quiddities (we are considering practical quiddities) are founded in the Form of the Good. The latter is expressed through the intelligent bringing to be of things that are good. But a good thing cannot simply be good: it must be a good F or G.[31] Hence the Form of the Good is expressed through one or another practical or productive specific quiddity, and is their common foundation. On the other hand: (2) these quiddities reach out to thickness by the directionality of their nature. Each concrete realisation of a quiddity has properties and relations that go beyond what is needed for it to be such a realisation. The thickness is not on the side of the eternal and intelligible, but on the perceptible and historical side.

Intellect is necessary for this metaphysical process, perhaps because the Good *is* an intellect, and the quiddities are 'in' it; but there may be other ways of articulating the role of intellect. For example, it might seem right to distinguish between world-making intellect and *the* Good, because world-making intellect interprets the Good in the way appropriate to its own function, i.e. in terms of the perfection and completeness of the cosmos that is to be made. There are also other intellects, in particular those of mortal rational beings, whose task is to interpret the Good in terms of arrangements that are good for humans and can only be humanly realised. These aspects of the Good would arguably not be part of the cosmic paradigm, because (on a simple understanding) if they were, the corresponding human arrangements would come about as elements of the *natural* universe, not through practices that depend on human culture. On this way of looking at it, the world-maker and the human agent are concerned with distinct practical quiddities and separate readings of the Good.[32]

On the other hand, we could instead say the following. Since humans are an essential part of the divinely made world, the most far-sighted human intellects, when thinking out the practical quiddities that should guide human affairs, will do their best to see the human good in relation to basic human nature and the nature and meaning of the surrounding

---

[31] The values of 'F' and 'G' etc. are selected with the proviso that a good F etc. is a good, or a good thing. This precludes examples that are merely attributively good, e.g. good terror-tactics.

[32] This and the next paragraph take in the fact that in the early Academy it was denied that there are Platonic Ideas for artefacts. For references and discussion, see Broadie 2007.

cosmos. Thus a humanly practical quiddity ideally incorporates reference to human physiology, human psychology, and the rest of nature insofar as this bears on the good human life. The quiddity's content will therefore include more than the goal that is to be humanly realised, because the goal appears against a background understanding of nature. So the humanly practical quiddity is, as it were, two-level: not an instruction through and through, but an instruction embedded in a scientifically declarative setting. We can also conceptualise the cosmic paradigm in the complementary way. According to this, its content includes not only the world of nature but also outlines of ideal human qualities and institutions (where 'ideal' means in part 'ideal given the nature of the cosmos'); however, the ideals-for-humans do not dictate tasks for the world-maker. From his point of view, these parts of the paradigm are, as it were, dormant (although not hidden), since they can only be activated by humans.[33] Thus his paradigm too is double-layered, with some parts directly addressing the practical side of the demiurgic enterprise, and others not. This picture, which places the humanly relevant quiddities within the cosmic paradigm but at one remove or as if in quotation marks, allows for a world-maker who cares how humanity manages its fate even though the particular developments are not under his control. Putting all this together, the far-sighted human cosmologist will look out for specific ways in which human nature has been divinely constructed so as to have the best chance of making good choices.[34]

3.5 SUMMARY

This chapter has focused on a contrast between two Platonically inspired ways of looking at the physical cosmos and its intelligible paradigm (sections 3.1 and 3.2). On one of these approaches, the cosmos is the subject-matter for the human scientist, and the paradigm is epistemically subordinate. This is because the scientist reconstructs the paradigm as far as possible just in order to have a well-reasoned theory of the cosmos. What makes it reasonable to hope for such a theory is the framework assumption that the cosmos was made in accordance with the paradigm. Moreover, the paradigm in this act of making (or the maker's use of the paradigm) is also subordinate – to the production of the best possible physical world. This world is the maker's primary objective, just as it is the natural scientist's primary object of study.

---

[33] For more discussion of 'parts of the cosmic paradigm', see the Appendix.
[34] For examples see Chapter 4, n. 16.

3.5 Summary

According to the other approach, the intelligible paradigm is the primary object for the Platonic investigator, and the physical cosmos is useful as conveying it by representation. This approach goes hand in hand with a drive towards a hyper-realism of 'thick' intelligibles, whereas the first one involves a more moderate realism of intelligible practical or productive quiddities.

I argued in section 3.2 that the evidence is strong that the *Timaeus* cosmology is governed by the first approach, even though there are some conspicuous passages whose language suggests the second. These, I hold, could be rephrased in accordance with the first approach without spoiling the argument. In fact, this would improve it as argument, if not as rhetoric.

In section 3.3.1, I briefly discussed the relation between the notion of thick intelligibles and the Third Man regress. I concluded that finding ways round the regress does not shut the door on thick intelligibles. Then in section 3.3.2 I discussed ways in which the two approaches, although clearly distinguishable, might nonetheless become confused. There is potential for confusion in the fact that mathematical objects or relationships can be objects of study in themselves, but can also be applied in designing and constructing non-mathematical things. Further potential for confusion lay in the mathematicising hope of some early Platonists of deriving the physical world from principles of mathematics.

In section 3.4 I compared the two types of Platonic realism which have emerged: hyper-realism and the more moderate realism of quiddities. The second does not entail the first; hence dislike of the first does not justify dislike of the second. Even so, the second is still sufficiently Platonic to be repugnant to naturalists: an interpretation of Platonism agreeable to them would definitely have gone too far. I then sketched a way in which practical and productive quiddities, although they are not thick intelligibles, possess even so their own foundation in the Form of the Good, and also their own connection with thick or concrete realisation – but in the physical sphere. I ended by sketching ways of conceptualising the content of the intelligible cosmic paradigm: ways that allow for the fact that some practical quiddities define human, not divine, projects.

CHAPTER 4

Immortal intellect under mortal conditions

4.1 PRELIMINARY

In Timaeus's story, mortals must exist because otherwise the cosmos would be incomplete. But mortals incorporate an immortal element: the rational soul or the intellect. The Demiurge creates these intellects from the same sort of incorporeal material as he used to create the cosmic soul: a complex blend of Being, Sameness, and Difference (35a1 ff.). He instructs them for life under mortal conditions, and hands them over to his ancillary gods who will provide them with mortal bodies. The aim of this chapter is to understand these themes. The most important points are that the immortal souls in question are distinct from the cosmic soul, although of similar composition; they are plural and individualised from their inception; and they are essentially oriented towards mortal embodiment and moral responsibility for embodied action.

Let us begin with an extended quotation, which I have divided into paragraphs corresponding to stages of the story:[1]

(1) [41a] When all the gods had come to birth, both all that make their circuits obviously and all that manifest themselves just as they will,[2] the generator of this universe spoke to them thus: 'O gods – gods of whom I am maker and of whose

---

[1] The passage is very dramatic, containing as it does the only speeches in Timaeus's monologue, namely the Demiurge's address to the ancillary gods (direct speech, with a remarkable number of occurrences of 'I/me' and 'you' plural), and his admonition to the new immortal souls (reported speech). The address to the ancillary gods is in some sense matched by what would have been the address (direct speech) of Zeus to the other gods, beginning at *Critias* 121c6 – except that the *Critias* breaks off just here.

[2] Taylor, 1928, 247, identifies the second group of gods with those of traditional theogonies, but Timaeus is quite dismissive of these at 40d6–41a3: we 'know' of them only through the claims of their self-styled descendants (such claims of divine descent are implicitly rejected by Timaeus at 41e3–4: 'the first birth would be ordained as one and the same for all of them'). The second group may include the demiurgic ancillaries; these could be said to manifest themselves at will to philosophers who infer to such principles from the teleological features of living things.

4.1 Preliminary

works I am father, nothing that has come to be through me can be undone unless I will it.³ What has been fastened can in all cases be undone, but [41b] what has been fitted together by fine workmanship and is in good condition <only> an evil being would will to undo. Therefore, although because you have come to be you are not absolutely immortal and indissoluble, you will not be undone nor will the fate of death be upon you, since your allotted portion is my own will: a bond greater and more sovereign than those by which you came to be fastened together when you were coming into being. So now take in what I tell you, showing you my mind. Mortal kinds, three in number, remain as yet ungenerated:⁴ but if these do not come into being the world [*ouranos*] will be incomplete. For it [41c] will not have within itself the totality of kinds of living beings: but it must have them if it is to be properly complete. But if it were through me that these came to be and got their share of life, they would be equals of the gods. Thus so that there should exist mortal beings, and so that this All should truly be the sum of things, it is for *you* to turn in accordance with your nature to the fashioning of the animals, imitating that efficacy of mine by which you yourselves came to be. And whatever in them deserves to share the name of immortals, <namely> a part called god-like which exercises rule in those of them whose will at all times is to follow righteousness and to follow you – this part I myself shall sow, and having thus made a beginning [41d] shall hand over; for the rest, do you, weaving mortal to immortal, bring to completion [*apergazesthe*] living creatures: bring them to birth, give them nourishment and make them grow, and as they perish receive them back again.'

(2) Thus he spoke, and turning⁵ again to the mixing bowl he had used before, the one in which he had blended and mixed the soul of the All, he poured in what was left over of the former <materials>, mixing them in a way in the same

---

³ On this sentence see Cornford, 1935, 367–70, and Taylor, 1928, 248–50. I adopt Cornford's punctuation (with the result that there is no interesting chime between 41a6 and *theos de ho theôn* at *Critias* 121b7, where another divine principal is about to address his inferiors), and I accept Cornford's emendation of *ha* to *ta* at 41a7 (*ha* leaves the sentence without a main verb); but my translation differs. Taking *theôn hôn* as a poetic reordering of *hôn theôn*, I understand it to be doing double duty, first as objective genitive governed by *dêmiourgos*, then as subjective genitive (or genitive of origin) whose scope is *ergôn*. (Thus the Demiurge tells his addressees that they themselves are authors of *erga* even before explaining what these *erga* are to be; and he simultaneously pronounces the assurance that he will be father of these *erga* too no less than of his own handiwork, as Cornford puts it. At 28c3–4 he was called 'the maker and father of this All'.) The Greek is rather awkward on this construal, but the sense is preferable to Cornford's: he takes *theôn* and *ergôn* as partitive genitives with *ta di' emou genomena* (47a 7–8), and translates: 'Gods, of gods whereof I am maker and of works the father, those which are my own handiwork etc.' (140). This implies that among the gods produced by the Demiurge there is a sub-class of gods not directly brought into being by him; but there are no such gods in the *Timaeus*. The awkwardness on my construal could have been eased by a repetition of *hôn* (and perhaps of *egô*) and a reordering of the words, resulting in something like: '*Theoi, theôn hôn egô dêmiourgos hôn te ergôn egô patêr*'; but such a reworking would have ruined the metrical pattern analysed by Cornford.

⁴ Cf. 39e3–40a1, where the Demiurge sees from the paradigm that the complete cosmos will contain heavenly gods made of fire, and mortal kinds that move, respectively, in the air, in water, and on land.

⁵ Reading with Cornford *kai palin epi ton proteron <iôn* or *trepomenos> kratêra*.

fashion, only this time <to form a mixture> not in the same way unvaryingly free of contamination, but of second and third quality. And when he had compounded the whole, he divided it into souls equal in number to the stars,[6] and [41e] assigned each soul to one particular star, and mounting <each> as if on a vehicle[7] he showed them the nature of the All and told them the fated laws: the first birth would be ordained as one and the same for all of them, so that no one would be disadvantaged by him;[8] and having been sown into the instruments of temporal lengths [*organa chronôn*],[9] each into the one that is proper to it, they must be born as [42a] the most god-revering of animals; and human nature being twofold, its superior part would be such a kind as would later be called 'man' [*anêr*]. So whenever they came of necessity to be implanted in bodies, and of their bodies something would be passing in and something passing out: first, sense-perception would necessarily arise, innate and the same for all, the effect of violent impacts; and second would arise passionate love [*erôs*][10] mixed with pleasure and pain; and in addition to these fear and temper [*thumos*] and [42b] all the feelings that go with these, and all whose nature is disparate from them and opposed. If they mastered these they would live in righteousness, but if mastered by them, in unrighteousness. And he who lived well for the appropriate amount of time would be conveyed back to the habitation of his companion star and would have a happy and congenial life; but if he failed in this he would at [42c] his second birth change to a woman's nature."[11] And if under these conditions he still continued in depravity, then in accordance with the similarity determined by the mode of his degeneration – by the coming about of that mode – he would at each stage change into some particular bestial nature resembling it; and the toils of these vicissitudes would not cease for him until he drew together into his internal circuit of the Same and Similar that chaotic mass [*ton polun ochlon*] of fire and water and air [42d] and earth – his

---

[6] That is, the fixed stars, whose motion is due to the circle of the Same (40a7–b6).
[7] This may imply that at this point, and after the soul has rejoined its star, the star (also created by the Demiurge himself) will stand to it as body, replacing the mortal body created by the ancillaries as its vehicle in the vale of tears: cf. 69c7.
[8] Plato is often said to be an elitist, which is true in a sense, but his cosmology is profoundly egalitarian about human beings; cf. *Theaetetus* 174e5–175b4.
[9] Usually identified as sun, moon, and the five known planets, but since the earth, 'our nurse . . . the first and most venerable of the gods within the heaven', is said to be 'maker (*dêmiourgon*) of night and day' (40b8–c3), it too is an instrument of time. One traditional interpretation identifies the ancillary demiurges with the instruments of time. But at 38e6 ff. the 'appointed tasks' of the instruments of time are described entirely in terms of their visible celestial motions.
[10] This puts Eros in its place in the cosmogony: it arises only as an aspect of mortals, rather than being, as Hesiod says, one of the earliest gods (*Theogony* 120); similarly Parmenides in the Way of Mortal Opinions: 'First of all gods she contrived Eros' (B13). 'She' refers to Necessity (cf. B10 and 12), which also figures in the present passage, 42a4–5; cf. 69c8 and d5. See Taylor, 1928, 636–7.
[11] Although the human female is a degraded form, Socrates in his discourse on the best constitution 'yesterday' proposed that women should have all the same activities as men, including military ones (18c1–4); cf. *Republic* IV, 451c ff.

new accretion, turbulent and irrational – and conquered it by reason, and so returned to the form of his first and best condition.

(3) After delivering to them all these ordinances so that he would be guiltless [*anaitios*] of their subsequent individual depravity [*tês epeita kakias hekastôn*],¹² he set about sowing: into the earth some of them, into the moon some of them, and the others into all the other instruments of time. After the sowing, he passed to the new gods the task of moulding mortal bodies; and the rest of the human soul, the part that still needed [42e] to be added and all that this implies, <he gave> to *them* to produce and hold in charge, piloting the mortal animal in the best and most expert [*kallista*] way they could except for such evils as it to itself would cause.

(4) He for his part, having delivered all these instructions, took up station in his own characteristic attitude [*emenen in tô(i) heautou kata tropon êthei*¹³]; and as he so stayed his children heeded their father's injunction and set about obeying it. Having received Mortal Animal's immortal principle [*athanaton archên thnêtou zô(i)ou*], they imitated their own maker: borrowing from the cosmos portions of fire, earth, water, and air [43a] on condition that these would be paid back again, they cemented the takings together – not with the indissoluble bonds with which they themselves were held together – but fusing them together by means of closely arrayed rivets so small as to be invisible they made in each case one body out of all of them, and bound the revolutions of the immortal soul into a flowing-in-flowing-out body. (41a3–43a6)

4.2 WEAVING MORTAL TO IMMORTAL

This section will look at ways in which Timaeus's story is designed to make sense of the paradox of human nature, i.e. our existence as a combination of contrary things: something immortal and something mortal.

Consider first the way in which the quoted account itself 'weaves mortal to immortal' (41d1–2).¹⁴ We are not shown a simple order of makings, with the Demiurge first creating the immortal souls and then telling the other gods to make the bodies and assemble the whole. Instead, the Demiurge leads in by addressing the gods he has created and guaranteeing to them

---

¹² Literally: 'the subsequent depravity of each of them', but this need not imply that each of them *will* be depraved; they are capable of overcoming as well as being overcome by the irrational forces (42b2). The meaning is: 'the subsequent depravity of whichever individuals among them become depraved'.

¹³ This is obscure, but minimally it implies that his good will towards the cosmos is unchanged.

¹⁴ Taylor, 1928, 254–5, explains nicely the relational direction: the immortal part is the warp, which is set up first on the loom, and the mortal is 'the *softer* and less *durable* threads of the weft' which are then worked in. Cf. the collocation of words at 42e7, 'Mortal Animal's immortal principle', with Heraclitus B62, quoted by Taylor, 1928, 253.

their immortality. He then speaks of the incompleteness of the cosmos without mortal creatures, and at once explains that mortals cannot be created by him, and must therefore be the work of the gods addressed. He speaks to them of mortals as though mortals would be unproblematically *units* (the only problem being that *he* cannot make them), even while he is about to explain that it will be he who gets the work started (*huparxomenos*, 41c8) by disseminating an immortal part which he will then hand over to the created gods for the next stage of production. What they are to produce is defined by him in terms of the essentially mortal attributes of birth, nutrition, growth, and death (41d2–3). Thus this passage begins with immortality, ends with mortality, and weaves the two themes together as it goes along. The weaving presents in one perspective (a) the causal gulf between the supreme agent and any wholly mortal product, (b) the former's immediate power-by-authority to mobilise subsidiaries for the purpose, and (c) the fact that he and they will be collaborators not merely in the global project of making a cosmos that is complete, but also in the more circumscribed task of creating the new kind of being needed to complete it. For the new being will be built up starting from an immortal ingredient provided by the Demiurge himself. The division of labour between higher and lower divinities comes across as making perfect sense, just as completing the cosmos makes perfect sense: with the result that we see the immortal ingredient as itself in a way *completed* through the body which the ancillaries will construct. It is not simply that they make the mortal body (along with the non-intellectual psychic powers), while he makes the immortal soul. The thought, rather, is that he and they take on different aspects of a single work, that of producing a single being: an immortal one living a mortal life.

Notice further that whereas the Demiurge's actual making of the souls (from a sort of matter), is recounted quite briefly (41d4–8), the very next stage is shown in much more length and detail: it consists of the various measures he takes to prime the souls for mortal existence (41d8–42e4). Thus we are not shown any stage straight after their construction at which they enjoy unencumbered immortal life for its own sake. The ride on the star as if on a vehicle is not a tour taken for its own sake: it launches their preparation for mortal embodiment.[15] Before embodiment, in fact from their very inception, the souls become mentally harnessed to the mortal future that lies ahead.

---

[15] *te . . . te* at 41e1–2 makes the tour part of the same process as the declaration of the fated laws, which are all about mortal incarnation.

4.2 Weaving mortal to immortal

Notable too is the precise way in which the ancillaries' role is realised. They will contribute as the Demiurge's agents, not as his blind instruments: they will operate not merely in accordance with his will but in the light of it. They will be responding to his explanation *to them* of what is needed to complete the whole. They will not be tunnel-visioned sub-systems each aware only of its own immediate task, but will share in the whole cosmic project as such.[16] In this way too the mortal-immortal is shown as a natural unity: the two causal streams which jointly account for its dual nature are carefully integrated by the device of the Demiurge's address to the created gods.[17]

As I have already suggested in this section, the unity of the mortal-immortal is also underscored by the idea that without this composite being the cosmos would have been incomplete. If we see it as natural and as making sense (1) that this cosmos ought to be and is complete, (2) that its completeness requires the existence of mortal rational beings, and (3) that reason is immortal: then we should accept it as *natural*, and not as a disturbing anomaly or paradox, that (4) the cosmos does include beings composed of something mortal joined to something immortal. On the other hand, the story itself throws up a conspicuous obstacle to easy acceptance. For it says that we mortal-immortals exist in a physical environment that (through our bodies) subjects the immortal element to a wild sensory onslaught, overwhelming its innate rhythms, so that our bodies move at random in response to every stimulus (43a6–44b1). True, this is not the last word; what has just been described is the condition of infants.[18] We can learn to get ourselves under control, and the senses of sight and hearing can become allies, not

---

[16] Later we see the ancillaries designing the human body with the immortal element's well-being in view; they interpret its well-being in ways that match the Demiurge's statement of its inevitable difficulties. See 47a1–e2 on the salvific purpose of vision and hearing; 69d7–70a7 and 70d7–71a3 on the anatomical segregation of the non-rational parts of the soul so that reason is as undisturbed as possible; the provision, necessitated by this segregation, of mechanisms of communication (heated blood, 70a7–c1; liver, 71a3–d4) needing maintenance in turn (cooling by the lungs, 70c1–d6; cleansing by the spleen, 72c1–d3); 72e3–73a8 on the alimentary system, where the bowels are coiled for slower processing to allow intervals of mental calm between bouts of hunger and replenishment; 75b2–c7 on the head, fashioned to promote intelligence at the expense of longevity, on which see the brilliant discussion by Solmsen, 1963. The last thing the Timaean cosmos needs is ancillary demiurges with some parochial criterion of their own for what counts as a good human head. Such is their cooperation with the main Demiurge that sometimes the plural reference to them becomes singular: e.g. 75c5 switching to 'the god' at d1–5, then back to the plural at d7, then to the singular at 76c6, then back to the plural at e1 ff. On the design of the human frame for maximum well-being see also Steel, 2001; Johansen, 2004, Ch. 7.

[17] Note too how this address characterises the rational soul in man as 'ruling in those of them who are willing to follow justice and *you*' (41c8): we might have expected 'justice and *me*', but he literally puts them in place of himself.

[18] Cf. Taylor, 1928, 267–8.

enemies, of the immortal part (47a1–e2). To which it might be retorted: so the gods or God may have given us something of a cure, but he or they gave us the illness. What good do they intend and achieve by plunging the immortal souls into an alien element and providing them with a means to swim in it? The whole dispensation may well seem a pointless and even cruel loop: if surmounting sensation is so important, why were the souls subjected to it in the first place? Why were they not kept in heaven, or not created at all?

The response that I think fits the Timaean context best is that the looping itself is the good intended: that reason's self-development from within a mortal body assaulted by forces not friendly to reason is just the kind of thing without which the world would be incomplete. I shall return to this suggestion in section 4.7. For now let us note that the notion of the world's incompleteness-without-us has more than one side to it. One can try to specify just what it is about us that the Timaean world needs if it is to be complete. But one can also look more closely at what Timaeus says about the world itself in order to measure the depth to which, on his story, it would be incomplete without us. This will be the focus of the rest of this section. We shall find that any inclination to regard the mortal-immortal combination as paradoxical must be balanced against a recognition that the coming to be of this supposedly paradoxical thing has all along been written into the basic nature of the cosmos. In other words, the coming to be of this creature is not in the least peculiar, odd, or surprising given what Timaeus relates about this cosmos long before he gets to the stage where the Demiurge takes the steps that culminate in the genesis of human beings. We can also turn this point round logically, and say: if the coming to be of this creature is a paradox, then so was the coming to be of the cosmos in which it has its home.

Having established that the cosmos is intelligent and therefore alive (30b1–c1), and that its nature as a living being is to contain all other kinds of living beings (30c2–31a1), and that it is unique (31a2–b3), Timaeus starts to discuss the cosmic body. Before turning to questions of its form and the nature of its movement (33b1–34a7), he discusses its matter. He opens with an explanation of its materials: why it is made of fire, earth, water, and air:

That which came to be[19] must [*dei*], of course, be corporeal, and visible and tangible; but in the absence of fire nothing visible would ever come to be, nor

---

[19] The tense of *dei* favours taking *to genomenon* to be a general description, 'whatever has been generated'. Even so I take it to refer to the cosmos. This is Proclus's understanding (*in Timaeum* III, 140A; 144C). The general statement would commit Timaeus/Plato to the view that since the soul comes to be, it is corporeal, visible, and tangible. Taylor's construal avoids this implication by taking *sômatoeides* as complement of *genomenon*, but the order of words is against it (Taylor, 1928, 93; cf. 293). See also Cornford, 1935, 43, n. 2.

<anything> tangible without something solid, and solid is impossible without earth. That is why, as the first step [*archomenos*] in constructing the body of the All, God began to make it from fire and earth. (31b4–8)

(Timaeus then explains why water and air are needed too: to function as means, hence bonds, in a geometrical proportion connecting the 'extremes' of fire and earth [31b8–32c4].) The important point is that sensibilia (instanced by the visible and the tangible), and therefore the sense-capacities themselves, have been catered for from the very beginning – from before the cosmic body was even constructed. In Timaean physics, fire and earth make their very first appearance as the *sine non quibus* of seeing and touching. It is on the basis of *that* connection that fire and earth are assigned the role of materials of the corporeal universe. In other words: that there is to be the possibility of perception is a more fundamental principle of physical reality than the exclusively corporeal properties and relations of the elements.[20] Remarkably, however, the cosmic body which the perception-providing materials compose is the body of a god without sense organs. Thus the most fundamental aspect of this god's body – that it is made of materials whereby things in the cosmos are perceptible – is not one that can make any difference to *its* mode of living out its life. The reason is that this god was created to be a perfectly self-sufficient living system; its completeness excludes its having a perceptible environment or sense faculties of its own (33c1–3). Even so, the cosmic god would presumably have remained fundamentally unfulfilled if it did not harbour mortal percipients to activate the possibilities for touch and vision that define the very materials of which its divine body is made.

Our argument needs one more step. Timaeus, for better or worse, does not recognise any kinds of animal that are straightforwardly non-rational and mortal through and through. The lower animals exist as suitable repositories for reincarnated immortal souls that first had human bodies but lived particularly brutish or mindless lives (42c1–4; 91d6–92c3; 76d8–e6). Thus there cannot be any perceiving animals at all in Timaeus's world unless there are mortal-immortal composites, and these are either human beings or they are mortal-immortal declensions from human nature. So: for the cosmos's nature to be realised, it has to contain mortal-immortals.[21] *Qua* mortal these look, touch, and point to things present and around them, and *qua*

---

[20] Thus it is not surprising that Timaeus provides a lengthy and detailed science of sensible qualities, along with some physics and physiology of sense-perception.
[21] Plants occur only briefly in the cosmology (76e7–77c5). They are said to be a kind of *zô(i)on* (usually translated 'animal' but here it means, rather, 'living thing'), created specifically to feed mankind. They lack reason, opinion, intelligence (*nous*), and self-locomotion, but they have rudimentary desires and

92   *Immortal intellect under mortal conditions*

immortal they are capable of thoughts and questions about their world as a whole. They, in short, are the natural users of the phrase 'this All'.[22]

4.3 THE REMAINDERS: A SURPRISE?

In this and the next two sections I shall continue to discuss what the story shows or implies about the origin of the immortal element in mortals, about its preparation for embodiment, and about relations in which the resulting animal stands to the cosmos.

Let us begin with the incorporeal soul-ingredients left over after the Demiurge fashioned the cosmic soul. By way of background, here is how he made that soul. (Stage 1): he started with indivisible and divisible Being, indivisible and divisible Sameness, and indivisible and divisible Difference, and in each case he mixed the indivisible and divisible kinds together. Then (stage 2) he mixed together the three mixtures from the previous stage. Then (stage 3) he marked out all the resulting material into two interlocking series of intervals mathematically determined. Then (stage 4) he took this entire compound stuff, split it into two along its length, arranged the two strips in a cross, bent each into a circle, and joined the ends and the circles to each other. Then (stage 5) he gave each circle its motion, which in the case of the inner one, the circle of the Different, he split into seven distinct revolutions. Finally, he fashioned the spherical body of the cosmos within this system of psychic movements, and united them centre to centre, the corporeal structure with the incorporeal one.

This account runs from 35a1 to 36e1, and not a word is said in it about anything being left over at any stage. We are not told that there were remainders or residua (*hupoloipa*) until the very moment when the Demiurge starts to use them to make the immortal souls that are destined for mortal bodies, i.e. not until 41d5–6. Why were remainders not mentioned before? The way they suddenly appear in the story is almost absurd. Plato cannot have thought of them only just now, any more than we can suppose that the Demiurge, the 'best of causes' (29a6), left them out of the

---

perceptions (the language suggests that the perceptions may only be sensations of their own pleasant or painful physiological conditions). Cornford writes: 'Galen observes that plants have the power of distinguishing and drawing to themselves substances on which they feed, while rejecting those that are harmful. But plants have no perceptions such as we receive through the special organs of sense enumerated, with the corresponding qualities, from 65b onwards. Nor have they anything corresponding to the rational revolutions of the immortal soul seated in the brain of man. It may be for this reason that they are excluded from Plato's scheme of transmigration, though they were admitted to that of Empedocles' (Cornford, 1935, 303). See Carpenter (2010) for an excellent discussion of the philosophical and exegetical problems posed by Timaean plants.

[22] See above, 'What lies ahead'.

4.3 The remainders: a surprise?

first soul-making through inadvertence. (That would have meant that the cosmic soul is missing a portion of what should have been used in its composition.) So why does the account of the genesis of the cosmic soul fail to hint that during this process – which is described in great detail – the Demiurge wisely saved some materials for use in a later round of soul-making? Why does the *narrative* at this point do what we later learn the Demiurge did, i.e. hold the remainders in reserve?[23]

Not only are we not told about them at the moment *when* they were left behind or set aside, but the process of the making of the cosmic soul is described in a way that helps to make it seem as if *nothing* was left over from that process. At 36b4–6 Timaeus states that the whole of the mixture that resulted from stage 2 was used up in stage 3 (*pan katanêlôkei*), and at 36b7 he states that the entire result of stage 3 was split into two at stage 4 (*tên sustasin pasan*). Experiencing this narrative for the first time, we could easily fall into imagining stage 1 as using up all the available basic ingredients, and stage 2 as using up everything that resulted from stage 1.[24] In fact such an impression has already been under preparation from even before the account reaches the making of the cosmic soul. The preceding episode (in the order of narrative) was the construction of the cosmic body (31b4–34a7). The first part of this was about the nature and inter-relations of the corporeal materials (31b8–32c4), and the last was about the cosmic body's form and motion (33b1–34a7). In between, there was a short and compelling part in which Timaeus argued that the body of this cosmos must contain all existent corporeal materials without remainder:

Each one of the four [sc. fire, earth, water, and air] in its entirety went into the construction of the cosmos. From all fire, and all water, and earth, and air, its constructor constructed it, leaving [*hupolipôn*[25]] outside no part or power of any of them, his reasoned purpose being: first, that it should be to the highest degree a whole – a complete living being <made> of parts that are complete; and in addition that it should be single, since no materials would have been left over [*hupoleleimmenôn*] from which another such being might come into existence; and further that it should be immune to ageing and disease, since he realised that, in

---

[23] Proclus asks this question at *in Timaeum* v, 316A *ad fin*. His complicated doctrinal answer could not be more different from the one suggested in this section, namely that the reason is essentially rhetorical.

[24] Moreover, *panta* at 35a7 could be taken to mean that stage 2 took over everything, not merely mixtures of all three kinds, that resulted from stage 1; and *holon touto* at 35b2 can mean either 'this in its entirety' or 'this whole' in the sense of a compound representing each of those three kinds. These ambiguities help to build the impression, on first reading, that nothing was left over at any stage; when we discover later that this was not so, the passage can be re-read consistently with the new information.

[25] Some sources have *kataleipôn* (and some *hupoleipôn*).

the case of a compounded body, if hot things and cold things and all things possessed of strong powers surround it externally and collide with it, they lead to its untimely dissolution and by bringing diseases and ageing to it they make it waste away. (32c5–33a6)

We are shown many parallels between the cosmic body and the cosmic soul. Each is perfect; each is unique in that there is no other cosmos of similar body and soul; each is framed in accordance with a series of proportions; there is nothing physical beyond the cosmos either to inflict wear and tear on its body or to occupy its soul in sense-perception[26] and other soul-governed functions such as breathing, nutrition, or place-to-place movement involving special organs of locomotion (33c1–34a7); the cosmic body and the cosmic soul fit together as two exactly interpenetrating spheres, one corporeal, the other incorporeal; and each is in circular motion (the body: 34a1–5; the soul: 36c2–d7 and 37a5[27]). All this seems to me intended to invite the thought that, just as the cosmic body comprises all the corporeal matter in the universe, so too the cosmic soul is the complete totality of rational and immortal soul.

The suite of details insinuating this parallel, along with Plato's keeping the incorporeal remainders up his sleeve until the very moment in the story when the Demiurge turns to use them, can only mean (as I see it) that their appearance when they do appear is a deliberate surprise. It is not inconsistent with anything said earlier; one has no cause for logical complaint if one drew the parallel that then turns out to be false. There has been no cheating. But there has been concealment up to the last minute. The aim, surely, is to give maximum emphasis to an intensely significant lesson and one that is new in cosmology: reason in man is *not* a part or manifestation of the great rational soul that informs the cosmos. This message is not likely to get us typical contemporary Westerners jumping to attention, since we do not recognise any such thing as the soul of the cosmos. This is as much anathema to the Western religions as it is to contemporary atheistic naturalism. But, as I argued in Chapter 1, section 1.3, it was not uncommon, when the *Timaeus* was written, to believe in a cosmic mind, and also to believe that human intelligence is somehow a part or a manifestation of it. Plato in his cosmology was on to something startling and arresting when he came out so strongly in favour of the first belief and equally strongly repudiated

---

[26] 'It had no need of eyes, for there was nothing visible left (*hupeleipeto*) outside, nor yet of ears, for likewise there was nothing audible', 33c1–3.
[27] For Timaeus the intellectual activity of the cosmic soul is itself rotation which gives rise to the visible rotations of the heavens; see Johansen, 2004, 138–42.

the second. But at the same time he saved something of the spirit of the second. Our intelligence and reason is not a fragment of cosmic intelligence and reason, but it is not something completely different, either. It is an inferior instance of the same kind, made of the same kinds of components less perfectly blended. To underline this sameness in kind but difference in number between cosmic immortal reason and immortal reason in each of us, Plato shows the Demiurge turning a second time to the mixing bowl and pouring into it residual materials deliberately left on one side when the cosmic soul was created.[28]

4.4 BORROWING FROM THE COSMOS?

In this section and the next, I shall look at how the *Timaeus* develops the conception of the rational souls of mortals as souls of individuals living their own lives distinct from each other and from the life lived by the cosmic god. This section is concerned with a contrast between the relation in which mortal bodies stand to the cosmic body, and that in which the rational souls of mortals stand to the cosmic soul. Then in section 4.5 I shall look at the way in which the souls are invested with individual responsibility for their future actions as mortals while at the same time shown as completely without responsibility for becoming mortalised in the first place.

As the account has it, when the ancillary gods set about making the mortal body, they used materials from the cosmos. They 'borrow[ed] from the cosmos portions of fire, earth, water and air, on condition that these would be paid back again' (42e8–43a1). We saw in section 4.3 how various details made it tempting although misguided to imagine the cosmic soul as comprising all the rational soul in the universe, just as its body contains all the corporeal materials. Now we are to resist another specious parallel. Why are the rational souls of mortals, in Timaeus's story, not borrowed portions of the cosmic soul, destined to merge back into it on death of the body? The obvious response is: it is because such portions would not be individuals, and Plato sees the souls as individualised – that's why he portrays them as having a distinct genesis. One could also point out that equating them with portions of the cosmic soul would cause difficulty in a system that includes the doctrine of reincarnation. Such portions would have the cosmic soul's

---

[28] 41d4–8 may imply that there was just one act of mixing for the human souls. If so this would correspond to Stage 2 of production of the cosmic soul, in which case the remainders were portions of the three mixtures resulting from stage 1 (35a1–6). We know, though, that there are details which Timaeus leaves out; e.g. the human souls possess the sequence of ratios (43d4–7), but the Demiurge is not shown providing these.

attribute of immortality, but it is hard to see what it would mean to say that *the same* portion having merged back was then borrowed again for life in a different body.

Still, this problem about reincarnation is probably not what mainly worries us if we worry that the portions would not be individualised. We may not care whether or not the *Timaeus* provides a coherent account of reincarnation, yet think it of very great importance that the *Timaeus* individualises the rational soul in man. For us to find this important it need not be the case that we ourselves are disposed to assert roundly: 'Yes! The *Timaeus* is right to individualise the soul of man!' It is enough if we think that the idea of individuality is momentous, whether or not we 'agree with' it. Now, the thought (see the last paragraph) that Plato depicts these souls not as portions of the cosmic one but as distinct creations *because* portions would lack the individuality that he wants the souls to have, gets us (in my view) hardly any distance forward; this is because the supposed explanation ('he wants the souls to be individualised') is too close to the *explanandum*. No doubt outside the context of the *Timaeus* Plato could take for granted what we are getting at with phrases such as 'human individuality' (he does so, for example, in the myth of Er, *Republic* x, 614b ff.); but I do not think that he could formulate it, thematise it, and implicitly hold it up for comparison with the contrary position (i.e. 'Through and through, body and soul, we are borrowed from the cosmos'), except by means of a myth such as Timaeus tells. The mythic presentation calls less for academic paraphrase by some term like 'individuality' (planted down and left at that), than for a detailed or concrete unravelling of what is presented, putting together Plato's philosophical theory of the divine cosmos with what we know about human life from ordinary experience.[29]

Let me explain by reverting to the image of our corporeal matter as 'borrowed' from the cosmos. The image implies that the basic materials of the mortal bodies belong throughout to the cosmos: it owns them all the time. By this I think is meant (in our language) that the laws of these materials in the cosmos at large hold as much when they are composing a mortal's body as when they are constituents of inanimate tracts of air, earth, water, and fire. Their properties and behaviour are the same, so that when the borrowings are returned they are in the same fundamental state as if they had never been borrowed. This is exactly what could not be the case with the rational souls of mortals in relation to the cosmic soul. These souls make

---

[29] These remarks about this portion of the *Timaeus* are not meant as any kind of basis for general conclusions on Plato's use of myth.

differences to themselves by how they live their mortal lives. They become stamped with their own ethical and intellectual conduct and misconduct. For Plato, these effects, in every case, are too important ever to be lost from the scheme of things. Hence it is impossible that these souls are mortal. But it is equally impossible that they are immortal through being portions borrowed from the cosmic soul. This is because the mortal animal does not live the life of the blessed cosmic god on a smaller scale. The cosmic god does not live, on some larger scale, the life of a mortal as we know it to be from ordinary experience: a life that is needy, effortful, and often tormented. These lives, mortal and divine, are radically different *qua* lives. Consequently, the rational soul of a mortal cannot be yielded up again to a cosmic soul from which it came. For this would mean one of two things. Either the cosmic soul must take into itself the twisted or at best untwisted lives of mortals: but nothing in *it* can ever have been twisted; or the mortal lives are wiped clean of what they have made of themselves: but then it is not true that these works of soul matter so much that they cannot be lost.

I suggested above that when Plato starts to focus on the topic of what we may want to call 'individuality', it is not the case that he generates the myth we are studying *because* he is focusing on that particular subject-matter as if these were separable thought-processes; rather, generating this myth *is* his focusing on that subject-matter. Thus his generating the myth is his fixing, for inspection, a *concept*. This myth, however, insofar as it brings together the idea of the individual human soul with the idea of immortality, is also instead of an *argument*. Plato has arguments for the immortality of the soul in other dialogues. But those arguments, except possibly the one in *Republic* x (numbered 6 below), signally fail to establish the personal individuality of the human immortal part. What most of them establish (to the extent that they work, which is highly dubious) is a general connection between soul, or rational soul, and immortality. For all that is shown, what turns out to be immortal is rational soul considered as a single impersonal force or incorporeal element that manifests itself in each of us.[30] Or if the idea is that each of us has or partly consists of a distinct portion of such an element, these portions could be portions of the soul or mind of the universe. Consider the four arguments in the *Phaedo*. According to the argument (1) from Opposites, larger comes from smaller and smaller from larger, etc.; so since living beings turn into dead ones, dead ones turn into living; otherwise there would be no new living beings coming on line in each generation, and

---

[30] This has often been noticed in connection with the *Phaedo* and *Phaedrus* arguments.

all would end in universal death (which is assumed to be impossible) (*Phaedo* 70c–72d). The argument assumes that the quantity of what lives, or of life, is constant throughout time. This no more individualises soul than a latter-day conservation principle individualises matter or momentum or energy. According to the argument (2) from Recollection (by itself it only proves life before birth), we recollect the Forms which we could not have encountered in this life; *ergo* there is something in us that encountered them previously (*Phaedo* 72e–77a). But why should that something be, so to speak, individual and personal to *me*, any more than some parcel of corporeal matter in me that was also present in my father and still bears traces of something that happened to it when in him? Then there is the argument (3) from Affinity: our soul cognises the Forms, so it like them must be incorporeal, eternal, etc. (*Phaedo* 78b–80b). But there is nothing individualising about this affinity; the argument would work equally well whether the soul in each of us is individualised in itself or whether each human body is united with a bit of the universal intelligence, these bits being individualised only by linkage with particular bodies. Lastly in the *Phaedo* there is (4) the Essential Connection argument which seeks to prove an essential connection between *soul* and *life* just as there is between *three* and *odd* and between *fire* and *heat* (*Phaedo* 102b–107a). This simply bypasses any question of individuality. The situation is not improved by (5) the *Phaedrus* argument which Plato inherited from Alcmaeon of Croton. It claims that soul must be immortal, because soul is 'self-moving' and therefore the source of all motion, so that if soul ever did not exist there would not be motion in the universe: which is assumed to be impossible. Hence soul is fundamental to the universe, and can therefore never cease to be within the history of the universe (*Phaedrus* 245c–e). Nothing here supports the thought that my soul is not just a portion of soul in the universe. In sum, arguments (1) to (5) in no way depend on the idea that our souls are essentially individual. Essential individuality is not built into the notion of soul at work in these arguments, and it makes no contribution to the derivation of the conclusion.[31]

Finally, there is (6) the argument in *Republic* x about injustice as the soul's worst and most proper evil. Since it is observable that seriously unjust persons do not in this life perish from the injustice that is in them, we conclude that the soul is indestructible. If it cannot be destroyed by its own

---

[31] The notion of soul no doubt varies between some of these arguments, but not in a way that affects the present point.

proper evil, nothing else can destroy it (*Republic* x, 608e–611a). This argument may seem more hopeful from the present point of view; i.e. given that injustice and justice are properties of individual persons as such, perhaps the argument shows that the soul that is immortal is personal and individual. But I am not sure, given the context, that we do Plato any favours by granting that injustice and its opposite are properties of individual persons as such. Earlier in the *Republic* Plato has argued that cities can be just and unjust, and there he seemed certain that justice and injustice in this case amount to exactly the same as these qualities when they occur in individuals (IV, 441d5–e2; 442d7–9). This important position is undermined by the immortality argument in Book X. For Plato could hardly deny that experience in this life shows that city-states are indeed sometimes destroyed by their internal injustice: which suggests that justice and injustice in individuals cannot be safely modelled on the justice and injustice of cities.

One can, of course, run these arguments for immortality on the prior and independent assumption that the soul of man is individual and personal. Then if we find the arguments convincing, we shall accept them as proving the immortality of distinct individual souls. The assumption is doubtless permissible in the context of ethical dialogues, since the question there is how we individuals should live or what our attitude should be to philosophy, wealth, political power, rhetoric, and so on. But, as I have argued, a context in which one would not have been entitled to take that assumption for granted was ancient Greek cosmology as conducted in the fifth and early fourth centuries.

A good case, it seems to me, can be made *a priori* for the conclusion that no argument for immortality that simply concentrates on the nature of soul and the nature of the immortal as such, is capable of proving (even if one accepts the premises) the immortality of an individual human soul. Unless this position is already included in the premises (and here we get back to the question of how, without myth, it could be formulated), it cannot logically appear in the conclusion. So the only way to establish it, in the sense of planting it in people's minds, is to construct an intensely serious myth like the one which we have been studying in the *Timaeus*.

That myth is not only serious but very precise in the comparisons it forces us to make between the cosmic body and the cosmic soul, and between the human body and the human soul, dangling plausible analogies before us and then showing us that they are not to be accepted. Let me end this section by comparing the subtle Timaean picture with the simple analogical argument at *Philebus* 29a9–30d8 to the effect that reason rules the universe: (1) The fire, water, air, and earth which constitute the bodies of animals are small, weak, and impure counterparts of these elements in the tracts of the universe. (2) The elements in us 'are nourished from and come to be from and are augmented by' corresponding ones out there in 'the All', and in general our bodies are nourished etc. from the body of the cosmos. (3) Our body has a soul. Therefore (4) the soul in us must have come from a greater cosmic soul; and since our soul takes care of our body in a rational way, the cosmic soul must be likewise the rational ruler of the universe. Here, reason and soul in us are on a par with our corporeal elements: they all 'come from' greater counterparts in the cosmos.[32] The language leaves it vague whether the fire and water, etc., in us are minute portions of the greater fire etc. which have been transferred to us and become impure because mixed with other elements, or whether they are mereologically distinct and intrinsically inferior derivative entities. The same vagueness holds of the relation between soul and reason in the cosmos and in us. The *Philebus* picture may or may not be pantheistic about cosmic and human reason. But the striking thing is that even if it is not definitely intended as pantheistic in that way, no effort is made to rule out such an interpretation.[33] This may be because the *Philebus* argument is meant to show that reason rules the natural world, and this conclusion is not in any obvious way strengthened by taking up a position on the individuality of reason in us.[34]

It is often said that for Plato the human being and the universe stand as micro- to macrocosm. This is borne out by the *Philebus* argument, but with respect to the *Timaeus* the statement, while true in a way, has to be heavily qualified. Here, Plato secures the affinities, psychic and corporeal, between the cosmic god and ourselves by devices that leave him remarkably free to emphasise fundamental differences such as living mortally *versus* immortally, and being plural and social *versus* unique of its kind and happy in solitude.[35]

---

[32] An abbreviated version of this argument occurs in Xenophon, *Memorabilia* I. iv. 8. See Sedley, 2007, 78, n. 8, for references to scholarship on the possible common ancestor, and 217–25 for discussion of the Stoic appropriation of Xenophon's version.

[33] Note that Protarchus, who represents common sense, finds the argument satisfying as it stands. Archer-Hind, 1888, 27–30 interprets it pantheistically and transfers this result to the *Timaeus*. Shorey, 1888, 300, replying to Archer-Hind, dismisses *Philebus* 29a6–30d8 as 'mere pious Socratic commonplace'.

[34] Nor does it matter in this context whether fire, water, etc., have the same natures both in us and in the universe at large, i.e. whether exactly the same physics applies to both.

[35] *Justice* is enjoined on the pre-carnate souls at 42b2; cf. 41c8. On the blessed solitude of the cosmic god see 34b5–9.

4.5 WHERE RESPONSIBILITY BEGINS

After the second mixing, the Demiurge divides the incorporeal material into souls equal in number to the stars, and assigns each to a star.[36] From the start these souls are plural (for instance, they are not pluralised through descending into bodies), and from the start they are individualised. Mounting them as it were on a vehicle, he shows them the nature of the All. He then expounds to them 'the fate-appointed laws' that will constitute the framework of their immortal existences (41d8–42d2). This vision of the universe, and the instruction conveyed in his address, are their immortal equipment, given them by the Demiurge just as the ancillaries will provide their mortal equipment. We may be reminded, through contrast, of the story of Epimetheus: the gods moulded the mortal animals from fire and water in a subterranean place, and when it was time to lead them up into the light, Prometheus and Epimetheus were ordered to equip the creatures from a repertoire of natural powers and protections. But Epimetheus took the whole task on himself and carelessly doled out all the natural endowments before getting to man (*Protagoras* 320c8–322a2). Timaeus's Demiurge provides all the accoutrements that its maker can give to an immortal incorporeal soul before it is born into mortal life. Intellectually, and we might say spiritually, these souls at mortal birth are the opposite of 'naked, unshod, without a covering, weaponless', which was the condition of man before Prometheus came to the rescue and endowed him with technology (*Protagoras* 321c5–6).

Even so, the Timaean story stresses the magnitude of the difficulties facing our rational souls. It is highly significant that this theme of difficulty makes its first appearance in the Demiurge's address to the already individualised souls. In dividing the second-mixed psychic material into separate souls, he sets up, so to speak, separate repositories of responsibility. The measures he takes next bring them closer and closer to the state in which they will *take* responsibility, thereby becoming actually responsible.[37] First: by the one–one assignment to stars he gives each to know that it is a separate

---

[36] Jackson, 1884, and Archer-Hind, 1888, 141–2, held that the Demiurge first divides the human-soul material into portions that are not yet individual souls, and assigns these portions to the stars: individualisation takes place through a subsequent division. Shorey, 1889, reports that Th. H. Martin, *Études sur le Timée de Platon* (Paris, 1841), held a similar view. As Shorey says (59): 'there is not a word in the Greek that suggests a further division'.

[37] Plato shows this but could not have said it in so many words. Just as there was no word for 'individual' in the loaded sense invoked in section 4.4, so there was no word meaning 'responsible' *simpliciter* as distinct from 'responsible for' some specific deed or outcome.

self, one of a human plurality but not the plurality of a herd.[38] Then: by giving them the vision of the universe he lets them know that they will always be more than bundles of dispositions to react to the dangers and lures of their intra-mundane circumstances and their embodiment. Next: for it to be true that they can make progress, it has to be true not only that they will if they try, but also that they have a will to try; and in order to have a will to try, they have to carry with them the belief that they can succeed, even if only incrementally. Thus he makes it clear that, despite the difficulty, they can. Finally: in order to make the maximum effort, they must not get stuck in the acquiescent delusion that the gods – or even their own pre-embodied selves – positively condemn them to flounder, or have left them to do so through neglect. Thus by emphasising to them that these great natural difficulties arise through necessity (41e2–4; 42a3–4),[39] hence not through anyone's fault, the god turns them away from blaming, and disposes them to regard these as things to be worked through by them. All his communications to them are acts of not-neglecting them, and ones by which they are in a position to know that they have not been neglected. By telling each soul all these things, he lets each know that it is to be a responsible agent, and in this way he primes it for the actual assumption of responsibility.

It is in this light, I think, that we should understand the statement that rounds off the Demiurge's rational preparation of the souls: 'After delivering to them all these ordinances so that he would be guiltless [*anaitios*] of their subsequent individual depravity, he set about sowing, etc.' (42d2–4). Even without his admonition they would in fact be individual causes of their own actions, since it was as individuals that he made them. There was no choice in the matter: the Demiurge is not shown *deciding* to divide the second mixture into individual pieces as if for some reason this was the preferable alternative. It is simply a fundamental fact that reason in mortals is reason individualised. So if the world is to be complete, there will necessarily occur in it actions (and the consequences of actions) of which neither the Demiurge nor any other god is the agent-cause. Since this is so because of the essential nature of reason in mortals, it would be so even if the Demiurge had divided the second mixture into souls and sent them straight into the world without any education from him, like an uncaring father. He instructs them – not so as to make it the case that he is *not the agent* of their actions, since that is already inevitable, but – so that they as

---

[38] The star of each is said to be its *sunnomos* (42b4), a word used of animals that pasture with their own kind. Here, it suggests that each soul will only be truly at home when on or with its star.
[39] For a close discussion of 'necessity' in this and related passages, see Johansen, 2004, 142–59.

independent agents will have been as well prepared as possible. His aiming to be guiltless of any subsequent depravity of theirs is his aiming to forearm them as best he can.[40]

We are told that the substance of these souls is a less perfectly blended mixture than was produced for the cosmic soul (41d6–7). This is one of the most interesting points in the story, because it means that the imperfection of reason in mortals goes back to *before* the soul-material was divided into distinct individuals. The inferiority of their material presumably reflects the fact that they are destined for life under conditions of mortal difficulty.[41] But this future is written into the fabric of their being. Mortal incarnation as such is not something that happens to some souls because they have made mistakes or are defective as individuals. The first birth is the same for all (41e3–4), and the story gives them no opportunity to *act* as individuals in advance of the first embodiment, which will be as humans, in fact human males. From then on, different histories lie ahead of them. Those who live well for a suitable time will return to their particular stars; those who fail to do so will be reborn as women; and further failure leads to rebirth as one or another lower animal (42b3–c4; 90e3–92c3).

This is radically different from the myth which Plato tells in the *Phaedrus*. There, the soul in general is likened to an 'inherently constituted winged system consisting of a team of horses and charioteer' (*sumphutô(i) dunamei hupopterou zeugous te kai hêniochou*, 246a6–7). Some souls are gods: these are the ones with only good horses; others have a good horse and an unruly one. The unruly horse is the would-be autonomous appetite (*epithumia*) for lower pleasures. The all-good souls fly up to the summit of the circuiting heaven where the rational part, the charioteer, feeds on the vision of the Forms and thereby strengthens the soul's wings. Some of the non-divine souls manage to become 'companions of gods', which means that they stay aloft at least for the current circuit. But many of them are dragged downwards by the weight of the disobedient horse; they miss out on most of the nourishing vision; their wings moult and fail; and despite an agonising struggle to stay aloft they fall to earth where they are born in the first

---

[40] Should we understand 'so that he would be guiltless' etc. as meaning that his concern is only that if they err, *he* will not be to blame, i.e. that his moral respectability will remain intact? Well, if we do, then perhaps we should interpret 'his children [i.e. the ancillary gods] heeded their father's injunction and set about obeying it' (42e6–7) as meaning that they only wanted it to be true that they obeyed his orders, as distinct from also entering into the spirit of the enterprise for which the orders were given.

[41] More specifically: these immortal souls had to be of material such that mortal parts, bodily and psychological, *could* be 'woven' on to it (41d1–2). The idea may be that if their soul-fabric were perfect like that of the cosmic soul, it would throw off any addition: the graft would not 'take'. If this is correct, even their soul-fabric was designed with a view to integrating mortality with immortality.

instance into human bodies; descents into lower animals may follow (246a3–249b5).

According to this *Phaedrus* picture, pre-carnate souls are all of the same general kind, but some are thoroughly sound and good while others are not. They are all the same kind of complex system, differing from each other in respect of internal co-ordination. Whether a given soul stays aloft or descends depends on how it manages itself.[42] In defective ones, the defect is primarily in the bad horse, although the charioteer is faulted too (248b2). But in any case it is by their individual failure to cope that some of the systems become weighed down with forgetfulness and defect (248c7), and fall even for the first time.

So in the *Phaedrus* the first descent is ethically and metaphysically on a par with any later descents into lower animals: in each case it occurs because of defect in the individual soul, and these souls are of the same general nature as those which are gods. Thus the fallen souls are failed gods. By contrast, in the *Timaeus* our souls have never been gods or parts of some god, and our primal psychic inferiority is no more personal than the brittleness of our bones.[43] We were all subject to the first descent because of the basic composition of our soul-stuff. It is only what happens next that depends on, and varies with, us as individuals.[44]

4.6 DIFFERENT KINDS OF RATIONAL ACHIEVEMENT PERFECT THE COSMOS

The foregoing sections raise questions or demand distinctions concerning the perfection of the cosmos. Given that the lives of mortals are individual and their own, it is clear that there are two senses in which the Timaean cosmos is complete. As an animal or organism it is complete, i.e. a complete unitary living being, having all that it needs, body and soul, to live its own

---

[42] At 248c6–7 the fall is said to be triggered by 'some sort of incident' (*tini suntuchia(i)*), which Rowe, 1986, 181, I think rightly, interprets as a collision with another soul (cf. 248a8). Such an event is part of the soul's career. The point is not that each soul is entirely the author of its own descent (this is clearly not a fair description, although it might be said that their jostling [248a6–b3] means that they are collectively to blame), but that the original descents stem from 'incompetence' (Rowe's translation of *kakia* at 248b2 and c7).

[43] In a world as perfect as the Timaean one there can be no room for failed gods as numerous as the stars (41d8).

[44] In the *Phaedrus* psychic complexity precedes the first descent and is in a way to blame for it when it occurs, but in the *Timaeus* the souls that first descend are simply rational. There is no non-rational part dragging the rest downward while reason struggles to stay up. The non-rational psychic parts come into existence as powers built into the human body, and they are mortal along with it (69c7–72d3). The first embodiment is what turns the rational soul into one element of a psychic complex.

4.6 Different kinds of rational achievement perfect the cosmos

divine life without the addition of mortal creatures. But without them this divine animal would be incomplete *as a world*. For the Demiurge created it to be not only a perfect immortal animal but also a home for mortal ones.

It is also now clear that we must distinguish the sense in which he made this world to be as good as possible. What he and the ancillary gods made was the best possible natural universe: not merely the best possible divine cosmic animal living its own life, but a natural world as friendly as possible, in its general design and operations, to the rational functioning of mortals.[45] But the existence of the first mortals, human beings, brings in a new dimension of good and ill. As well as the world of nature there is now the sphere of ethical life. The mortalised immortal souls live in the very real possibility of making bad choices instead of good ones. Through these souls there is space in the world for ethical differences and human ethical concern about those differences. No doubt it is due to our common natural endowment that we can choose better and worse; but how we do choose on a given occasion is not just a working out of our common natural endowment.[46] Plato is scientific about nature, and like any scientist he assumes that, barring external interferences, nature necessarily works in the same way. But ethically we do not necessarily work in the same way under the same natural circumstances. This, I think, is his view. Hence the totality of things may not be as good as possible *simpliciter*; i.e. it may be that not every state of affairs is superior to all possible alternatives. And obviously Plato holds that in any generation wrongs are *in fact* committed, vile political decisions taken, brutal or small-minded measures followed in bringing up children, where the choice could have gone better.[47] Moreover, nothing in Plato's thought-world commits him to some theory to the effect that every human action, right or wrong, inevitably by a secret connection to consequences makes the sum of things better *simpliciter* than would otherwise have been the case. Hence logically his position should be that the sum of things is less

---

[45] See section 4.2, note 16.
[46] According to Timaeus, conditions of the body often make immediate self-control difficult or impossible, and living under bad institutions is responsible for a great deal of bad character; but he still sees it as our task to improve ourselves through the right upbringing and education (86b1–87b9). 'Our' here includes a collective and diachronic reference: the person prone for physical reasons to incontinence is not necessarily unable to choose a life-style which will make him less vulnerable in future; and when individuals go wrong through bad upbringing, this is a human fault even if not primarily theirs (87b4–6).
[47] In fact, since the physical completeness of the universe requires that it always contain every kind of mortal animal, there can never be a time when all rational souls of mortals have passed beyond reincarnation and returned each to its star. When the immortal soul rejoins its equally immortal star, the mortal-immortal has gone beyond the conditions of mortality. Thus cosmic completeness necessitates the incompleteness of ethical goodness.

good than it might have been, even if it is as good as could reasonably have been expected.

The distinction just indicated between the natural and the sphere of ethical life implies that human nature is dual in two ways. On the one hand, it consists of a mortal and an immortal part. The latter is definitely natural – not 'supernatural'.[48] Its creation and existence fall under the whole divine scheme for nature, and it is natural too because its constituents are the same in kind as those of the cosmic soul, which is an intrinsic aspect of the nature that englobes us. On the other hand, human nature involves the dualism of the ethical and cultural *versus* the natural. As the individual immortal soul interacts with its physical and human environment, it generates distinctive ethical dispositions and *mores* that shape our bodily as well as our mental existence into forms un-prefigured in the basic natural endowment. It seems reasonable to see the Timaean story as hinting that human potential for ethical and cultural achievement is the reason, or at least a pre-eminent reason, why the Demiurge made the to-be-mortalised immortal souls.[49] That, in my view, is why the account of their making, and of the weaving of mortal to immortal, is studded with so many details, fertile with meaning, which usher 'into the light', in a cosmological setting, the notion of human individuals as ultimate agents of their own paths in the world.

This is bound up with the thought that there are two quite different fronts on which reason can overcome disorder, and that both kinds of rational victory must be won if the cosmos is to be the completest triumph of rationality. There is the operation of divine demiurgy, a mode of causation unmediated by physical instruments and in its operation entirely unaffected by the vicissitudes of the unordered materials with which it has

---

[48] I first heard this point made by Thomas Johansen at a conference.

[49] (i) The distinctive status of ethical and cultural achievement is not called into doubt by the fact that Plato uses the same vocabulary of 'symmetry', 'proportion', 'measure', 'balance', etc., to characterise both naturally good arrangements and ethically good ones, or by the fact that the *Timaeus* sets up the mathematically ordered rhythm of the cosmic soul as an exemplar for our self-improvement. The distinction lies not in the nature of the good in each case, but in the difference between its being realised effortlessly, and through struggle.

(ii) The dating of events is a signal example of the interconnection of cultural and natural spheres. The astronomical system provides units of temporal measurement (37d5–e7), but events are not naturally endowed with handy dates. Dating by Olympiads, magistracies, annual festivals, etc. is by humans for humans. (We learn that the conversation between Socrates, Timaeus, Critias, and Hermocrates is taking place in Athens at the time of one of the Athenaic festivals: 26e3; cf. 21a2.) Dating sets up a connection (not the only one) between Timaean cosmology and the Athens–Atlantis story. The story dates the foundations of ancient Athens and Egyptian Sais where the story was preserved at, respectively, nine thousand and eight thousand years (astronomical units) before Solon (cultural icon) (23d4–e5). See Sattler, 2010, for an excellent discussion of time and rationality, cosmic and human, in the *Timaeus–Critias*.

to deal; and there is the achievement attained from within the physical *milieu* by rational souls made for mortal incarnation. That in the *Timaeus* they are made *for* mortal incarnation is clear from the fact that the pre-carnate state is shown not as a condition desirable in its own right but as an interlude entirely occupied with preparation for life in the body. Hence a soul that does well enough to rejoin its star will not be *returning* to a paradisal situation which it actually enjoyed at leisure before it was somehow ousted. On the contrary, the pre-carnate interval is dedicated to providing the souls with a basic moral outfit for mortal life. This means that their mortal embodiment will come as a fulfilment, even though one fraught with dangers. Thus we have the strange but nonetheless carefully made out fact that the immortal soul will enter into the mortal condition as if into its inheritance, and in living the mortal condition it will be engaged in a life genuinely its own. The body is not to be a bunker in which it is trapped against its nature and from which its most rational wish would be to be allowed to escape.

Through entering into mortality the soul encounters difficulties of a completely different nature from the purely intellectual problems that might be imagined gripping the Demiurge, as when, for instance, he determines the best series of ratios for the intervals in the cosmic soul-material and in the sister material of human reason (43d3–6). That sister material and its revolutions are now bound into a body that 'flows in and flows out' (43a5–6):

Fastened as they [i.e. the revolutions] were into a vast river, they neither mastered nor were mastered by it, but rushed and were rushed along by force, so that although the living creature did move as a whole,[50] it went along at random and without rule or reason, with all the six motions:[51] forward and back, and again right and left and up and down, wandering every way in all the six directions. Vast as was the nourishment-bearing billow flooding in and ebbing back, still greater was the disturbance brought about by the effects of what was dashing against each one, when a creature's body happened upon and collided with alien[52] fire outside it or indeed with a solid mass of earth, and with liquid slippings of waters, or when it was overtaken by a gust of air-driven winds, and the movements set up by all these would be transmitted though the body and dash against the soul . . . (43a6–c5)

---

[50] That is, it was not torn apart.
[51] The seventh motion, the only one possessed by the cosmic animal, is rotation without change of place (34a1–5).
[52] 'Alien' because the mortal body is itself compounded from the four elements. As Taylor points out, 1928, 269, 'alien' logically applies to all four external elements.

But worse is to come:

> [the gods] gave [to the immortal soul, enshrined in the head] the whole body as its vehicle, and in it they additionally framed another kind of soul, the mortal kind, which has within itself dreadful and necessary affections: first, pleasure, men's greatest enticer into evil; next pains, which send them fleeing from goods; also boldness and fear, a pair of witless counsellors; and temper, hard to talk men out of; and hope which easily leads astray. Compounding these with unreasoning perception, and lust [*erôs*] which stops at nothing, they [the gods] bowed to necessity and constructed the mortal kind. (69c7–d6)

Life on the second front is shot through with non-rational necessity, because mortal physiology and psychology are designed not only to foster reasoning but also for feeding, reproduction, and every kind of coping with the physical and social environment. Any climb to rational victory on this front must start with reason under these conditions picking itself up so as not to be at the mercy of these conditions. Human reason, unlike that of the Demiurge, cannot *begin* from an intellectually clear paradigm of its goal. It has to get itself *to* that, under the deformations and distractions inflicted by mortal conditions, building a psychological platform from which it sustains itself and becomes free to 'feed on' its own kind of objects: intelligible connections or the structured fitness of some purposed arrangement. Moreover, even when reason on the second front has won some success, it remains exposed to an endlessly repeated risk of failure, because each mortal life is a distinct battleground, and the generations will always be renewed.

Timaeus speaks only of the risks common to all. But in the background of his speech lies Critias's contribution to the opening dialogue, prefiguring the story to be told at length in the *Critias*. As we shall see, this carries no shortage of reminders that mixed in with the universal challenges there will be different ones besetting different souls according to the variety of human existence, with particular geographical, cultural, and historical contexts contributing new and not *a priori* imaginable shapes to the mortal rational enterprise.

4.7 PROBLEMS ABOUT HUMAN REASON

I shall consider two problems arising from the fact that Timaeus presents human reason as a sort of junior and vastly inferior sister to the cosmic reason that moves the stars.

The first problem, which I shall state in a moment, arises because Timaeus also draws on our general understanding of craftsmanship in order to get the cosmology off the ground: we are invited to think out what sort of world the best of craftsmen would make (see Chapter 2, section 2.2). And in the previous section I pressed further the parallel between successful human reason and the divine Demiurge, in speaking of the victory of reason on two different fronts, intra-mundane and transcendent. Thus human reason is a term in two resemblances, with the Demiurge and the cosmic soul as the other term respectively.

The two resemblances work differently, even though each uses something familiar to illuminate something remote or hidden. In the resemblance with the Demiurge, we start with our own experience of human craftsmanship[53] and apply this in an enquiry about the genesis of the cosmos as a whole. In the resemblance with the cosmic soul we start with something familiar but external, namely the movements of sun, moon, planets, and stars; we then interpret these as manifesting a cosmic psychic activity; and then on this basis we theorise about something extremely obscure, namely the inner nature of human reason. However, the difference in explanatory direction does not affect this discussion.

We may think it unproblematic that Plato illustrates the divine reason of the world-maker by reference to the rationality of human craft, and also explains human rationality in general on the model of the world soul. Why shouldn't he attribute different similarities to the same thing in the same discourse, as for instance when he speaks of the Demiurge (craftsman) also as 'father' (28c3; 37c7; 41a7; 42e7)? There is nothing wrong with this in general, but the present case may cause difficulty for an argument earlier in this book. The difficulty, if there is one, comes under the heading 'fundamentals of Timaean anthropology', which is why it makes sense to discuss it in this chapter on mortal-immortals. But the threat would be a threat to the argument of Chapter 1, section 1.3, on the separateness of the Demiurge from the cosmic soul.

That argument depended on the assumption that the Demiurge and the cosmic soul are different types of causes, one–many and one–one respectively in relation to their immediate effects. The Demiurge and his ancillaries bring about many effects of many kinds from materials in which they are not immanent principles, whereas the cosmic soul is a cause immanent in one body, and source, by its own kinetic intellection, of that body's life and astronomical movements. I argued that the difference between their types of causality was a sufficient reason, in the theoretical context of the fundamentals of cosmology, for not identifying the Demiurge with the

---

[53] Timaeus's accounts of particular phenomena also assume acquaintance with a very wide range of specific human craft techniques. See Solmsen, 1963, 481–3; Brisson, 1998a, 35–50; Pender, 2000, 237–8.

cosmic soul, i.e. for rejecting the idea that the cosmic soul can be assigned the function which the letter of the text assigns to the Demiurge. However, this conclusion becomes less secure if we find that Plato, through Timaeus, is happy to think of the rational soul in man as equally a lesser version of the Demiurge and a lesser version of the cosmic soul. If this is allowed to make sense, or if Plato allows it to pass even if it doesn't, then there is less reason to insist (on the ground that it gives him a clean theory) that the difference between the Demiurge himself and the cosmic soul itself is much more than a presentational device. This is the first problem of this section.

The second problem stems from the doctrine of reincarnation. This part of the Timaean account seems to undermine the assimilation of human reason to the cosmic soul. Human reason may resemble the cosmic soul by consisting in circular or would-be circular motions in the head, but, given reincarnation, human reason is surely related to the human body quite differently from the way in which the cosmic soul is related to the cosmic body. The cosmic soul is what *animates* the cosmic body, but a reincarnatable mortal soul seems to be more loosely related to its current body than that. I shall discuss this second problem first.

The right response to it, I think, is to grant the obvious differences between an immortal soul that can be reincarnated and the cosmic one whose one and only body is fully informed with its rational life for ever, but to argue even so that there is a body-ward orientation sufficiently alike in the two cases for it to make sense to picture the two kinds of soul as akin. I shall press for the view that despite the possibility of reincarnation, the rational soul in a given mortal body can be understood as intimately related to that body, or to part of it, in a way that approximates the relation of the cosmic soul to the whole cosmic body.

We can start to build a case by registering support from the fact that with the rational souls of mortals there is clearly a one–one relation of each to the mortal body it possesses for any given stage of its immortal existence. However, the case-building now becomes more difficult. Timaeus says that the mortal body has in it appetitive and thumetic soul 'framed in addition' (69c8). The thumetic and appetitive aspects perish when the particular body perishes. Timaeus explains that the basic animation of a living mortal body depends on the bone-marrow: the marrow 'anchors' the soul and keeps it 'bound' in the rest of the body.[54] The gods compounded marrow from

---

[54] This binding of the soul is strongly emphasised at 73b3–4, and d5–6; see also c3; 43a5; 44b1; d5. If the argument in sections 4.5 and 4.6 is on the right track, then the binding has positive significance: the soul is *secured* to the body, not chained to it as a prisoner. Its being bound to it is natural and good, just as it is

4.7 Problems about human reason

particularly excellent samples of the four corporeal elements. They fashioned some of it into a globular mass to receive the immortal soul, and they surrounded this mass with the cranium. Thus the circlings of the immortal soul are located in the roughly spherical human head. The rest of the marrow, which binds in the mortal parts of the soul, was made into shapes that were 'rounded and at the same time elongated', which were then given bony casings making up the rest of the skeleton (73b1–e1). The picture implies that the marrow, wherever it is in the body, is the basis of vitality and soul in that part of the body.[55] Now, the vitality or soul that is anchored in the encephalic marrow is a rational activity to the extent that the psychic circlings are not shaken about or impeded by disturbance from sense-perception or from elsewhere in the body. However, the head does not become *biologically moribund* when the circles are badly impeded. Something still keeps it physically alive (usually). So does this mean that when the rational circling goes more or less as it should there are two separate kinds of life going on in the head: (a) the activity of reason, and (b) the biological life anchored by the encephalic marrow? Plato does not give any help with this question, even for formulating it and certainly not for answering it. But I do not see that the answer has to be 'Yes'. Perhaps we can think of the encephalic marrow's maintenance of biological life as nothing other than its maintenance of the mortal's potential for rational activity, with this potential continuing even when the circles are disturbed by non-rational impulses. Then when those impulses fall back and the circles run correctly, that very same rational life is going on, but now in full actuality. If this makes sense, we can say that the rational soul is not just loosely connected with its physical location like a person in a room to which the electricity is supplied completely independently. On the contrary, the presence of the rational soul is the presence of a biologically vitalising principle. In short, the fact that the rational soul will be reborn in another body does not force us to think that it merely dwells in its present body without in any sense animating it.

Let me turn back to the first problem of this section. In dealing with it the question to ask is whether it is true that Plato through Timaeus presents the rational soul in man as equally a lesser version of the Demiurge and a lesser

---

natural and good that the four corporeal elements are bonded by a proportion (31c1–3; 32b7; c3–4), and that the ancillary demiurges built the mortal body by bonding together minute portions of those elements (42e8–43a6). See also 45b4 where they bound 'light-bearing eyes' on to the organism, and 74d7 where they bound the bones together by means of sinews. Bonding the rational soul to the body *via* the marrow is just what a good craftsman does when constructing a mortal-immortal animal. Compare the negativity of the soul-bound-to-body theme at *Phaedo* 81e2; 82d9 ff.; 83d1 ff., where it is the bad person's non-rational desires that do the binding. See Pender, 2000, 165–82.

[55] See Johansen, 2004, 137–59, esp. 150–52.

version of the cosmic soul. Now, we have already noted how the pre-carnate souls are no sooner made by the Demiurge than he prepares them for life in mortal bodies. Their basic task is to live a good mortal life, or as good as possible: and the goodness in question is explained as self-control and justice (42b1–2). From this we see that their primary business is ethical *praxis*, not skilled *poêsis*, to use Aristotle's distinction (*Nicomachean Ethics* VI, 1140a1–23). Just as the cosmic god exists to live a certain sort of life and engage in a certain form of 'behaviour', namely its thinking which is also its rotation, so the rational mortal creature exists to live a certain sort of life and engage in a certain sort of behaviour, namely rationally ordered, thought-informed, human *praxis*. The rational soul must first and foremost deal (one–one) with and through the body and the non-rational psychic tendencies that come with the mortal body. Only when a measure of reason has got the mortal-immortal organism under some control can human craft-activities begin to help perfect our lives.

The craftsman's planning and his controlled activity are of course utterly characteristic of human reason. Even so, from what we can gather from the *Timaeus*, this is secondary for us. Our first task is not to make products but to live excellent lives in which, and subordinate to which, any products play their parts. This is why Timaeus's Demiurge says nothing at all about human craftsmanship in his admonition to the pre-carnate souls. (He never, for example, tells them that they will be free to 'borrow' materials from the environment in order to make themselves shelters or do clever things with fire.) This seems to me to answer the first problem, which essentially was: if the human immortal part is fundamentally demiurgic and is also fundamentally a version of the same kind of thing as the cosmic soul, then we are free to suppose that the same divine being takes care of the functions of cosmic soul and Demiurge, and so to shrug off the argument in Chapter 1, section 1.3. The answer denies the antecedent: the human immortal part is not fundamentally demiurgic. That it will start to turn to the skills and crafts under mortal conditions no doubt follows from its essence, but this is not the core of its essence.[56]

---

[56] (i) More support for this last point: when a soul gets back to its star in the circle of the Same, it will not be to engage in craft-activities; but it will engage in some kind of activity, perhaps identifying with the star's movement and thinking its thoughts.

(ii) It may be worth noting that prioritising ethical *praxis* over skilled *poiesis* reverses the order of gifts in the *Protagoras* myth, already referred to in the text. When man came up from underground with no natural equipment, Prometheus thought to rescue him with the gift of stolen-fire technology; but man could not get on with justice and shame or respect (*aidôs*), which were given to him only later, by Zeus.

4.8 SUMMARY

This chapter has examined certain major aspects of the Timaean anthropology: the relation of the human immortal soul to the cosmic one, a relation of affinity but also of fundamental difference; the individualisation of this soul and its endowment with the capacity for moral responsibility;[57] the way in which immortal and mortal are integrated through the former's mortal-ward orientation; and the resulting creature's specific contribution to the completing of the cosmos. The aim has been to show how, through a multiplicity of telling details, these inter-related themes are realised in the *Timaeus* with coherence and precision.

Section 4.1 consisted mainly of a quotation of the central text, 41a3–43a6. Section 4.2 began the task of explaining the coherence of 'weaving mortal to immortal'. It pointed to the way in which these themes are themselves woven together in the Demiurge's address to the created gods and in his dealing with the new immortal souls. It brought to the fore the fact that the fundamental corporeal constitution of the cosmos prefigures its role as habitat for beings such as those which the Demiurge and his ancillaries now create: immortal souls subject to sense perception.

Section 4.3 focused on the soul-ingredients left over from making the cosmic soul and used to make the immortal souls of mortals. I argued that there is nothing accidental about the suddenness with which these remainders appear. It is a deliberate surprise that they have been waiting in reserve. The point is to tauten attention so that the meaning will be absorbed and the importance grasped of a major new theme in cosmology. We are shown how the new soul's affinity to the cosmic one is the affinity of something whose separate genesis makes it also indelibly distinct, and we are shown how this is because the new souls will essentially lead lives of their own.

Section 4.4 studied the contrast between the borrowed-from-the-cosmos status of the materials of mortal bodies, and the original, not borrowed-from-the-cosmos, status of the new immortal souls. A comparison was drawn between this treatment and the *Philebus* argument that reason in us comes from reason in the universe. Section 4.5 then looked at how the Demiurge prepares the new souls for life under mortal conditions, making them repositories of responsibility: also at the way in which their mortal-ward orientation is reflected in the very texture of the pre-individualised psychic material from

---

[57] The capacity will not be activated until they are in a position to make choices, which will be when they have entered mortal life.

which each soul is made. A comparison was drawn with the *Phaedrus* myth, where mortal embodiment is a mishap befalling defective individual souls.

Section 4.6 addressed questions arising about the perfection of the cosmos. A distinction was drawn between the biological completeness of the cosmos as a divine organism, and its completeness as a world. A distinction was also drawn between the divinely made excellence of the natural realm, and the risk-fraught possibilities of ethical excellence that open up for souls operating from within the conditions of mortality. I argued that the contrast between these two different kinds of rational achievement shows, specifically, how the cosmos would have been incomplete without mortals. Thinking about the universal difficulties which mortality brings should lead us also to think of the variegated difficulties thrown up by diverse human conditions. Such a theme has already been sounded in Critias's prefatory *précis* of the story for which (it was said at the outset[58]) the Timaean cosmology was to be in fact the overture: the story of the ancient clash between Athens and Atlantis.

Section 4.7 discussed two problems that centre on the supposed affinity between the rational souls of mortals and the cosmic soul. First, if human reason is radically demiurgic in nature, as well as being of similar nature to the cosmic soul, then the argument in Chapter 1, Section 1.3, for the separateness of the demiurgic god from the cosmic soul becomes less convincing. Second, the fact that the rational human soul is subject to reincarnation seems to imply that it is only ever cobbled together with its current body in a way quite different from the integrated animation whereby one and the same body always belongs to the cosmic soul. Resolution was perhaps clearer for the first problem than for the second.

---

[58] 27a2 ff.; cf. *Critias* 106b6–8.

CHAPTER 5

The Timaeus–Critias *complex*

5.1 PRELIMINARY

The *Timaeus* comes to us as part of a single huge complex. What remains of the rest is the unfinished *Critias*, which also mainly consists of a monologue, the 'history' of the ancient confrontation of Athens and Atlantis. The *Critias* is not linked to the *Timaeus* as a distinct although dramatically sequential dialogue in the way the *Sophist* (coupled with the *Statesman*) is to the *Theaetetus*. The *Sophist* discussion is assigned dramatically to the day following that of the *Theaetetus* discussion (*Theaetetus* 210d3–4; *Sophist* 216a1–2), and it brings in a major new speaker not present 'yesterday'. By contrast, the discourses of the *Timaeus* and *Critias* unfold on the same day dramatically speaking, and the characters are the same throughout. Plato may not have had the *Sophist* and *Statesman* in view at all when he wrote the *Theaetetus*; stylometry shows that they were written at a later period. By contrast, the *Timaeus–Critias* from the start was planned and written as a complex unit.

Even in a book devoted mainly to the cosmology, we should try to find a perspective, perhaps more than one perspective, that gives point to the coupling of the *Timaeus* with the *Critias*. The presentation of the Athens–Atlantis 'history' is so deeply puzzling in so many ways that it may well seem that there is more to be learnt about the *Critias* than about the *Timaeus* through looking at them together. And that may indeed be true. Even so, it remains a fact *about the cosmology* that it is set in the context of Critias's story, and this fact is a surprising and unsettling one. It should be enough to motivate interpreters of the *Timaeus* to attempt an explanation.

The perspective reached in section 4.6 of the previous chapter is surely a promising one from which to begin. According to this, the cosmos as divine construction represents one kind of victory of reason over disorder, and the cosmos once constructed will be the scene of other such victories achieved by mortals among the ever-present possibilities of defeat. Critias's historical-seeming story of the foundation, growth, and clash of two geographically distant nations carries forward this theme by tracing supposedly real concrete examples of the second kind of victory, the human kind. His contribution will feature one morally pre-eminent example and many technological and organisational ones.[1] Thus from this point of view Critias represents something that makes a natural pair with the Timaean cosmology and continues in a natural way from where the latter leaves off. But this takes us only so far. For we must also make sense of the relation or relations between the cosmology, the Athens–Atlantis story, and the presence of Socrates as somehow the head and motivator of the whole complex. And we must try to shed light on the further fact that Critias presents his story as a true history, and, what is more, a history about the original and hyper-archaic *Athens*.

One of the aims of this chapter is to bring out what seems to me to be a single relation in which what Timaeus represents and an aspect of what Critias represents jointly stand to what Socrates represents. Another aim is to discuss the status (truth versus fiction) of the Athens–Atlantis story, and certain aspects of Plato's purpose in staging it. In this connection I shall discuss some interpretations of other scholars. The last forty years have brought a number of illuminating advances on interpreting the Athens–Atlantis story, and some of these treatments have also focused on how to make sense of *Timaeus–Critias* as a single enterprise. It somehow characterises this set of questions that diverse approaches are compatible. Particularly with Critias's story, it seems clear that Plato, as so often, kills more than one bird with one stone. And he may be implementing more than one purpose in putting together the whole *Timaeus–Critias* complex. For this reason, although I shall be arguing against a few proposed answers to some of these questions, the interpretations which I put forward make no claim to be exclusively right.[2]

Yet another aim of the chapter is to show in different ways that Critias and his story represent the ongoing need for Socratic philosophy. Here,

---

[1] The *Critias* account of ancient Athens mentions farming, building, gymnastic training, making gardens, managing their own land 'and the whole of Greece'. The *précis* in the *Timaeus* also mentions military skills, study of the cosmos, divination and medicine. For Atlantis there are many more examples, mostly on a grand scale: mining, carpentry, building (temples, palaces, harbours, docks, channels, fortifications, bridges, roads), planting of trees, irrigation and making reservoirs, shipbuilding, metallurgy, architecture, statuary, many kinds of decorative craftsmanship, horsemanship, organising an army and its equipment. In both places the basic political dispensation was laid down by local gods: Athena with Hephaestus for Athens (*Timaeus* 23d6–e2; *Critias* 109c6–9), Poseidon for Atlantis (113c2 ff.; 119c1–d2).

[2] I have particularly learnt from the studies by Vidal-Naquet, 1986 (1964); Gill, 1977, 1979, 1980; Brisson, 1998b (1994); Pradeau, 1997; Naddaf, 1998; Johansen, 2004.

however, the situation is complicated by the fact that 'what Critias and his story represent' does not stand for something simple. To put the matter very crudely for now, Critias represents something positive, and also some decidedly negative things.[3] The positive aspect of Critias's story has already been sketched in terms of the second kind of rational victory. That sketch will be supplemented by a more specific and less grandiose claim, about the validity of historiography. But a negative aspect of Critias will also come to the fore. What is positive and what is negative about the Critias-character will be developed in terms of a positive or complementary, and a negative or oppositional, relation to the figure of Socrates. What will emerge on the negative side is a striking disassociation of Critias from Socrates. As for the relation between Critias and Timaeus: this too is not simple precisely because Critias is not simple. As I have indicated, the positive Critias is to be grouped with Timaeus in a relation in which both stand to Socrates. By contrast, when it comes to the negative Critias, we shall see Timaeus standing rather to one side of this character, but not completely aside.

5.2 CONNECTING SOCRATES, TIMAEUS, AND CRITIAS

The main textual clues to the connection between these figures are laid down at the beginning of the *Timaeus*, as follows: (1) Having 'yesterday' regaled the other three companions, Timaeus, Critias, and Hermocrates, with a philosophical discourse on the ideal city (it has some striking resemblances to the Callipolis of the *Republic*[4]), Socrates expresses a longing to hear a saga that shows such a city proving itself in war and in diplomatic interactions with other cities (19b3–c8). His companions' charge is to return hospitality by joining together to provide such an account (20b7–c1). (2) It emerges that Critias already has the wherewithal to do so (20c4–d1): a narrative of actual events, matching Socrates's request, has been handed down in Critias's family (20d7–21d8). This is the story of the victory of the original Athens over the aggressor Atlantis, of which Critias now gives an outline (24c4–25d6; cf. 26c5–7). (3) Critias next proposes to tell that story in detail, and says, speaking for himself, Timaeus, and Hermocrates collectively, that the three of them will make a concerted effort, 'dividing the task

---

[3] I shall claim that the positive Critias largely resides in the 'history' of Athens and Atlantis undertaken in the *Critias*, whereas the negative persona is expressed in the *précis* version of the ancient encounter given at the beginning of the *Timaeus*. The *précis* is bound up with an explanation of how the nuclear story survived.

[4] But internal evidence shows that yesterday's discourse is not the huge speech by Socrates that is the body of our *Republic*.

between them', to give Socrates his wish (26d5–6). (4) Socrates welcomes the proposal (26e5–27a1), and (5) Critias lays out this plan: Timaeus will speak first, beginning with the birth of the cosmos and ending with the generation of humans; Critias will follow with the saga of Socrates's ideal city, which he now asks the assembled company to identify with ancient Athens (27a2–b6; cf. 26c7–d5).

Between them, (1), (3), and (5) tell us that although Socrates has simply requested a story of the ideal city in gallant action, the request cannot be properly fulfilled by giving him just that: the story must be introduced by a cosmo-anthropogony. It is also clear that the cosmo-anthropogony, and the account of the ideal city in action, will be parts of a single whole, and that of the two the ideal-city story was originally meant to be the principal part.[5] These points follow from the fact that in (1) and (3), the repayment of Socrates by the others is said to be a single shared task, and that in (3) the whole task is described by reference to just one of its proper parts: the telling of the political and military story desired by Socrates. It is never described just by reference to its other proper part, i.e. as giving a cosmology. So we have to look out for reasons why the ideal-city story might have been meant to be the principal part of the whole; and also why it is told better when prefaced by the cosmology – or why the cosmology is told better as a preface to it. There is also the question of what sort of preface the cosmology is supposed to be: does it simply get us to the point from which Critias's main story begins (the very earliest human settlements on earth, *Critias* 109b1 ff.), or does some theme that has emerged from the cosmology continue to reach into Critias's contribution? (I have already, in terms of the two kinds of rational victory, argued in favour of this.) We shall also, of course, adverting to points (2) and (5) above, have to consider (although not in this section) why Socrates's ideal city is identified with ancient Athens.

It is helpful in approaching these questions to keep an eye on the fact that the complex of the two discourses is offered as homage to Socrates in

---

[5] 'Originally', because in deciding to leave the *Critias* unfinished (if it was by a decision rather than because of some accident), Plato not only may have realised that the *Timaeus* would now loom proportionately much larger in the resulting *Timaeus–Critias* complex than in the original design, but may now even have intended just such a different proportion. (I am assuming that Plato did not intend the *Critias* to be a fragment all along, although this assumption is not universal. For a full discussion of the 'unfinishedness' see Nesselrath, 2006, 34–41.) Critias announces at the beginning of his long account that 'concerning the many barbarian nations and all the Greek tribes that existed then, the course of the narrative, being progressively gathered up together [or 'unrolled', *aneillomenē*] so to speak, will show case by case what was encountered in each place' (109a2–4). If he had told the entire Athens–Atlantis epic in the same detail as he tells the preliminary part in *Critias* 108e1–121c5 (cf. 26c5–7), his story might have been two or three times the length of the cosmology. Plato also originally intended the complex to have a third part, delivered by Hermocrates; we can only guess at its nature.

grateful return for his political-philosophical contribution of the previous day: the table-guests (*daitumones*) of yesterday are to be the banquet-givers (*hestiatores*) of today (17a2–3; cf. 20b7–c3; 26e7–27a2; b7–8). What is the point of representing Socrates, who stands for abstract, dialectically conducted, ethical and political enquiry, as being offered such a gift and happily welcoming it? In what sense is the offering as a whole, or either of its parts, *for* Socrates? What exactly is it that the Socrates-persona wishes for, what does he get, in what way is what he gets an acknowledgement of him, in what way is it an addition *to* him? According to one proposal, Critias's share of the gift is a 'rather desperate attempt … to pretend that [the society portrayed in the *Republic*] *could* exist and indeed *had* existed, but far away and long ago'.[6] But is the supposed pretence being mounted for the benefit of characters in the dialogue-world, or is it for the benefit of Plato's anticipated real-world audience? Not the latter, since (as I shall argue in section 5.3) Plato's audience would have known that Critias's story is a fiction. And not the former, because it is clear in the *Timaeus* that the Socrates-character's wish to see his city in action would be satisfied even by a story that counted as fictional within the dialogue-world. Thus the Socrates-character is not wishing to be shown real (in the dialogue-world) evidence for the premiss of an inference *ab esse ad posse*.[7] That he is actually to receive a piece of real history is a bonus for him. Here is a passage that makes it clear that what Socrates yearns for is not history-based reassurance that the ideal city can be realised, but the imaginative experience of having its actions unfold under his gaze:

Now about the constitution which we have covered, let me tell you next the condition I find myself in with regard to it. It seems to me to resemble the condition of someone who, on enjoying the spectacle of beautiful creatures, whether wrought by a draughtsman or even alive in truth but keeping still, develops a longing [*epithumia*] to witness them in motion and pitting their efforts in one of those contests considered to be fit challenge for their physiques. (19b3–c1)

In keeping with this, he goes on to specify what he wants told about his city by means of a series of present participles. He wants not to be informed

---

[6] Lee, 1971, 166. A more nuanced version of this claim is put forward by Johansen, 2004, 44–5.
[7] At 19d3–e8 Socrates complains that the poets and the sophists cannot give him what he wants, the former because they are only good at representing what is familiar to them, and the latter because their cosmopolitanism deprives them of a sense of what it is like when *your own city* is at war. Here he is clearly talking about *producing a certain kind of vivid narrative*. The fault he finds with the poets and the sophists is *not* that neither group *knows enough actual-world history*; in fact, some of the sophists probably did know more of this than most. See Gill, 1979, and Johansen, 2004, 28.

that this and that did happen, but to have the happenings conjured up for him as he listens (19c2–8).[8]

That Socrates is allowed to desire this and be given it indicates the important recognition on Plato's part that story, imaginative spectacle, and speculation about the causes of things, speak to needs that exist in intellectually responsible adults, not just in children and the frivolous; that these needs deserve to be addressed in their own right; and that this cannot be properly accomplished except by moving beyond the territory of Socratic practical philosophy. By prefacing Critias's Tale of Two Cities with Timaeus's cosmology, Plato puts on the table a pair of genres conspicuously concerned with matters over which we have no control whatsoever, as they are universal necessities of nature or are happenings sealed in the past. These genres are beyond the competence of Socrates.[9] So elaborate examples of them are now offered to him in a joint tribute of grateful thanks for what he represents; and Socrates receives it with welcome. By this device of the 'return-feast' Plato signals that cosmology, and historiography or the empirically informed systematic study of peoples, lands, and institutions, are enterprises which the Academy itself should now count as coming under the general heading of *philosophia*.[10] They are enterprises which from now on are not to be looked upon as outsiders' business; on the contrary, it is now signalled through the examples presently offered that these are possibilities deserving to be realised in works coming up to the highest Platonic standards of exactness, thoroughness, comprehensiveness, and rational organisation.[11]

Given the perspective which I have just suggested, we can see a reason why, for the historiographical example, Plato chose not to practise with a piece of (literally) real history. The symbolism of 'tribute graciously received by Socrates' means that the material of the *Timaeus–Critias* return-feast had to exhibit a natural and very pronounced connection with the figure of Socrates. Plato effects the connection by laying it down that the heroine of Critias's story is a *polis* of a type that recalls the ideal of the *Republic* and is further associated with the Socrates-character by having been his topic

---

[8] Bury, 1929, understood this when he translated *hêdeôs an tou logou diexiontos akousaim'an* (19c2–3) as 'Gladly would I listen to anyone who should *depict* in words' (my emphasis).

[9] For his incapacity to produce a story of the ideal city in action, see his words at 19c8–d3: 'I myself in my own eyes stand convicted of complete inability to celebrate the men and their city in appropriate fashion'; for his turn away from cosmology see *Phaedo* 96a5–100a3.

[10] *Philosophia* and cognates occur at 18a5; 19e5; 20a4; 24d1; 47b1; 4; 88c5; 91e3; *Critias* 109c7.

[11] See Gill, 1977, 1979, 1980, for stimulating discussion of the Critias story as an essay in both historiography and fiction. See Pradeau, 1997, 55–66 and 246–76 for exhaustive discussion of the geography, economy, town-planning, etc. of Atlantis and ancient Attica.

'yesterday'. This is a condition which material from *known* real-world history would hardly be able to meet![12] I am arguing, in sum, that Plato's choice of a fictional stretch of history as subject for Critias's contribution to the feast is dictated by the need to establish an intimate association between the Critian offering and what we take to be the meaning of 'Socrates'.[13]

By the same token, a cosmology prefacing a tale from known real-world history, however coherent such a complex might be in itself, would lack the link to Socrates: it would not be a cosmology that emphatically elicits the Socratic blessing. We can also see from this point of view that, certainly for the cosmology, it does not matter at all that Critias's story breaks off unfinished. By association with what there is of it, the cosmology already has the Socratic blessing. Nor does the break-off necessarily vitiate the welcome signalled to historiography; Plato may have abandoned the *Critias* with good conscience, thinking that what there is of it was enough to make his intended point.[14]

What does Socrates learn through receiving a heroic civic story prefaced by Timaeus's cosmology? Let us look first at what he himself brings to the moment of reception. If we allow ourselves to draw on the Socrates of earlier dialogues, we can say this: Socrates equates virtue with a state of rational order in the soul; for him, the virtuous soul is the one ruled by the wisdom of reason. He is unconditionally dedicated to the cultivation of this state. He is well known for warning that if people are to pursue virtue properly at all, they must do so for its own sake, and, like him, with complete single-mindedness.[15] Again, when it comes to particular actions as distinct from virtuous dispositions and institutions, Socrates must belong with moralists who say that we act most finely when, under difficult conditions, we do what is called for from the sense that nothing matters more than doing what is called for. He presumably also thinks that when citizens are required to fight in defence of their city, the appropriate sense of doing what is called for is nothing other than the sense of patriotism.[16] He must further think that of all patriotic deeds of valour, the most precious are those where the risks are taken and the sacrifices suffered on behalf of a genuinely good city,

---

[12] As Burnyeat, 1992, has emphasised, the non-existence (if so it be) of the ideal city of the *Republic* is a fact of history, not metaphysics. (On the possibility that such a city has been realised 'in the limitless past' or is even now in existence 'in a foreign land far beyond our ken', see *Republic* VI, 499c7–d1, quoted from the translation of G. M. A. Grube, revised by C. D. C. Reeve, in Cooper, 1997.)

[13] The import of this association will be further worked out in sections 5.6–5.8 below.

[14] Note that the argument of this and the previous paragraph only explains why the historiographical part has to be about Socrates's ideal city; it does not explain why that city gets to be pseudo-historically identified with ancient Athens.

[15] E.g. *Republic* x, 617e3–4.   [16] Cf. *Crito* 51a7–c3 on piety towards one's *polis*.

a civic way of life that recognises, practises, and understands the worth of the true virtues. Since Critias's story of ancient Athenian valour exactly fits this template, it should indeed be a story after Socrates's own heart. Given what Socrates stands for, it should not be hard for him to agree that Critias's sources (quoted in advance of the story itself) were not exaggerating when they described the victory over Atlantis as the greatest episode in the entire history of Athens, and the one that by rights should have been the most famous of all (21d4–5; cf. 24d6–e1; 25b5–6).

What Socrates stands for (what we gather from his discourse of 'yesterday') does not, however, logically lead to an organised, coherent, theory, such as Timaeus's prefatory cosmology will establish, that virtuous human struggle has a cosmic purpose. From Timaeus's distinctive contribution, Socrates will now learn with rational comprehensiveness not only that the enterprise of human reason is enacted in a natural world whose maker's mind is akin to ours, and whose arrangements for the human race are as conducive as possible to its rational success, but also that our human enterprise is of fundamentally the same kind as that which the world-maker carried out when he formed the cosmos. Socrates of the *Phaedo*, the *Gorgias*, and the *Republic*, has himself given a metaphysical rationale for why the practice of 'justice with wisdom'[17] matters more than anything else: because our souls are immortal, their condition matters more than all physical and worldly goods. He was not reduced to saying simply 'It matters most because it matters most.' But now in the *Timaeus–Critias* Socrates is introduced to a further rationale, one that emerges in the burgeoning of a new branch of *philosophia*: by acquitting ourselves with justice, wisdom, temperance, and courage in this natural life we bring additional glory to the god-made world. *As a system of nature for cosmology to study*, the cosmos is already complete regardless of how we, the mortalised immortals, actually fare in our particular lives; it is a self-sufficient immortal animal, perfect in all its parts and stocked with the gamut of mortal animal kinds. But thought of also as the world *in which we live*, the cosmos is the scene for possible rational enrichments of kinds quite new to it. And, as was argued in the previous chapter (section 4.2), one thing intended for the cosmos from inception was that it would be where we live.

So it is not the case that we, in rising to the challenges which reason now faces being planted within the natural universe, add finishing touches to the world in the sense of completing it as a system of nature, insofar as 'system of nature' means the subject-matter of cosmology. Consider these points:

---

[17] *Republic* x, 621c5.

5.2 Connecting Socrates, Timaeus, and Critias

(1) Our rational activities do not complete the world by being intramundane expressions of the divine life of the immortal cosmic animal scattered here and there within the space and time of the whole. If that were so we would not be rational individualities, and it would not be true that a god is not responsible for the evils that come about through us (42d2–4). (2) Nor does humanity complete the world (designed as it is from ground up for sense-perception to occur) merely through our activity as sense-perceivers. If that were so, we need not have been created as anything more than one kind of percipient mortal creature: the humanoid kind. But instead we also have, or are, immortal rational souls. It fits in with these points that (3) intelligible Forms of human excellences and excellent institutions are not straightforwardly 'in' the cosmic paradigm.

The reason for re-emphasising these rather metaphysical considerations from previous chapters,[18] is that they ratify a radical distinction between cosmology and ethics. For example, to say that Forms of human excellences are in the cosmic paradigm would be to imply that human ethical and political philosophy is simply a sub-division of cosmology. But that is not at all the relationship between these disciplines. Nor is cosmology simply an ancilla to ethical and political philosophy. But doesn't Plato move in the direction of merging or conflating these studies (although this would surely be to the detriment of both)? Doesn't he do that when in the *Timaeus*, via Critias's story with its special interest for Socrates, he deliberately forges a link running from Socrates to cosmology? No: on the contrary, he takes special care to secure the Socratic connection in a manner that scotches any suggestion of conflation. Plato effects this through a strong and precise emphasis on the reciprocal distribution between Socrates on the one hand, and Timaeus, Critias, and Hermocrates on the other, of entertaining and being entertained. Socrates is sole recipient today because he was sole entertainer yesterday, while on both days the others occupy the converse role as a group. Each side stands for the distinctive entertainment it *gives*. Hence what the others stand for, whether collectively or individually, is not part of what Socrates stands for; nor is his territory a whole of which the others' territories are parts.

These last remarks have to do with the relations between various genres of human intellectual discipline. But before continuing the discussion of

---

[18] On the distinctness of human rational souls, see Chapter 4, sections 4.2–4.5. On the world as made for sense-perception, see Chapter 4, section 4.2. On what is in the cosmic paradigm, see Chapter 3, section 3.4 *ad fin*. For background on the distinctness of the ethical sphere, see Chapter 4, section 4.6.

this, let me summarise how things stand on the level of ontology, metaphysics, and world-making. In forming this natural world, the Demiurge reworked the eternal intelligible paradigm in a generated sensible medium, giving concrete expression to the intelligible and making *this* cosmos, the one which he, the Demiurge, admires (cf. 37c6–d1), and which the human cosmologist tries to understand. Next: the natural world having been instituted complete with human animals, human reason gets going from within it. Within the sphere of human life possibilities provided by nature are actualised in a vast number of determinate and physically concrete ways through human ethics and culture. In the great canvas of the *Timaeus–Critias*, the metaphysical shift effected by the Demiurge from the intelligible to the sensible is not in my view more momentous than the next shift, effected by us, from the merely natural to the ethical and cultural. We by our divinely endowed individual rational activities add a new kind of reality to the world. Examples of the kind of reality that only mortal-immortals can add include: the achievements of the ancient Athenians in Critias's story; the impressive (in a different way) achievements of the Atlantideans; non-fictional instances of such things and similar things, great and small; the conversation between Socrates, Timaeus, Critias, and Hermocrates; the accounts, theories, narratives, or arguments produced by human cosmologists and historians whether fictional or real, and also by mathematicians and moral and political philosophers; the propagation and discussion of these theories; Plato's own composition of the present work; and the reception of it by his own and later audiences.

Now let us look more closely at the link established between Socrates and cosmology via Critias's story. The cosmology is sandwiched between a *précis* (complete with lengthy wrappings concerning transmission) of the climactic event in the story, and what is left of the full version. Critias is shown presenting Socrates with the *précis* by way of pilot: on its basis Socrates is to decide whether the ancient Athens–Atlantis episode meets his desire to see his ideal citizens in action; if so, Critias will recount the longer version. One very striking thing is that only *after* Socrates has expressed satisfaction with the abbreviated story from his own point of view (26e2–27a1) does Critias announce that the longer version will be prefaced by an account, the task of Timaeus, of the world of nature starting from its beginning and ending with the 'nature of human beings' (27a2–7). Socrates does not turn a hair at this surprising development. He says only: 'It seems that I am about to receive a complete and splendid feast of discourse in return for mine', and then hands over to Timaeus (27b7–9). What we are being shown here is not merely that Critias's story about fine human beings in action would be incomplete

5.2 Connecting Socrates, Timaeus, and Critias

without some sort of framing by cosmology, but that the Socrates-character is already committed to accepting the cosmology even before he is made aware (through Critias's announcement which he does not question) that this must be an essential part of a 'complete return'. Thus the Critian story comes in under Socratic auspices through a kinship, obvious to all the characters, between its topic (the ancient Athenian *polis*) and the subject-matter of Socratic ethical and political philosophy; but along with the Critian story, embedded between the abridged version and the long one, comes in something wholly unforeseen by Socrates but immediately welcomed by him as soon as it shows itself: the Timaean cosmology. It of course makes sense to look for and identify, as scholars have done, connections between the areas of thought covered by this cosmology and the philosophy of the *Republic* and other ethical dialogues. However, here I am less concerned with the kinship of the areas than the symbolism whereby Socrates, in welcoming what will be Timaeus's comprehensive and detailed discourse on the natural world, welcomes a discipline *dis*continuous with the philosophy *he* represents.

We may be impressed by a contrast, implied in the preceding paragraph, between the two new kinds of discourse in their relation to the Socratic one of 'yesterday'. Both are new kinds, one about universal cosmological actualities, the other about particular and supposedly historical ones. But the latter kind, in the form promised by Critias, is congenial in advance to the Socrates-character because it answers to the shape of what he longed for when he explicitly longed to see the fixed structure of his ideal *polis* breaking out into action; whereas the cosmology is not presented as answering to any pre-existing desire of his. On the other hand, on closer inspection this contrast looks a bit superficial. There is thematic unity between the ethics and politics of the *Republic* etc. and passages in Critias's story that spotlight ethical and political characteristics of the human beings and societies involved. But these Critian passages add up to a very small proportion of the whole which Plato has left us. This is especially true of such passages in the longer version as compared with the rest of it.[19] In fact, concerns about ethical character and political institutions provide just two among a great variety of perspectives which the full Critian story brings to bear on human life and history. The account sets out to exhibit the rise and fall of societies

---

[19] *Timaeus* (précis): 23b7, 23c5–d1, 24b7–d6, 25b5–7, i.e. 20 lines in a total of about 100 (running from 23b3 to 25d6); *Critias* (full version): 109d1–2, 111e3, 112c3–4, 112e4–5, 120e1–121c2, i.e. 33 lines in a total of about 503 (running from 108e1). We may of course speculate that overtly ethical material would have been more frequent in the missing part of the full Critian story.

not merely as manifestations of the soul-states of the citizenry but as processes shaped by geography, history, natural resources, and technology. It musters a vast range of empirical (even if fictional) detail. To the extent that it considers institutions, it does so not simply with reference to their ideal purposes but as concrete facts in a wider world. It may be that one of its purposes is to bring out ways in which institutions conducive to virtue, and therefore to happiness, are deeply dependent on and vulnerable to empirical conditions over which individuals have little or no control; and to send the message that for this reason statecraft should study history, geography, economics, town-planning, and a great deal more that lies beyond philosophical ethics. Even so, my point now is that Critias's contribution turns out to be vastly more than the story of fine citizens in action which Socrates desired.[20] Thus Critias's fuller discourse has something important in common with the cosmology, namely that both offer Socrates massively more than he is represented as looking for; and in both cases he approves these offerings in advance.

If we think that the affinity or correspondence, such as it is, between the discourse which Critias provides and the story that Socrates desired is more important than any disparity between them, we may find puzzling the fact mentioned above that he is not presented as having any pre-existing desire for a *cosmology*. (His discourse of the day before seems to have contained nothing that might have led anyone's mind in that direction.) Whatever we make of it, there is something to think about here: for Plato could rely on his readers to be familiar with the *Phaedo* story of Socrates's youthful interest in cosmology, his disappointment with Anaxagoras's book, his logical bafflement over physical causal explanations, and his turning to the method of *logoi* as 'a second voyage in the search for explanation' (99c9–d1). Even if this phrase means not 'a second-best' enterprise, but one (perhaps in fact the best) resorted to only because the previous one got nowhere, the *Phaedo* leaves us with a sense that in turning to *logoi* Socrates set aside his cosmological interest rather than lost it altogether. After all, Plato has Socrates at the end of the *Phaedo* speaking at length (while disclaiming authorship of the account, *Phaedo* 108c8) about the true nature of the earth and the geography of the underworld (108c5–113c9) – as if it was a shame to show him dying in a state of total cosmological unfulfilment. So in the *Timaeus* it

---

[20] My focus here is on the disparity *in content* between Critias's full version and what Socrates desired. In section 5.8 I shall be concerned with a very different disparity between Socrates and Critias. In that discussion, Critias's *précis* with his surrounding remarks about the transmission of the story will be more important than his full version.

5.2 Connecting Socrates, Timaeus, and Critias

is presumably deliberate on Plato's part not to have the Socrates-character admitting to an unsatisfied (and by his own efforts unsatisfiable) desire for cosmology.

However, if this is puzzling it becomes less so in the light of the fact that the fit between Critias's provision (the full version) and what Socrates called for at the beginning is really not close at all, since the provision vastly and in unexpected ways overflows the template held out by Socrates. To the extent that Critias's contribution is *not* heralded by the words of the Socrates-character, we should find it unsurprising that Timaeus's contribution is not heralded by words from the Socrates-character. In each of the two cases what we are shown is the introduction, under auspices represented by the Socrates-character, of a discipline non-continuous with the ethical, political, and dialectical thinking that we identify with Socrates.[21] Institutional piety towards the figure of Socrates does not require dining only at the Socratic table, with a succession of courses coming always *from* the Socratic kitchen. The piety can also be expressed by a return-feast dedicated *to* Socrates, for him to smile upon, with its courses coming from new kitchens.

I have been underlining the way in which the symbolism of the return-feast allows for a circle of new disciplines to appear as all in some sense inspired by Socratic philosophy but also as clearly not later versions of it, but enterprises with their own aims, standards, and methods. There is surely a challenging tension in presenting the whole position cleanly, perhaps for the first time: too much emphasis on ties to and continuities with the Socrates of earlier dialogues risks blurring the lines between what he and what the others respectively stand for. I think that this perspective helps with a puzzle about Socrates's discourse of 'yesterday'. The *resumé* given of it by Socrates 'today' speaks only of various *Republic*-style institutions (there is nothing about *Republic*-style psychology or epistemology or metaphysics), and the *resumé* is said to have covered everything, i.e. presumably, all the institutions and the rationales for them (19a7–b2). Strangely, though, there is no mention of philosopher-rulers.[22] The reason for this, I suggest, is that mention of them would have brought to mind the topic of the rulers' philosophical education, with the associated epistemology and metaphysics. But in the *Timaeus* Plato wants to give that epistemology and metaphysics

---

[21] This is not to say that the Timaean cosmology is not Plato's answer to Socrates's frustrated gestures towards cosmology in the *Phaedo*; on this see Chapter 6, Section 6.1.

[22] As Cornford, 1935, says (4), 'The summary is confined to the external institutions of the state outlined in *Republic* II, 369–V 471.' The idea of philosopher-rulers is introduced at V, 473c.

to Timaeus to use for founding his cosmology (27d5–28a3; 29b3–c3; 48e4–49a1; 51d3–52a7). It would have been crass to put philosopher-rulers into the Timaean Socrates's discourse of 'yesterday': doing so might well have suggested that the Socratic feast yesterday already of itself was promising the cosmology, hence that Timaeus today offers nothing new but only serves up to Socrates a piece of what Socrates had already served up to him.

As it turns out, Socrates will never be accorded the spectacle he longs for and which it is beyond his competence to produce for himself: the imaginative spectacle of the ideal city up and running. Critias's full version never gets as far as the extraordinary events befalling hyper-archaic Athens. And Critias's *précis*, although lavish with superlatives ('the greatest deed, the one most deserving to be most renowned' (21d4–5); 'the finest and best race among men' (23b6–7); 'a city most excellent at war and pre-eminently well-governed in every way, whose deeds are said to have been finest, and finest too whose institutions,[23] of all beneath the heaven of which we have heard tell' (23c5–d1); cf. 20e4–6; 23e5–6; 24c5–d6; 25b5–6), is short (to put it mildly) on interesting details of heroic action and sagacious leadership.[24] However, it may or may not be fanciful to point out that Socrates *is* given, in return for 'yesterday', the more intellectual spectacle of two new Platonic disciplines up and starting their running.

I have emphasised the distinctness of the two new genres from the Socratic one, and this has involved putting weight on the fact that Socrates is or has been represented as incompetent to perform adequately in them himself. But we should not downplay the complementary fact that Socrates is represented as an intelligent appreciator of performances in genres not his own. By this I do not mean the point which has already been underlined: that in graciously accepting the offerings of Critias and Timaeus Socrates extends to these genres an official blessing, thereby inaugurating their practice in a sort of institutional space historically identified by reference to him. I mean, rather, that Socrates is also shown taking the sort of interest in such offerings that is presumably to be expected from any well-educated person, not merely one with the power (because of his unique authority) to withhold inaugural permission. The symbolism of the return-feast only makes sense on the assumption that there are and should be lively connoisseurs who are not themselves expert practitioners. This tells us something about what, in Plato's view as

---

[23] The translations by Cornford, 1935, and Zeyl, 2000, do not convey the flowery chiastic repetition of 'finest'.
[24] On the 'scantiness' of the *précis*, cf. Rosenmeyer, 1956.

it comes across in the *Timaeus–Critias*, the expert practitioner should provide: like a playwright or theatrical producer, he or she should provide what an intelligently appreciative laic audience would judge well done and worthwhile.[25]

5.3 ATHENIAN HISTORY WITHOUT MARATHON (1)

The last section was concerned with the genres represented by Timaeus and Critias, and their relation to the one represented by Socrates. It did not attend to one of the strangest features of the *Timaeus–Critias* complex, a feature which has received intense discussion in the modern period: the fact that the story offered to Socrates is a purportedly historical account of events centring on Athens nine thousand years before Solon. Socrates simply wishes for a story with a certain kind of heroic content, and it is clear that he is not expecting a piece of history. Critias responds with what is, *inter alia*, a narrative matching Socrates's description – but (he says) it does not just match the description: it is historically true, and it is about Athens! What are we, Plato's readers, to make of this?[26]

Logically, one might ask why the supplied account is about an 'historic' event at all before asking why it is about one involving Athens rather than some other city.[27] But no one doubts that Plato composed the *Timaeus–Critias* with his own city-state in his sights all along; so 'historicity' as such is not a separate issue. But in fact, of course, what is not a separate issue is the story's *pseudo*-historicity. The story is unashamedly pseudo-historical. By this I mean that whereas in the dialogue-world the characters respectively present and receive the Athens–Atlantis story as true and historical, not only is it really pure fiction, but it advertises itself as such to recipients in the real world. Plato's contemporary readers or audience would have recognised it at once as pure fiction, and he would have known that they would. This is despite the fact that the names of at least three of the *Timaeus* characters, 'Socrates', 'Critias', and 'Hermocrates', belong to historical individuals well known by repute to the readership. There are two reasons we can be sure that Plato knew that this readership would understand the Athens–Atlantis story as fiction.

---

[25] Timaeus calls his audience *kritai* ('judges') at 29d1, echoed at *Critias* 108b3–5 and d6.
[26] In the last section I was mainly concerned with the genre represented by Critias's long version. In this section the focus will be on his *précis*, where the drama of Athens's finest hour is pinpointed.
[27] Cf. Johansen, 2004, 38.

(1) The story is an obvious pastiche of the real historical record of 490 BCE when an army of Greek hoplites, almost all from Athens,[28] stood up to the Persian invaders and defeated them at Marathon.

(2) The story comes swathed in an account of its own transmission right up to the moment when Critias is about to present it to Socrates. This transmission-account embraces a thousand years between the founding of the original Athens and the time when the story arrived in Egypt with the foundation there of Sais (23d7); eight thousand years of preservation in Saitic priestly records up to Solon's visit to Sais (23e2–4); Solon's return to Athens with the story (21c5–d1); the passing of the story from Solon to Critias's grandfather, also called Critias (20d8–e4);[29] its passage from ninety-year-old grandfather Critias to his ten-year-old grandson, the present Critias (21a7–b1; 25d7); the resuscitation of this childhood story in the present Critias's mature mind 'yesterday' (25e2–4; 26b1–2); and his rehearsal of it to Timaeus and Hermocrates 'yesterday evening' and 'early this morning' before they were due to join Socrates for the current meeting (20c6–d1; 21a1; 26a7–b1; 26c3–4).[30] Now, the real-world veracity of the nuclear story stands and falls with that of the associated transmission, and the transmission-story is ridiculously incredible by real-world standards. It is true and believed only in the dialogue-world, being designed to explain to the characters there how one of them is in a position to tell a story as yet unheard of by the others about the brilliant Athens of over nine thousand years ago. People in Plato's real-world circle of early audience or readers in a way stand to the author of the *Timaeus–Critias* as Socrates and the others stand to the Critias-character; for the real audience too had certainly never heard of this brilliant nine-thousand-year-old Athens until they opened these pages or heard them read. The difference is that none of those real people would have believed the dialogue-world explanation of why this great event had been unheard of by practically everybody. In particular, they

---

[28] Of the ten-thousand-strong army, nine thousand were Athenians, one thousand Plataeans. Thus the event of 490 was slightly less flattering to Athens than the one in Critias's summary in the *Timaeus*, where Athens alone of all the Greeks took a stand against mighty Atlantis (25b7–c6). But in the *Critias* version it seems that Athens was at the head of an alliance (*Critias* 108e4–5).

[29] Solon had a family connection with this Critias and hence with his descendants (20e1–2; cf. *Charmides* 155a).

[30] In the *Timaeus* Critias speaks as if the transmission from Solon down to himself had been purely oral. But at *Critias* 113a3–b4 he says that Solon wrote a translation of some of the material in the Egyptian records, with a view to working it into a poetic composition of his own (cf. *Timaeus* 21b4–d3), and these notes passed to grandfather Critias, were studied by the present Critias as a child, and are still in his possession today.

5.3 Athenian history without Marathon (i)

could not have believed for an instant that knowledge of the event not only had been buried from the Greeks for thousands of years before this knowledge arrived in Athens – arrived back home – but *had then existed in Athens since Solon's time even while remaining a secret to virtually everyone*. That situation is confined to the dialogue-world of Plato's authorial stipulation, where Critias *divulges* the story to Timaeus and Hermocrates, and then to Socrates, and hardly knew himself that it existed deep inside him until something just happened to remind him of it.

So in the real world of Plato and his readers the Critias-character's Athens–Atlantis story is a transparent fiction, a pastiche of the victory at Marathon in 490 projected into the hyper-archaic past. By contrast, for the characters of the *Timaeus–Critias* the ancient Athens–Atlantis story is true: and *they* have one less reason than real-world readers for doubting its truth. For in the dialogue-world the victory in 490 at Marathon, the most celebrated event of Athens's real-life history and famous throughout the Greek world, is absent from any historical record in the background of the conversation – a conversation which takes place in Athens (cf. 21a2; 26e3), with participants who are all Greeks, among them two Athenians. These personages are in no position to dismiss the Athens–Atlantis story as a pastiche of the early fifth-century triumph at Marathon, because theirs is a world in which that event *has never been heard of.* We can infer this from the fact that if in their fictional world that event was a known part of the (relatively recent) past of the Athens where they meet and hold their conversation, then the similarity between it and the nuclear episode of Critias's tale must have been remarked on by one of the characters. (Critias, at least, is not blind to 'miraculous' [*daimonios*][31] coincidences; cf. 25e4–5.) In the dialogue-world, Socrates the Athenian listens to Critias's Marathon-style story with completely fresh ears. Here is how Critias announces it to Socrates: 'Listen, then, Socrates, to a story that is very strange [*logou mala atopou*] but nonetheless completely true' (20d7–8).[32]

---

[31] Cornford's translation, 1935, 19.

[32] Christopher Gill has pressed me on whether Critias's story might not carry a 'silent allusion' to the real fifth-century Marathon. Certainly, Plato's staging the story is a silent allusion *by him* to that event. The question is whether in the dialogue-world Critias silently alludes to a fifth-century Marathon there in the background for him and his interlocutors, about which they remain as silent as he. Response: (a): if none of them mentions it, why should we suppose that it is there for them? It is not as if we outside the dialogue-world can just *see* that feature present inside it. (b) Its presence in the dialogue-world would undermine Critias's intention in telling his story. He means to *honour* Socrates by translating the Socratic ideal into hyper-archaic Athens, but the honour is diluted if the characters are aware of a rival to the hyper-archaic victory. That victory is supposed to manifest the unique virtue of the Socratic *politeia*; but if Critias and co. know of a similarly spectacular victory achieved when Athens had a very different constitution (that of Cleisthenes) they cannot admire the Socratic one as

So Plato's contemporaries would not only have known at once that the Athens–Atlantis story is a blatant fiction: they would also have known at once that 'present-day' Athens in the dialogue-world – the Athens nine thousand years or so later where Socrates and the others are meeting – is deeply and transparently unreal: it is an Athens for which Marathon has never occurred or is completely missing from the record. Plato's contemporaries, predictably by him, would have seen this as soon as they grasped (a) Critias's sketched outline along with (b) the accompanying explanation of why the story, although true, is complete news to the Greeks. From these two points they would have deduced that among the facts of the dialogue-world is the fact that an event with *this* profile is no part of recent[33] known history. And from this they would have deduced that the real-world Marathon-event of 490 is not on record in the dialogue world. For the profile in question belongs uniquely to *this* recent real-world event.

Once we are clear that the Athens–Atlantis story is pseudo-history, and obviously so, it may seem that the natural next step is to consider what message its content sends. What does Plato mean to convey by this overtly mythical clash of hyper-archaic Athens with Atlantis? However, rather than turning straight to this question, let us look first at what is to be learnt from the fact that the presence of this duplicate of Marathon in the dialogue-world implies (given the lack of comment on any duplication) the absence from it of what we know as the real-historical actuality of Marathon. I shall begin by considering what the absence of Marathon implies for scholarly questions about the dramatic date of the *Timaeus–Critias* and the identity of the Critias-character. This will take up the rest of this section. Then in section 5.4 I shall discuss what the absence of Marathon suggests about Plato's philosophical and moralistic purpose.

If in the dialogue-world no publicly known and constantly recounted Marathon-event occurred within, let us say, the presumed lifetime of any parents of the Socrates-character, then there is no reason to assume that any of the major events of actual fifth-century Athenian history have occurred in the dialogue-world: for instance, what we know as the second Persian invasion, Athens's investment in maritime strength, the constitutional reforms of Ephialtes and Pericles, the rise of the Athenian empire, the

---

so uniquely superior after all. (See section 5.5 on an analogous problem affecting certain other interpretations of Critias's story.) While admitting the need for caution in resting weight on an inference about hypothetical responses of characters in a fictional world of which *we* are not the authors, I nevertheless think that the obvious, and cleanest, conclusion to draw is that fifth-century Marathon, and the memory of it, are not features of the *Timaeus–Critias* dialogue-world.

[33] Recent by comparison with nine thousand years ago. Plato's great-grandfathers and the grandfathers of the real Socrates would have been of an age to fight at Marathon.

5.3 Athenian history without Marathon (i)

particular policies of Pericles, the Peloponnesian war, the Sicilian expedition, the rule and expulsion of the Thirty, the trial and death under similar-to-actual-circumstances of Socrates. For there were causal linkages between these episodes, starting with Marathon. So, for example, we are free to suppose that *in the Marathon-free dialogue-world* 'Socrates' never goes on trial and lives to be eighty-five years old instead of seventy like the actual Socrates.

We know from internal evidence that the meeting of the four characters takes place in Athens during a festival of Athena (26e3; cf. 21a2). But internal considerations not only give no clue on where to place this meeting in the chronology of, say, the last third of the fifth century BCE, but additionally they show why there cannot be such clues in the work as actually written. They show this by showing a dialogue-world in which Marathon never happened. Some of the actual sequel to Marathon might have happened even if Marathon had not, but we have no particular reason to think so, nor any conceivable way of identifying what would have been the same and what would have been different. Hence some of the parameters which scholars use to narrow down the possible dramatic dates of this and other dialogues have no application here. The parameters I have in mind consist of events and situations in real-world fifth-century Greek history. 'Could Hermocrates, given that we identify him with the Hermocrates who was or would be the Syracusan general, have been received in Athens on the peaceful and friendly terms of the dialogue-world after Athens launched the Sicilian expedition in 415, or after the débacle of that expedition? No; so the dramatic date must be earlier, probably no later than the peace of Nicias in 421.'[34] Other speculations about when Hermocrates might have visited Athens are similarly based on likelihoods themselves based on our knowledge of post-Marathonian Athenian history.[35] Then there is the identity of Critias. Which real-world Critias is the person in the dialogue-world? By the same token, there are fewer data than is usually realised for discussing this question. For example, it has been argued that since the dialogue-character seems to be an old man (he remembers what he heard long ago in childhood, not what he heard yesterday, 26b4–7), he cannot be Critias of the Thirty (son of Callaeschrus), who was a contemporary of Socrates and an older contemporary and relative of Plato, and who appears in the

---

[34] This is the view of Taylor, 1928, 14–17. For discussion of the question as applied to the Epizephyrian Locrian, Timaeus (cf. 20a1–2), see Lampert and Planeaux, 1998. (Epizephyrian Locris was allied against Athens during most of the Peloponnesian war.)
[35] E.g. Brisson, 1992, 333–4. See also Nesselrath, 2006, 57–9.

Charmides: the reason being that this Critias was in his fifties when he was killed in 403 in civil strife, an aftermath of the Peloponnesian war.[36] But it does not follow. Plato can place in his dialogue-world someone who in the real world died a violent death in middle age: for in the dialogue-world Plato can have this individual live tranquilly for eighty or more years.[37]

5.4 ATHENIAN HISTORY WITHOUT MARATHON (II)

I shall continue to press the thought that the fictional episode of hyper-archaic Athens is significant not only for its positive import but also because of its exclusion of what it excludes in the fictional world, which is to say the Athenian victory at Marathon and (I am suggesting) the sweep of consequent fifth-century Athenian history. Our four characters, celebrating in their own way the festival of Athena in Athens, are set against a background muffled in darkness, resistant to even the vaguest imagining of recent historical details. One thing we do gather, however, is that Athens in the fiction has retained what the Athenians felt to be its goddess-given identity:[38] Athens has not, for example, been swallowed up in a Persian empire stretching now over the Greek mainland; there are still free men philosophising at Athens. There are still festivals of Athena, and still the ancient system of phratries ('brotherhood groups') with its annual Apaturia festival and Cureotis ceremony (21b2; 7).[39] There is still a Socrates; still a Critias, scion of a great Athenian family[40] with its ancestral tie to Solon; still a Hermocrates visiting Athens from (we assume) Syracuse; still a figure such as the highly distinguished Timaeus (20a1–5), he too visiting from Western Locris in Italy; still the hospitality that a Critias could offer to men such as Timaeus and Hermocrates as his house-guests (20c7). But in this fiction-world the goddess-given identity of Athens has been secured without lustre

---

[36] Cornford, 1935, 1; Lampert and Planeaux, 1998; Nails, 2002, 106–13 (under 'Critias III' and 'Critias IV'); Nesselrath, 2006, 43–50.

[37] This consideration only rebuts arguments based on the relatively early actual death of Critias of the Thirty. A different objection to straightforwardly identifying him with the *Timaeus–Critias* character is that a grandfather of his could not have lived in the time of Solon, who died seventy years before Marathon. See Taylor, 1928, 23–4; Cornford, 1935, 1–2; Osborne, 1996, 182, n. 8; Lampert and Planeaux, 1998; Nails, 2002, 107. The objection depends on assuming that Plato would have been reasonably accurate about the chronology; but see Nesselrath, 2006, 47–8, on anachronism generally in Plato and in connection with Solon in a variety of authors. I shall say something on the possible 'trans-generational identity' of the Critias-character in section 5.7 of this chapter.

[38] Underlined by Critias: 24c4–d3 and *Critias* 109b1–d2.

[39] At the Apaturia adolescent boys were introduced into their phratries. The name is connected with 'deceit' according to the ancient etymology. At the Cureotis, which was the third day, children born within the previous year were registered by their fathers or guardians.

[40] This was Plato's family on his mother's side. The Critias killed in 403 was his mother's first cousin.

5.4 Athenian history without Marathon (ii)

from any Marathon in the relatively recent background; nor, until the moment when Critias opens his mouth (20d7–21a3), has it to any degree been enhanced by the glorious similar event of nine thousand years ago, since the memory of this had been all but lost from the Greek world until Critias started to resurrect it the evening before (cf. 25e2–26a2).

Plato may well have viewed Marathon not, as so many of his countrymen had done, as a straightforwardly happy source of continuing Athenian self-congratulation, but as the prelude to the disastrous trajectory of his city's rise to naval predominance and imperial power, its development as a full democracy, its embroilment in a thirty-year-war ending in its abject defeat. In Critias's story, the Athenian victory is followed by the physical obliteration of both sides in a day and night of earthquakes and floods (25c6–d3): project this whole scenario forward in time nine thousand years or so, and we have a symbolic curtain falling on real Athenian history some time after the Marathon victory, a curtain extinguishing Marathon from the record. We do not need to suppose that anyone literally wished that things had gone thus. For Plato simply to host the thought, to hold it up for inspection – the thought that a subsequent history without the memory of Marathon would have been a better history for Athens – sets the real-world history in a cold and sceptical light. Among the effects, and to Plato perhaps chief among the effects, which the real-world Marathon victory brought in its train was the proud Athenian remembrance of it that helped fuel Athens's subsequent spectacular rise while masking the possibilities of dangerous overreach.

These possibilities, revealed in harsh enactments of real-world history, are brought to the fore for readers of the *Timaeus–Critias* by the *personae* of Critias and Hermocrates. Their names evoke two of the most lamentable and shameful episodes in Athenian history, both having occurred within living memory of Plato and many of the original readers. Plato's contemporary kinsman Critias, son of Callaeschrus, was prominent in the brutal though short-lived oligarchic regime of the Thirty which the Spartans helped to install in Athens after the Peloponnesian war.[41] And 'Hermocrates' was the name of the Syracusan general, a man of great

---

[41] This is far from being all we know about Critias son of Callaeschrus *c.* 460–403 (on whom see Nails, 2002, 108–13, under 'Critias IV'). For a time he was an associate of Socrates (on which see more below). He was a leading rhetorician and poet (there may be a reference to his plays in the image of the 'theatre audience' and 'poet' at *Critias* 108b4–5; cf. d6). He was the author of verse and prose compositions (the *Politeiai*) on customs and institutions of various Greek city-states; thus it is apt that the 'historian' in the *Timaeus–Critias* should bear his name. For Plato, he would have been a prime example of a man of philosophical gifts corrupted by bad associates and bad institutions (*Republic* VI, 489d–495b).

resourcefulness and leadership and highly talented also as a diplomat,[42] who had led the successful resistance against the Athenian expedition to Sicily (415–13). The failure of this exercise in Athenian overreach had been catastrophic for Athens. And then there is the Socrates-persona. *His* name evokes the historical individual whom Plato had Phaedo describe as a man 'who was the best, and also the wisest and most just, of all in his day with whom we had personal contact' (*epeirathêmen*; *Phaedo* 118a16–17), and whose return-feast at the hands of his fellow Athenians was – not free maintenance at the Prytaneum which Socrates facing the dicasts said was the sentence he deserved, but – execution in prison for the crime of impiety.[43]

To the extent that these and any other actual events came about through forces fuelled by the cherished memory of Marathon, a hypothetical early fifth-century Marathon-victory which through some natural disaster left no mark on subsequent Greek minds would have been the equivalent of something that never happened at all. And this almost holds in the dialogue-world for the brilliant achievement of hyper-archaic Athens. As measured by its impact (in the dialogue-world) on history through Greek remembrance, the brilliant feat too might almost not have happened. Its one effect on latter-day Athenians has been to provide a story: a story for Solon to tell, and then Critias the grandfather, and now the current Critias. There may be an important purpose in the story, and it is surely important in the dialogue-world that no one in that world disputes its truth. Even so, even in *that* world the real event which renders the true story true has made virtually no difference to the souls of any Greeks who lived later. For after the story reached Athens with Solon it created no new condition in any souls except, in an élite few, a state of unquestioning belief and a solemn power of story-telling transmission. Yet it was only because of the dispositions of the souls in question that the story could affect them in this way. The actual event behind the story could not reach out and affect them itself, somehow causally bypassing the story-medium. Hence when the four characters meet 'today' in the dialogue-world, everything is the same for them as it would have been if – still in the dialogue-world – the story were (as in that world in fact it is not) some long-ago individual's fabrication. The nine-thousand-year-old event behind the story is as functionally null in the context created by the coming together of Socrates, Timaeus, Critias, and

---

[42] At 19c7 Socrates refers to *dihermêneuseis* ('parleyings'), i.e. diplomatic activity.
[43] Cf. *Apology* 36d1–37a1.

Hermocrates, as it is non-existent in the actual world of Plato and his readers.

Let us look at this matter by means of two contrasts: one with the purely physical effects of an event such as the battle of Marathon, and the other with the psychic responses of individuals involved in such an event on either side. The physical effects would spread out anonymously into the surrounding environment in accordance with the nature of the materials from which the Demiurge made this universe. They would make the same difference to physical nature whether or not anyone knew of them and talked about them. The psychic responses of the individuals involved would be emotions and struggles with pain and emotions, exercises of attention to perceptual information, exchanges of information, acts of imagination, self-exhortations, resolutions and refusals, deliberations, calculations of chances, decisions, giving commands, taking in commands, outward actions: also succumbings to pain or emotion, failures to decide, losses of nerve, lapses of attention, and so on. (We can surmise that the Socrates-character was hoping to hear about such things amongst others in the story that he requested.) Under the impact of the surrounding events individuals would respond in accordance with their personalities and their training. These ethically engendered responses not only lead to external behaviour; they also have effects within the soul (for Plato, the person's immortal soul), reinforcing or redirecting or undermining its pre-existing ethical dispositions. Such responses are, of course, real events and their effects on the soul are real, helping to shape responses in the future, or laying down dispositions to respond in certain ways even in situations that were never to arise. However, unlike the purely physical effects of a battle, and the underlying physical materials and forces, the ethical responses and dispositions are formed, directed, and moulded through symbolic thinking and linguistic interaction with others and self. It belongs to their nature to be effected and affected in part by words. Even so, when an ethically engendered response occurs, its effect on the soul whose response it is does not depend on its being known or talked about by people beyond the fray. Even if the responses and their ethical effects on the agent become lost to recorded history, things can never be as if they had never occurred: the difference remains in the psychic world of immortal souls, just as the physical difference made by an event survives in some form or other in the world of corporeal nature. These psychic differences made by the real battle of Marathon to participants would have existed even if an earthquake or tidal wave had erased all news of Marathon from the human record. The same would have been true of Critias's nine-thousand-year-old counterpart battle had something like that happened in the real world, but the news never got out.

However, suppose that a certain event did occur; also that there are people who believe that it did, but nonetheless tend to treat this event, understood by them to have happened, as having no significance beyond the fact of its being the subject of a fascinating story for the nations to take in and believe, and as having no effects or ripples in the world that are not mediated through this fact. To the extent that these people have the attitude just mentioned towards the event, to that extent they behave as if it makes no difference whether it really occurred or not. For they behave as if they could have the story and their belief in it, and everything they want from the story and their belief, even without the actual event.

Yet as well as believing the story – which means, of course, that they take it to be true – they may for some reason think it an extremely important and noteworthy fact, a fact that deserves to be emphasised, *that* the story *is* true (and would have been true even if no one at all had lived to tell it, since the event – it is assumed – would still have happened). Even so, if they behave as if all that matters about this wonderful event is that it is the ultimate source of a wonderful unquestioned story, then in fact they behave as if the event might just as well not have happened provided they would still have the story and their belief in it. And in that case, they cannot in logical consistency think or say, given their behavioural attitude, that it is important that the story they believe in is true – even if they do say or think this sincerely.[44] That inconsistency, it seems to me, is not far from being the predicament of Critias in relation to the Athens–Atlantis story as it appears in the *Timaeus* – Critias whose excited first words at the meeting are: 'Listen, then, Socrates, to a story that is very strange but nonetheless completely true [*pantapasi ge mên alêthous*]' (20d7–8; cf. 26c7–d3). However, the reasons for charging Critias with approximation to this inconsistency must wait until section 5.8 of this chapter.

In this section I have looked at differences that would or would not be made by, as it were, pulling the battle of Marathon out of Athenian history. The interest in this was prompted by the twofold fact that (a) the dialogue-world with its history of ancient Athens and Atlantis is obviously in some sense a counterpart to the real Marathon-containing world as seen from Plato's and his readers' point of view, and (b) any battle of Marathon that

---

[44] We are no doubt too rational to be able to assert in thought or word: 'I believe that it is true that *p* whether or not *p*'; but we can sincerely ascribe to ourselves a certain attitude even while engaging in some pattern of behaviour inconsistent with having that attitude.

took place say in the generation before the historical Socrates was born has (as I argued in the previous section) been blanked out of Athenian history in the dialogue-world. I considered what else of importance to Plato and to Athens would have been subtracted from actual history by subtracting the actual battle. I then turned to drawing out the fact, as I see it, that although in the dialogue-world the Athens–Atlantis story is true (that it is true is part of the fiction) its truth makes virtually no difference, even in that world. Although true there, it functions there *only* as a story.

Such considerations come naturally as one thinks about Critias's narrative in the *Timaeus*. While any interpretation of Plato's purpose here remains speculative, it is hard to believe that it was not one of his intentions to induce reflection on the uses of *logoi* and the importance and unimportance of truth. In general, human use of a given *logos* affects, or is intended by the user to affect, recipients in all sorts of ways other than merely disposing them to pass on the *logos* in the precise way in which it was passed on to them. Suppose the *logos* is a statement that p: it may be used to give someone a piece of practical information, or to give them some entry into a theoretical discussion in which they would connect p with other beliefs, or to indicate a standard to be aspired to: or so on and so on – depending on the content of p and the context. This fact, that the statement is used for so many more purposes than the purpose of its own replication on someone else's lips or in a new recipient's ears, is so ordinary and pervasive that the idea that a *logos* should exist only to be told and retold without change seems to be the idea of something not really human, or only stuntedly human. There may not be much difference between treating a certain *logos* in this way, even in the firm belief that it is true, and regarding the event which has made it true as having occurred only so as to be told about. This is to treat any *other* effects of the event, whether it is the shadow-Marathon of nine thousand years ago or the real Marathon of 490 BCE, either as non-existent, or as irrelevant, or as trivial and minor by comparison with the event as recounted, or as real and important effects of other causes and never of *it*. The real Marathon of 490 was, undeniably, a magnificent achievement for the victors; but recounting it over and over with that sole emphasis abstracts it from real history. The iconic event takes on the status of a Platonic Form of Athenian excellence. Just as beautiful particulars have that property by their conformity to the Form of the Beautiful, so it is with Marathon. If Marathon is adopted as a paradigm of Athenian excellence (it would be a sensible rather than an intelligible paradigm according to Timaeus's contrast at 28a6–29a6), then in the eyes of believers in this paradigm it or their use of it cannot lead to degradation: if arrogance and misjudgement are bad things, then reliance on the paradigm automatically (in their own view) prevents its adherents from being overtaken by arrogance and misjudgement: that only happens to people with quite different standards. Obviously this lesson is an exemplary philosophical simplification and a warning, rather than a description of any complicated political realities recent or prevailing when Plato wrote the *Timaeus–Critias*. The lesson is general: it would apply to any unthinking use of a historical event, constitution, or person as iconic of wisdom, courage, or justice.

5.5 SOME OTHER PERSPECTIVES ON THE ATHENS–ATLANTIS STORY

In the last two sections I mainly discussed matters arising from a negative or privative implication of the story: namely, that in the *Timaeus–Critias* dialogue-world, no battle of Marathon lies in the relatively recent past prior to the occasion when the characters meet. I now turn to a number of views on how to understand the story's affirmative content, i.e. its portrayal of ancient Athens and of Atlantis.

According to an illuminating and influential interpretation, Atlantis has a double role: it signifies on the one hand imperialist Persia of the first quarter of the fifth century and on the other hand imperialist Athens of the last quarter. Athens in the story stands for the real Athens which fended off the Persians at Marathon. Like Athens in the story, and in this respect also like Sparta in much of the Peloponnesian war, Marathonian Athens fought on land, not at sea. Imperialist Athens by contrast was a maritime power which in 415, in a westward extension of the Peloponnesian war, launched the Sicilian expedition reminiscent of the Persian sea-borne invasions (also westward) at the beginning of the century. Thus Critias's story re-enacts both Persian and Athenian imperialism.[45] It re-enacts the Sicilian expedition, and it also re-enacts the Persian invasion putting recent Athens on the wrong side. It identifies imperialist Athens with an alien, barbarian, power, a threat to the freedom of the Greeks in general[46] – but a power that was ultimately self-defeating. In pitting one historical Athens against another,

---

[45] This line of interpretation, proposed in the twentieth century by Vidal-Naquet, is summed up by Gill, 1980, xvii–xx, and by Brisson, 1992, 322–5. It was anticipated by Giuseppe Bartoli, *L'essai sur l'explication historique que Platon a donnée de sa République et de son Atlantide*, 1779, on which see Vidal-Naquet, 2007, xxi; 89; 92–4; Pradeau, 1997, 71–82.

[46] Thucydides (VI. 76. 4) reports a speech by Hermocrates to the people of Camarina in 415–14, saying that contemporary Athens has replaced Persia as enslaver of the Greeks; see also VI. 33. 5 for a speech where Hermocrates pointedly mentions disasters that can overtake great expeditions far from home, whether Greek or barbarian.

5.5 Some other perspectives on the Athens–Atlantis story

Atlantidean against Marathonian, it shows the values represented by the latter as threatened and encroached on by those of the former, but finally (in the normative symbolism) vanquishing them. As these are the same city at different causally connected stages of its history, the story proclaims that Athens has a split identity; also that latter-day Athenians should not bathe in the glory of the Marathonian defeat of Persia or be thereby emboldened to new risky ambitions while refusing to remember the pattern of Athenian rise, overreach, and downfall which unfolded in the fifth century.[47]

It seems overwhelmingly plausible that his original readers would have seen these meanings in the text, hence likewise that Plato intended them. But locating these meanings does not fully plumb the interpretative puzzle. What a reading of the above kind does not really address is the significance of the fact that Athens in the story *has precisely the character of Socrates's political-philosophical ideal*, and indeed is actually identified by Critias as a concrete case of this ideal (27a7–b6). This is considerably more than is needed for Plato to express, pamphlet-wise,[48] his criticism of the real career of Athens. For that, he needed a story similar to the one Critias tells, with a modest and decent Athenian protagonist-city acting heroically (as indeed the real Athens did at real Marathon, and in some other crises) and later being obliterated.[49] But this does not set up an intrinsic demand that the Athens of the story actually exhibit a detailed match with the philosophical ideal of Socrates. Yet *this* match is what the whole of the *Timaeus* dialogue prior to the cosmology is constructed so as to emphasise. (The interpretation just discussed has also the limitation of not suggesting any obvious link between the Athens–Atlantis story and the cosmology.)

The Socratic character of Athens in the story is addressed by the line of interpretation that sees the tale as Plato's synthetic charter-myth for Athens. The Athens that was founded by gods, was given the ideal constitution, and from that basis heroically defended the Greeks against Atlantis, is a Socratic

---

[47] The *Timaeus–Critias* was probably composed in 360–56. Several scholars have seen the Athens–Atlantis story as (amongst other things) a warning to contemporary Athens in light of the city's resurgence as a maritime power beginning in 377. See Pradeau, 1997, 224–9; Morgan, 1998; Nesselrath, 2006, 63–6.

[48] Cf. Pradeau, 1997, 13, 229, and 236.

[49] In *Laws* III, 698a9–699d2, the passage most likely to express his own views on the Athens of Marathon, Plato does not lavish praise on the city's constitution at the time (nor does he glowingly applaud the event). He characterises the constitution as ancient and as based on four property-classes; he attributes the morale that resulted in victory to internal solidarity on the part of the Athenians that arose from a combination of law-abidingness and fear of what the Persians would do to them if they lost; and he attributes the law-abidingness to the fact that the Athenians of that time served *sôphrosunê* as their mistress. It is not suggested that the laws were ideal, or that the laws were directly responsible for the *sôphrosunê*.

Athens precisely because it is Plato who fabricates the charter-myth. However, this line of interpretation, as I understand it, includes the suggestion that Plato created this charter-myth as something to be adopted by the historical Athens of the actual world in which Plato and his readers lived. The question is: how realistic could such a purpose have been? It is one thing to create what one intends to become a charter-myth for Athens in the real world, quite another to sketch a fictional world in which a story is brought to the fore in order to take on the status of a charter-myth for Athens *in that fictional world*. Since Plato has seen fit to write a play in which serious, highly educated men such as Socrates, Critias, Hermocrates, and Timaeus simply accept the Athens–Atlantis story as true,[50] he may indeed be suggesting that, given the authoritative endorsement of these characters, the story will now become the charter-myth of the city in which they are holding their conversation. It is highly imaginable that Plato composed the piece as an example of the kind of myth that a better and happier Athens, an Athens not puffed up by an early fifth-century Marathon, might have been in a position to tell about itself. Such a counterfactual Athens would have been an internally stable state that had not acquired a navy and an empire to the fear and envy of others; Hellenic freedom from Persia would have been maintained in some other way; Athens would not have been embroiled in a Peloponnesian war. Such a quiet and restrained Athens would probably have won no particular fame or notoriety for its deeds in the counterfactual fifth century; why, indeed, not balance this humdrum fictional Athens by endowing it with a glorious tradition according to which it *once* carried out 'the greatest deed, the one most deserving to be most renowned' (21d4–5)?

Such a tradition, believed and passed on in this counterfactual Athens, would certainly fit Luc Brisson's characterisation of myth as 'a message by means of which a given collectivity transmits that which it preserves in memory of its past from generation to generation'. Brisson also observes that '[a] community presents itself as a model to itself through the myths that it transmits'.[51] But note that, according to these very criteria for 'myth', the Athens–Atlantis story is *not* a beloved tradition of the real Athens of Plato. In the real world, the story is a pastiche, not merely of historical

---

[50] For Socrates, see 26e4–5, discussed in section 5.6. Hermocrates and Timaeus do not openly affirm its truth; but when Critias does so at 20d7–8 and 26d1–5, they do not dissent. Critias's emphasis on his and their joint responsibility for the return of hospitality makes it impossible that they not share his assumption of veridicality (26d5–6; 27a2–b6; cf. Timaeus at 17b1–4, echoed by Hermocrates at 20c4–6; also Socrates at 19e8–20c3 looks upon the others as sharing a single task).

[51] Brisson, 1998b, 13 and 9. The characterisations quoted are not intended by Brisson to cover everything deemed a 'myth' (see, e.g., the examples at 63), and he would no doubt accept putting 'in memory of its past' in inverted commas.

5.5 Some other perspectives on the Athens–Atlantis story

writing such as that of Herodotus,[52] but also of civic *myth*, given the supposition that civic myth functions in the ways which Brisson has emphasised. Such functioning depends on a receptive civic audience, which is precisely what does not exist in the real world where Plato publishes the *Timaeus–Critias*. For 'receptive' means that the audience is willing and able to sing along with the story being told about itself. But for real Athenians this would require suspending or discounting common knowledge of the last century and a half of their own history. (It would be like asking us, today, to celebrate – not: pretend to celebrate; what could be the point of that? – an immemorially ancient epic confrontation between a Winston Churchill and an Adolf Hitler, while blotting World War Two out of our knowledge of the twentieth century.) Certainly, Plato may have wished that his real Athens *had* been a *polis* possessing a charter-myth about itself as a Socratically ideal city beating back the forces of barbarism. But whatever may be true of philosopher-rulers in the *Republic*, Plato in real Athens was not in control of a state-wide propaganda-machine. There was no way in which he could have reasonably hoped to implant Critias's story into his fellow Athenians' psyches so that it would be for them an actual, functional, edifying tradition about themselves.[53]

Proponents of the 'charter-myth for real fourth-century Athens' interpretation (including any who fudge the difference between a charter-myth functioning as such in the fictional dialogue-world and one that would function as such in real fourth-century Athens) might lean on the fact that, in real life, the epistemic standard for a society's accepting some tale as its charter-myth is very far from being that of the serious historian assessing what may really have happened. In entering into civic identity-myths, even sophisticated people are allowed to be uncritical and childish. Granting this,

---

[52] This applies to Critias's longer version rather than his *précis*.
[53] That this was Plato's aim in composing the story, and in fitting it out (for the dialogue-world) with the trappings of an authentic tradition, seems to be the thesis of Naddaf, 1998, and Lampert and Planeaux, 1998. Supposedly, the purpose was to make up for the fact that real Athens lacked an epic celebrating its ancient glory; heroes such as Cecrops and Erechtheus are 'almost totally ignored by Homeric tradition' (Naddaf, 1998, xxx–xxxi). See also Morgan, 1998, 109. Morgan, following Gill, 1993, compares the Athens–Atlantis story with the Myth of the Metals, which in *Republic* III, 414b–415d, Socrates suggests as a charter-myth for Callipolis (while recognising the problem of inculcating it into the first generation; 415c6–d2). But this by itself leaves it quite unclear whether the Athens–Atlantis story is supposed to be the charter-myth for the fictional Athens which is the setting of the *Timaeus–Critias*, or for Plato's historical Athens. (Morgan's paper provides, however, more food for thought than can be addressed here, especially in relation to the parallels between elements in Critias's story and themes in Isocrates, on which see also Loraux, 1986.) Brisson, 1998b, does not confront the question of Plato's aim in constructing the Critias story; his treatment perhaps suggests that the purpose was somehow to thematise and meditate on the nature of myth.

let me turn now to a different theory, namely that Plato mounted the Athens–Atlantis story in order to persuade his fellow citizens to look more favourably on the Socratic civic ideal, or to persuade them not to dismiss the ideal out of hand as impossible. It seems to me that Plato would have had to be a fool if he hoped to persuade the *Athenians* to look favourably on a philosophically constructed political ideal by pointing to a mythic case that both fits that ideal *and* manifests Marathonian heroism. Athenians would retort: 'We have already pulled off Marathon in real life, without at that time or any other conforming to your philosophically constructed political ideal.' As for the question of possibility, the response might well be: 'Who cares about the possibility of the Socratic ideal, given we already have at least one great instance of the actuality of civic virtue in the shape of our own Athens as she was when she fought the land-battle at Marathon? Let that continue to be our tried and familiar ideal example,[54] not Socrates's new-fangled city of words!' And those who gave this second reply could fairly add the taunt that when Plato for some reason decided to serve up a particular illustration of his philosophic ideal in action, his imagination ran so dry that he had to borrow a piece of existing Athenian history.[55] So much for his pretensions to hold up *a priori* standards for Athens. Still worse, Plato risked being interpreted as after all deliberately extending his full philosophical blessing to the actual Athens as she was at the time of Marathon.

Much the same difficulty besets Nicole Loraux's theory that the Critias-story is Plato's serious philosophical eulogy to the Socratic *politeia*.[56] The problem is that the episode which the supposed eulogy uses for illustration is copied from Athens at Marathon, when Athens at Marathon, for everyone whom Plato can be supposed to be addressing, was a salient episode of public history. Again the question arises for Plato and whoever he is addressing: if mythic Athens in the story no more than matched the performance of Athens at Marathon, why suppose that its *politeia* is superior to that of Marathonian Athens? Why should anyone listen to a eulogy of the Socratic political ideal, rather than to traditional eulogies of Athens at the time of Marathon?

No such problem arises *within* the *Timaeus–Critias* dialogue-world, because in that world there has been no Marathon, nor therefore a Marathonian Athens. In the dialogue-world the event in Critias's story is a nonpareil. So there the story might function as a eulogy to the Socratic

---

[54] As it is in Plato's send-up of the *epitaphios logos* in the *Menexenus*.
[55] Providing more material for the traditional charges that Plato plagiarised.
[56] Loraux, 1986, 296–303.

5.5 Some other perspectives on the Athens–Atlantis story

politeia, just as there it might function as a charter-myth.[57] But the fact that it could have these functions in the dialogue-world does not explain what Plato, writing in the real world, meant to teach his real-world readers by staging Critias's story.

What blocks the mapping of dialogue-world verities into the real world inhabited by Plato and Plato's readers has been contingent historical actuality and the actual public memory of it. By contrast, when Timaeus is shown eulogising the cosmos and the wisdom of its maker we can also, I think, safely assume that Plato means this as his own eulogy to the cosmos too. Thus Timaeus and Plato genuinely engage in one and the same kind of performance and to the same effect. Why may we safely assume this congruence? It is because there are no contingent and newsworthy real-world facts, matters which Plato and his readers know and know each other to know, that clash with anything that Plato makes Timaeus say. By contrast, the well-known historical reality of the battle of Marathon does clash – in two ways – with the Marathon-stamped story which Plato has Critias tell. (1) For anyone in Plato's real-world audience who was simple-minded enough to accept the Critian story as real-world true, there would be a clash in the sense of a rivalry between the event in the story and the real battle: they compete for the status of exemplar. If virtues and good institutions manifest themselves in fine deeds, then the qualities and institutions of Marathonian Athens were as good as any that Socrates can delineate, since the deeds referred to were just the same. So why pay attention to Socrates? If the instance of *his* ideal is intrinsically no better than Marathonian Athens, surely we should prefer the recent one which books and speeches have been written about, and which our own great-grandfathers and their fathers were involved in, to one that perished nine thousand years ago and which no one has ever heard of? Supplying people with the premisses of this argument is hardly a way of eulogising the Socratic ideal. Alternatively, and to my mind more probably, (2) people would have understood the Athens–Atlantis event in the Critias-story as being *instead* of its counterpart in real Athenian history: this is a clash such that the presence of one in a narrative does not merely crowd the other but actually excludes it. So people would

---

[57] By similar reasoning, Critias's story could be a real-world eulogy to that ideal *politeia* on the fantastic assumption that the place where Socrates presented the *politeia* yesterday and where Critias is telling its ancient story today, is some far off real-world corner of the earth that has been shielded from news about Athens from Marathon onwards, or where such news is only a faint rumour not to be taken seriously! Alternatively, the story could be an Athenian real-world eulogy to the Socratic *politeia* in the context of a future, differently historied, differently memoried, Athens in which, perhaps through an intervening cataclysm and a great lapse of time, knowledge of the Marathon of 490 BCE has disappeared without trace or survived merely as a folk-story.

have inferred straight off that the Critias-story is a fiction and such an obvious one that Plato never expected them to believe it. He is pretending to believe it and inviting them to share his pretence. The pretence is that once long, long ago there was a city that instantiated the Socratic ideal and exercised its Socratic virtue in achieving a great victory. But if we think that the way to eulogise the Socratic ideal is by pointing to great deeds it accomplishes, how does it help to pretend-point to a deed that never happened? If someone says: 'But to function as an exemplar it doesn't have to have really happened', one can answer: 'Yes, but not having really happened – this being the kind of thing that might happen and might not – doesn't automatically make it a better exemplar than something similar that *has* happened'; and then the door is open again for the actual Marathonian episode to be installed as paradigm. Again, a strange way to eulogise the Socratic *politeia*.

5.6 PARADIGMS AND BOUNDARIES

I shall now suggest that in identifying the Socratic ideal city with prehistoric Athens Plato puts forth a message about the ongoing need for Socratic philosophising. In a way the message is single and simple, but Plato in my view frames it in terms of three oppositions corresponding to three ways of engaging with the past, or with memory and history.[58] First (1), there is the use of the past as a source of paradigms, especially positive paradigms. This use is political in intent, hence carries practical implications for the wider society: bits and pieces of the past are commandeered as tools of political persuasion. Then (2) there is the historian's engagement with the past for its own sake: investigation that aims to be comprehensive and objective. This is worthwhile because its results are a form of knowledge: or – if that seems too strong (especially for Platonic circles) – because its search for the best account is governed, in fact defined, by a set of demanding impersonal internal standards. (It also contributes, as I have suggested, to the grand story of the cosmos by having in its scope the vast unfolding network of moral and intellectual victories, and also defeats, on the mortal-immortal front.) Thirdly (3), there is the telling of some splendid piece of the past in order to link it with the story-teller and his audience, and them

---

[58] References in the *Timaeus–Critias* to memory, records, and preservation and loss of information through time: 17b5–7; 18c7; 18d6–8; e4; 20e4; 21a1; c3; 22a1–b8; e4–5; 23a1–b6; c2–3; d1; e3–4; 24d6–e1; 25e2–4; 26a1–2; b1–7; c2–3; 27b4; *Critias* 108d1–4; e1; 109d2–110a7; 110b1–2; 112e8; 119c6–d1 (cf. e2–4); 120c3–4. See also 21d1–3 and the references to fame in n. 77.

5.6 Paradigms and boundaries

with each other and with previous rounds of tellers and audiences: here, the value lies in the individuals' enriched sense of identity and belonging, and their enhanced sense of importance as connected with the splendid past and as conduits of a precious tradition. I shall argue that in the *Timaeus–Critias* Plato confronts these ways of engaging with the past with an eye to the potential each has to usurp the ground that rightfully belongs to Socratic philosophising.

The Critias-character represents all three ways of relating to the past, and this multiplicity is a large part of the reason why interpreters have found it so hard to pin down the nature of his contribution. There is no such single nature. 'Critias' stands for a certain mode of political ideology; for historiography; and for entrancement with one's own tradition. (And as well as referring to these different mental attitudes towards the past, the name also points to a lamentable relatively recent episode in the external arena that was just one of a series of deeply questionable episodes which had among their causal antecedents the Athenian victory of Marathon; see section 5.4.) Of the three past-oriented attitudes, the first and third are more akin to each other than either is to the second, but they are different enough, at least in the context of the *Timaeus–Critias*, to need separate discussion. As I shall explain, their differences enable us to see the first attitude as a degenerate analogue of the thinking done by the Demiurge, and the third as a degenerate analogue of Timaeus's tale of the coming to be of the cosmos.

The difficulty of this plurality of meanings of 'Critias' does not end here. In the dialogue-world, Critias is, of course, a single character; and his companions all welcome all his interventions with friendly politeness. But Plato in the real world of his time regards the first attitude as hopelessly wrong-headed; shows (in my view) biting scorn for the third (at least as instanced by his Critias); but legitimates the second in a manner that simultaneously stands as a warning against a certain possible misconstruction of its role. Thus we have Critias in the dialogue-world receiving a uniformly smooth reception from the impeccably admirable Socrates, Timaeus, and Hermocrates, whereas the things which he stands for in the real world are meant to arouse contrary reactions in readers with good judgement.[59]

---

[59] At 20a6–7, when pointing out his companions' qualifications to provide a good account of the ideal city in action, Socrates characterises Critias as follows: 'Critias, I suppose [*pou*], is known by everyone here [sc. at Athens] to be far from unqualified in all the things of which we speak [*oudenos idiôtên*]' (i.e. in philosophy and politics; cf. 19e5–20a1). This accolade is noticeably more restrained than the one Socrates accords to Timaeus, 20a1–5, and perhaps a bit cooler than what he says about Hermocrates at a7–b1.

Plato has, however, given some help for disentangling worthy from unworthy Critiases. He has done this by placing the whole expanse of the cosmology between the Critian *précis* of the Athens–Atlantis story (which comes encased in the elaborate account of its own transmission) and the full and detailed version undertaken in the *Critias*. The former text largely represents the two base attitudes – pastwards-pointing political ideology and entrancement with tradition – while the latter represents respectable historiography. The texts, isolated from each other by the cosmology, differ not merely as outline and filled-in treatment. In the outline, the intellectual personality of Critias comes across as excitable, passive, and uninterested in factual detail, while his speech in the second reflects a mind that is on the whole keen and thoughtfully in control of his mass of material.[60]

With these preliminaries on the table concerning the plurality of Critias, let me turn to the three ways of relating to the past, and their respective differences from Socratic philosophising. I shall consider the first two ways in the rest of this section, and my discussion of the third will be developed in sections 5.7 and 5.8.

(1) We are surely never to forget that the Socratic ideal was constructed in discourse by analysis and argument *a priori*. By identifying this ideal with a fictional Athens (and even in the fiction an Athens sealed off from living Greek history by nine thousand years of oblivion), Plato, I suggest, is saying that *no* Athens belonging to real history should be taken as political exemplar.[61] This is in response to the practice, common in politics of the time (and perhaps of any time), of nostalgically harking back to this or that supposedly superior civic arrangement from one or another period in the

---

[60] We are not given a decisive way of telling how much of this mind (in the dialogue-world) belongs to Critias himself, and how much belongs to whoever or whatever composed the story which he inherited. Does he fill in outlines himself or only repeat what he had been told? His plea for indulgence at 106b8–108a4 is tailored to the particular present context, but the rest of the account could all have come via his grandfather.

[61] I argued this in Broadie, 2001. Even if one grants that Plato was in some sense pro-oligarchic (although this does not logically follow from his hostility towards the Athenian democracy) I do not see the evidence for holding that by means of the Critias story he preaches a return to 'the ancestral constitution established by Solon' (Brisson, 1992, 324–5; so also Gill, 1980, xix–xx. If this had been the message, why would Plato not have invested the ancient opponent of Atlantis with something like the Cleisthenean constitution (or the Solonian, especially as Solon is crucial to the fictional transmission of the story) rather than with one devised by a fifth-century dialectician? As I understand it, Plato would have thought that pointing to Marathonian Athens for light on what a *polis* should be was as *methodologically* misguided as pointing to fully democratic Athens for the same purpose (as Pericles virtually did in a speech reportedly made to the Athenians in 431; Thucydides, II. 37. 1: 'Instead of our polity being one that emulates the laws of our neighbours, we ourselves are an exemplar [*paradeigma*] to certain people rather than being imitators [*mimoumenoi*] of others'). This does not entail that Plato would not have deemed Marathonian Athens to be in fact morally superior to the Periclean city, and therefore a no doubt less dangerous (although still false) *paradeigma*.

earlier history of the state. For instance, the Critias-persona reminds us by his name of recurrent efforts by some factions to get full-blown Athenian democracy replaced by an oligarchic set-up touted as the restoration of a supposedly more pristine ancestral constitution.[62] Anyone persuaded by such rhetoric has, in effect, accepted some extremely shaky assumptions: for instance, that historical memory, such as it is, can accurately identify historic paradigms worth following today; that great deeds such as those of Athens against the Persians in the early fifth century do bear adequate witness to the underlying political excellence of the city as she was when she performed those deeds; and, supposing the first two assumptions satisfied, that no special discernment would be additionally necessary for determining, first, which of the chosen exemplar's distinctive characteristics were relevant to its success under its own historical circumstances, and next whether those circumstances sufficiently resemble the situation of Athens today. Such unanalytical promotions of this or that real-historical example are surely part of what Plato is targeting when he stages a fictional world where the true Athens-of-Marathon, the truly exemplary Athens, existed not twenty years before the birth of Socrates, nor a hundred years or so before that when Solon brought about a new order in Athens, but lost to history in the furthest reaches of hyper-archaic time. For the true paradigm of what Athens should be has no more place on a real-historical time-line than any other intelligible Form F has a place in a group of perceptible fs.

This is not the unverifiable and pointless existential claim that the ideal city (according to Socrates's specification) has never been exemplified (or even that there has never in the whole of time been such a city where Athens now stands). It is a claim about how to access the civic ideal. Here again is the general principle, which Timaeus applied to the making of this world:

Whenever the craftsman looks towards what is always changeless, and using a thing of that kind as his paradigm reproduces in his work its form and meaning, everything that he completes in this way is, of necessity, beautiful. But whenever the craftsman looks towards something that has come to be, using a paradigm that has been generated, beautiful his work is not. (28a6–b2)

Socrates has no theories about the genesis of the world, and in the *Timaeus* he is presented as nescient of the language that Timaeus will use to bring out the metaphysical and epistemological distinctions between the good craftsman and the bad one. Nor was Socrates ever granted an opportunity to make, in reality, a city. But he implicitly knows and practises the right way

---

[62] Marathonian Athens was iconic to the anti-democrats.

of determining the city-maker's objective: it is a matter of thinking out argumentatively and analytically what a city-state should be. Philosophy done in the tradition of Socrates may reject or modify some of its previous conclusions. For example, the philosopher may not continue to view the polity of the *Republic* as the right ideal.[63] The important thing is that philosophers should treat the question as philosophers' business, and should investigate it by way of the method which Plato's first audience will have associated above all with Socrates in the *Republic*. The principle governing this method is that a true account of a given institution must be built up by way of teleological reasoning from fundamental principles of human nature.

(2) Moreover, now that some in Plato's circle may be adding to their projects the more empirical and *a posteriori* study of human events and institutions, it is particularly important not to forget the distinctive character of Socrates's practice. In the long version of Critias's story Plato clearly shows a lively sympathy for the writing and reading of history. First, he himself by writing a fictional history packed with lively, coherent, and often exotic detail gives us something of one kind of pleasure to be had from reading certain kinds of history, such as Herodotus on the customs of the Egyptians and the layout of the great cities of Ecbatana and Babylon. Plato would hardly have known how to create that sort of pleasure if he had not appreciated it himself. Second, beyond that sort of pleasure the account in the *Critias* points to many categories for organising historical information so as to generate theoretically fruitful comparisons and generalisations about the development of human culture and society. Furthermore, Plato may have originally intended to focus too on the reasons and motives[64] which activated cities and leaders on each side, showing how reasons and motives, developing as they would under pressure of events and in the melting-pot of debate and negotiation, provide interesting and perhaps satisfying explanations. Thus he may have intended episodes of speech-making, crafted to fit the various contexts, that would link episodes of military preparation and action in the manner characteristic of Thucydides. That would have helped answer the wish Socrates expresses at *Timaeus* 19c2–8.

However, Plato's manifest understanding of various kinds of natural interests that are expressed and strengthened through reading and writing history must have been balanced by a sharp sense of the difference between

---

[63] Thus by the time he wrote the *Timaeus–Critias* Plato may have had second thoughts about the content of the political ideal in the *Republic* while continuing to endorse the method exemplified there.

[64] Cf. *prophasis* at 20c5 and *Critias* 120d8, often used in this sense by the historians and orators; see Nesselrath, 2006, 429.

5.6 Paradigms and boundaries

this discipline and the enterprise of Socratic philosophy, and of the need to make that difference officially clear. As we have already seen (section 5.2 of this chapter), this move is effected by the device of the return-feast. Socrates is positioned on one side, and the others in a group on the other. Their plan, in which Socrates fully concurs, is to present *to* him a complex offering of their own. Their *act* of offering-in-return establishes an endorsed-by-everybody institutional collegiality between them and Socrates, while at the same time making it clear that no part of *what* they offer was already contained in what he presented yesterday. Hence the new disciplines come on to the Platonic stage wreathed, so to speak, in disavowal. What the manner of introducing them says is that they are *not* new and improved forms of what Socrates stands for: which in turn means that they neither collectively nor severally compete with or supersede what Socrates stands for.[65] It would of course be the crudest misunderstanding to think that the division of duties between 'yesterday' and 'today' shows that the Socratic task is now a thing of the past, whether because it has been completed or because it has been discarded in favour of an improved version of itself. In fact, the symbolism conveys that since Socrates is present as a necessary component of today's proceedings, his kind of task and method are still alive and needed. For symbolically there is no distinction to be drawn between Socrates and the philosophising he stands for. His expressed wish occasions the others' collective response, but this tribute of theirs is not being paid to the wishful Socrates, deficient in resources to imagine a tale for himself, but to the philosophical master who shared the fruits of his distinctive intellect yesterday and is the same person today.

The lesson of the return-feast symbolism perhaps needs special underlining for people who pursue history. History is about human affairs, and in traditional forms it often highlights ethically salient contours of individuals and communities as their careers shift about between the ethically charged poles of *eudaimonia* and *dusdaimonia*. Moreover, normative political science must if it is to be at all practical contain an internal impulse towards the study of existing and past institutions, if only to see what under what circumstances does or does not work, is or is not possible. Normative political science at these outer edges of itself, so to speak, joins hands or merges with historical studies. This is fine as long as no one takes it to mean

---

[65] Such a disavowal would have been particularly necessary given that the *content* of what Socrates stands for has not been static throughout the dialogues preceding the *Timaeus–Critias*. Plato needed to be able to rethink the specific intellectual commitments (about subject-matter, method, doctrine) that he desired to associate with 'Socrates' while avoiding any suggestion that his 'Socrates' is simply a symbol for higher learning in all its different kinds.

that history has *superseded* fundamental thinking about the good of man and society. The ceremonious symbolism proclaims boundaries so that each discipline may enjoy its own space, as well as a measure of complementarity.

The division of the disciplines, Socratic, Timaean, and Critian, does not closely resemble the joint operation of creating the complete cosmos which the Demiurge has to call upon divine ancillaries to share. For that shared task had a very clear single purpose specifically pre-figured from the start. The disciplinary division is more like the original partitioning out of the earth between recognised gods such as Athena and Poseidon shown near the beginning of Critias's long account:

> Now, gods once upon a time took over the whole earth by due division of the regions – *not* in strife: for it would not be in accordance with right reason that gods should be ignorant of what belongs to each of themselves, nor yet that they recognise what belongs rather to others but severally attempt to get possession of it for themselves through outbursts of strife. So: as each received by the allotments of justice their beloved portion, they began to settle [*katô(i)kizon*: the word also means 'they began to colonise'] the lands; and having settled them, as shepherds their flocks they began to nurture *us*, their own possessions and nurslings ... (109b1–c1)[66]

No doubt this passage indicates *inter alia* a picture of the gods whereby humans could exercise their distinctive religious bent from the very first (cf. *Timaeus* 42a1), before they had reasoned theories of the divinity of the cosmos and the stars; but one of its several meanings must be that the habitable earth diversely but peaceably came under human settlement through diverse gods because human potential was destined to take root in diverse starting points of terrain, climate, etc. (cf. 24c4–d3) so as to develop in importantly diverse ways.

Finally in this section, recalling some of the discussion in the previous one, we should ask whether the symbolic division of disciplines in the dialogue-world is meant to carry over into the real world of Plato and his readers: or whether it is like the idea of Critias's story as charter-myth or eulogy of the Socratic ideal: viable, no doubt, for the dialogue-world but absurd for the real one. The right response is surely to accept the carry-over. The same goes for the logically related point about respect for historiography. Is respect for it only an element of the Plato-created world where no one doubts that Critias's account is true? No, no more than respect for the

---

[66] It is obvious but important that these gods are not cosmogonic or identified with natural forces. They are distinctive *genii locorum*, whereas the forces of nature are the same everywhere. They appear after nature has been completed, and have a purely cultural role. For a fascinating discussion of the gods of the *Critias*, see Thein, 2008.

Timaean cosmology itself. These happy features of the dialogue-world do not stay trapped inside it because they are not at odds with anything that Plato's readers know about the real one.

5.7 PHILOSOPHY AND REMEMBRANCE (I)

In this and the next section I shall focus on what we learn about Critias in the *Timaeus* as a link: both a link in the story-telling chain and a link in a family-chain. As last link in the story-telling chain this figure in a way stands for or summarises the whole tradition and its transmission. And the figure may also be meant to represent a fusion of several generations of historical Critiases,[67] or to personify an intergenerational abstraction, a sort of *daimôn* of the house.[68]

In any case the name naturally brings to mind its most notorious bearer: Critias son of Callaeschrus (c. 460–403 BCE), a cousin and older contemporary of Glaucon, Adeimantus, and Plato, and for a period one of the circle round Socrates. Plato had already made him a minor character in the *Protagoras* and a principal interlocutor in the *Charmides*, where he appears as a person of lively ideas with a love of linguistic and conceptual distinctions. The short-lived oligarchic regime of the Thirty (404–3), led by this Critias, was lawless and ruthless, and after its overthrow in which Critias was killed his was amongst the most disgraced names in Athens. According to Xenophon, Critias at some earlier point had a falling out with Socrates and turned implacably against him.[69] The Thirty, quite possibly at the express suggestion of Critias, ordered Socrates and four other citizens to bring in Leon of Salamis, an innocent man, for arbitrary execution. (Their purpose was to lay hands on Leon's property while incriminating others, thus building their own support.) Socrates refused to have anything to do with it. This firmness would probably have cost him his life if the Thirty had not fallen shortly afterwards.[70] Also according to Xenophon, Critias helped draft laws for the Thirty and with Socrates in mind he put in a clause criminalising the teaching of the 'art of *logoi*'.[71]

---

[67] This covers more than two generations of the family, for the name, as was the custom, went from grandfather to grandson.
[68] Brisson, 1992, 332, suggests that Plato may deliberately leave the identity of Critias indeterminate as between Critias of the Thirty and one or more of his forefathers.
[69] Xenophon, *Memorabilia* I. ii. 29–31.
[70] Plato, *Apology* 32c4–d8; for references in other ancient authors see Burnet, 1924, 135 ff.
[71] *Memorabilia* I. ii. 31 ff.

If Critias's grudge was indeed as intense as Xenophon describes, Critias might have got grim satisfaction could he have known that his own earlier friendly association with Socrates, like that of the equally disgraced Alcibiades, would posthumously contribute to the train of events that culminated in Socrates's execution as a criminal in 399. After the democracy had been restored, the image of Socrates as 'educator of traitors' helped fuel the orchestrated suspicion that led to his indictment and conviction. A few years later, the Athenian Polycrates, a teacher of rhetoric, published a 'Denunciation of Socrates' attacking him for his connection with Alcibiades and Critias. As we gather from Xenophon, Polycrates claimed:

Critias and Alcibiades, having become associates of Socrates, the pair of them, brought down a host of evils on the city. For Critias became the most rapacious and most violent and most murderous of everyone in the oligarchic regime; and Alcibiades became the most intemperate and most arrogant and most violent of everyone in the democratic regime. (*Memorabilia* I. ii. 12)[72]

The odium was still very much alive well into the middle of the fourth century. As late as 345 the orator Aeschines was invoking it as an accepted attitude when he (assentingly) declared to an Athenian jury: 'Men of Athens, you put Socrates the sophist to death because he was shown to have educated [*pepaideukôs*] Critias, one of the Thirty . . .'[73]

The point of these remarks is partly to show the kind of reputation Critias of the Thirty left behind him in Athens echoing down through the years,[74] and partly to indicate that both his actions and the reception of them must have had complicated and troubling effects on someone indissolubly linked both to him and to Socrates: to him by unalterable facts of kinship, to Socrates by philosophy. For instance, we can imagine a family milieu in which certain of Plato's relatives, being Critias's relatives, in some cases refused ever to mention Critias after his death, and in others were in bitter dissension within and among themselves over the meaning of his career: whether he was swept along by events, whether his ignominy was due to enemies rather than to his own conduct, and of course whether it was partly through some sort of provocation or other unlucky influence from

---

[72] Xenophon does not name his source for this quotation, but the scholarly consensus attributes it to the pamphlet of Polycrates.
[73] Aeschines, *Against Timarchus*, 173.
[74] This Critias and Alcibiades were said to be obsessed with making names for themselves (*onomastotatô genesthai*, Xenophon, *Memorabilia* I. ii. 14). See n. 77 on the same superlative in the *Timaeus–Critias* as applied to ancient Athens.

5.7 Philosophy and remembrance (i)

Socrates that Critias's life turned out as it did.[75] With these considerations as background let us return to the telling of the Athens–Atlantis story in the *Timaeus*.

Plato would surely have assumed that his *Timaeus* readers are familiar with the *Charmides*, which is about *sôphrosunê* (moderation). In that dialogue the character Critias makes the interesting claim, central to the second half of the work, that *sôphrosunê* is nothing other than the self-knowledge enjoined by Apollo at Delphi.[76] Whatever may be the state of Critias's self-knowledge as revealed in the *Charmides*, the *Timaeus* character is displayed as in a way strangely nescient about something at the core of himself. The 'something' is ancient Athens in the story and his own relation to it. This point will be developed in the next section, but first let us note the motif of self-nescience present in the story itself before it ever reaches Critias. The story is elaborately knowing about its own pedigree, but to the Athenian Solon it came as unheard of and wonderful news about his and his countrymen's origin (22a2–4). At the same time the story suavely explained how it had remained unheard of.

According to the story, Solon was retailing to the Egyptian priests the Greek account of the origin of man, taking it back to before '*the* Deluge' (22a5–b3), when a very old priest broke in:

Oh Solon, Solon, you Greeks are always children; no aged Greek exists.... You are all young in your souls. For you possess there not a single belief brought from long ago by ancient hearsay, nor a single piece of knowledge hoary with time. The reason is this: there have been and there will be many and many kinds of destructions of human beings ... (22b4–c2)

The genealogies you recounted just now of the people in your [plural, i.e. 'of the Greeks'] part of the world are scarcely more than children's tales, first because you [plural] remember a single deluge upon the earth when many had happened before, and then because you do not know that in your land was born the finest and best race on earth, from whom come you [singular] and the whole of your present-day city – for once upon a time a small measure of seed was left over; but you people know nothing of it, since for many generations the survivors lived and died voiceless because illiterate [*grammasin ... aphônous*]. So once upon a time, Solon, before the greatest destruction by water ever, the city that is today the Athenians' own was most excellent at war and pre-eminently well-governed in

---

[75] We are focusing on Critias, but to compound such effects there was the memory of Plato's maternal uncle Charmides, once a youth of extraordinary physical beauty and (according to Critias in the *Charmides*) of remarkable *sôphrosunê* (*Charmides* 157d3–5), who came to be associated with the Thirty and was killed in 403.

[76] See especially *Charmides* 164c5–165b4. The connection between *sôphrosunê* and self-knowledge is recalled at *Timaeus* 72a4–6; cf. Taylor, 1928, 513–14.

every way: its deeds are said to have been finest, and finest too its institutions, of all beneath the heaven of which we have heard tell. (23b3–d1)[77]

After outlining those institutions the priest continued:

> So this was the entire ordering and system [*diakosmêsin kai suntaxin*] which in those days the goddess gave first to you when she founded your habitation, having selected the place of your birth with an eye to the temperateness of the seasons therein, because it would bring forth men of superlative wisdom. Accordingly, she being both a lover of war and a lover of wisdom, the place that was to bring forth men most acceptable to her [*prospherestatous autê(i)*] was the one which the goddess selected and first founded. So you lived under laws and customs such as I have described – and under better ones still [*eti mallon eunomoumenoi*] – outranking [*huperbeblêkotes*] all mankind in every virtue, as befitted your birth and education at the hands of gods. Well, many and great were the city's deeds held in written record here for men's wonderment, but there is one that surpasses them all in greatness and nobility . . . (24c4–e1)

Surrounding such eulogistic utterances is the priest's explanation of his own knowledge and Solon's complete ignorance hitherto of the wonderful origin of Solon's city. One of those disasters that nature recurrently brings swept away the original Greek civilisation; whenever such a thing happens, all that remains of the Greeks for many ages is an illiterate posterity of mountain-dwelling herdsmen and shepherds. Greek culture has to begin over and over; but in the temples of geophysically protected Egypt great deeds from every country are preserved in written annals (22c1–23d1; 25c6–d3).[78]

Here are the salient items for us in all this. First, in two great stages of its transmission, the story of Athens and Atlantis came from *remote or external* sources: from ancient Athens to Egypt, and from Egypt back to Athens via Solon. Secondly, it was *by luck* that Solon received the story of ancient Athens. No doubt he travelled to Egypt, and visited the priests, for some wise reason (20d8–e1; 21c1), but he did not go to Egypt in order to find out about Athens! Thirdly, it was *through no one's fault* that records of the great event were lost to the Greeks for all that time. It was no one's fault that the original Athens lacked the ever-to-be-remembered fame[79] that just judges

---

[77] See also the superlatives in grandfather Critias's speech to his *phratêr* Amynander, 21d4–5: 'the greatest of all deeds, the one that would most deserve to be most talked about' (*onomastotatês pasôn*); and at *Critias* 112e4–6: 'because of their beautiful physical features and their possession of every kind of excellence of soul [the original Athenians] were famous throughout the whole of Europe and Asia, being the most talked about of all peoples [*onomastotatoi pantôn*] of that time'.

[78] Thus the Egyptian priests are in a position to systematise important events belonging to different cultures in a single chronology. There may be an implicit contrast with the chronicles of the various other cultures, where for each its own history would have been the exclusive or central subject.

[79] *doxa aeimnêstos*, Thucydides II. 43. 2.

would have accorded her (cf. 21d4–5). It is because of natural disasters that the Greeks revert again and again to cultural infancy (22b6–8; 23b4–5; cf. 23c3[80]); no child is to blame for being a child.

For the Critias-figure the first two items are reversed. The story came to him (1) from within his family, and (2) not at all by luck. Passing on legacies including oral and written records is one of the things that define the family. The third item does not apply to Plato's fictional Critias-figure, because he has been born into a family in which the record had been *kept*. However, as we shall see, it had been kept and was then received and kept in turn by him in such a way that, for all the ethical illumination the record has brought him, it might as well have died out thousands of years ago. And the fact that this extant record has shed as little ethical light as a completely forgotten story is *not* due to a natural disaster or the physiological immaturity of a child. I shall develop this in the next section. But finally here we should note how the third item by a multiple reversal becomes a negative finger pointing at the historical Athens into which Plato was born, and at Critias of the Thirty. They won for themselves by their own deeds the not-soon-to-be-forgotten infamy that just judgement accords.

5.8 PHILOSOPHY AND REMEMBRANCE (II)

The story which the Critias-character has been carrying about inside him since childhood (21b1) contains specifications of various civic institutions of ancient Athens (24a2–c5). And the story, as we have seen, rings with superlative praise for that city. Critias like all his predecessors in the chain of transmission (and like his own audience today), takes the story to be true. So all these years Critias has held within him what he takes to be truth, a good deal of detailed, descriptive truth, concerning the nature of the best *polis*. What he accepts unquestioningly is, actually, that a certain particular *polis*, the ancestor of present-day Athens, was both superlatively excellent and had such and such institutions. But Critias, I suggest, has never used this information to move to the universal. It might at some point have come to him: 'Now I see: in general a very excellent *polis* would be one with these and these institutions.' But it has not. And this can only be because he has never really asked himself the universal question 'What is the nature of the excellent *polis*?', or entered into the enquiry of someone else who was asking this. If you have some particular information that would supply an answer to the universal question 'What is it for something to be *F*?', and the

---

[80] *aphônous*; the word is used of an infant (by the infant itself!) in Sappho, fr. 118.

information is clear and you are contemplating it, then if you are still devoid of any rudiment of answer to the universal question, this can only be because your mind-set is not that of someone who has been seeking an answer to *that* question.

But is it fair to claim that this Critias-character, the character which Plato has created, is without interest in the universal question and its answer? What is the evidence for this? The evidence, I consider, lies in the fact that Critias is shown as having no interest in *why* the ancestral Athens whose institutions the story describes was supremely excellent. He knows from the story that this city (1) had characteristics *A*, *B*, and *C*, and (2) was supremely excellent.[81] But he gives no sign of interest in what the middle term or terms might be whereby (2) is consequential on (1).[82] For all he cares, having *A*, *B*, and *C* might be quite incidental to the excellence. But he knows, or he has all the wherewithal for knowing, that the city's excellence was in fact grounded on and explained by its having *A*, *B*, and *C*. For Socrates the day before had presented to the others various features of the best *polis*: it is a *polis* that has *A*, *B*, and *C*. And we know from the fact that these were results reached by *Socrates* that they were reached by argument from fundamental principles in answer to the Socratic question 'What is the best *polis*? Of what sort of men does it consist?' (17c1–3). So the middle terms and chains of connecting argument had been supplied. But Critias shows no grain of interest in such explanations, explanations that arise in answer to the universal question. He does not say today: 'Socrates, thanks to your discourse, I yesterday saw (or began to see) why the old priest was right to extol ancient Athens in those brilliant terms.' So not only is Critias not interested in the universal question for its own sake: he is not even interested in applying the reasoning by which it was answered to the particular case which perhaps alone commands his interest for its own sake, that of the original Athens. If he contemplates this Athens for its own sake, it is not so as to *understand what made* the city deserve the kudos lavished on it by the story. His companions report no expression from him the evening before of explanatory curiosity raised and satisfied (cf. 20c6–d1). In this Critias appears as a maimed counterpart of Timaeus, who analogously begins from the non-negotiable fact that his subject-matter – this universe – is as excellent as anything of its kind can be, and proceeds on that basis to derive

---

[81] It is true that Critias proposes to identify by stipulation the citizens of Socrates's ideal state with the hyper-archaic Athenians (27a7–b6), as has been emphasised by Johansen, 2004, 37. But the *excellence* of the hyper-archaic Athenians and the *characteristics of their polity* are not stipulated by Critias: these data were already in the Egyptian record.

[82] Alternatively: whereby (1) is grounded in (2), with (2) treated as the final cause explaining (1).

5.8 Philosophy and remembrance (ii)

its actual nature. His account tries to *explain why* a world of that description is superlatively good.

Critias, by contrast, not only fails to construct any such explanation himself concerning ancient Athens, but fails to engage with the clues to such an explanation provided yesterday by Socrates. Critias is interested only in the resemblance between his long lost jewel and the Socratic ideal, and in how hearing about the latter reminded him of the former. He says to Socrates:

> While you were speaking yesterday about the political constitution and the citizens whom you were describing, I began to marvel in recollection [*anamimnêskomenos*] of the very things which I now relate; I began to realise how miraculously some chance had brought it about [*daimoniôs ek tinos tuchês*] that in most points you were not off target [*ouk apo skopou*] <but> in coincidence with what Solon said. (25e2–5)[83]

Critias is impressed by the *fact* of Socrates's convergence with the Solonian story which he already knows to be correct. He actually sees this convergence as a miraculous piece of luck. But if it was through good Socratic reasoning that the Socratic account converges with the truth about the nature of the best city (which just happens to have been realised in ancient Athens), this is not because of luck, certainly not on the side of Socrates – whom Critias patronisingly congratulates as 'in most points not off target' – but because of Socrates's skill as a philosopher. For Critias it is independently established in and through the story that the original Athens both had such and such features and outranked all mankind in every virtue. Hence Critias knows in advance that any philosophically well-constructed ideal *polis* would be bound to have many of those features. He (from his own point of view) is in a position to praise the Socratic discourse of yesterday – not because of any of its internal features, but – because it has delivered what he already knows to be the right answer about the nature of the ideal polity.

Critias knows that Solon's account was backed by impeccable authority. It was the goddess Athena who founded Sais in Egypt on the same political model on which she had founded Athens a thousand years earlier (23d6 ff.; *Critias* 109c6–d2). It must have been she who originally furnished Sais with a record of the characters and deeds of Athens and Atlantis, and with the practice of preserving records. The evaluations (that Athens with its Sais-like institutions was the most excellent city ever; her victory over Atlantis

---

[83] Whereas in Platonic reminiscence a particular *f* brings to mind the intelligible *logos* of *F* which it resembles, Critias moves in the opposite direction: on being presented with the *logos* of the perfect *polis* he is reminded of (the story of) a similar particular. Cf. Cristiani, 2003, 263.

the noblest deed) must have been part of the same god-given record. Where else could they have come from and still carried authority? But if Athena is *philosophos* in any sense reckoned valid by Plato then she at least, even if not any of the mortal links in the chain of testimony, must have possessed rational understanding of why a supremely excellent city would have characteristics A, B, and C. The convergence by Socrates is of one rational being with another on the same topic, a mortal with a goddess, Socrates thereby becoming someone highly acceptable to her like the citizens of the Athens she personally founded (24c5–d3).[84] It is no accident for Critias that the original citizens turned out to be of a character highly agreeable to their goddess: the story has her choosing their habitation for its conduciveness to that character. But in Critias's eyes it is only by luck, even if 'miraculous' luck, that the Socratic ideal converges on that of the goddess. And the Critias empty of interest in the reasons why Socrates endowed his ideal with A, B, and C must be equally empty of interest in the principles explaining why the goddess's ideal had these features. For to the extent that Socrates philosophised well yesterday (and Critias with the others treats that performance as deserving a magnificent return) Socrates's reasons and the goddess's principles would have been the same. Thus given what Critias independently knows about the divine foundation of the original Athens, he is in a position to be aware that entering into the Socratic reasoning would be a way of seeing something of Athena's mind.[85] But either he is aware of this but not interested, or he is not aware of it. And if the latter, this can only be because he is not on the lookout for such insights; but that, again, is the mark of a mind for which they hold no interest.

Of course, it may be that he did enter into the Socratic reasoning while it was going on *yesterday*; but all trace of such attention seems to have been wiped away from him overnight. For in fact, without embarrassment and for the sake of a sweetly reminiscent contrast, Critias lets the company know

---

[84] On the convergence: at 24d6 the story which Critias believes and repeats speaks of the men of the original Athens as *educated by the gods*. At 27a8 he describes the citizens of the Socratic construct as *outstandingly well educated by Socrates* (*para sou . . . pepaideumenous*). (In both cases the meaning is that the education was designed by the agent in question.) Then at 27b1–4 he pronounces the latter citizens identical with the former. ('Educated by Socrates' is possibly meant to recall the common slur that Socrates had educated Critias of the Thirty; see section 5.7 on Polycrates's Denunciation.)

[85] And perhaps of the minds of the original Athenians too. For if we understand wisdom on the Socratic model, we may take the story to imply that the wisdom of the original Athenians (24c7) included reflection and discussion on why Athena had endowed them with their actual institutions. But in the eyes of a character like Critias, the ancient Athenians' wisdom (matching the 'wisdom' embodied in his own story-telling, with its blind faith in the authority of testimony and its concern for propagating the identical tale) could only have consisted in accepting the institutions on divine *fiat* and taking care to keep them the same.

5.8 Philosophy and remembrance (ii)

that he is not sure that he even remembers everything that was said yesterday.[86] Addressing himself to, of all people, Socrates (25d7; e2–3; 26a4), whose discourse yesterday is the *raison d'être* of today's whole show, Critias idiotically frames his repayment with these words:

> Just see how true the saying is that children's lessons have a wonderfully memorable quality. Take *me*, for instance: what I heard [*ēkousa*] yesterday I don't know that I could completely lay hold of again in memory; but in matters where a long, long time has passed since my listening [*diakēkoa*], I should be utterly amazed if anything has escaped me.[87] It was a great pleasure and great fun [*paidia*] to be hearing and hearing it long ago with the old man eagerly teaching me as I questioned him over and over; thus it has come to be fixed in me like indelible encaustic paintings. (26b2–c3)

If Critias is oblivious to anything it is not because he is generally lazy. For, as he explains, after Socrates's discourse jogged his memory he worked hard last night to recall the whole account and he practised it on the others, just as he worked in childhood to extract it all from his grandfather (26a1–b2; cf. *Critias* 113b2–4). Nor is Critias indifferent to the truth of things. For him it is all-important that his account of the original Athenians is true, i.e. reports historical fact. By contrast, what Socrates presented yesterday was just a 'story' of a city and its citizens. In effecting the *rapprochement* between Socrates's subject-matter and his own, Critias sees himself as bestowing on the former (as if it needed it for full perfection) the precious property of historical truth. Addressing Socrates, he says:

> The citizens and the city which you were describing yesterday as if in a story [*hōs en muthō(i)*] – we shall now translate them into the truth [*epi t'alēthes*]: we shall place them here [*deuro*],[88] making *that* city [sc. yours] be *this* city here, and the citizens which you were intending we shall pronounce to be those true forefathers of ours, the ones in the priest's account. They will fit perfectly, and we shall not be out of tune if we declare them [the Socratic citizens] to be the very ones that were real in that time back then [*autous einai tous en tō(i) tote ontas chronō(i)*[89]]. (26c7–d5)

In contrast with Critias's earnest excitement about the historical truth of the story, Socrates displays a mood of relaxed acceptance. When Critias asks

---

[86] Thus when Socrates at the beginning checks to find out whether the details of yesterday's offering are still remembered by the rest of the group today, it is Timaeus whose memory he interrogates, and who does not let him down (17b5–19b2).

[87] Note the contrast between the aorist *ēkousa* (b4) and the perfect *diakēkoa* (6), the latter but not the former implying that the state logically resultant on listening has not been cancelled.

[88] Critias seems to be referring to the Athens in which this conversation takes place, this being more or less the same geographically as hyper-archaic Athens. But he may also be referring to the relocation of the Socratic citizens within his, Critias's, story.

[89] Understanding *autous* as referring to the citizens of Critias's account.

him whether the outlined saga fits his expressed wish, or whether they should look for some other account instead, Socrates replies:

> Why, what other should we substitute in preference to this one, Critias? Its close link to the goddess makes it splendidly appropriate for her festival which is now taking place; and the fact that it is not a fabricated story but a true account is enormously important, I suppose [*to te mê plasthenta muthon all' alêthinon logon einai pammega pou*]. So how and where shall we find other men if we let go of these? Impossible. So it is for you [plural] to speak (may your effort be successful), and for me in return for my discourse of yesterday to keep quiet now and take my turn at listening. (26e2–27a1)

Socrates accepts Critias's word that the story of ancient Athens is historically true, but he does so with a slight curl of the lip or shrug of the shoulders: that it's true is 'enormously important, I suppose'. Does that glint of sarcasm in fact express scepticism about the claimed historicity? Or does it express a reservation about the propriety of using 'true' at all of propositions about things in the realm of becoming?[90] I think not the latter, because Socrates in the *Timaeus–Critias* is not represented as possessing the meta-philosophical vocabulary for marking off what philosophers are about when they think something out from eternal first principles, as this Socrates was doing yesterday. What he was doing can indeed be described as 'looking to an eternal and intelligible paradigm' and his results can be called 'truth' (which is 'related to assurance [*pistis*] as being to becoming') (29c2–3). These distinctions are emblematic of Socrates's method, but to operate the method Socrates needs only a nose for the method itself: he does not need to be able to theorise *about* it in explicit terms which compare it with other methods or fraudulent methods. In the *Timaeus–Critias*, talk of eternal paradigms is left entirely to Timaeus (cf. section 5.2 above). As for whether Socrates's 'curl of the lip' shows scepticism about the veracity (in the ordinary sense) of Critias's offering: on the level of the return-feast symbolism, this would suggest that least urbane of moves, the impoliteness of looking a gift horse in the mouth; while on the level of the symbolised it could convey approval of what on that level is illegitimate, namely the interrogation by one discipline of another discipline's performance.

Hence I conclude that Socrates is to be understood as simply and straightforwardly accepting *that* the story of ancient Athens is true to fact, as Critias affirms. What the glint of sarcasm conveys is that to him, Socrates, this uncontested historicity is no big deal. Of the two advantages he sees in Critias's offering – its truth, and its suitability for Athena's festival – the

---

[90] As Johansen suggests, 2004, 45–6.

5.8 Philosophy and remembrance (ii)

second is the one that Socrates mentions (without sarcasm) first. The truth of it is not something for him to get excited about, he indicates. This is because, first, he has been given no reason to recede from the original spirit of his request, which was for *a* story that would waken the ideal city into concrete action and bring it before the eyes of the imagination. It did not have to be a true story, and the story he is now to be given by Critias might just as well not be a true one for all the difference this makes to Socrates, even though true it happens to be. And, secondly, if Socrates as philosopher desires mental access to the ethical and political structures underlying the imagined heroism of the perfect city, he and others like him can achieve this on their own whenever they wish, through a method unperturbed by the truth or falsity of existential claims that such structures have been or will be instantiated in actual history. The practice of this method does not depend on any historical record, which is as much as to say that nature and time are powerless to obliterate the ethical reality which the method discovers. A perfect city may once have existed and been wiped out without trace, but what should matter to us now about any such city, namely what the features are that would have made it so excellent, is always freshly accessible at first hand to a mind that really seeks answers to such questions.

With Critias, by contrast, it is as if the ethical reality which his story conveys is as local and perishable as the physical and human substructure of that ethical reality. The ethical reality is summed up by such statements as: 'Ancient Athens was the best city, and performed the most fame-worthy exploit, that the world has ever known.' Epistemologically speaking, the truth of these ethical predications is guaranteed for Critias by precisely the same second-, third-, and *n*th-hand hearsay as guarantees the existential claim that there was an Athens with such and such descriptive features nine thousand years ago. And, metaphysically speaking, for Critias it is as if what makes those ethical predications true is wholly situated in that particular ancient city and its citizens, or is wholly situated where they were situated in space and time. For Critias behaves like one for whom there is no such thing as an eternal, universal, principle or set of principles connecting ethical excellence with the empirical characteristics of the particular city in question. Hence for Critias it is as if the truth-maker for the proposition that ancient Athens was the best city etc. has nothing eternal and universal among its constituents.

One also gets the impression that for Critias the importance of this true ethical predication is entirely bound up with the fact that its logical subject is ancient *Athens*, the forerunner of *his* city. He would not be interested in its possibly being true of some other particular city instead. For Socrates, that would make no difference: or the only difference would be that a saga composed about an alternative city, whether historically real or not, might be less suitable for performing at an Athenaic festival in present-day Athens of the dialogue-world. But why in fact would it therefore be less suitable? If the alternative citizens were the same except for not being identical with any geographical Athenians ever; and if therefore they were (non-Athenian) lovers of war and lovers of wisdom (cf. 24c7–d2); and if Athena's nature is necessarily the same so that she remains the divine lover of war and lover of wisdom: then it surely follows that a tale of such anonymous alternative citizens would be a fine offering for Athena even at her festival in Athens. But for Critias it is as if the only real courage and wisdom are *Athenian* courage and wisdom. Lucky Socrates should be heartened to learn that *his* philosophical studies of abstract courage and wisdom have zeroed in on the real, Athenian, qualities.

At any rate, the Critias-character's cognitive position blocks him from access to any standard of courage and wisdom that transcends or is more universal than the ancient Athenian versions. This is because what he counts as his knowledge of these qualities has essentially arrived in him as a tradition passed down, and the tradition speaks only of ancient Athenian courage and wisdom, praising these to the skies but never asking what the abstract qualities are or how in general they are grounded. For once these questions come to be asked and different answers compared and criticised, with the strongest answers being made the bases of further investigations – then there is the risk of departures, and willingness to countenance departures, from the all-precious tradition.

Critias is depicted as perfectly untroubled by the fact that since Solon's time the males directly in line with him – part of the core of Athens's aristocratic core – have known themselves to be the city's repositories of truth about superlative courage and wisdom and civic excellence, yet have not tried to do anything (according to ordinary understandings of 'do') with their wonderful possession. For if they had, the knowledge of it could not have remained one dynasty's perquisite.[91] So the knowledge has never in all these years been mobilised by its lucky possessors into a practical ideal or a set of shared standards for evaluating existent practices. If – a possibility of which Critias seems brazenly unaware – there is something shameful in this: Athenian aristocrats in Athens conducting themselves in a matter of highest importance as esoterically as Egyptian priests in Egypt – the shame (in the

---

[91] And the story could not have figured as a very special gift for Socrates, since Socrates would have been in possession of it already, and so would many others.

5.8 Philosophy and remembrance (ii)

dialogue-world) touches even the great statesman Solon, 'wisest of the seven sages' (20d8–e1; cf. 21c1).[92] For there is no sign in Critias's inherited story that Solon ever understood the priestly account as having the slightest practical import for him. In this story Solon visited Egypt *before* he carried out his reforms in Athens (21b6–d3).[93] This must be a very deliberate touch by Plato, because the well-known account of Herodotus placed these events in the opposite order. Thus Plato's version is designed to insinuate that Solon already knew the political ideal when he set about his reforms, yet did his own political work unguided by that knowledge; for the famous Solonian constitution was very different.[94] Still, whatever we may think of the effeteness in this respect of the Solon-figure and the intermediate Athenian links of transmission, the present Critias, their representative, outshines them all in failure to use the legacy: for he is the only one of that line whose life has been exposed to the philosophising of Socrates.[95]

But shameful or not, we should not be at all surprised that the preciously hoarded story had never been used as a template for political thought or action in the fictional recent Athens of the dialogue-world. For to use it thus, especially in a city which, however indeterminately characterised, is bound to have been very different from the template (why otherwise would the Critian image of the original Athens arouse any special interest?),[96] must have involved some modicum of precisely the kind of thinking that Critias and all whom he replicates have been so determined to ignore.

The Critias-character's self-exclusion from all such thinking is rooted in the fact that for him the be-all and end-all of the story's content is to exist as a possession handed down through the generations. That it is factually true matters to him enormously because it means that the story is about *his* city, *his* original ancestors. Each telling glorifies them and the tellers and recipients. So in his childhood long ago the relay of glory joined this Critias to

---

[92] On the invidiousness of concealing wisdom, cf. Nightingale, 1995, 125–6.
[93] This is indicated by the pluperfect at 21c6 and the perfect participle at c7. Cf. Morgan, 1998, 109–10.
[94] It is interesting too that grandfather Critias assumed that if Solon *had* 'done' anything with the Athens–Atlantis story besides pass it on in its bald form, this would have been to turn it into a poem that would have made him more famous than all other poets, Hesiod and Homer included (21c4–d3). So if it was a pity that Solon did virtually nothing with the story, the pity lay wholly in the fact that Athens thereby missed out on the creation of an Atheno-centric epic that would have more than compensated for the paucity of attention to Athenian heroes in the *Iliad* and the *Odyssey*. See n. 53.
[95] It is unremarkable that the citizens of Sais never used their knowledge of the perfect Athens to reform or criticise their own institutions: for their city had been founded on a similar model by Athena a thousand years after the original Athens, and it still had its original institutions when Solon visited eight thousand years later. On Solon's failure to apply the Egyptian lore to his own legislation, cf. Rowe, 1999, 273, n. 25.
[96] It is Italian Locris, the city of Timaeus, that Socrates commends as *eunomôtatê* in the present-day dialogue-world (20a2); the priest says the same of the original Athens (23c6; cf. 24d4).

Critias his conduit-grandfather, and now this Critias by telling it in turn renews not only the hyper-archaic glory but the happy intergenerational bonding in glory of that grandfather and that child.[97] Since Critias in the dialogue-world is a real being, his identity can only be fed in this way by an original source that is real. Thus the subject of the story *must* have existed, and the story *must* be true. So: to the extent that his identity is fed from that source, he cannot afford to question the reliability of the transmission. He cannot, for instance, afford the humility of considering that the quality of his knowledge of it, hearsay of hearsay, must be a shadow in comparison with the first-hand experience of the protagonists who perished so long ago. He revels in the multiplicity of links of transmission like one who also cannot afford to let cross his mind the thought that the information might have degraded in the process, even though from the more detailed Critias-history we know that he knows that deterioration of things over time is in general possible (cf. *Critias* 110e3–111c8 on the geological deterioration of Attica; 121a8–b1 on the moral decline of the Atlantideans). To the extent that his identity is fed from the Athens in the story his epistemic connection with it must be safe with a supernatural, adamantine, safeness. Only a transmission magically safe could measure up to the trustingness of Critias, as childish now as when he received the story at the age of ten. One could, however, also say: to the extent that Critias's identity is fed from that source, any brittleness in his connection with it is a brittleness in him; and (by the same token) he is only as real as the vanished source itself even though he walks and talks in the present with Socrates.

This Critias of Plato's imagination is the personified paradigm of one sort of unreason.[98] Plato left it to his audience to use the paradigm as a measure of any individuals or any trends or practices they knew or knew about; or to see in it an image of the Athens of their own and their parents' and grandparents' life-time. They might see in it an Athens oblivious to its own capacity for fundamental self-criticism – oblivious to the benefit held out to it by the historical Socrates – because mesmerised by its own good stories about itself. They might also see it as calling for a more general meditation on ways in which culture, tradition, and civilisation, achievements of mortalised reason, can breed their own sophisticated forms of rational self-enslavement.

---

[97] It is interesting that Critias remembers with such pleasure the ritual, obviously exclusive to their family, of learning the story from his grandfather, given that in the perfect Athens which the story is about there are no exclusive family relationships in the ruling class (18c6–d5).
[98] On the 'anti-paradigm' cf. *Theaetetus* 176e3–177a8.

5.9 SUMMARY

In this chapter I have attempted to interpret the *Timaeus–Critias* complex as a whole, and have looked for ways of answering the following questions. (1) What do the contributions of Timaeus and Critias have to do with each other? (2) What do they, jointly or severally, have to do with Socrates? (3) Is it meant to be obvious to Plato's audience that the Athens–Atlantis story is fictional? (4) If so, what are we to make of the fact that the characters in the dialogue-world, even including Socrates, treat it as true and historical? (5) If the story is transparently fictional, what is the point of Plato's staging it? (6) If the story is transparently fictional, what does this imply about other elements in the *Timaeus–Critias* complex, in particular the cosmology? Is its credibility or seriousness to be questioned too? (7) Why does Critias tell a story featuring a nine-thousand-years-ago replica of the defeat of the Persians at Marathon in 490 BCE? (8) Could this hyper-archaic replica of Marathon be part of a supposedly historical record of which the Marathon of 490 is also a part? (9) Why is Critias's story of ancient heroism about *Athens* in particular? (10) Why does the Athens in the story have institutions of the same description as those of the political ideal which Socrates has explained 'yesterday', so that Critias (with the others' agreement) actually stipulates identity between the Socratic ideal citizens and the supposedly historical Athenians of the story? (11) What are we to make of the portrayed transmission of the story, and of the characters' attitudes to this strange transmission?

In approaching this set of problems, I have relied on three mainstays: (A) the symbolism of the return-feast for Socrates; (B) the impossibility of combining in a single historical record *both* the replica-Marathon of nine thousand years ago in which Athens beat Atlantis *and* the 490 BCE Marathon in which Athens beat the Persians; and (C) the fundamental difference of intellectual stance *vis-à-vis* moral and political ideals between the Socrates-character, given what we are entitled to assume about him, and the Critias-character, given the way he is presented in the *Timaeus*.

A. I suggested (sections 5.2 and 5.6) that the return-feast for Socrates stands for a Socratic or Academic sanctioning of certain non-Socratic genres of discourse, in particular cosmology and historiography. These genres must be shown to be both *non*-Socratic – they neither continue nor develop what Socrates stands for – and at the same time not at all *anti*-Socratic: they must be visibly welcomed by Socrates as in no way alien to him. Such a friendly connection with Socrates is secured by (i) making the historical element focus directly on a city-state just like Socrates's own ideal, and (ii) coupling this history with a cosmology so that the latter through association with the former shares the former's connection with Socrates. This coupling is effected by treating the history as the principal part of the return-feast, and the cosmology as a run-up to this principal part. Because the history is connected with Socrates by being about a *polis* matching the Socratic ideal, the history is necessarily pseudo-history. However, a pseudo-history, and even an incomplete one, can serve to demonstrate the point that historiography is a welcome though non-Socratic genre.

B. I argued (section 5.3) that the dialogue-world contains no record of an Athenian victory at Marathon occurring in the equivalent of 490 BCE. This claim rests on two pieces of evidence: (i) everyone in the dialogue-world accepts Critias's story as historically true; and (ii) the resemblance between this story's topic and the real-world Marathon victory is too striking to have passed without comment from one or another of the characters. Since they make no such comment it is reasonable to infer that the real-world Marathon victory is no part of recent recorded history in the dialogue-world. This consideration triggers reflections, which it surely makes sense to suppose that Plato meant to induce in his early readers, knowledgeable as they were (unlike various later ones) about the history of Greece in the fifth century, on how Athens might have fared better in those years if real-world Marathon had never occurred or had occurred but somehow, like the victory over Atlantis, left no mark of Athenian fame on subsequent history (section 5.4). Such reflections reinforce the Platonic message about the arrogance and disastrous misjudgements of actual fifth-century Athens: a message that has been well identified by Vidal-Naquet and others who see the hyper-archaic city as standing for the pre-imperial, pre-naval, Athens of Marathon, and Atlantis as standing for that same Athens in its later and ultimately catastrophic involvement with imperialism (cf. section 5.5).

C. I argued that in the *Timaeus* at least the Critias-character is devoid of interest in any political and ethical illumination available to someone who, like him in the dialogue-world, is informed about the institutions that characterise the best *polis* and also knows that a *polis* with those institutions is indeed the best that has ever existed (section 5.8). Neither this Critias nor anyone preceding him in the Athenian line of transmission has done what one might have expected from Athenian recipients of the information, namely use it as a basis for political reform or at least political criticism of Athens. Critias also has the wherewithal to engage in a theoretical project of the same methodological type as that of Timaeus, in which we begin with the assumption that a certain object O is the very best of its kind K, and on that basis proceed (i) to make new discoveries about O's characteristics, and

(ii) to explain why it has the characteristics which it is already known to have. But Critias is uninterested in that kind of thinking too. He only wants to describe the ancient Athens and underline how magnificent it was without grounding value in fact or explaining fact by reference to value. But notwithstanding this striking contrast between Critias and Timaeus, the contrast between Critias and Socrates is more striking still, because whereas *O* for Timaeus is this cosmos, which is not Critias's concern, *O* for Socrates and *O* for Critias are in a way identical. For them the content of *O* is the same: for each it is the ideal *polis* with its institutions *A*, *B*, and *C*. This identity of content in their focus of interest frees us to contemplate the depth of difference between the types of interest on each side. Locked together by that strange sharing of content, Critias and Socrates, the two Athenians in the group, are infinitely far apart.[99] The *Critias* framed in this way is truly an anti-Socrates.

Or so it seems. But are we justified in going with the appearances on this and other features of the *Timaeus–Critias*? This question (cf. section 5.5) is posed by the fact that some salient and apparently serious features of the dialogue-world are evidently at odds with what we know of the real world, in particular the Athens–Atlantis episode and the absence of early fifth-century Marathon. So on what principle do we decide which aspects of the dialogue-world are meant by Plato to carry over into the real world? Such a question can be asked about any Platonic dialogue, but is particularly pertinent here for two reasons. First, it is not at all clear what messages are being sent by the Athens–Atlantis story and by the fiction of its transmission and final telling by the Critias-character: consequently, it may be necessary to distinguish between real messages meant for the world in which Plato is writing, and mock-messages meant as a send-up of some kind or as anyway exhausting their literal significance within the dialogue-world. And a criterion or criteria would be needed for making such distinctions. Secondly, there is the well-known question of the 'literalness' of the cosmology. Naturally, it is sometimes wondered whether the blatant fictionality of the Athens–Atlantis story, including the account of its weird transmission, might not be a signal (one of several, it might be thought) that the other monologue is in certain respects not to be treated too seriously. So, for instance, should we take the Athens–Atlantis fictionality

---

[99] The situation throws a sardonic light on the proverb 'friends have things in common'; cf. *Critias* 112e9–10. (For the proverb elsewhere see *Republic* IV, 424a1–2; Aristotle, *Nicomachean Ethics* VIII, 1159b31; IX, 1168b8; *Eudemian Ethics* VII, 1237b33 and 1238a16, to mention only philosophical contexts.)

into consideration when we ponder what to make of '*eikôs muthos*', Timaeus's description of his cosmological account, or when we argue (on whatever other principal grounds) that Plato does or doesn't really mean it when Timaeus speaks of the cosmos as having begun? After all, the characters of the dialogue-world completely accept both monologues at face value: on what principle should *we* then discriminate, saying that Plato thoroughly endorses what is said in one and only pretends to endorse what is said in the other?[100]

I have operated on the assumption that Plato seriously intends any messages of the *Timaeus–Critias* that do not collide with obvious facts of the real world (section 5.5). Common sense together with basic knowledge of Athenian history tells us and would have told Plato's early audience that the Athens–Atlantis story and the account of its loss and restoration to Athenian memory are pure fiction; also, in my view, that the fifth-century victory at Marathon is missing from the dialogue world; also that the lofty Critias-persona is very probably full of ambiguity. By the above simple criterion the following are meant seriously: the symbolism of the different genres of intellectual discipline; the implied counterfactual fantasy-wish that the Marathon of 490, whose glory was a turning point for Athens, had never happened or had somehow been written out of history (for a message conveyed by a counterfactual *wish* is not at odds with known facts); the implied condemnation of the use of historical particulars as paradigms of the political ideal; the implied condemnation of civic self-eulogy whose ritualisation ring-fences it against rational criticism; the implied gulf of disconnection between Critias of the Thirty and Socrates. By the same criterion, I argued, Plato could not have meant the Marathon-like Athens–Atlantis story as a serious charter-myth for Athens, i.e. as a charter-myth for the real Athens, since real-world charter-myths must not be blatantly incredible in the real world. Nor could he have meant by that story to sell

---

[100] Menn, 1995, 5 (see also 71–2, n. 5), says: 'Timaeus is said to have received [his account of the cosmos], through an obviously fictional chain of transmission, from Solon, who learned it from the Egyptian priests, who had it in their sacred writings'; i.e. Menn claims that in the dialogue-world the cosmology and Critias's story have a common provenance in what Solon learned in Egypt. Even if this were part of the fiction it of course would not imply that the cosmology and Critias's story are meant to be received in the same way (as equally serious, literal, reasonable, etc., or the contraries) in the real world (not that Menn draws this inference). But nothing in the fiction says that the cosmology came to Timaeus via Solon. There is no mention of any link between Solon and Timaeus. Menn combines the fact that the *Timaeus* says (Critias speaking) that Solon was the wisest of the Seven Sages, 20d8–e1, with the fact that Socrates says elsewhere that 'all the wise agree that *nous* is king for us of heaven and earth' (*Philebus* 28c6–8), to get the result that since Timaeus's Demiurge is *nous*, the account of this Demiurge and his works must (fictionally, at least) have come from the wise, hence from Solon *par excellence*.

5.9 Summary

or eulogise the Socratic *politeia* to his real fellow citizens. Such strategies, I argued, could have no rational hope of success in an Athens which in Plato's day remembers herself as she was at the real Marathon-time, and knows that she then both behaved spectacularly well and had institutions very different from those of the Socratic ideal. Each case must be judged on its own merits. As for the cosmology: by the above criterion its claims, both first-order and methodological, are of course meant seriously. This, however, tells us almost nothing about how precisely to interpret '*eikôs muthos*' and the apparent cosmic beginning. The most that one can conclude about this case, and in general, is that the obvious fictionality of 'Athens–Atlantis' is never by itself a reason for suspecting that some other puzzling feature of the *Timaeus–Critias* is not meant seriously.

One conclusion to have emerged in this chapter is that the Critias-character stands for disparate forms of memory and interest in the past: the historian's interest; the uncritical use of past constitutions as political paradigms for today; and the even more uncritical memorialising of past achievements for the sake of civic or family self-glorification. 'Critias' stands too for Plato's kinsman Critias of the Thirty, friend of Socrates and then his enemy, who would have fared better had he lived quietly and never made history rather than leaving a long and ugly memory behind him in Athens. And 'Critias' stands for forgetfulness as well as for memory: for Plato's kinsman's forgetfulness of any good that he might once have received at the hands of the historical Socrates, and for his and the city's obliviousness to the eternal intelligible ethical norms whose proper effect is human self-correction in the light of them (sections 5.6, 5.7, and 5.8).

This obliviousness is the condition removed by Platonic *anamnêsis*. But do we really have a firm grip on what this *anamnêsis* is? We are bound to connect it with the method of Socrates. But how do we bring out the difference between Socrates and the Critias-figure, who is also all about a kind of remembering? The difference is not captured merely by identifying Socrates with an esoteric activity called 'recollection' that brings the soul into non-sensory contact with changeless and perfect objects (cf. *Phaedo* 73a–76c). For in the dialogue-world we see the Critian kind of remembrance bringing the soul into non-sensory contact with such an object: the vanished Athens of nine thousand years ago was a perfect city, unique of its kind, and like everything in the past it and its perfection are changeless. If literal remembering is of what one has done or experienced oneself in this life, then Platonic *anamnêsis* of the Forms is not the only kind of non-literal 'remembering'; for there is also harking back to past exemplars through testimony and tradition. So how do we adequately distinguish Platonic *anamnêsis*? This question certainly ought to have occurred to Plato as a philosopher, and the contrast of Critias and Socrates in the *Timaeus* seems a likely starting point for taking it further.

For now, however, it is enough to see that so far as Critias treats his ancient Athens simply as a focus of wonderment reaching back into the depths of the past, rather than as a reasoned norm for self-correction in the present, he renders his perfect object as idle in the present as if it had never existed.[101] (The same would hold of a supposed Platonic philosopher who simply gazed in wonder at an ethical Form – a practical quiddity [cf. Chapter 3, section 3.2]. By letting it stay idle the philosopher would be making a mockery of its eternal reality even while extolling it. And what if the god who in fact made the universe had decided instead to stay contemplating the beauty of its Form?) Had Critias brought his ancient Athens into play as a reasoned norm for self-correction in the present, his relation to it would have become like that of Socrates: a relation that he would have known remains equally substantial and dynamic should it even turn out that no such perfect city has ever existed anywhere in space and time. Critias could then have let the mythistoric ancient Athens go under completely. His *logos* of its perfection could have lived on as something other than a tale for children; it could have become a prolific origin of rational change in him and those around him, instead of being the echo of an echo of something extinct.

---

[101] On the 'wonderful' in Critias's story, see 20e5; 23d2; 24d7; 25a6; *Critias* 115b5–6; 117a6. *Philosophia* begins with wonder (*Theaetetus* 155d2–5; Aristotle, *Metaphysics* I, 983a12–21), but anyone who just stays on happily wondering has missed the point (cf. Aristotle, *ibid.* 982b14–20). Critias's fuller account draws attention to all sorts of natural and man-made wonders, but it does so systematically and is not fixated on them in the way his *précis* is fixated on the glory of the Marathon-like event.

CHAPTER 6

The genesis of the four elements

6.1 TWO KINDS OF CAUSES

The concerns of this chapter have their roots in the moment when, in Timaeus's narrative, the divine demiurgic ancillaries 'take over' (*paralambanein*) the immortal souls created by the supreme Demiurge, and begin their task of 'weaving' mortal bodies on to them (42e6 ff.; cf. 41d1–2). Timaeus launches this episode by focusing on the entirely new kinetic and cognitive situation in which the immortal soul is placed when joined to the mortal body. At first the soul is in near chaos because of the impulses from the body and from the environment. But in the natural course of things, the 'stream of growth and nutriment' becomes less violent with time; the soul's immortal revolutions take advantage of the calm and become more stable (43a4–44b7). The narrative now bifurcates into a path about what human education can do to perfect the revolutions in mortals, and a path about the help afforded by nature, i.e. the demiurgic provision. The first path is only sketched at this point (44b8–c4; cf. 47b6–e2; 90c6–d5), and now for a while we follow the second. We begin to be shown specific anatomical arrangements. The immortal revolutions are naturally housed in the head, and the rest of the body is to serve the head. First and foremost, limbs of locomotion are needed for transport, as required by the head, and a distinction is needed between forwards and backwards motion, and therefore between the front and the back of the body. The front is distinguished by the face, into which the gods bound 'organs'. First they created 'light-bearing eyes'. Timaeus now proceeds to explain the formation of the eyes (*toia(i)de aitia(i)*, 45b3–4). These organs are constructed so that a pure, non-burning, kind of fire (and no other kind) within the body may stream out to coalesce with the external daylight along its path, as a result of which the visual stream collides with external objects and distributes the consequent motions through the whole body to the soul – whereby there is seeing of those objects (45b2 ff.). Timaeus confirms this theory of the physics of vision by showing how it explains why we cannot see in the dark (45d3–e2); how it helps to explain dream-images; and how it explains various mirror-image phenomena (45e3–46c6).

Timaeus now breaks off to declare that 'all these things' are only *auxiliary* causal factors (*sunaitia*, 46d1; *summetaitia*, e6), which God employs to serve the project of the best. Thus he implies that he was wrong to say that his theory of visual fire gives the *cause* or primary explanation (*aitia*, 45b4) of vision. Most thinkers, he says, make the mistake of attributing causal status in the fullest sense to fire and air etc., factors that work by cooling and heating, condensing, dissolving, and so on. The fire that makes seeing possible is just such a factor. Timaeus goes on to argue that since fire, water, earth, and air are visible, they are without soul (since soul is invisible),[1] and therefore they are without intelligence. Causes that come under the category of intelligence are the ones to be treated as primary, he states, whereas those that belong in the class of things 'moved by other things and movers of yet others by necessity', must be considered secondary. Both kinds must be discussed, but the distinction between the types of causality must be observed as fundamental (46c7–e6).[2] Then, as if in tribute to the primacy of intelligent causes, Timaeus immediately goes on to spell out the intention of the divine intelligent cause of our visual apparatus: the greatest good for which we were given it was to see the alternation of day and night and the revolutions of the stars, and thereby come to numbering and time-measurement, and to the *philosophia* that leads us to enquire about the whole universe and brings well-being to our rational soul. For contemplation of the 'revolutions of Intelligence in the heavens' is our kindred soul's mimesis of the cosmic one. This mimesis steadies the revolutions in us into their proper courses (46c7–47c4).[3] Here Timaeus glances along the first of the forking paths mentioned above, the one that reflects on how it depends on us and the direction we take in our education whether we make best use of our natural endowment.

As all interpreters agree, Timaeus's prioritising of the two kinds of cause is meant to recall that moment in the *Phaedo* where Socrates complained

---

[1] Not a good argument: it proves that fire, etc. are not souls, but not that they are soul-less.
[2] One must bear in mind that Timaeus draws the contrast between Intelligence and Necessity in the context of explaining the formation of organic creatures from earth, air, fire, and water. Timaeus returns to this contrast at 68e6–7 at just the moment when he is about to resume discussion of organic formations. Thus Intelligence in this contrast is divine demiurgy, the principle of organic formation (cf. 68e2). Some readers, I believe, start by taking the contrast at 46c7–e6 to be between all operations or effects of divine rationality and those of some completely non-rational factor; they are then surprised when Timaeus goes on to show how divine rationality, at a prior stage, constituted the four materials by geometrically ordering certain rudiments (53b1–5). See also n. 49.
[3] This is also said to be the purpose of voiced sound and hearing, 47c4–e2.

that Anaxagoras started out positing the primacy of cosmic Intelligence, but failed to use this principle in his explanations of particular cosmic arrangements, falling back on 'airs and aethers and waters' in such contexts. This, Socrates said, was like first announcing that Socrates does everything he does because of reason, and then trying to explain why Socrates is sitting and conversing (here in prison, on his last day) wholly in terms of the properties of bones, sinews, and joints, and those of voiced sounds, aural sensations, and air currents (*Phaedo* 98b7 ff.). For Socrates in the *Phaedo* the missing explanation would have referred to his decision that awaiting execution was the best action open to him (98e1–99a4). This was the true cause, whereas (according to Socrates in the *Phaedo*) the physical infrastructures of his sitting in the Athenian prison do not deserve to be called 'causes' at all: they are only necessary conditions for the true causal factor to function as such (99a4–b6).[4]

Let us see how Timaeus improves on what Socrates said in the *Phaedo*.[5] Socrates was right when he declared that a discourse about human anatomy would point only to necessary conditions – not to any sort of causes – of his sitting in prison. This is because the *explanandum* in this example is a human action, a phenomenon of *ethical* significance. An account of bones and tendons contributes nothing to our understanding of Socrates's posture as implementing a human decision.[6] And as well as saying too little, the anatomist's account says too much. We do not have to be experts on human anatomy to know all we need about the actions by which Socrates realised his purpose. Moreover, if Socrates had decided instead to decamp to Megara (99a1), the same anatomical expertise, if relevant at all, would have been just as relevant for 'explaining why' Socrates would have been sitting in Megara.[7] However, Socrates in the *Phaedo* discussion extrapolated from his own sitting in prison to the cosmological perspective. He did so because he saw that the Anaxagorean starting point implied that cosmic arrangements are as they are because it is better so (98a6–b3), just as he knew that he was staying where he was because it was better so. Extrapolating, he drew the conclusion that a supposed explanation of some cosmic fact in terms of its material conditions is likewise no sort of causal explanation at all (99b2–6). That is to say: knowing in detail the nature of those conditions adds nothing to any understanding that it makes sense for us to seek.

---

[4] They are not causes at all because they shed no light on the nature of what they make possible.
[5] See Strange, 1985, and Johansen, 2004, ch. 5, for useful discussions.
[6] For such a case, what Aristotle calls the dialectician's explanation (inadequate for the *phusikos* considering a physical phenomenon) is enough: *On the Soul* 1, 403a29–b2.
[7] Cf. Johansen, 2004, 103–6.

This is the point on which the *Timaeus* corrects what Socrates said in the *Phaedo*. Anaxagoras may have been at fault in not explaining the specific ends which cosmic Intelligence had in sight which the 'airs and aethers and waters' were supposed to produce.[8] But it is also a mistake for the *cosmologist* to dismiss the material conditions of the phenomena he studies as in no way genuine causes. These do not stand to cosmic objectives in the way in which the anatomical condition of Socrates stands to his ethical purpose. They *are* causes, albeit only auxiliary ones, since cosmology cannot understand the phenomena properly without expertise in the physics and chemistry of inanimate matter. Furthermore: in trying to understand and indeed to identify a human action as such we can well afford to ignore its anatomical *sine quibus non*, because we typically have an epistemic route that goes through the *logoi* of the agent. If it is our own action we know what it is and understand it because we intend it and know our reasons for doing so; if it is another's we get to identify and understand it by asking the agent, and being told, what he or she is about. But since the Timaean natural scientist cannot question the Demiurge, there may be cases in which we can only proceed by trying to infer the specific purpose of some phenomenon from considering its material details.[9] In this way by considering the fragility of the human cranium Timaeus draws the conclusion that its thin-ness of bone is conducive to intelligence (*Timaeus* 74e10–75c7). If the Platonic scientist modelled his approach to nature on that of Socrates in the *Phaedo*,[10] declaring that a proper interest in the good attained by some physical arrangement precludes all interest in the material aspect, he would risk denying himself what may sometimes be the only route to exactly the kind of explanation he desires.[11]

---

[8] However, Sedley, 2007, ch. I, argues that Anaxagoras's teleology is much more substantial, even though somewhat implicit, than we would gather from the *Phaedo*.

[9] At 46d7–e2 Timaeus says that the true lover of knowledge must *seek for* the intelligent causes first and for the necessary ones second, but this is not a promise that the seeker will necessarily *find* the former before the latter.

[10] Or on that of a geometer who rightly ignores the materials of a diagram.

[11] Cf. 68e1–69a4 (the end of the enquiry into the physics and chemistry of matter): 'So all these things, being naturally constituted thus by necessity, came to be taken over by the Demiurge of that which is fairest and best in the realm of what comes into being at the point when he was starting to bring to birth the self-sufficient and most perfect god. <The Demiurge> used the causes in this domain as subservient, whereas the good in all that was coming to be was of his own devising. That is why we must distinguish two kinds of cause, the one necessary, the other divine, and why we must seek the divine one in all things for the sake of as blessed a life as our nature allows, and the necessary one for the sake of the former, reckoning that without these <necessary> things those very ones that command our devotion cannot on their own come into view nor yet be grasped or in any other manner fall to our share.'

6.1 Two kinds of causes

Let us now turn back to Timaeus's explanation of the greatest good that God conferred by endowing us with vision. This passage (46e7–47c4) grows out of his repudiation of theories that reduce everything to the effects of heating and cooling, condensing and dissolving, etc., and his consequent declaration that these are only secondary and auxiliary causes, whereas the intelligent cause is primary (46c7–e6). I think it is worth considering in what way the specific explanation of the purpose of vision adds to, strengthens, or deepens the general declaration. Perhaps, however, it is not meant as a strengthener, but is simply something important which Plato naturally places next. But we can say more than that. Two observations can be made.

The first is that, having implicitly criticised Socrates of the *Phaedo* for his methodological *naïvety* over natural science, Timaeus now pays him tribute. When Socrates sat fast and awaited execution, this was not simply an example of doing what one deems it best to do: it was also the action of the philosopher that Socrates was. He chose this course on philosophically reasoned grounds concerning his debt to the laws of his city;[12] he chose it out of faithfulness to his own mission of bringing philosophy to the Athenians;[13] and as he followed through on it he was philosophising to the last on the meaning of the step he was about to take from life to death.[14] Now in the *Timaeus*, with vision's highest benefit explained as specifically *philosophical*, Plato elevates to universal and cosmic significance the (to most people) crazy and quixotic values of one eccentric Athenian, Socrates. The immortal cosmic animal, the mortal rational animals, and the organic parts of animals, are designed as they are for the sake of the activity of wisdom.[15] True, Socrates failed to understand in full the path to cosmology, and he himself turned away from this kind of causal enquiry.[16] Even so, his own philosophising was one great example of what the world as studied by cosmology is ultimately all about.

The second observation will take a few steps to develop. Plato may think that as long as one is content to believe that the purpose of vision is fully explained as perception of nearby objects (as distinct from the heavenly bodies) it is easier to slip into imagining that a story about corporeal materials could fully account for vision: that such a story could explain

---

[12] *Crito* 44c–54c.   [13] *Apology* 20d–23b; 30d–e; 37e–38a.
[14] *Phaedo passim*.   [15] See Chapter 4, n. 16.
[16] *Phaedo* 99c8 ff. He speaks of this turn just after saying that he would gladly become the pupil of anyone who could explain why the position of the earth is for the best (99c6–8). In the *Timaeus*, where Socrates reappears as a character, that kind of wish is granted. Sedley, 2007, 91–2, points out the strangeness of the wish in the *Phaedo* setting, where Socrates has scarcely an hour to live, and speculates that 99c6–8 actually alludes to Plato's future work on cosmology and Socrates's presence in something like the *Timaeus*.

not only the intrinsic nature of the optic ray, but also, somehow, the development of the fine-tuned optical apparatus that produces this ray. Plato may consider his audience less ready to accept that the elemental materials and forces are wholly devoid of intelligence, including even what might be thought of as a purely intuitive, inarticulate, quasi-intelligent tendency (perhaps not operating, like the reason of the Demiurge and his helpers, by steps that *we* can distinguish and understand), *if* the audience is allowed to stay with the commonsense assumption that the eyes are above all for seeing things on our own level. It is this – seeing the cliff-edge in front of us, or the predator before it sees us – that matters for physical survival. Focusing on this benefit of vision helps foster a certain picture of the corporeal elements and powers of nature. According to the picture (a rather traditional one), these mighty pervasive beings have engendered the organic species that dwell in natural habitats of land, water, and air. These species are very different in appearance and operation from the corporeal elements and forces themselves, but through and through they seem to be rooted in them, to feed off them, to live and move and have their being in them; so why (perhaps, even, how?) can it not be true that through some elemental creativity the organisms also originally emerged from them, and emerged having just the physical equipment they needed in order to make their way in their environment? So perhaps it is in contrast to this sort of view that Plato insists that the mortal faculty of vision is principally designed to forward not our corporeal survival but our incorporeal and immortal reason's self-salvation. *This* end, unlike our corporeal survival, is not imaginably within the competence of the great corporeal materials of the cosmos to encompass even by blind teleology: the reason being that this end is too dissimilar in nature to them and all that they provide. Even if they had inchoate comprehension of anything, they could not inchoately comprehend *this*! In sum: once it is clear that the four elements cannot remotely account for what is most important in the design of mortal animals, then if other aspects of the design are rationally related to the most important (which in the best possible cosmos must be the case) there can be no temptation to imagine the corporeal elements as having any part at all in that design. Thus by insisting at *Timaeus* 46e7 ff. that vision is mainly for the sake of rational salvation, Plato consolidates the doctrine of 46d4–e6 that fire, earth, water, and air are completely devoid of intelligence, and therefore can *only* be assigned the status of subordinate causes.[17]

---

[17] The lesson of 46c7–e7, on the difference between primary and auxiliary causes, is sometimes (I think) taken to be just this: *given* (1) that fire and water and earth and air are unintelligent, it follows (2) that they are no more than *auxiliary* causes. The ensuing passage, 46e7–47e2, on the greatest benefit of

6.1 Two kinds of causes

If this interpretation is not off target, it means that Plato could not presume that this dualistic doctrine would automatically appear self-evident and completely unsurprising to all to whom he addressed the *Timaeus* cosmology. The dualism which I mean is encapsulated at 46d4–7, where he says this about the agencies that cool and heat, condense and dissolve, etc.:

> They are not capable of possessing any <kind of> reasoning [*logos*], nor yet intelligence [*nous*] with a view to anything. For the only entity that is properly endowed with intelligence must be declared to be soul: but this is something invisible, whereas fire and water and earth and air have all come to be as visible bodies.

This insistence that body as such is devoid of soul and intelligence may seem reminiscent of Cartesian dualism. But the difference is at least as great as any resemblance. From the point of view of Cartesian dualism it is deeply problematic that mind (or intelligent soul) has any effects at all on the domain of *res extensa* (and vice versa). This sort of puzzle is the last thing that Plato wants, if he could even have envisaged it. Instead, for him and surely for many in his audience the thought that intelligence expresses itself in ordered motions of visible bodies, and in beautiful or beneficial corporeal structurings, would have come as completely natural.[18] But this very naturalness also makes it not implausible to think that corporeal things – even corporeal things as such – are invested with intelligence, and therefore with soul (since everyone is likely to accept that soul is the bearer of intelligence). So even if for Plato this is not an option, he cannot take it for granted that the same is true for all whom he hopes to reach with the cosmology. Thus he must make some move to exclude this possibility.

---

vision and hearing is then read as simply explaining what the distinct primary intelligent cause had in view when creating those sense faculties, it being taken as already completely settled that (1) and hence (2) are true. As I read it, however, 46e7–47e2 is in part, at least, an implicit confirmation of (1) and hence of (2). Thus the argument as a whole is: since (1) fire, etc. *are* unintelligent – which is overwhelmingly plausible, given that the nature of the greatest benefit that they through vision etc. provide is such as to make it utterly implausible that *they* would intelligently aim for *that* – it follows that (2) they are no more than auxiliary causes.

[18] So far removed is he from Cartesian dualism that he sees the psychic activity of the cosmic soul and human reason in the human head as literally consisting in incorporeal but nonetheless circular (hence, spatial) movement. In the cosmic case this gives rise to visible celestial rotations (see Chapter 4, n. 27). In the human case, as someone pointed out at the 1997 Cambridge May Week seminar, Plato should explain why our heads are not visibly spinning (anyway when we think aright). The answer must be that the mortal-immortal's best movement of its body as a whole, i.e. that which expresses human reason at its best, (a) is complicated and variegated because of the complications of our bodies and lives compared with those of the cosmic god, and (b) would not be helped by a human head spinning on its own: voluntary forward movement in any one direction would be impossible, because 'forward' is defined by reference to the face (45a3–b2).

It is not enough for him to aver that soul is invisible and in general not perceptible, for this fails to secure his desired conclusion that soul, or at any rate the kind of soul that is vehicle of intelligence, is wholly incorporeal. After all, Empedocles had emphasised that his corporeal forces of Love and Strife have to be contemplated by the mind as distinct from the senses.[19] The same is true of the corporeal micro-structures which Timaeus will later invoke to explain sensory experiences (cf. 56b7–c7; 64a2–68d7, on which see note 48 below). As Plato develops his own scientific interest in the invisible forces and basic structures of matter, it becomes less convincing of him simply to assert that the invisibility of intelligence-bearing soul spells its radical incorporeity.[20] He has to inject a new consideration to invigorate his own dualistic paradigm (in the Kuhnian sense) according to which the corporeal elements are completely devoid of intelligence. In the passage we have been considering, he makes a move to that effect (so I suggest) by insisting that the chief benefit of intelligence-crafted vision has nothing to do with the well-being of our bodies.[21]

Now for a curious postscript on Timaeus's remarks about the chief benefit of vision. Whatever the intention behind this passage, Plato must have regarded his point here as well worth making: for it comes with a cost of which he can hardly have been unaware. If the chief benefit of vision depends on contemplating *all* the visible regularities of the heavens, Timaeus's physics of vision cannot be adequate. The theory that postulates an optic fire that coalesces with daylight can explain only daytime vision (45b4–d7). By itself it cannot explain how we see the moon and stars by night. Almost as soon as Timaeus has uttered his account of how vision works, it turns out to sit badly with his account of the ultimate purpose of the faculty.[22] At best the account of the working is shown to cover only a sub-class of cases; hence it stands out as needing to be developed in some

---

[19] B17, 20–1.
[20] See *Phaedo* 79a6–c1. The qualification at 79b7–11, that soul is invisible *to human beings*, is presumably meant to allow that the divine judges can see our incorporeal souls: *Gorgias* 523e1–6; cf. *Phaedo* 80d5–7.
[21] However, particularly in the *Timaeus* any dualism of body and rational soul is criss-crossed with serious philosophical potential for a kind of mathematical monism, since both rational soul and corporeal matter are given mathematical analyses.
[22] I have not found this incoherence discussed by the commentators I have consulted. Burnyeat, 2005, suggests that internal but not external coherence is a necessary condition for a Timaean *logos* (i.e. section of the cosmology on a specific subject-matter) to be *eikôs*. The vision example casts doubt on this, if (as I am supposing) it is internally incoherent – unless Plato missed the difficulty.

way on which nothing is said. Timaeus is silent about the difficulty. We can only suppose that Plato believes the theory offered to be at least as plausible as anyone else's on this topic (29c7–d3), and therefore he allows it to stand.[23] He did take care to make Timaeus warn at the outset that total self-consistency and exactness is more than mortals can reasonably expect from a mortal cosmologist (29c4–7).

6.2 APPROACHING THE SECOND BEGINNING

After discoursing on the mechanics and purpose of vision, Timaeus moves in great strides to a major turning point of the cosmology, the 'second beginning'. The relevant text is 47e3–48e1. I divide exposition into numbered points.

(1) Up to now, Timaeus says, he has mostly been displaying the craftworks of Intelligence in the universe: but we should also in our account 'set alongside' these (*parathesthai*, 47e5) the effects attributable to Necessity; otherwise we shall not do justice to the fact that the coming to be of this cosmos was a compound operation involving Necessity and Intelligence in combination (47e3–48a7). In other words, having firmly denied Necessity and its effects the status of first or only causes, Timaeus now declares that they are absolutely not to be marginalised. He takes the views of 'Necessity-only' theorists seriously enough to give great weight to their favoured causes. For instance, it is not as if the capacity for vision is a functional structure describable perhaps in abstract mathematical terms and reproducible in many different materials. It is because of what *fire* contributes to vision that vision is possible. In general, we need to study the nature of fire, water, air, and earth to see what they in themselves contribute to the production of animals (including, of course, the cosmic animal) and their parts. This study turns out to be immensely comprehensive: it concludes only at 68d7. Timaeus squares it off there with a reprise of themes from which it began, namely: the twin cosmogonic contributions of divine demiurgic Intelligence and natural Necessity; the latter's subservience to the former; and the need for cosmologists to observe the distinction and priority of those two kinds of cause (68e1–69a5). The two kinds of cause, Timaeus says, now lie at hand (*parakeitai*)

---

[23] Timaeus seems to adhere to the earlier theory of vision when discussing colours at 67c4 ff. The caution sounded at 68d2–7 is aimed at specific proposals (or experiments) concerning colours, not about the general theory of vision.

for us like material for builders; now that they have been separated off from each other we can weave them together so as to produce the rest of the account, thereby completing the cosmology (69a5–b2). He then reminds us of where we were when this long disquisition about fire and water etc. began: we had just started on the psychological predicaments of the mortally embodied soul, and the anatomical arrangements made for it by the ancillary demiurges (69c5–6). The anatomical enquiry is now at long last resumed, with many of its points made clearer as a result of the intervening account of the corporeal elements and their compounds.

(2) As Timaeus puts it, the study of the four materials will focus on their nature and their properties as these were 'before the coming to be of the cosmos [*ouranos*[24]]' (48b3–5). See also 68e1–4, where he says that the Demiurge 'set about taking them over' (*parelambanen*; cf. 30a4) for his use in crafting the cosmos. Minimally, this means that we are to study their independent contribution to the product. Imagine fire and earth, water and air, as they would be if no portions of them had been taken up in the fashioning of mortal bodies and if the large portions from which these portions were 'borrowed' (cf. 42e6–43a1) had not been fashioned into the spherical non-mortal body of the cosmos itself: the elements as they would be, or would have been, in this supposed situation are what we are now to examine.

(3) The emphasis on the materials' subservience to cosmos-building Intelligence (which includes their subservience to the ancillary divinities that fashioned the mortal animals[25]) by no means allows us to picture them as just waiting about to be picked up and used. Far from it: in the pre-cosmic situation which we are now to envisage, they were in a state of disorderly motion. Timaeus terms them collectively 'the wandering cause' (48a5–7; cf. 30a2–6). But the disorderliness and the wandering do not mean chaos or total absence of determinate motions. The point, rather, is that the materials taken for use by cosmos-building Intelligence were astray and random in relation to the cosmic desideratum. Thus 'wandering cause' and 'disorderly motion' in the passages just mentioned either repeat or prepare for what is laid down at 46d4–7: i.e. that the elements themselves lack the intelligence which, if present, would reliably aim to produce the beautiful organic formations of the cosmos. But this is not to deny that on their own they would still behave in quite determinate and possibly even predictable ways such as we often

---

[24] For this meaning of *ouranos*, see Aristotle, *On the Heaven*, 1, 278b18–21.
[25] The Demiurge and the ancillaries are often not distinguished in the later pages; see Chapter 4, n. 16.

6.2 Approaching the second beginning

observe today, and would be in possession of their own definite natures.[26] Only because they have their own natures are they able to make their important causal contribution to the cosmos, one requiring a distinct scientific study.

(4) This means, however, that when Intelligence harnessed them for its purpose, it could not just let them go on as they would have been going on without it. They had to submit to a direction not their own. It is hardly thinkable in the Timaean system that Intelligence should force the corporeal elements against their nature.[27] It would have to be forever holding them down or holding them back; but such a state of affairs can hardly be calculated to contribute to the tranquil permanence of a blessedly immortal cosmos. Nor could elemental non-resistance be the non-resistance of the completely broken; to serve the cosmic project, the elements must show up with their identities and powers intact. To encompass the required relation between Intelligence and Necessity, Plato has Timaeus speak of 'persuasion':

> With Intelligence ruling over Necessity by persuading [*tô(i) peithein*] it to bring towards the best most of what was coming into being, in this way and on these terms, through Necessity's yielding to wise persuasion, this All came to be constituted. (48a2–5)

According to this image, Necessity could not tell itself what to do to contribute to the cosmos, but it 'listened to' Intelligence, and complied 'willingly' and of itself.[28]

(5) The separate study of the four corporeal materials is so important that in broaching it, we in effect begin our cosmology a second time over:

> So we must go back again; we must take up a beginning [*archên*] proper to these very things, a second one starting over; and just as we did with those previous concerns so we must again do now with these: we must begin from the beginning. The task now is to survey the nature of fire and water and air and earth <as it was> before the coming to be of the cosmos – their nature itself and their properties as they were before then. (48a7–b5)

---

[26] This interpretation is in line with the expositions of Morrow, 1950; Gadamer, 1980, 176 ff.; Gregory, 2000, 113–15; Johansen, 2004, 92–5; cf. 74–5. See also D. Miller, 2003, 66–70, on Necessity and the wandering cause. See Mason, 2006, on predictability and on light shed on Necessity by modern chaos theory.

[27] Although this, we are told, is what the Demiurge had to do to the 'hard to mix' Different when getting it to blend with the Same to form the material of the cosmic soul (35a7–8).

[28] Cf. 56c5–6, in the geometrical account of the elements: '... in whatever way the nature of necessity gave way willingly and because persuaded [*hopê(i)per ... hekousa peistheisa te ... hupeiken*]'. On the translation of *hopê(i)per* cf. Sedley, 2007, 119, note 57.

Timaeus here alludes to his first beginning (27c1–29d3; at 29d5, Socrates called it his proem or overture). A few lines on Timaeus states that he will continue to adhere to its epistemic demand for 'likely accounts', and will try from the start, as before,[29] to give on each topic and on all of them collectively an account no less likely than anyone else's but in fact more so (48d1–4; cf. 29c7–d3). He also, as at the first beginning, utters a prayer for the success of his enterprise (48d4–e1; cf. 27c1–d1).

(6) So far, we may think that this new beginning simply launches discussion of the nature of the four materials. But the last quoted sentence, about the pre-cosmic nature of the four elements, is immediately followed by this declaration:

> For no one has ever yet revealed their genesis; instead, we talk as if our listeners know what fire and what each of them is; we posit them as first principles [*archas*, starting points], the A, B, C [*stoicheia*] of the All, whereas even a person of meagre intelligence would not in likelihood [*eikotôs*] find their likeness [*apeikasthênai*] even amongst the forms of mere syllable. (48b5–c2)

So fire etc. too have a genesis, like the things that are fashioned from them; and, this being so, we can hardly claim to know their nature unless we have explored the starting points of *their* genesis. Thus the second beginning not only inaugurates the entire subject of the corporeal materials, but does so by promising to look into the beginnings of, the principles behind the genesis of, those very materials themselves. What was to have been an investigation of them as they *were* when at hand in their immediately pre-cosmic state has just turned into an investigation of their *origin* in something more primary.

(7) In the quotation in (6) above, Plato through Timaeus swipes away 'our' assumption that the four materials are first principles: he does so with the air of pulling the rug out from under someone's feet.[30] By the end of the sentence he has also quashed any thought that even if the four are not absolutely primary principles of reality they are fundamental enough to constitute the second level up, standing to the absolutely first things as syllables to the letters of the alphabet. In other words: do not imagine that you reach the primary principles of reality by reducing the corporeal materials to their constituents. (By contrast, Democritus not only reduced fire to spherical particles, but postulated such particles as literally indivisible atoms, and so, with the void, as ultimate constituents of reality.) Then Plato makes Timaeus go on:

---

[29] Accepting Cornford's conjecture *hê(i)* before *emprosthen* at 48d3.
[30] Presumably Empedoclean feet; see Taylor, 1928, 305–6; Cornford, 1935, 161–2. In having Timaeus say '*we* talk etc.'(48b7), Plato may allude to the character's Italian origin.

But for now let the matter rest thus, at least as far as *we* are concerned: the principle – or principles, or however one sees fit to speak of them – *of all things* [*hapantôn*] is not a matter for the present discourse, if for no other reason then because of the difficulty of making clear the views <in question> while keeping to the present kind of exposition [*tropon tês diexodou*]; therefore just as you must not suppose that I ought to state them, so I could not persuade myself that I should be right to attempt taking on such a major task. (48c2–d1)

This is immediately followed by the announcement (see [5] above) that in what comes next we are to continue to observe the standard of the *eikos*. If 'keeping to our present kind of exposition' also refers to this, then it is implied that an enquiry into first principles of *everything* would demand a different epistemic standard. However, I am inclined to think that 'our present kind of exposition' points not only to the epistemic standard for cosmology but also to its subject matter. Timaeus is saying that the study of first principles *of everything* lies outside his remit. Thus Plato here signals a division like Aristotle's between first and second philosophy.[31] This tells us two things. First: Timaean cosmology is complete (as cosmology) without going back to absolutely first principles. Cosmological science of the four corporeal materials needs to take account of their immediate origin, but not of whatever lies further back.[32] Second: in studying what lies ahead, interpreters should look at all the themes, however 'metaphysical' some of them may be, through the lens of this question: what do they contribute to the cosmology?

6.3 TWO ACCOUNTS

What lies ahead consists of *two* accounts of the genesis of the four materials. I shall summarise them in this section, and shall discuss various relations between them in section 6.4. The first is the famous Receptacle-passage, running from 48e2 to 53a7; the second explains the geometrical formation of the four. The most fundamental part of this starts at 53a7 and reaches a pause at 56c7, but Plato draws consequences from it throughout the rest of the cosmology, particularly when explaining the properties of inanimate matter, and also on occasion when discussing the anatomy and physiology

---

[31] Aristotle, *Metaphysics* VI, 1026a16; VII, 1037a15. This is not to imply that Plato places the division where Aristotle does.

[32] The contrast at 48c2 ff. is between principles relevant for cosmology and principles of all things. Then at 53d4–7 Timaeus contrasts the cosmologically relevant basic triangle with 'higher principles known <only> to God and to that man who is dear to God'. Whether or not these latter principles are 'of all things', they are presumably treated by a more rigorous standard than the *eikos*, and in themselves shed no special light on cosmology.

of mortal animals. If we include in it all the implications about inanimate matter (ending with the enquiry into visible qualities at 67c4–68d7), the second account is almost four times as long as the first.

6.3.1 *The Receptacle-passage (48e2–53a7)*

The initial claim is that while a dichotomy sufficed for the cosmology's first beginning, we now need a 'more ample' division. Before, the fundamental distinction was between two kinds (*eidê, genos*; 48e3–49a4), namely *intelligible changeless model*, and *generated sensible copy* (*mimêma*). These metaphysical kinds or categories were then exemplified by the case of the paradigm of this cosmos and the cosmos itself (27d5–28a4; 28e5–29b2). But now our discourse 'seems to force' recognition of a third kind as well.

Comment: it is important to be clear that Timaeus is here speaking of kinds or categories, not instances.[33] Thus the continuity of the first two kinds as between the first and the second beginning does not entail that the instances of those kinds are the same in both beginnings. And indeed the instances are not the same. At the first beginning, as has just been said, the instances are the intelligible paradigm of the cosmos and the sensible cosmos itself. At the second beginning (as I argue in the course of this chapter) the instances are the intelligible paradigms of the four corporeal elements and the sense-perceptible elements.

The third kind, or the third thing, Timaeus emphasises again and again, is obscure and difficult to explain (49a3–4; 51a7–b2; 52b2). The best way to grasp its competence (*dunamin*) and nature is to think of it as 'Receptacle [*hupodochê*[34]] and so to speak nurse of all becoming'. But to make this clear,

---

[33] I am indebted to Dana Miller, 2003, 37 ff. for this essential point, which has helped me to think more clearly about the Receptacle-passage. Neglect of it naturally leads to the assumption that *instances* of the first two kinds are the same throughout both beginnings. This in turn has fostered the assumption (closely bound up with the 'ontological' interpretation of the Receptacle, discussed below in sections 6.5 and 6.6) that at both beginnings the first two kinds consist respectively of intelligible Forms in general and sense-perceptibles in general. This (I shall argue) leads in a false direction. For Miller, however, the main importance of the distinction between kinds and instances is this: since it implies a conceptual distinction between the third kind as such and its instance, the Receptacle, it allows for the possibility that the Receptacle is not the only instance. On this basis Miller argues that the *Timaeus* recognises a distinct member of the third kind, namely *chôra* (see esp. 61–2 and 197–213). This neatly solves difficulties which interpreters since Aristotle have experienced in trying to make sense of a single entity that is both *chôra* and has the attributes of the Receptacle. I cannot, however, believe that Plato with his penchant for enumerating importantly different entities would have applied it only to the three kinds rather than (also) making it explicit that the third kind has *two* cosmologically important members.

[34] On the connotations of this word ('container', but also 'haven', 'refuge', 'act of friendly reception'), see Sallis, 1999, 99–100; Reynolds, 2008.

6.3 Two accounts

Timaeus says, we must first face something puzzling about fire and the other elements (48e2–49b2). What is puzzling, he says, is this:

> With respect to each of them, which should one say is really water rather than fire, and which <one should call> any given one rather than <calling it> all and each? To do this using a terminology[35] that is trustworthy and firm is a difficult thing. (49b2–5)

He spells this out by stating that (as it seems) they visibly turn into each other: we *see* (49c1; d4) what we have named water turning into stones and earth through condensation and into air by relaxing and dispersing; air by combustion becomes fire; fire by contracting and being quenched becomes air again; air through condensation becomes cloud which through further condensation becomes water; and from water come earth and stones again; and so on round. This – the fact that none of them ever[36] keeps the same appearance – is the reason why, if we firmly insist of any one of them that it really is *this*, whatever that may be (e.g. that it really is *fire*), we end up feeling foolish (49b7–d3). How to speak of fire and the others in a way that is safe and unembarrassing? This is how: we must understand the terms 'fire', 'water' etc. not as *this*-words, i.e. nouns each referring to a *this*, but as adjectives indicating a qualification, or that something is qualified. (On the latter formulation, 'fire' stands not for the subject as such that is qualified, but for the subject qualified in a certain way.) Expressions indicating *this* or *that* are properly used of a subject that is stable in the sense that its nature is permanently what such an expression implies. It is a mistake to use 'fire' etc. as if they were *this*-referring nouns, precisely because 'fire' applies and then ceases to apply; and so with the other terms for the corporeal materials. The applicability of these terms constantly goes round and round (*aei peripheromenon*, 49e5), i.e. their applicability is on and off and on again, and so on unremittingly, because the referents are subject to genesis (sc. from each other) (49d4–e7).[37]

Question: why does Plato problematise the inter-transformation in this linguistic way, floating the impression that our ordinary use of 'fire', 'water', etc. as nouns opens us up to an embarrassing puzzle and paradox? This would be true only if our ordinary use had built into it the rule that if such a

---

[35] Bury's translation.
[36] *oudepote*, 49c7–d1: I take this to mean that there appears to be transformation in every case, not that they appear to be transforming at every moment (this is not what we see or even seem to see [49b8–c1]).
[37] 49b2–50a2 on 'this' and 'such' allows for different choices of translation and interpretation. See Zeyl, 2000, lvi–lxi, for a clear exposition of the different possibilities and references to previous scholarship. It will be clear that I have accepted what he calls the 'traditional' interpretation.

noun applies, it applies for ever; but no such rule is built in. With our ordinary use we can equally state the theory that the four materials turn into each other and the theory that each always continues present with its own unchanging nature. However, Plato is aiming to win acceptance of his notion of the third thing, the Receptacle. He is committed to the view that the four materials are not ultimate: they have a genesis which it is the business of cosmology to understand. This idea of their having a genesis is helped forward by the claim, supposedly based on observation, that they do turn into each other in regular cycle.

However, this in itself will not get us to the Receptacle. The idea of the Receptacle is the idea of something more fundamental *in which* they come to be and pass away (49e7–8). But why should one suppose that the transformation has to take place *in* anything? Why should it not just take place? Or why not (in somewhat Aristotelian style) locate the metamorphosis of a given portion of fire into a portion of air *in* the place where the particular fire was or the air now appears, saying (if more detail is wanted) e.g. that this happened at the mouth of such and such a volcano, and generalising to the conclusion that for every piecemeal transformation there is a place in which it occurs – but not a place constituted or determined by anything more fundamental in nature than the empirical objects involved in the transformation? To motivate postulating the Receptacle, Plato has to exhibit fire and the others as essentially qualifications, the terms for them as essentially adjectival. Once this is accepted, then the picture cannot be complete without postulating a subject which they qualify, a fundamental *this* on which they depend. For qualifications, like adjectives on the linguistic level, are essentially dependent on something of a different category. But how does he show that fire and the others *are* no more than qualifications, their names no more than adjectives? He does not show it, at least not by anything we can call a good argument. He simply insists on it by dramatically pressing the claim that the transformational cycle makes nonsense of our use of 'fire' etc. as nouns. But this claim is easily shrugged off unless one already wants to believe in the Receptacle.

At any rate, it is now established in Timaeus's account that there is something *in which* the materials appear and pass away. This alone is the proper referent of 'that' and 'this', and we are also told that terms such as 'hot and 'white', and 'any of the opposites, and anything consisting of them' do not apply to it (49e7–50a4). Timaeus now offers an image by way of explanation. This strange new principle is like a piece of gold which someone ceaselessly moulds into different shapes (*schêmata*, 50a6; b2; cf. c3): if someone points to one of them and asks what it is, the safest thing is to say: 'It is gold', and to refuse to speak of the triangle and the other shapes as if they 'are', since they disappear as one applies the name; instead in their case one should be content to say *'suchlike'* (e.g. 'triangular', not 'triangle'). So it is with the 'nature that receives all bodies'. It alone must always be called by the same name, since it never departs from its own nature (*dunamis*, 50b8), its function being always to receive all things, and to take on no shape like any of the things coming into it. It is like a moulding-stuff for every nature; it is moved and configured by the things going into it, and through them it has now one appearance, now another; but these going-in-and-out things are in each case only copies (*mimêmata*) of realities (50a4–c6). Timaeus now recounts the three elements of the second beginning: 'that which is coming to be, that in which it comes to be, and that from which it comes to be, of which it by nature is a likeness'; this last should be likened to father, the recipient to mother, and the nature generated between them to child (50c7–d4). Timaeus goes on to emphasise again how the recipient itself must be completely devoid of all the characters it receives: otherwise it could not be the universal recipient, since having any of them would make it unreceptive to the opposite character. It must be like the odourless base of scented ointments, or a soft material for moulding figures, which is required to be as homogeneous as possible (50d4–e10).

By now it is clear that the items received are likenesses of the eternal Forms (51a1–3; cf. 50c5 and 50d1–2).[38] Mention of the Forms recalls the first beginning's contrast between intelligible paradigm and sensible copy. So now there is the question of placing the new principle in terms of that contrast. Well, it is mother and Receptacle of whatever has become and is perceptible; but in its own way it differs from the perceptible as sharply as the intelligible paradigm does, not being any of the four materials, nor anything composed of them nor anything from which they have come to be[39] (51a4–6). After a sentence emphasising the difficulty of grasping the nature of the Receptacle (51a7–b2), Timaeus now captures the main point without imagery:

The enflamed part of it shows up as fire each time, while the liquefied part shows up as water, and <it shows up> as earth and air to the extent that it receives copies of these. (51b4–6; cf. 52d5)

This makes a good conclusion to a passage that began with our 'seeing' (as we think) water being condensed into earth and dissolved into air, and air

---

[38] Even though the text seems disturbed at 51a1.
[39] According to Cornford, 1935, 186 n. 3, 'the things from which these have come to be' (51a6) refers to qualities such as hot and cold which were fundamentals of some earlier systems; cf. 50a2–3; e2–4. According to Taylor, 1928, 330, it refers to the triangles of the geometrical account. This is less plausible since the point is that the Receptacle *per se* has nothing *perceptible* about it (cf. 51a7): those triangles are in any case necessarily not perceptible, since they account for sense-perception and sensible qualities; cf. n. 48.

through combustion becoming fire, etc. (49b7–c7). Initially the empirical materials were naïvely presented as subjects of physical processes by which one becomes another; but now we are shown something closer to the underlying metaphysical truth: the Receptacle is the real subject; the empirical materials are its qualified parts *qua* qualified; and their appearance in it is due to the Receptacle's receptivity in presence of the Forms.

Next there comes a long passage (51b6–52d4) that announces itself as a more 'conceptual' or 'discursive' (*logô(i) de . . . mallon*) enquiry about fire, water, etc. This begins with the question whether there is a Form of fire and each of the others, or in other words whether the entire 'truth' (51c3) about fire and the others is given by body-based sense-perception. To recognise the Form is to recognise *two* things, an eternal intelligible and its sensible likeness (51e6–52a6). But the latter comes to be and passes away in a place (*en tini topô(i)*, 52a6–7; cf. 52b4), so there are in fact *three* things to keep distinct and to tally, the third one being now called space (*chôra*)[40] and described as 'providing a basis [*hedra*] for all things that have genesis' (52a8–b1; see also 52d2–4 for the tally of three). I shall return to this passage in more detail in section 6.6.

Next and finally in the first of Timaeus's two accounts of the genesis of the materials, the Receptacle, filled as it is with 'powers neither similar nor in equipoise' (52e2), is shown undergoing a shaking motion whereby the different materials, some dense and heavy, some loosely packed and light, travel to different regions of the universe (52d4–53a7). This separative motion, we are told, was going on even before the cosmos (*ouranos*) was formed from the four elements (53a6–7). But the motion still goes on today on a lesser scale.[41] I shall return to this topic in section 6.7.2.

6.3.2 *The geometrical account (53a7 ff.)*

The text continues, introducing the geometrical account:

And before this, these things were all in a state devoid of reason and measure [*eichen alogôs kai ametrôs*[42]]. But when the ordering of the All started to be undertaken, fire

---

[40] I follow Taylor, 1928; Cornford, 1935; and Algra, 1995, in using 'space' to render *chôra* at *Timaeus* 52a8 and d3. This is very far from a perfect translation, but any other English word is yet more misleading. On uses of *chôra* in other contexts in Plato, see Sallis, 1999, 115–18 and 121, n. 29; and Pradeau, 1995, for a comprehensive study.
[41] See 57a7–c6 and 58a2–c4; the main verbs in both passages are present tense.
[42] Reading *eichen* rather than *echein* at a8. On either reading the transition from the Receptacle to the geometry is marked by a change from indirect to direct speech. The fact that the whole of 52d3 *on te kai chôran kai genesin . . .* to 53a7, *. . . . .genesthai* depends on *Houtos . . . . .dedosthô logos* at 52d2–3 is lost in translation.

first and water and earth and air – which, while possessing certain traces of themselves were even so in every way in the state one would expect of anything when God is absent – just this being their natural condition, they were first configured by God [*dieschêmatiseto*] by means of forms and numbers. And that God constructed them so as to be as beautiful and good as possible out of what was not so, must remain our constant declaration at all points in our account. (53a7–b7)[43]

Timaeus refers back to this passage on completing his geometry-based discussion of the four materials in themselves. At that point he gives a summary prefacing his re-entry into the account of the construction of the bodies of mortal animals:

So, as was said at the beginning,[44] when these things were in a disorderly state [*ataktôs echonta*] God implanted in each of them in relation to itself and in relation to each other all the proportions and modes [*hopê(i)*, 69b5] by which it was possible for them to be rationally conformable to each other [*analoga*] and proportionate [*summetra*]. For *then* neither did anything partake of these properties except by chance, nor was there anything meriting in any way a name of the things which are named today [*nun*], such as fire and water and any of the others. However, first he ordered all these things, and then from them he constructed this All, a living being having within itself all living beings both mortal and immortal. And of the divine things he himself takes on the role of [*gignetai*] craftsman, while crafting the coming to be of mortals was a task that he laid upon his own offspring. And they, his imitators, took over <from him> the immortal principle of the soul, and next they encircled it with a mortal body, and gave it the whole body as vehicle . . . (69b2–c7)

This passage makes clear what was not altogether clear in the introduction to the geometrical account: that Timaeus envisages two pre-cosmic stages. First, only rudiments ('traces') existed, and then there were the configured fire, water, etc., not yet formed, but ready to be formed, into the cosmos. Equally, there are two transitions from less to more organised: first, the geometrised transition from rudiments to fire, water, etc., and then the transition whereby the cosmos was formed from these.

In the geometrising of the rudiments the four material kinds were constructed as regular polyhedra with sides composed of triangles chosen so that the resulting solids would be (a) most beautiful, (b) dissimilar from each other, and (c) capable of turning into each other through re-assembly

---

[43] All three sentences in this passage are *about* fire and water, etc. It was these that God configured (i.e. brought into full being by configuration). The passage does not grammatically imply that there were traces to which God did something, namely he configured them. This is clear in Bury's and Cornford's translations, not so clear in Zeyl's.
[44] That is, 53a7–8.

of the triangles. The triangles in question are the isosceles half-square and the scalene half-equilateral. 'So this [i.e. this pair of triangles] is what we assume as principle of fire and the other bodies as we move ahead with our account in which the likely is joined with necessity'[45] (53d4–6; cf. 54b2–5). It now turns out that condition (c) cannot be completely satisfied, since on the basis just stated only three of the solids in question can turn into each other (54b5–d3); the cube, which will be equated with earth, is odd man out for geometrical reasons. Timaeus next explains the formation of regular polyhedra from the triangles; the numbers by which God was said to configure the rudiments (53b5) are now shown to be answers to 'How many?' when asked (i) about the triangles needed to compose the face of a given solid S, (ii) about the faces needed to compose a solid angle of S, and (iii) about the solid angles of S (54d3–55c4). This account yields the tetrahedron, the octahedron, the icosahedron, and the cube, shapes respectively assigned to fire, air, water, and earth by matching the geometrically more and less mobile shapes with the different observed mobilities of the materials (55d6–56b6). Now and only now is it divulged that observable fire etc. are collections of imperceptibly minute particles having those shapes (56b7–c3).

Timaeus then sweepingly declares that proportionalities pertaining to the amounts of the four and to their movements and other powers have all been fully and exactly provided for by the god in his original structuring (56c3–7). From now on, the geometrical genesis of the four materials is a given, and on this basis many things are explained, beginning with elemental intertransformation. It also turns out that the geometrical starting point allows for differently sized particles of the four kinds. Because of this there are many different types of each of the four materials (57c7–d5; cf. 58c5–e2).[46] Not only does this help to bring a great deal of empirical variety under just four headings; it also means that earth is not completely unsusceptible to transformation, since different types of earth can turn into each other. Using this elegantly small handful of geometrical assumptions, Timaeus

---

[45] That is, geometrical necessity. It is *eikos* that beautiful (because regular) polyhedra were selected, also that as many as possible are composed of just the triangles that allow inter-transformation; the rest follows by geometrical necessity. See Chapter 3, n. 27.

[46] See Cornford, 1935, 230–9. From the fact that the elemental particles must be 'most beautiful' geometrically speaking, it follows that they are not homoeomerous, i.e. randomly divisible into smaller *bodies* of the same kinds as themselves. A tetrahedron is not randomly divisible into tetrahedra. More generally, it seems that the only way in which Timaean particles can turn into other particles is via reassembly of the triangles. Although we can imagine a cube yielding eight smaller cubes by direct division in three dimensions, Timaeus's physics seems to rule this out as a mode of change for his particles. Three-dimensionally speaking, they are atoms or indivisibles.

6.4 Looking at the accounts together

goes on to sketch explanations of a vast range of the phenomena of inanimate nature, from the interactions of the four materials to their powers to affect sentient creatures with physical pleasure and pain, and with perceptions across all the sense modalities.

6.4 LOOKING AT THE ACCOUNTS TOGETHER

The two accounts of the genesis of the materials have important things in common.[47] (a) They both take off from the transformations of the materials. The relation of this starting point to the geometrical account is obvious: the latter supplies the systematic explanation of how transformation is possible amongst the three of the four that do turn into each other. In the Receptacle-passage, by contrast, transformation is not an *explanandum*, but (as we have seen) a fact that supposedly requires that the four materials be understood as qualifications: this then motivates the postulate of a subject *in which* they are. (b) Each account features some kind of problem concerning the application of the names for the four materials (49b1–50a2; 69b6–8). More generally: (c) the accounts resemble each other in that each shows a way of upholding a general assumption from which the whole cosmology began: that the perceptible is generated from or by, and is dependent on, principles not themselves perceptible (27d5–29b1). Thus the geometrical account reduces the four materials to elements that are necessarily imperceptible: first to minute three-dimensional particles, and then to the triangles (which are incorporeal because two-dimensional; cf. 53c4–6).[48] The Receptacle-account makes the materials dependent (in different ways) on the Receptacle and on the Forms of Fire and the others. And (d): both accounts presuppose something indeterminate and characterless that is in one or another way prior to the genesis of the four materials. In the first

---

[47] I should warn that this discussion of the two accounts prescinds from the question of dual Timaean explanations of heaviness and lightness, one centring on separative regional movements involving the Receptacle, the other on numbers of triangles composing the geometric particles. The idea of the separative regional tendency will be important in section 6.7.2 below, but the argument there will not depend on its implications for a theory of heaviness and lightness, nor, therefore, on how such a theory may be reconciled with one based on numbers of triangles. The separative regional tendency is a datum for the *Timaeus* independently of implications for explaining heaviness and lightness. See O'Brien, 1984 for a minute examination of Plato's dual theories of heaviness and lightness (and analogously dual accounts of hardness and softness, heat and cold, sweetness and sourness). See also Code, 2010.

[48] The physical particles are necessarily imperceptible because they constitute the causal bases of sensation in subject and object. See e.g. 64a7–c3, recalling 55d8–56a3; 64e4–5; 65d2; 66a4–5; 67c7; d3. To perceive the particles we should need micro-sense organs made from and susceptible to the action of yet smaller particles.

account it is the Receptacle itself, and in the second it is certain rudiments that had to be geometrically ordered by God before anything appeared that deserved the names of fire, earth, air, and water. But there is a big difference between the two cases. The rudiments, whatever they were, simply give way to the divine ordering; they are wholly superseded thereby, and immediately disappear from the story. By contrast, the Receptacle's function keeps it massively *there* throughout the surrounding account, and (a point to which we shall return) throughout the cosmic careers of fire, earth, air, and water.

Moreover, very importantly (e): each account makes it clear beyond doubt that the four materials owe their genesis to the same kind of divinely rational dispensation as the one that subsequently formed them into the cosmos complete with mortal animals. In the geometrical account this is plain from the references to God configuring the 'traces' into shapes, numbers, and proportions (53b4–7; 56c3–8; 69b2–c1). Only once, at 69c3, is the god responsible for this pre-cosmic ordering identified with the Demiurge of the cosmos, but whether the divine being is numerically the same or different in the two cases is unimportant from the point of view of cosmology; the same values of rational beauty prevail in both.[49] The Receptacle-account makes no distinct reference to a god, since divine rationality is here identified with the impersonal principle of the Forms of fire and the other elements. Any mention of a god (perhaps as distinct efficient cause, looking to the Forms, as at the first beginning) would have raised, unnecessarily, the arguably awkward question whether the Receptacle too is a god or goddess. (Elsewhere, the gods other than the Demiurge of the cosmos – and other than the god of pre-cosmic geometrical formation – have been created by the Demiurge [29c4–5; 34a8–b1; 39e10–40d5; 41a3–7].) However, by speaking of the formal principle as *father* and the Receptacle as *mother* in relation to the four materials as *offspring* (50d2–3), Plato makes it as clear as possible that the Receptacle is co-operative with the formal principle. Hence if the formal principle relevant to the generation of the materials is in the same camp, as it surely is, as the cosmic paradigm consulted in making the cosmos, the Receptacle is clearly on the same general side, so to speak, as the rational god who crafted the cosmos in accordance with this paradigm. In my view, the most

---

[49] Taking it to be the same god in both contexts does not license saying: 'The *Demiurge* configured the traces' (as e.g., Crombie, 1963, 224 ff.; Strange, 1985, 403 [the reference is to the 1999 reprint]; Johansen, 2004, 95–6; Sedley, 2007, 97 and 117–18; Harte, 2010). Plato seems to reserve 'Demiurge' for the distinct function of forming the cosmos; this is clear at 68e1–3 and 69c3–4. The Demiurge as such 'takes over' the pre-cosmic materials, 30a4. This is in line with the explanation of Johansen, 2004, 82–3, on why the Demiurge is absent from the Receptacle-passage.

6.4 Looking at the accounts together

important point to emerge from these relationships is this: since (a) the Receptacle co-operates with divine rationality, and (b) the four empirical materials used in crafting the cosmos are in the Receptacle's stable (being totally dependent on it for existence as a child in the womb), they too, when it comes to crafting the crafted cosmos, are on the same general side as the god who crafted it. The four materials constitute a *principle* of this cosmos alongside the principle that is the cosmic paradigm and the principle that is the Demiurge. But unlike the latter two principles, the materials are dependent on something more fundamental, namely the Receptacle. Or, more precisely: whereas anything prior on which the Demiurge or the cosmic paradigm may depend is cosmologically irrelevant (and therefore not discussed in Timaeus's discourse), the Receptacle underlying the empirical materials is cosmologically important.

What does the Receptacle-theme tell the cosmologist? Given the considerations assembled just above, it is surely meant to bring home the point that the four empirical materials in their pre-cosmic state were *amenable* to being used in cosmopoiesis.[50] What is the perspective from which emphasising this point is important for cosmology? It is a perspective, I think, from which the alternative scenario – where the four materials are simply given, having no prior metaphysical origin or none that is relevant – presents itself as offering no reason to suppose that the four would lend themselves easily to cosmopoiesis, and perhaps even as offering reason to fear that they would not. More on this in section 6.7.2.

To return to the comparison of the two accounts: they are clearly complementary. The Receptacle gives no analysis of the four that might explain their transformations and account systematically for their many phenomenal properties and powers, whereas the geometry does just this. Conversely, the geometry can explain what Timaeus speaks of as relative mobilities of the four – differences of solidity and liquidity – by the different structures of the particles (55d8–56b3); but it cannot explain their characteristic local motions towards different regions. For this the Receptacle is needed. At 57b7–c6 the geometrical account explicitly invokes it to explain why, when a portion of one element is generated within a mass of another, it does not stay where it is but goes to the region where the bulk of its kind collects.[51]

---

[50] So it is seriously misleading when writers make the following sort of statement without qualification (as is typical): 'The good intentions of the Demiurge are limited and often frustrated by the recalcitrant matter with which he must work, but which he had no part in creating' (Hasker, 1998) For a contrary but nuanced view see Sedley, 2007, 114 ff.

[51] This is in the present tense; i.e. a phenomenon observable by us is being explained. The separation of the elements is also discussed at 58a2-c4, where it is said to be an everlasting phenomenon. For an

What exactly is the narrative relation between the accounts? The Receptacle-passage shows the four elements in the grip of processes still going on in the world today. The metamorphoses and separative movements which *we* see were happening in the pre-cosmic era. The pre-cosmic separation was on a vast scale, giving rise to the great tracts of earth, air, etc. in their distinct regions, whereas now the separations are smaller scale – at first sight, this is the only difference. The Receptacle-scenario is never over, and there is no hint that it ever had a beginning. By contrast, Timaeus speaks of God's pre-cosmic structuring of the traces as a sort of one-off event. In narrative terms, when is this event supposed to have taken place? Here is how Timaeus presents it. He has just explained that what I am calling the large-scale separation of the materials was happening 'even before the All came to be from them as an ordered system' (53a7). Next he says:

And before this, these things were all in a state devoid of reason and measure [*eichen alogôs kai ametrôs*]. But when the ordering of the All was starting to be undertaken, fire first and water and earth and air ... were first configured by God [*dieschêmatiseto*] by means of forms and numbers. (53a7–b5)

Does 'before this' mean 'before the cosmos had its genesis', or does it have the more precise meaning of 'before the large-scale separation'? Well, if that separation had never *begun* (for the text says nothing about such a beginning), the meaning must simply be 'before the genesis of the cosmos'. Timaeus then makes this reference more determinate by tying it down to 'when the ordering of the All was starting to be undertaken'. He is saying, in effect, that the geometrising was the first step of cosmopoiesis.[52]

It follows from this that the pre-cosmic contents of the Receptacle were the pre-geometrised 'traces'. These were the original child of the Forms and the Receptacle – a child which developed somewhat (or became less embryonic) through being geometrised, although never to the point of becoming independent of the Receptacle. The Receptacle-account presents the processes of separation and transformation as pretty well continuous between what is observable today and the pre-cosmic situation. But putting the two accounts together we have to recognise a certain discontinuity: the

---

explicit backward reference to the Receptacle-passage, see the clarification at 54b5–8: previously it was said (*to prosthen* ... *rhêthen*) that all four elements seemed to convert into each other, but this turns out to be impossible for earth. There are no obvious forward references from the Receptacle-passage to the geometrical account, although some scholars see hints of it in the mention of 'shapes' and 'shaping' at 50a6; b2; and c3.

[52] Geometrising prepared the materials for demiurgic use. Whether we regard preparation of materials as prior to the whole constructive process or as its first stage, seems rather arbitrary. The summary at 69b2–c3 suggests that nothing intervened between the geometrising and the construction of the fully fashioned cosmos.

subjects of the spectacle today are full-blown fire, water, etc., whereas the entities in the pre-cosmic situation were rudiments not 'deserving the names' of these materials; they did turn into each other but in ways 'devoid of reason and measure' (53a8), i.e. without the present-day benefit of the geometry.[53]

Once God has introduced the geometry, the rudiments disappear from the picture. These indeterminate entities were only pre-cosmic. This is by contrast with the Receptacle even though it too, in a way all its own, is empirically even more indeterminate. *Its* role as matrix of its contents and their movements is as real today as it was in the pre-cosmic era. There is also an important difference between the 'naming problems'. The rudiments as such gave rise to a naming problem because (through lacking the geometry) they *lacked the clear empirical distinctions* that guide our actual use of the terms 'fire', 'water', etc. But an entirely different naming problem arises from trying to apply 'fire', 'water', etc. to the contents of the Receptacle considered *as such*. The contents as such, Timaeus asserts, *are in the wrong logical category* to be properly named by substantives. And this is equally true of the contents as we see them today in their full empirical character.

The text is silent on the relation between the formal factors in the two accounts, i.e. the Forms of fire etc. in the Receptacle-scenario, and the geometry presented next. One can speculate that the Forms stand to the geometrical constructions as the prescription of an objective to a determination of the most suitable means of realisation. The Forms would dictate the cosmological roles, properties, and relations of the four elements, and the geometrical passage shows the most rational way of realising these so far as geometrical structure allows.[54]

6.5 THE RECEPTACLE AS ANSWERING TO SOME GENERAL ONTOLOGICAL REQUIREMENT?

By its multiple imagery and shifting turns of phrase, the Receptacle-passage suggests an entity that is the ultimate subject in which physical things

---

[53] Thus Mohr, 2005, 111–17; Johansen, 2004, 126–7.
[54] Vlastos, 1969, 322–3, esp. n. 86, speaks of a 'purely contingent connection' between the two Forms, Fire and Tetrahedron; but he was writing before Kripke prised 'necessary' apart from '*a priori*'. Vlastos also remarks that once the existence of the elemental Forms has been proved, they are 'quietly ignored in the rest of the treatise where the workings of nature are explored'. This is as it should be according to Vlastos, since the only scenario in which he imagines those Forms *not* being 'ignored' is one in which they are misguidedly treated as (*per impossibile*) the bases of 'dialectical' (purely conceptual and *a priori*) deductions of elemental phenomena. This, however, is far from being the only story about how recognising those Forms can contribute to the cosmology; see sections 6.6.2 and 6.7.2 below.

inhere; the prime matter from which things are made; a medium into and out of which things appear and disappear and in which they move about; place; and space. But surely nothing can be all these; perhaps nothing can be any combination of these. *We* are in a position to voice such conceptual misgivings in the light of all the work, beginning with the early Academy and notably Aristotle, by which these notions were hammered into precise conceptual tools serving distinct (sometimes overlapping) philosophical and scientific purposes. Perhaps the Receptacle's greatest service to philosophy has been to launch the effort of disentangling those distinctions from each other, or of carving them out from the proto-concept that held them all suspended *in potentia*.[55]

But what concerns us here is a different question. Within the framework of the preoccupations and assumptions which Plato himself brought to composing the *Timaeus*, what determinate function can we assign to the Receptacle, even if in historical retrospect and in the light of problems formulated later we perceive this notion as in some ways highly indeterminate? In this and the next two sections I shall discuss two kinds of approach to this question, which I label 'ontological' and 'cosmological'. According to the ontological kind, the Receptacle is postulated to meet some difficulty or other that lies at the heart of Plato's general ontology of Forms and images (i.e. particulars that exist as likenesses of the corresponding Forms). An example of this ontology was brought to bear at the first beginning of the *Timaeus*. According to the other type of approach, the Receptacle fills a specifically cosmological need. In this and the next section I discuss the ontological approach, concluding that the evidence tells against it. Then in section 6.7 after discussing some examples of the cosmological approach I shall offer my own proposal, which falls into this class.

The ontological kind of interpretation starts from Plato's metaphysical dualism of Forms and images. This is clearly in some way crucial to the question of the Receptacle, because this duo, as the Receptacle-passage declares with repeated emphasis, is what has to be supplemented by a third kind of thing (48e2–49a4; 50c7–d2; 51e6–52b1; 52d3–4). Now, Plato, of course, had already forged the dualism in non-cosmological contexts such as the central books of the *Republic*. Hence if one sees this dualism as

---

[55] A number of contemporary interpreters see the Receptacle as above all a medium for its contents, and I too tend to accept this, although see the difficulties raised by Algra, 1995, 99 ff. Brisson, 1998a, 208–20, shows in detail how Plato's representations of the relationship fall into semantic 'spectra' such that transitions between (to us) signally different extremes can be effected by relatively unsurprising small steps. See Zeyl, 2010, for a detailed account of the Receptacle as a 'material medium or field' (124). See also Harte's 2010 study.

6.5 The Receptacle as answering to some general ontological requirement? 199

somehow *directly and of itself* motivating the Receptacle-postulate, then in effect one has identified the postulate as belonging first and foremost with the general Platonic ontology of Forms and images. One will take it that the problem to which the Receptacle is a solution, or the unfinished business which it carries to completion, is first to be found in that ontology: in other words, it does not arise from any specifically cosmological source. On this sort of view, although the Receptacle-idea appears only in the Timaean cosmology, its philosophical *raison d'être* lies outside that system. Logically speaking, its relation to the cosmology is like that of the Forms–sensibles contrast:[56] it is drawn upon for magnificent service to the cosmological enterprise, but does not originate in a demand peculiar to that context.

One prevailing version of this approach emphasises the ontological frailty of the images as such: they need something else in which to subsist, and this is the Receptacle.[57] According to another version (the difference may really be one of emphasis), there has to be something that metaphysically differentiates the Form from its image, the sensible particular, and the difference is that the latter but not the former is *in* something other than itself; now, this thing-in-which cannot be the Form (a sensible cannot be in a Form), hence it must be a third kind of thing.[58] In yet another variant of the same general approach, the Receptacle is introduced to solve an already existing

---

[56] See particularly the use of this at 27d5–29b2.
[57] Cornford, 1935, foreshadows this interpretation in his comment on 51e6–52d1: 'In this passage Plato comes nearer than anywhere else in the *Timaeus* to the problem of the *eidôlon*. He contributes towards the solution an important factor which did not come into view in the *Sophist*. Space, as eternally self-existent, provides the copy with a "room" or situation where it can cling to existence as *on pôs* and escape being nothing at all' (196). (The *Sophist* reference is to 240a7–c5, where the *eidôlon* is paradoxically displayed as not really being [sc. what it is of], although it is 'in a way' and really is an image.) For a fuller articulation, see Cherniss, 1962 (1944), 172–3: 'It is to save the possibility of sensible phenomena as such, the essential characteristic of which is instability and which, because they have no steadfast being of their own, must be imitations of the real ideas, that Plato assumes a receptacle, *chôra*; this receptacle is the field required by phenomena because they are merely "likenesses".' Cherniss again, 1945, 23: 'Plato himself explains [sic] that his theory of space as the participant or receptacle is a consequence of his doctrine that physical particulars, being constantly in process, are *imitations* of reality, for as such they imply not only real entities – that is, the ideas, *of* which they are images – but also a field or medium *in* which they can, as images, appear and disappear.' See also Cherniss, 1956. Lee, 1966, reads *Timaeus* 48e2–52d4 as 'one of Plato's major and most careful metaphysical pronouncements – a fundamental statement not only on the notoriously obscure Receptacle, but on his entire metaphysical theory of phenomenal being' (342–3; cf. 361). Mohr, 2005, 87 (cf. xxiv and 255), sees the Receptacle as resolving 'the problem, left over from the *Republic*, of how becoming holds a middle ground between being and non-being'. Algra too in his nuanced 1995 study is inclined to see Plato's 'overall perspective' in the Receptacle-passage as 'metaphysical rather than physical', and as offering a way of conceiving of *methexis* (76; 91; 95; 105–6; 118). Zeyl, 2009, § 6 *ad fin.*, is in the same vein. Waterlow (= Broadie), 1982, 349–50, also saw the problem as one of general ontology.
[58] See Patterson, 1985, 7 and 86 ff.; Brisson, 1998a, 177; 195–7; 202; 207; and 2006, 218; Sallis, 1999, 122–3.

ontological problem concerning the nature or possibility of participation (of sensible particulars in Forms).[59] These interpretations are united in assuming that the Receptacle is meant to solve a problem generated by Plato's pre-existing commitment to the general dualism of Forms and sensible images. They differ in their precise identification of the problem, some seeing it more in terms of the ontological status of the sensibles (given that they are not the primary realities), others in terms of the relationship of sensibles to Forms.[60, 61]

It is worth remarking that on any such interpretation the account at 52d4–53a7 of the Receptacle as implicated in the regional movements of the four materials has something of the appearance of being tacked on, since what it explains is a distinctly cosmological fact. However, it could be said that having fashioned the concept of the Receptacle for one sort of purpose Plato exploits the tool for a heterogeneous one in the spirit of economy.

Before turning to any positive evidence for the general type of interpretation just sketched, I shall look at some difficulties it faces.

---

[59] For Lee, 1966, *Timaeus* 48e2–52d4 establishes an 'ontology of the insubstantial image' that rescues Plato's metaphysics from the regress arguments of *Parmenides* 132a1-b2 and c12–133a7 (361–3). (With a number of scholars, I think that the regress arguments can be overcome without additional metaphysics, through more careful formulation of the doctrines targeted.) Sayre, 1983, 238–55; cf. 13–14, sees the Receptacle-passage as an ontological exploration (as distinct from a finished doctrine) in which Plato experiments with a figurative answer to 'the problem of participation' imported by his earlier ontology of sensibles as images of separate Forms. See also Sayre, 2003, 198. Fronterotta, 2001, 390–1, locates the problem for which the Receptacle is supposedly a solution in the separateness of the Forms (cf. *Parmenides* 130b1–3); according to Fronterotta, separateness at *Parmenides* 133b4–134e8 implies that sensibles and Forms can stand in no relation at all; hence participation is impossible (278–83). According to Kahn, 2007, 38, one of Plato's projects in the late dialogues was to reformulate his metaphysics so as to avoid the *Parmenides* objections to 'participation', and the solution is in the *Timaeus* if it is anywhere. Silverman's 2002 interpretation of the Receptacle is no less ontological – it sees the *Timaeus* as 'propounding a theory of particulars' (292), particulars as such being contrasted with Forms as such (15–22; 246–84) – but it is distinctive in discerning complementary Timaean accounts of particulars, one at the first beginning, the other involving the Receptacle and the geometrical particles (273–82). Silverman's interpretation is not liable to the two objections that follow in the main text.

[60] For a blast of cold air on this entire approach see Solmsen, 1942, 41: 'There is little to be gained by seeing, in this new concept of space, Plato's answer to criticisms levelled at his earlier theory (or theories) concerning the relation between the Forms and their counterparts in the visible world.' Solmsen goes on to say: 'The origin of the departure eludes us . . .'.

[61] At 50c6 Timaeus says that 'we shall return on another occasion' to the hard-to-articulate and wonderful way in which the copies in the Receptacle are 'imprints from' the Forms. No subsequent passage in the *Timaeus* clearly takes this up. Taylor, 1928, 324–5, thinks that the phrase may be a 'polite formula for the dismissal of a subject', but also suggests a possible reference to the unwritten doctrine of the One and the Dyad. Some (e.g. perhaps Gadamer, 1980, 173) see here a postponement or setting aside of the problem of participation itself. If that is correct, it seems unlikely that the Receptacle is put forward as the *solution* to that problem.

6.5 The Receptacle as answering to some general ontological requirement? 201

There are two major objections to any hypothesis that sees the Receptacle as rescuing or intended to rescue the general ontology of Forms and images from a metaphysical incoherence into which it otherwise falls. The first is that if such proposals are on target, the Receptacle ought to have been introduced at the first beginning of the cosmology.[62] Here, let us recall, Timaeus lays down a set of generalities: (G1) the distinction between the changeless being of what is intelligible and the becoming of what is perceived by sense; (G2) the principle that what is becoming must have had a cause, assumed to be a maker who makes in accordance with a paradigm; and (G3) the principle that something is made well only if its maker looks to a changeless paradigm. Timaeus then applies all this to the coming to be of this cosmos, and thereby establishes his methodology. Since (these next premisses are independently laid down) (C1) this cosmos is perceptible by sense, and since (C2) it is the most beautiful thing in the realm of becoming, it follows via G1–3 that (C3) this cosmos was made in accordance with a changeless paradigm. Consequently, (C4) this cosmos is a likeness or image of such a paradigm. C4 follows via a fourth generality (G4): a made thing is a likeness of its paradigm.[63] (G4 is either a natural assumption or is implicit in G2, in the idea of making-in-light-of-a-paradigm.) G3 and G4 yield a fifth generality (G5): any well-made sensible thing is a likeness or image of a changeless paradigm. Now if there is some sort of ontological difficulty about the viability of G5, the same difficulty infects C4. If (as is naturally assumed in the kind of interpretation we are considering) Plato had already perceived this supposed difficulty in G5 when he set about writing the *Timaeus*, and then saw that the solution is to posit a third kind of thing over and above the two kinds that figure in G5, a thing such as the Receptacle, he would have brought the third kind forward at the start of the cosmology. *At that point* he would have laid it down, still as a generality, that the making of at any rate a well-made thing (for these are the ones that must have changeless paradigms) depends on there being something of the third metaphysical kind. For otherwise, he would be letting the account of the genesis of the cosmos go forward on ontologically insecure foundations. Even if the solution, based on the third kind (or, indeed, the supposed problem along with its solution) only occurred to Plato when his work on

---

[62] E. N. Lee, a proponent of the ontological interpretation, sees this difficulty, and tries to meet it by stressing the need for 'structural completeness and balance' of the passage 48e2–52d4, which he regards as 'a coherent structural whole' that 'stands outside the coherent general pattern of the rest of the dialogue' (Lee, 1966, 348 n. 16 and 349).

[63] I have made the argument more succinct than Plato does: he adopts 'the maker of this cosmos was the best of causes' as a separate premiss, but it surely also follows from the premisses I have listed.

the cosmology was already under way, he would surely have gone back and revised the first beginning so as to include the third kind. Not only has Plato *not* done this, but he has specifically endorsed the adequacy of the first beginning for its own purposes. For he opens the Receptacle-passage with a declaration by Timaeus that the dual division of changeless, intelligible, paradigm and generated, sensible, copy (*mimêma*) was *sufficient* (*hikana*) for the first beginning (48e4–5).[64]

The second objection is that when the Receptacle finally *is* introduced, it is clearly introduced to explain the genesis of fire, water, earth, and air. *These* are what it is the Receptacle's function to receive; these are its proper contents. The Receptacle is not represented as needed to contain or uphold all physical things indiscriminately, including mortal animals, stars, the finished cosmos itself, and for that matter the cosmic soul and other souls (since these are images of parts of the paradigm). Yet this is what would have to be the case if the Receptacle were invoked to solve a perfectly general problem about Forms and images. It is true that such things as mortal animal-bodies and stars are in the Receptacle because they are in space or in a place, and the Receptacle some of the time is identified with space or place; but overwhelmingly the passage identifies it just in relation to fire, earth, air, and water.[65] It is also true that the Receptacle is called the omni-recipient and nurse of all becoming (49a5–8; 49e7; 50b6–8; c2; e5; 51a1–2; 7; 52b1; cf. 88d6), but these expressions may mean either that every fundamental empirical material is in it; or that everything corporeal is in it either directly as fundamental materials or indirectly as made out of them; or they may mean both these things. That being so, the expressions do not license the

---

[64] It is not hard to find expositions that group the third thing with the paraphernalia of the first beginning. Alcinous, who identifies the third thing with Matter, puts it at the head of the trio whose other members are the Forms and God (see Dillon, 1993, 8–10). Ps.-Timaeus Locrus starts off with Mind and then Matter, which in short order he identifies with the Receptacle and *chôra* (Marg, 1972, 93a–94b). Similarly, Brisson, 1998a, places his chapter on the Receptacle, which he identifies with the spatial medium, straight after chapters on the Demiurge and the world of the intelligible Forms, and before those on the cosmic soul and the cosmic body, contrary to the order of the *Timaeus* itself. (See e.g. 177 on the third thing's supposed role in the Demiurge's construction of the cosmos starting at 29a.) M. Miller, 2003, 22, has the same collocation. There is no reason to hold with Johansen, 2004, 195, n. 29, that *nomisantes ta duo hexein hikanôs* at 49a2 shows Timaeus now retracting the original assumption that the first two kinds would be enough. (a) This would contradict his statement at 48e4–5. (b) Johansen bases his view on the tense of *hexein*, which he thinks refers to the whole of the cosmology to follow. In fact it refers to the task defined by the first beginning, i.e. that of explaining the work of (specifically) demiurgic Intelligence.

[65] Thus D. Miller, 2003, 73. By contrast, Lee, 1966, 346–7, assumes that all Forms (or all cosmologically significant ones?) are copied in the Receptacle, the sense-perceptible elements being mentioned only as examples of such copies. At 5022–4 Timaeus says that the Receptacle has no characteristics of the four materials *or of anything made of them*; but this does not entail that the class of things whose Receptacle it is includes objects made from the basic materials.

6.5 The Receptacle as answering to some general ontological requirement? 203

indiscriminate metaphysical egalitarianism needed by the sort of proposal we are considering, according to which everything whatever that is an image of a Form needs, precisely because it is the image of a Form and for no other reason, to be in the Receptacle.[66]

Having looked at two difficulties facing standard versions of the ontological interpretation, I shall conclude this section by pointing to what seems to be an important piece of evidence in its favour. This is the passage 52a8–d3. Here Timaeus speaks of the 'third thing' as *chôra* (place or space). He switches into this mode of presenting it just as he is about to respond to the benighted assumption that 'everything that is real must be somewhere, in a place [*topô(i)*] and occupying a space [*chôran*]' (52b3–5). The response consists in the following declaration: the *perceptible* object (e.g. perceptible fire) must indeed be in something other than itself – it must be in the third thing, now called *chôra* – precisely because it is only an image of what is really real; by contrast (he implies) the really real is nowhere – not in any third thing – precisely *because* it is really real, i.e. because it is primary and not a derivative image.

So: Plato makes Timaeus say (P): the perceptible thing must exist in something else (or else not be at all) because it is only an image (52c2–5). And the ontological interpretation says: Plato postulates the third thing in order to make sense of the fact that the metaphysical image exists at all (which is the same as the fact that it exists only as image of or participant in the Form). Surely P is pretty decisive evidence for the ontological interpretation?

The answer is No, because Timaeus's statement P can be understood as making one or other of two alternative points: (A) '[First premiss] the perceptible thing is not a full reality, but a mere image of one. [Second premiss] the image of a full reality (like any image) must exist in something other than itself.[67] Therefore [postulate] there must be something else for the perceptible to exist in, and therefore [conclusion] the ontology must include the third thing.' That is how ontological interpreters read P: they take it to be both postulating the third thing and explaining the need for this postulate: it is needed because (as has already been agreed) the perceptible is

---

[66] If everything perceptible is in the Receptacle, then since Plato classifies the cosmos as perceptible (28b7–c2) he is committed to the conclusion that the cosmos is in space/place, and is somewhere. There would have to be very good evidence for saddling Plato with this. I imagine that if Aristotle had glimpsed any ground for reading the *Timaeus* as implying what for him would be such an absurdity, he would have been on to it like a shot.

[67] That the existence of an image, simply because it is an image, depends on its being in or on something in the way in which (or analogous to the way in which) a reflection is in or on a surface, is not in fact self-evident. But this is a question for another occasion.

a metaphysical image, and metaphysical images have to exist in something else. The alternative reading is as follows: (B) '[First premiss] the perceptible thing can exist only in something else (this is what the Receptacle-passage has been showing us for some time). [Second premiss] the sort of thing that cannot exist except in something else is only an image of a full reality, not a full reality itself. Therefore [conclusion] the perceptible thing is only an image of a full reality.' The reasoning moves in opposite ways on the two readings. In A it assumes the mere metaphysical-image status of the perceptible, and from this deduces the need for and therefore the existence of the third thing. In B it assumes the existence of the third thing as the *sine qua non* for the being of the perceptible, and from this deduces that the perceptible thing has metaphysical-image status. Since readings A and B go opposite ways, accepting one means rejecting the other. Reading A suits the ontological interpretation of the Receptacle or third thing. Therefore it would be a blow to the ontological interpretation if B turned out to be the more plausible reading. More on this in section 6.6.3 below.

6.6 THE DISCURSIVE PASSAGE, 51B6–52D4

It is time to look more closely at the part of the Receptacle-account, namely 51b6–52d4, that is most explicit and most doctrinal on the relations of Forms, their sensible images, and the Receptacle. Here, Timaeus speaks in a 'discursive' mode (51b6). What he says here has been the inspiration for the ontological kind of interpretation discussed in the last section.

I bring to the passage this question: does it aim to establish, whether by dint of argument or by dint of carefully crafted assertion, that the Receptacle is required in order to make possible the existence of sensible particulars, these being assumed to be mere images of Forms? Or does it aim to establish a different conclusion?

I shall discuss the discursive passage in two parts, I and II, placing the division at 51e6. But let me introduce it via a summary of the preceding context.

6.6.1 Leading up to the discursive passage

(a) Timaeus has argued that the inter-transformation of the four materials should lead us to see that they are all qualifications (*suches*), and hence that there must be something else, a *this*, in which they are (49b2–50a4). (We may hope that there is going to be a further argument for equating

6.6 The discursive passage, 51b6–52d4

this fundamental subject with a totally non-empirical principle, since the present argument falls short of that. Why should one not suppose that the four simply turn into each other: that the fundamental thing is not any or all of them individually, but them as mutually constituting and constituted by just such a cycle of metamorphosis? Or why, at this point, should one not suppose that the *this* is an underlying but nonetheless empirical material – empirical enough to be subject to the condensation and dissolution etc. repeatedly mentioned at 49b7–c5?[68] It would not be *outré* at this stage to call such a thing by the phrase already used at 49a5–6, 'the Receptacle and, as it were, nurse of all becoming'.)

(b) The point about the permanent *this* and the changing *suches* is then 'made clearer' by the moulded gold illustration of 50a5 ff., and next we are told that the *this* in question is 'the nature that receives *all* bodies' (50b6) and that it is there as 'the impressible' (*to ekmageion*) for *everything natural* (c2; cf. 51a4–5); so the possibility that it is some sort of empirical material has now been ruled out – although by no new argument. At this point the features that 'come into it and go out of it' are said to be 'imitations' (*mimêmata*) of, impressions taken from, the 'things that are'[69] (*tupôthenta ap'autôn*), (50c4–5; cf. 48e6; 51a1; b6). Here for the first time since the triple distinction at 48e5 ff. there is implied reference to Forms.

(c) Next, the triple division is repeated in abstract terms: 'that which comes to be, that in which it comes to be, and that from which it has its nature, being made in its semblance'; and these are immediately compared to offspring, mother, and father (50c7–d4). Now that we are presented with the Receptacle as one of a pair of co-operative and (for all we know) coeval parents, it is clear – given that the 'father' is the formal factor, known to be inaccessible by sense – that the 'mother' too must be totally non-empirical.

(d) The same theme continues at 50d5–51b6: nothing can display a whole variety (*poikilou idein pasas poikilias*, 50d5) of sensible appearances

---

[68] 'What [*ho*] we have named water becomes stones and earth (as we think) through solidification, and again by relaxing and dispersing into air this very same thing becomes air; and air by combustion becomes fire; and again fire by being pressed together and quenched returns to take on the character of air; and again air by coming together and being condensed becomes cloud and mist, and from these as they are packed together still more there comes to be liquid water, etc.' The relative pronoun *ho* (b7) could be taken to refer to an underlying empirical material which is what we call 'fire', with the same reference continued by *t'auton touto* (c1–2). This could be understood as setting the main theme of the passage, even though *aera* (c2), *pur* (c4), and *aera* (c4) then become referents in their own right.

[69] Or: 'of the things that always are'.

unless it is devoid of any such features itself – compare the odourless perfume base, the perfect homogeneity of well-prepared moulding-material. Hence empirical natureless-ness must be the nature of the Receptacle. It is no mistake to speak of it as having what intelligibility it has[70] only 'most puzzlingly', and as being extremely hard to grasp. (The most correct way to present its nature in positive terms is as: that whose enflamed part from one to another occasion shows up as fire, whose liquified part shows up as water, and so on for all the 'imitations' it receives.)

Notice that so far it has been laid down that there *must* be a non-empirical principle in which fire, water, etc. are, as *suches* to its *this*, and that fire, water, etc. are imitations of the beings that always are. But it has not been explained why fire, water, etc. must be in a non-empirical principle of the third kind, or why it is important that they are. Perhaps these questions will be answered in what comes next.

6.6.2 *The discursive passage, Part 1: 51b6–e6*

Now, at 51b6, Timaeus moves into a different phase.[71] He begins:

But let us, rather [*mallon*],[72] pursue our enquiry about them [sc. fire, water, etc., just mentioned at 51b4–6][73] in a discursive way [*logo(i)*, emphasised by its position and by *dê*], by determining the answer to this question: . . . [*toionde diorizomenous*]. (51b6–7)

What precedes has almost entirely relied on imagery: the nurse, the gold, the father, mother and offspring, the perfume- and moulding-bases, and of course the very image of receptacle itself. What ensues is, by contrast, 'discursive' because it will eschew imagery and will proceed by steps. For instance, as we shall see, Part 1 of the discursive passage starts by asking a

---

[70] *metalambanon tou noêtou* at 51a7–b1 is equivalent to *on noêton*.
[71] D. Miller, 2003, 116, claims that 51b6–52d1 is a digression, and acknowledged by Plato to be so. There is no such acknowledgement in the text, nor any other evidence that the passage is a digression. Timaeus's unwillingness at 51c7–d1 to add to the length of his current discourse a 'further length that would be to one side of the main purpose' (*parergon allo mêkos*) does not imply that the immediate context is a digression. The passage indeed constitutes a new phase, partly because it is discursive as I explain in the main text, and partly because it highlights the metaphysical and epistemological distinctions laid down in the *Republic* and invoked at the start of the cosmology. The familiarity of these contrasts with the unfamiliarity of the Receptacle.
[72] *mallon* could also be taken closely with *logo(i)*, to yield 'more discursively'.
[73] The translations of Bury, Waterfield, and Fronterotta do not make it clear that the reference is to the elements; those of H. D. P. Lee and Zeyl omit the reference altogether. Presumably this is in order to smooth a transition, for it could be argued that here Timaeus starts to talk about Forms in general, using fire as an example not of the elements as such but of a wider class of empirical objects.

6.6 The discursive passage, 51b6–52d4

question; then a criterion is set up for deciding the question; then the criterion is applied and the answer generated. And in Part II Timaeus executes a dialectical move: he summons up a contrary position – a received opinion – and exposes its error.

How does the whole discursive passage relate to what precedes it? It is surely meant to support the tenet presented through several of the images, i.e. that in the case of the four elements the three-fold distinction applies: intelligible Forms, sense-perceptible particulars, and something on which the perceptibles depend for their being.[74] We shall return to the three-fold distinction in 6.6.3. For the moment let us look at Timaeus's question:

> Does there exist a fire [*ti pur*] itself by itself, and <do there exist> all the things of which we speak in this way, time after time, as 'themselves by themselves' in each case? Or these things which we *see* [emphatic *kai*, 51c1], and everything else that we perceive through the body – do they alone exist, their reality being like this [*toiautên echonta alêtheian*]?[75] Is it that there do not exist – not at all, and not in any way – other things besides these ones [*para tauta*]? Are we, instead, talking idly each time whenever we speak of the intelligible Form of a given thing, and all along this has been nothing but words? (51b7–c5)

Timaeus then says that on the one hand this metaphysical (as we would call it) question deserves more than sheer insistence by him that the answer is thus and so: i.e. it deserves to be brought to trial and adjudicated (*oute . . . to paron akriton kai adikaston aphenta axion* etc., 51c5–6). On the other hand, he says, it would be out of place to add a long digression to an already long discourse. So this is just the moment to introduce a major but briefly statable criterion (*horos*) for deciding – and he has one: it is epistemic:

---

[74] Stating this tenet leaves open the crucial question: which part of it is the point at issue? (Cf. section 6.5 *ad fin.* on readings A and B.) It is indisputable that perceptible fire, etc. exist, i.e. that there is something in the second category. So the question is: does Timaeus link the three categories together in order to maintain (A): 'Given that we accept that perceptible fire is an image of something in the metaphysically prior first category, we cannot avoid postulating a third thing on which too, but in a different way, perceptible fire metaphysically depends'? Or is he maintaining (B): 'Given that we accept that perceptible fire is metaphysically dependent on the third thing, we cannot avoid postulating something in the first category of which perceptible fire is an image'? A is the backbone of what I have called the 'ontological' approach to the Receptacle. Taylor, 1928, 333 ff., endorses B, apparently without even noticing that A is an option. Read carefully, the discursive passage supports B, as I shall argue in section 6.6.3.

[75] I follow Taylor, 1928, in punctuating with a comma after *estin*, and understanding *toiautên alêtheian* as equivalent to 'perceptible reality (or: truth)'. Alternatively, follow Burnet in omitting the comma, and with Stallbaum, Martin, and Archer-Hind understand *toiautên alêtheian* as meaning that perceptible fire etc. have the reality of the *auta kath' hauta*, i.e. they are the metaphysically ultimate fire etc. See Taylor, 1928, 335 ff.

So this is the way in which [*hôde*] I cast *my* vote: if intelligence [*nous*] and true opinion are two kinds,[76] then, without any question, there exist by themselves these <Forms> which we cannot perceive but can only grasp by intellect [*nooumena monon*]; but if, as some people believe, true opinion is in no way different from intelligence, then all the things we perceive through the body must be regarded as ultimate constants [*bebaiotata*]. (51d3–7)

'My vote', of course, continues the forensic imagery of trial and adjudication at 51c5–6. Notice that what Timaeus has just said is that he will cast his vote *in accordance with* the criterion; i.e. he is not here voting, or saying that he votes, *for* the criterion![77] (His actual vote is not cast until 51d2.)

Next, Timaeus states his answer to the epistemic question, giving reasons:

Now, *two* is the number to give them [sc. intelligence and true opinion], because they come into being separately, and are dissimilar in nature. (i) The one is engendered in us through teaching, the other by persuasion. (ii) The one is always accompanied by a true account, while the other lacks an account. And (iii) the one cannot be moved by persuasion, while the other can be persuasively overturned. And (iv) the one, it must be said, is something in which every man [*andra*] partakes, whereas intelligence belongs to the gods and to a small class of human beings. (51e1–6)

The initial question is whether there are Forms of Fire, etc., besides the sensibles (cf. *peri autôn*, 51b7). This is determined by deciding whether intelligence and true opinion are two kinds. If and only if the answer to this is 'Yes', the answer to the initial question is 'Yes'. And Timaeus gives four stock arguments proving 'Yes' to the second question. Notice that so far there has been no trace of concern about strengthening grounds for postulating the Receptacle, or explaining why it must be part of the picture. No doubt this is because people had already heard Plato and his circle talking about *X* by itself and *Y* by itself, and some had dismissed this as empty chatter, whereas no one had heard about the Receptacle before, so no one

---

[76] We might think it obvious that they are two kinds in that the objects of *nous* are intelligibles, whereas the objects of even true opinion are presumably sense-perceptibles (28a2–3; c1; 51c2; d7; 52a7); thus we may think that Timaeus ought to be asking whether *nous* has its own proper objects in the case of fire, etc. However, the term *nous* is primarily an accolade (as distinct from the name of a distinct cognitive faculty), meaning the most excellent form of cognition. If there are no Forms of fire and the others, then true opinion (sc. based on sense-perception) is *nous* in relation to fire etc.

[77] But the latter is what is conveyed by the translations of Bury ('This, then, is the view for which I, for my part, cast my vote') and Cornford ('My own verdict, then, is this'). Taylor, 1928, *ad* 51c5-d3 and 51d3–7 (337–8) has the correct interpretation: Timaeus sets about answering the main question by reducing it to another question. Taylor cites *Meno* 86e1 ff. as a parallel.

could have questioned *it*. Before saying more about the Receptacle, however, let us look at the way in which Timaeus reaches the present point.

He seems to argue that if, in general, intelligence about X is different from true opinion about X then there is the corresponding metaphysical distinction between, on the one hand, the Form of X, always existing itself by itself, the true reality of everything called 'X', and, on the other hand, the sensible X whose reality is the Form. But how can the general principle show that the metaphysical distinction holds for the particular case of fire and the other three elements? Either the general principle is already assumed to cover this case, or it is not. If it is, then Timaeus in effect is taking it for granted that there are Forms for fire, etc.;[78] but in that case why does he need a criterion for answering his own question? Why does he even raise the question? If, on the other hand, he is using the premiss that the principle holds in a lot of cases as a ground for extending it to the case that concerns him, what justifies this extrapolation?

Let us approach this question by considering why a very early Platonist would postulate the Form of this or the Form of that. Let us think about this with the epistemic criterion in mind. Minimally, the reason for postulating a given Form is surely this: with very many topics it is easy to tell that there is much more to know and understand about them than could be gained simply by attending to sensible instances. For example, this might be clear from debates that have already gone on in the culture, as in the case of ethical values and the nature of the good. Or it might be clear from contradictions that seem to arise from the very terms themselves: the large is also small, the like is also unlike, etc. This is just the kind of situation that assures the Platonist that there is more to the term (or what it stands for) than meets the eye of superficial opinion, let alone the sensory eye. Compare *Republic* VII 523a1–524d5 on the difference between unsurprising, logically obedient, terms like 'finger', and terms like 'large' and 'small' that awaken intellectual activity by 'summoning' the soul, spurring it into enquiry through bafflement at the simultaneously contrary deliverances of sense-experience.[79] In other words, some topics or terms naturally catapult

---

[78] Cf. *Parmenides* 130c2–4, where it is an open question for the youthful Socrates whether there are separate Forms of fire and water.

[79] 'Vision, however, saw large and small not as separate but as mixed up together, didn't it? – Yes. – And in order to get clarity about this, understanding [*noêsis*] was forced to see the large and small [i.e. to take them as its objects] not as mixed up together but as distinguished – the opposite way from <that of> vision? – True. – Then it's from this source, isn't it, that it first occurs to us to ask "What is the large, and, again, <what is> the small?" – It most certainly is. – And that is how we came to call one of them [i.e. one object termed 'large'] intelligible and the other visible. – Exactly right, he said' (524c3–d1).

us into intellectual enquiry under the aegis of a 'What is X?' question; and to move forward on a path marked out by that question simply is, for an early Platonist, to postulate that there is an intelligible Form of X.[80] That being so, it is a real question what could jolt us into a similar enquiry about fire, etc. The non-philosophical culture possesses no reservoir of conflicting views about those things. Everyone agrees that fire is hot, that it melts some things and consumes others, and so on. And for the most part we can simply decide by using our senses whether some given thing is a fire or a pool of water or a heap of earth. (In fact it would be extraordinary even to ask this question about something near enough to perceive clearly; cf. *Republic* VII 523b5–7; c1–4; 8.)

So there is no easy-to-hand exoteric controversy or obvious paradox to get anyone started along an intellectual track marked out by 'What is fire?' – i.e. in early Platonist terms to get one postulating a Form of fire. (To the extent that fire is easy to pick out by sense-perception, it is *already* fire 'itself by itself', not mixed up with some opposite.) The intellectual impulse has to come from a more esoteric source. For instance: if you are already wedded to intellectual enquiry in general – no longer needing to be jolted into it by bafflement at some clash of opinion or sense-based appearance – and if, in addition, you are convinced that the universe is such that it makes sense for enquirers about it to be always trying to push forward the frontiers of physical theory, then why not simply try your hand at theorising about the hidden essential natures of fire, water, etc., by having a go at working out an account such as Plato's geometrical account? To the extent that you make some progress on this, to that extent you have some reason to postulate an intelligible fire itself by itself, etc.[81]

My purpose in discussing how a Platonic enquiry into the intelligible nature of fire, etc. might get off the ground is to bring home the following point: whether such an enquiry can make good progress, i.e. whether postulating the corresponding Forms will turn out to have been justified, cannot be decided by *a priori* appeal to a general distinction (based on other cases) between intelligibles and sense-perceptibles, or between the corresponding modes of cognition. The question can only be decided by

---

[80] I am of course not suggesting that the early Platonist reduces the Form to an aspect of human rational enquiry, e.g. equating it with the intentional object of enquiry.

[81] It is true that to get such an enquiry started, the Platonic scientist must ask 'What is Fire itself by itself?', thus already postulating – perhaps simply in the general spirit of scientific enterprise – an intelligible Form for fire. But managing to move forward in a rational way from and guided by that question is what shows whether it was a good question in this specific case, i.e. whether the initial postulate was fortunate, so that we have reason to keep it alive in seeking further results.

6.6 The discursive passage, 51b6–52d4

attempting the specific enquiry itself.[82] That is why there is no logical bridge allowing Timaeus to pass from the general distinction to an affirmative answer to his question 'Is there a fire itself by itself?'

The absence of any such logical bridge together with the reason for its absence leads me to think that Timaeus's epistemically based response to his question 'Is there a Form of fire?' is not really intended as an *argument* for the answer he desires. I am inclined instead to think that the passage 51c5–e6 adds up to a stately announcement that *it will be shown by concrete example* that we can successfully theorise about non-sensible properties of fire, etc., and therefore do have reason to postulate corresponding Forms (and reason, too, to continue in the general faith that for every kind of natural object there is a Form beyond what appears to sense-perception, and that every kind of object is accessible to intellectual understanding, not only to sense).[83]

But why should one think that the passage, in fact, does no more than promise a soon to be provided concrete example of exact theorising about the four elements? Here is why. The metaphysical question (1) whether there exists a Form of X is so closely bound up with the epistemic question (2) whether it makes sense and is possible to carry out intellectual enquiry about X, that it is a puzzle how Timaeus's answer to question 2 can be a *way to* answering question 1, as if answering 2 were somehow easier than immediately trying to answer 1. When the questions are so tightly linked, how can it make sense to think that we can first get a handle on the epistemic question, and then, *by that means*, deal with the metaphysical one? Don't the two questions stand and fall together methodologically? Well, perhaps they do if we take them at face value, i.e. as requesting propositional answers and instructing us here and now to determine which proposition in each pair of possible answers is the true one. But there is a clear temporal priority if we think of the epistemic question as pointing towards the taking of *action*: the action in this case would be the intellectual one of human beings actually setting themselves to theorise about fire and the others, and seeing how this goes. As I said, to the extent

---

[82] *hekastote* and *hekastou* at 51c4–5 suggest that Forms were postulated on a piecemeal basis, i.e. enquiry by enquiry, and *aei* at b8 may make the same point. See also Frede, 1996.

[83] I have assumed that on the surface the text presents an argument: 'Since in general there is intelligence about a topic over and above mere sense-based true opinion of the objects, this holds in the case of fire, etc.' But it is possible that even on the surface what is intended is not an argument but an asseveration: 'As sure as I am that this is true in cases where we all already agree that it is true, so sure am I that it is true of fire etc.' We need not understand this as basing the second of the certainties on the first; it can be a mere comparison. The main point still holds, i.e. that justification of the second certainty depends on the success of a theoretical investigation of fire, etc.

that such an activity does progress, to that extent we find we have a grip on, hence some assurance of the existence of, Forms of fire and the others. One cannot discover that metaphysical fact unless the epistemic *action* is *first* attempted. I am not suggesting that Timaeus's epistemic question is a disguised imperative – a rally to epistemic action. Perhaps it is more like a disguised authorial declaration that Timaeus is going to undertake such action and will be successful. After all, Plato has the geometrical account of the elements up his sleeve.

Let us move on, noting three things. (a) Up to this point (51e6) the discursive passage has been concerned just with the metaphysical difference between intelligible Form and sensible particular, and with the corresponding epistemic difference. Nothing has yet been said in it about any third thing. (b) Timaeus has been operating as if the business of establishing the metaphysical difference for fire consists in establishing that there *is* an intelligible Form over and above sense-perceptible fire (i.e. the existence of the latter is taken for granted). Correspondingly, on the epistemic side he has been operating as if the task is to establish that even in the case of fire, etc. sense-perception is *not* our best, most effective, most probing mode of cognition. Now notice (c) the absence so far of the slightest breath of any puzzlement that goes in the converse direction, i.e. puzzling that goes: given that there are eternal, incorporeal, intelligibles, *how can there be, besides*, sensible, perishable, images of them? Given that there are intelligibles, how can there be (related to them) the kind of objects that sensory cognition would be cognition of?

6.6.3 *The discursive passage, Part II: 51e6–52d4*

Timaeus now passes from the difference between the intelligible and the sense-perceptible, to an expanded enumeration[84] in which these two are joined by a third thing, now called *chôra* but previously spoken of as the Receptacle. The third thing's return to the spotlight at this point indicates that Plato regards it as somehow bound up with the reasonableness of maintaining the duality of the first two kinds. The third thing somehow secures that duality. As we have already seen, the explanation for this could come from either of two directions. The thought could be (A) that although it is now completely established that there is the Form as well as its perceptible image, we do not yet understand *how* there can be the image as well as the Form. In this scenario the third thing is invoked in order to

---

[84] Compare 51e1 '*Two* is the number to give them', with the triple enumeration at 52a1–b2.

shed light on that. Alternatively, the thought could be (B) that the case is not yet completely established that there *is* a Form of which the perceptible is image: in which case the third thing is pointed out as providing an additional ground for that. Notice that on B, the problematic would be exactly the same as it has been right up to the triple enumeration. Since 51b7 the question has been: '*Are* there intelligible Forms of fire, etc., or are there only the sense-perceptibles?', and according to B the third item in the triple enumeration helps consolidate the desired affirmative answer. On A, the triple enumeration takes off from a *new* problem: 'Given that there *is* the image as well as the Form, how is that actually possible?'

It may seem that there is no evidence for preferring one alternative over the other, or none that has come to light so far. But I think that we already have some evidence (E1), albeit from silence, against A and therefore in favour of B. It is that Timaeus does not wind up the passage immediately preceding the triple enumeration by stating that now we have achieved the result that the Form exists over and above the sense-perceptible; and he does not say: 'However, a further question now emerges: what else does there have to be, for that duality to be possible?' Instead, he says 'Given these findings . . .' (51e6), and then he simply follows on with the triple enumeration.[85] If interpretation A is right, one would expect him to have said: 'Given these findings, we must further consider whether something else is needed beyond the two.' So: if interpretation A is right, Plato has not properly articulated all the stages of this self-consciously 'discursive' stretch of discourse. In particular, he has not signalled the turn to a further (although obviously closely related) question, and he has not explicitly asked that further question – even though it would have cost nothing to make such clarifications had they been in order.

Let us turn to the triple enumeration itself:

Given these findings, it must be agreed that there are: *one* thing, that which keeps its form unchangingly, is ingenerable and imperishable, neither receives into itself anything else from elsewhere nor itself enters into anything else anywhere, but is invisible and in other ways sensually inaccessible, being that which intellection [*noêsis*] has for apportioned object; whereas *second* is that which has the same name as the first and is similar – sense-perceptible, generable, always borne along, both

---

[85] That he does this is hard to see in Cornford's version, where more than two pages of commentary separate the translation up to *brachu ti* at 51e6 from the resumption at *toutôn houtôs echontôn* on the same line (Cornford, 1935, 189–92). Zeyl, 2000, lxv, seems to accept interpretation A when he writes 'Having established to his satisfaction that Forms do exist, Timaeus turns next to discussing the epistemic status of each of the items in his now tripartite ontology.'

coming to be in a sort of place[86] [*en tini topô(i)*] and again perishing from out of it, the object of opinion with sense-perception; and a *third* kind too, that of space [*chôra*], a kind that always is, admits of no destruction while providing a seat for all that comes to be, is itself non-sensually encountered by a bastard sort of reasoning,[87] and is almost beyond credibility. (51e6–52b2)

Timaeus now points out and explains a fundamental human error. Referring to the third thing, he continues:

It is with reference to this that we, dreaming, say that everything real must be somewhere [*pou*], in some place [*en tini topô(i)*], and occupying some space [*katechon chôran tina*], and that what is neither on earth nor anywhere [*pou*] in the heavens is nothing.[88] Take all these and other kindred points concerning the waking[89] and truly existing nature [*alêthôs phusin huparchousan*]: we are disabled by this dreaming from breaking out of sleep and bringing them into definition[90] in a statement of the truth, which is this: to an *image* – since the very principle on which it has come to be[91] is not in its own possession, and it is an ever-moving appearance *of* something other – it belongs to be *in* something other, thereby clinging to reality [*ousias*] as best it can on pain of not being at all; whereas that which is really real has for its defender [*boêthos*][92] the true, because exact, statement that as long as

---

[86] Or: 'in some place'.
[87] 'Bastard' perhaps because the third thing is grasped in a functional way ('that in which'), and largely through imagery and negations. Cf. Algra, 1995, 79–81. 'Legitimate' or paradigmatic philosophical intellect focuses on 'What is X?' where X is some subject, e.g. justice, that has already come up for attention in an informal way and pre-theoretically. By contrast, we grasp the Receptacle only as a (supposed) theoretical necessity. Still, the legitimate child and the bastard are close blood-relatives.
[88] Rivaud, 1925, 66 and translation *ad loc.*, takes this sentence to mean that in affirming that everything must be somewhere, we apprehend *chôra* in a dreamlike way. He takes 'the waking and truly existing nature' to refer to the nature of *chôra* as it is in itself, which we cannot grasp properly. Algra, 1995, 107, has a similar suggestion; also Sallis, 1999, 121; 153–4. Apparently, this interpretation goes back to Martin, 1841; see Taylor, 1928, 346. Following Archer-Hind, 1888, 185, and Taylor *ibid.*, I take it that (a) 'Everything is somewhere' is what we dreamingly affirm, referring to *chôra* by 'somewhere', whereas (b) 'the waking and truly existing nature' denotes the Forms. (But by a slip of the pen Taylor has written 'Forms' instead of 'ultimate realities' *vel sim.*)
[89] That is, it is not a mere appearance in sleep.
[90] *diorizomenoi*; 'definition' as in 'high-definition', 'low-definition'.
[91] Here, following Cornford's understanding of the passage (1935, 370–1), I also borrow his translation. For minute discussion of *oud'auto touto eph' hô(i) gegone heautês*, see Cherniss, 1956.
[92] 'Defender' continues the forensic imagery (cf. Taylor, 1928, 349). See also the punning *ousias* . . . *antechomenên* at 52c4–5, which, in line with Bury and Cornford, I have translated 'clinging to reality'; but the phrase also means 'laying claim to reality' in a sense that implies disputing another's claim to it; see Taylor, 348–9 and LSJ s.v. *antechô* III. 4. For good measure, *ousia* also means an estate, e.g. a farm, from which one gets one's living – just the kind of thing subject to ownership disputes. Since the object claimed in such a dispute and the person from whom one claims it are both in the genitive, *ousias* can be taken twice over so that the image puts in a claim *for* being true reality *against* the reality that is the genuine title-holder. On this line of metaphor, the image is nothing other than a sort of reified claim to be the original thing (i.e. the sense-perceptible is a reified claim to be object of truest cognition). That its existence is supported by the thing *in which* it is, both gives the claim its appearance of truth and proves it false.

6.6 The discursive passage, 51b6–52d4

something is one thing and something else is another, neither will ever come to be in the other and so become at once one identical thing and two.[93] (52b3–d1)

Timaeus has just explained why people benightedly assume that everything real must be somewhere.[94] This is as much as to assume that there is no reality apart from sense-perceptible things, and that talk of the *X* itself by itself is futile chatter (cf. 51b7–c5). Here we have a second piece of evidence (E2) in favour of alternative B distinguished above. (On this alternative, when Timaeus moves to the triple enumeration he has not yet completed the case for holding that there *are* intelligible Forms of fire, etc. over and above the sense-perceptibles; he completes it by invoking the third thing.) Explaining why a widely held view is mistaken is a time-honoured way of bolstering one's claim that it *is* mistaken. Thus there is reason to think that Timaeus is still working to uphold the position that there *is* a fire itself by itself.

Let us look at Timaeus's explanation of the error. It is an ingenious piece of table-turning.[95] It says in effect: the objects of sense, which seem such natural paradigms of 'that-which-really-is', are not only not the only things that are, they are also not principles of being for anything of a different kind from themselves; for they are not fundamental and self-subsistent: on the contrary, they are ontologically frail dependants on the third thing. When we take seriously their appearance of metaphysical power and solidity – and so deny reality to anything of a totally different order from them – we are dreaming: for the appearance derives precisely from the fact that they are in and upheld by something wholly other than themselves. By contrast, the

---

[93] I take this to mean: 'The criterion that saves that-which-really-is [sc. from being misidentified] is this: let "*Y*" stand for that-which-really-is; then, for any *Z* such that *Y* ≠ *Z*, *Y* cannot come to be in *Z* nor *Z* in *Y* so that one and the same thing becomes two.' Plato probably assumes (a) that no intelligible can 'come to be' in anything, not even another intelligible; and (b) that there are two ways (which for the present purpose he need hardly distinguish) for *A* to come to be in *B*: either *A* comes to inhere in *B* as in a subject, or it comes to be in *B* as in a place. If *A* comes to be in *B* as subject or place of *A*, we have something that is *B* and *A* (i.e. we have *B* qualified by *A* or characterised by its presence), so one thing has come to be two, and two one.
[94] This *endoxon* was developed into a paradox by Zeno of Elea, A24. It is an important target in Aristotle's discussion of place; see *Physics* IV, 208a29–31; 209a24–5; 210b21 ff.; 212b28–9. A contraposed form occurs in Gorgias B3 (see Sextus Empiricus, *Against the Mathematicians* 7.70). See Algra, 1995, 50–1, n. 61. For close discussion of the puzzle in Aristotle, see Morison, 2002, ch. 3.
[95] But the turn will not convince materialists or empiricists or, for that matter, mere commonsensical dreamers, that they are wrong to accept the *endoxon*. Since the rebuttal takes for granted the third thing, which is necessarily nowhere, such people can simply shrug it off as question-begging. Perhaps the rebuttal is meant just for Platonists or would-be Platonists, giving them an in-house reason to be unmoved (a) by the fact that so many people see *them* as postulating imaginary objects, and (b) by any tendency in themselves to find it viscerally incredible that sense-perceptible objects are not as real as real can be.

nowhere-ness of the Platonic intelligibles now shows up as confirming their self-subsistence and hence their greater reality than that of the sense-perceptibles. The 'dreaming' assignation of reality and unreality gets things exactly the wrong way round.

Notice that this involves no argument or explanation showing that we need to postulate that there *is* that third thing. On the contrary, the dialectic starts from the assumption that this is so. That it is so has already been rammed home in advance of the discursive passage. The only reason, such as it was, for positing the Receptacle was given in the initial *this-such* passage. From then on it was unquestioningly repeated that there is something utterly non-empirical which fire etc. are necessarily *in*. Timaeus now puts this position to use in defending yet again the tenet defended in 51b6–e6, namely: the four elements as we perceive them are not the whole story about the four elements: there are also, and more fundamentally, intelligible Forms of which those are only copies.

We are almost at the end of the discursive passage. Let us see how Timaeus rounds it off:

Let this, then, in summary form, be the reckoned reckoning [*logistheis . . . logos*] evinced by *my* vote: <it is that> there are being and space and becoming, three things by triple division, even before the heaven came to be. (52d2–4)

Here we have a further piece of evidence (E3) for the hypothesis that Part II of the discursive passage continues the trajectory of Part I, i.e. it aims to establish that there are intelligible Forms of fire, etc. over and above the sensory phenomena. Only now at the end does Timaeus cast his vote. When he mentioned his vote before, it was to explain the criterion he would follow in casting it (51d3–7). But the issue to be decided by that criterion was whether there are Forms for fire, etc., or whether the story ends with the sense-perceptible elements. So *this* is the issue on which Timaeus finally votes.

His criterion for voting was to consist in his answer to the epistemic question 'Are intelligence and true opinion two kinds?' He determines his answer to *this* question, and then on that basis[96] moves into Part II of the discursive passage. He takes the triple roll call, starting with intelligible being – perhaps because it is the most honourable of the three, but also perhaps because it is the reality of this more than anything else that he wants to proclaim. But why didn't Timaeus cast his vote sooner? Why didn't he declare immediately on completing his answer to the criterial epistemic

---

[96] 'Given these findings', 51e6.

6.6 The discursive passage, 51b6–52d4

question (i.e. at 51e6): 'Now I cast my vote in favour of the reality of fire itself by itself, etc.'? Surely because something still remained to be added to the case for this verdict. We do not vote until the whole case has been laid out. The addition, which essentially involves the third thing, is the error-explanation, E2 above.

If we read Part II as continuing on the same trajectory as Part I, we must understand the concern in Part II as focusing on, and even perhaps as restricted to, the question whether there are intelligibles corresponding to the four elements specifically. For the starting point of Part I is: 'Is there a fire itself by itself?' (51b7–8). I say this now notwithstanding the generality of the Part II presentation, a matter to be addressed in the next sub-section. Meanwhile, let me state the conclusion reached in the present sub-section so far. It is that internal evidence shows that the purpose of the discursive passage as a whole is to establish the reality of intelligibles (or of intelligibles corresponding to a certain subject-matter), and to do so by demoting sense-perceptibles to the status of metaphysical images. (Thus the direction of thrust is the same as in the Cave parable in the *Republic*: do not be fooled into believing that the shadows in the Cave and the man-made statuettes etc. that cast them are the ultimate realities.) In Part I the case is argued by applying the epistemic criterion, and there is no mention of the third thing. The epistemic criterion and the corresponding metaphysical dualism have of course long been familiar to Plato's audience. Then in Part II the case continues to be argued by reference to something quite unfamiliar and strange: the third thing which was introduced only a few pages back. The basis for the case is now the existential frailty of the sense-perceptible. The latter can exist only in something utterly unlike itself; but such incapacity for self-subsistence is just what we should expect of something whose characteristic nature has its source beyond itself. In short: the incapacity for self-subsistence is a sign or manifestation of the fact that e.g. sense-perceptible fire exists only as an image of something else. It follows that there is a real intelligible being of which the sense-perceptible item is the image.[97] That, I think, is what the whole passage means to establish.

Notice that on this interpretation it is assumed or presupposed as a premiss that the sense-perceptible is existentially dependent on the third thing. In my view, this is because the point is supposed to have been secured

---

[97] A more spelled-out version of the reasoning might go as follows: the sense-perceptibles can *exist* only in something other than themselves. So from what does each get its *specific character*? Not from the that-in-which, since this is devoid of specific distinctions; hence from a source distinguished by the *corresponding* intelligible character; hence the sense-perceptibles are images of those sources.

already, in the preceding Receptacle-scenario. By contrast, according to what I have called the ontological interpretation of the Receptacle or third thing, we start from the assumptions (i) that the sense-perceptible is image of an intelligible, and (ii) that its image-status requires the picture to be completed by postulating a third thing to give it such existence as it has. We now have a proof that there must be this third thing and, at last, an explanation of why this puzzling entity has been introduced at all. Now, without question it would be good to have it explained why the third thing is in the picture; but the explanation just outlined is not supported by the evidence. On the contrary, the evidence supports the view that the proposition 'The sense-perceptible is merely an image of an intelligible' is the conclusion sought, rather than an assumption from which some other conclusion is sought.[98]

Let me quote again from Plato's declaration of that truth which we shall not see until we wake up from our dream:

> Take all these and other kindred points concerning the waking and truly existing nature: we are disabled by this dreaming from breaking out of sleep and bringing them into definition in a statement of the truth, which is this: to an image – since the very principle on which it has come to be is not in its own possession, and it is an ever-moving appearance *of* something other – it belongs to be *in* something other, thereby clinging to reality as best it can on pain of not being at all. (52b6–c5)

It is undeniable that these wonderful phrases, taken by themselves, seem perfectly suited to carry the solution to an ontological problematic that *starts* from the position that intelligibles are true realities, and then puzzles over how sensibles, being only their images, can manage to exist at all, and over how this imaging-relation is metaphysically possible. Not a word of the statement has to be changed for it to start to shoulder this completely different argumentative burden. In this new structure of argument one assumes intelligible Forms, and one assumes that sense-perceptibles – by contrast with or in relation to intelligibles – are metaphysically problematic. They are supposed to be images of intelligibles, but it is difficult to see how they can be. One then invokes the Receptacle as that on which they depend for their existence, and now it is clear that and how these images, the sense-

---

[98] Scholars who see Part II of the discursive passage as supporting the ontological interpretation of the Receptacle are partly driven, I believe, by a sense that the text up to that point contains no satisfactory explanation for the Receptacle-postulate. That is, they do not see it as properly explained by the initial *this-such* argument. I share this part of their view. The *this-such* argument is a way of introducing the postulate, but not of convincingly justifying it. A sceptic about the postulate would have no difficulty in rejecting the *this-such* argument as pseudo-logic. I also share the assumption that the postulate does demand explanation; for a different way of meeting this demand, see section 6.7.2 below.

perceptibles, manage to have being. (The Receptacle enables the images to overcome their wretched existential predicament.) If we were justified in attributing this reasoning to Plato, we should certainly have in it an explanation of why he postulates the Receptacle. I have argued, however, that our passage's actual problematic moves in the opposite direction. Here one starts by assuming the Receptacle and the dependence on it of the sense-perceptibles; one explains this dependence as proving the latter to be mere images of something else; and from this one secures the conclusion – not nailed down previously, or not completely – that there exist corresponding originals, the Forms. (The Receptacle proves that the sensible materials *are* existentially 'wretched', and thereby relieves the Platonic cosmologist of a major anxiety: on which see section 6.7.2.)

6.6.4 Questions arising

(1) My first question arises from the main conclusions reached in 6.6.3: that the discursive passage as a whole aims to establish that sense-perceptibles (or a certain class of sense-perceptibles) are images of intelligibles, and that in Part II their dependence on the third thing is made a basis for that thesis. So has this all along been Plato's reason for introducing the Receptacle, i.e. to help make the case that the sense-perceptibles in question are images of intelligibles? I certainly hold that this has been *a* reason, but there may also be another. One important attribute of the Receptacle has not come into view at all in the discussion so far, namely its kinetic function *vis-à-vis* the four elements. Timaeus turns to this subject immediately after the discursive passage (52d4–53a7). If, as one might suppose, this is a new and independent function, then the point of the Receptacle goes beyond anything explained so far. I shall return to the kinetic function in section 6.7.2. Meanwhile, our discussion so far raises several other questions.

(2) What are we to make of the fact that Plato speaks of the third thing as *chôra*, and what of the fact that he does so only in Part II of the discursive passage (52a8; b4–5; d3; and by implication at a6)? Representing the third thing as place, or space, or that in virtue of which every sense-perceptible thing is somewhere, is not incompatible with its earlier representation as that-in-which and the Receptacle. But why was it not explicitly called *chôra* sooner, if – as some interpreters seem to assume – its being *chôra* is what matters most about it?[99] Does the idea of *chôra* enter the picture at a

---

[99] I mean: if its being *chôra* is what matters most to Plato composing the *Timaeus*. From the point of view of those (including Aristotle himself) who treat this part of the *Timaeus* as background for

fundamental level, i.e. because Plato, through having a degree of independent interest in whatever it is in virtue of which things are or are able to be *somewhere*, is moved to include it in the ontology of the second beginning? If so, then in effect he says: 'We are to understand *chôra*, or that whereby things are somewhere or in a place, as the third thing in relation to the Forms and the particulars, standing to the latter as co-parent with the former, etc.' On this reading, the purpose of the 'more ample' ontology announced at the second beginning (48e2–49a4) is (*inter alia*) to assign a theoretical position to *chôra* as such. But it is inexplicable in that case why *chôra* is not mentioned as such for *a hundred and ten lines* after the second beginning, at 52a8.[100]

Hence I conclude that Plato's reason for eventually presenting the third thing under the heading of *chôra*, is not that he is theorising (however briefly) about *chôra* as such or as a topic in its own right. The real purpose is to present the third thing – which right from the second beginning has been established through various images and analogies as a metaphysical *sine qua non* of the sensible objects – as that which we dreamingly have in view when we roll out the old dictum (D) 'Everything real must be somewhere and in some place and occupying some space.' This piece of supposed wisdom appears in Timaeus's argument not (as in Aristotle's *Physics*) to help shape an enquiry into 'whether place exists, and in what way it exists, and what it is' (*Physics* IV, 208a27–29), but because it contradicts the reality of the Forms. It is to counter D from this point of view that Plato presents the third thing as *chôra*. He confronts D because it provides an opportunity for table-turning too good to resist: but by accepting D as his target, he lets D itself shape the content of his response. In other words, it is *from D* that the notions of 'somewhere' and 'place' and 'space' leach into the discursive passage and

---

relevant discussions in Aristotle perhaps no argument is needed for treating the *chôra* appellation as the most important. So too for those who study the material as a chapter in the longer history of concepts of space and location.

[100] Assigning a theoretical position to *chôra* as such is a way of explaining or starting to explain the nature of *chôra*. But I do not think that Plato in the *Timaeus* is interested in explaining, even in a brief and pregnant or sketchy way, the nature of *chôra* as such. I say this *pace* Aristotle, who states, referring (or so it seems) to the *Timaeus*: 'Everyone says that place [*topos*] is something, but [Plato] alone tried to say what it is', *Physics* IV, 209b16–17. Cf. 11–13, where Aristotle claims that in the *Timaeus* Plato identifies *chôra*, glossed by *topos* (15–16), with matter. Aristotle's impression that the *Timaeus* tries to say 'what *chôra* is' seems no better founded than his simplistic impression that it identifies *chôra* with matter, on which see Ross, 1960, 566. (Aristotle, 209b14, may also misunderstand *metalambanon tou noêtou* at 51a7; see Ross 1960, 566.) The fact that place or space is an essential aspect of the physical world is not sufficient ground, in the absence of positive textual evidence, for thinking that the *Timaeus* would naturally contain an attempt to 'say what it is'. Contrast the Timaean discussion of time (*chronos*): it does give an explicit answer to the question 'What is *chronos*?' (37d5–7), whether or not this is its primary aim. (On the precise textual scope of the answer, see Brague, 1982, ch. 1.)

6.6 The discursive passage, 51b6–52d4

become attached to the third thing, previously called 'Receptacle'. Plato is making the type of counter-move in which you take over, as it were, your opponent's position, and give it a devastating twist. For instance (a simple example): the opponent has stated that obeying the laws of the city is carrying out the interest of the stronger, and you reply by saying: 'True, except for just one small difference: obeying the laws of the city is carrying out what the stronger *believe to be* the interest of the stronger.' In the present case, Plato introduces the notion of *chôra* at 52a8 because he is about to knock down D, which says 'Being somewhere etc. necessarily belongs to whatever is real', and his knock-down is going to be: 'Yes, being somewhere etc. necessarily belongs to ... whatever is real just in the tenuous way in which images are – images which indeed are necessarily somewhere because otherwise they would have no shred of reality at all' – from which it follows that the really real things are nowhere precisely because *they*, to exist, have no need to be anywhere. Anticipation of this passage of arms (and nothing else, I believe) prompts Plato to identify the third thing with that in virtue of which the things that are necessarily somewhere *are* somewhere – i.e. with *chôra*.

Since he has already taken for granted that the third thing is metaphysically prior to the objects that are in it, identifying it in one stroke (*sans* argument) with *chôra* implies an equal taking-it-for-granted that *chôra* is metaphysically prior to the objects that are in *chôra*. It is worth noting that from the perspective of anyone who is interested in *chôra* for its own sake – asking, e.g., what it means for something to be somewhere – Plato's opting without argument for the view that *chôra* is metaphysically prior to the empirical objects seems pretty obtuse. Plato brings in this principle to defend the reality of Forms against an opponent who attacks it using D; but such an opponent can and should equally wield D against Plato's metaphysically prior *chôra*.[101] Having done this, the opponent would do well to interpret the occurrences in D of 'place', 'space', and 'where' in a relational sense, rephrasing the dictum as 'Everything real is locatable in relation to something or other empirical.'[102] He or she can then dismiss the Forms on the ground that none of them is locatable in this way: to which

---

[101] The opponent should use D to argue that the metaphysically prior *chôra* is in another *chôra* (infinite regress) or else is unreal (cf. Aristotle, *Physics* IV, 209a23–5).

[102] The words in which D is presented at 52b3–5 fit a relational interpretation: 'Everything real must be somewhere, in some place, and occupying some space, and ... what is *neither on earth nor anywhere in the heavens* is nothing'; cf. Algra, 1995, 106. It is true that according to Aristotle, *Physics* IV, 208b29–209a1, there were people who, from accepting D, were led to regard *chôra* as a 'first principle of existent things'. But Aristotle thinks this naïve; he implies that it is primitive thinking (see his reference to Hesiod's *Theogony*), and ironically comments: 'If such a thing is so, place would have a wondrous sort of power.'

Plato would have left himself no effective reply. The predictability of this situation from the point of view of someone inclined, even if only briefly, to attend to *chôra* for its own sake, is further evidence that Plato, in the passage under discussion, is not occupying such a point of view.[103]

To return to his actual confrontation with D as I have analysed it: however ingenious, his response comes with a price. He takes on D, the inherited dictum, in the form in which it comes, and it comes without special connection to the four corporeal elements. Thus he detaches the third thing from that special connection when, acceding to D's suggestion, he presents the third thing as *chôra*. For that whereby things are somewhere is not more closely related to the masses of the elements than to organised corporeal things. A mortal organism is as much somewhere – in a place, taking up space – as a piece of rock or a pool of water. And the organism no less than the rock or pool is somewhere in its own right. It has to be somewhere not merely because it is made of inanimate materials that have to be somewhere, but because, for instance, it needs a habitat and room for its characteristic locomotion and sufficient proximity to its objects of sense-perception.[104] At the beginning of the discursive passage Timaeus singled out 'fire itself by itself' with special reference (51b7–8). At that point he maintained the emphasis, so noticeable in the run-up to and aftermath of the discursive passage, on the four elements above all. But then his language became unrestricted, and he seemed to be asking about the reality of Forms in general (51b8 ff.). And then (52a5 ff.) the third thing reappeared as *chôra* with dictum D in its train – a dictum that is likewise unrestricted in its support for the reality of all and only empirical things. These moves boost the philosophical impression that the function of Plato's metaphysical third thing is to be that which everything empirical is equally 'in'. So the third thing's brief appearance in *chôra*-guise has certainly helped promote the ontological interpretation, which hails the third thing as a general solution to a general problem about Forms. If I have been right in arguing that the ontological reading is not well founded (see sections 6.5 and 6.6.3), then it has to be admitted that Plato's run-in with D has warped his exposition in the magnificently written peroration of the discursive passage.

(3) Next there is a question about the Forms of the four elements. If we discount the warping effect just explained, then they are the real focus throughout the more discursive passage. What would be the reason for a

---

[103] This contrasts with his focus at *Parmenides* 138a2–b6.
[104] When Aristotle first introduces D, he shows it plausibly used to make the cut between imaginary and real *animals*: 'Where is the goat-stag or the sphinx?' (*Physics* IV, 208a29–31).

special concern with them? In section 6.7.2 I develop an answer to this question, arguing that the corporeal elements present a unique problem for the Timaean cosmology. If that argument is convincing it should dispel doubts (understandable at this point) about the fairness of not taking the appearance of generality at face value.

(4) I end with a question arising out of the discussion of Part 1 of the discursive passage (section 6.6.2 above). There I argued that the way towards showing that there are intelligible Forms corresponding to a certain empirical subject-matter is simply to try one's hand at working out a theory of the subject-matter – a theory that focuses on some datum of the subject-matter as standing in need of explanation, and shows in a formal and perspicuous way, for example by a mathematical model, how the datum is possible. Now if, as I assume, there is for some reason a special concern about whether there are intelligibles corresponding to the four empirical elements, then, given that Plato has the geometrical account at his fingertips, why does he not simply meet the concern by presenting that account *without more ado*? What do I mean by 'without more ado'? Well, I have also been maintaining that the Receptacle-postulate is meant to support the thesis that certain sense-perceptibles, i.e. the four elements, are images of intelligibles. So the question arising from 6.6.2 is this: why doesn't Plato simply get on and present the geometrical account *tout court* (thereby demonstrating by actual theory-construction that there exist corresponding intelligibles)? *Why does he not move straight to the geometrical account instead of first taking on board the paraphernalia of the Receptacle?*

Given the weakness of the ontological approach, it is clear that we have not laid our hands on a satisfactory interpretation of the Receptacle as long as this last question remains unanswered.

6.7 THE RECEPTACLE FULFILS A COSMOLOGICAL REQUIREMENT

In this section I shall argue that the Receptacle appears in the account for a specifically cosmological reason, or specifically on behalf of Platonic cosmology. I shall start by looking at some ways in which this might be so, but shall then put these on one side and develop a different proposal.

6.7.1 Some suggestions and their difficulties

First: it may be natural to assume that if the Receptacle is postulated for a specifically cosmological purpose, that purpose is to supply a sort of universal framework within which every corporeal object and process exists and unfolds; a framework underwriting the idea that everything corporeal constitutes *one realm* (even before the fully fashioned unique cosmos came to be) with the same powers of motion, interaction, and transformation. Arguably, the Forms by themselves cannot underwrite this idea; nor can the sensible copies of the Forms: considered *singulatim* they cannot add up to a single *domain*.[105] But if a universal framework is what Plato is reaching for with the Receptacle,[106] why are there not more traces of the corresponding problematic? It is true that Plato makes Timaeus emphasise that the Receptacle is nurse of *all* becoming, the *omni*-recipient, but by themselves these phrases fail to tell us what particular problem they are supposed to alleviate. They do not, for example, express the specific anxiety that without such a universal framework any phenomenal objects could stand in no relations to each other, whether spatially or through interaction or as stages of one or another single process. In short, if this or something like it is the puzzlement that the Receptacle is intended to resolve, it has to be admitted that the puzzlement remains unarticulated. The text declares over and over the sheer dependence on the Receptacle of what we call fire, water, etc., but it does not emphasise any dependence on it for their *com*presence or *co*existence. In fact, Timaeus starts by taking it for granted that they coexist in one domain, since we are first shown them turning into each other, and never once during the progress of his account does he open up the question of how this coexistence is possible.

Secondly, Thomas Johansen has suggested[107] that Timaeus (or Plato in the *Timaeus*) cannot make sense of the genesis and perishing of the elemental bodies otherwise than as an *entering and exiting*. The Receptacle is therefore required as being or providing the space or place which they enter (*eisienai*) on coming to be and which they depart from (*exienai*) on perishing (cf. 50c1–5; e1). The suggestion is *not* that e.g. a mass of fire comes to be by entering the Receptacle from somewhere else where it was before, and perishes (when it

---

[105] This is a sort of Kantian parallel (minus the idealism) to the supposed metaphysical problem about the very existence of sensible objects as images of Forms (discussed in the last section). In both cases the sensible particulars are regarded as incapable by themselves of composing a genuine realm of sensible particulars. We may also be reminded of Berkeley's system in which God is needed to uphold the regularity of the ideas that constitute the real world (as distinct from figments of our imaginations).

[106] This supposition would not be undermined by the fact that, if it were correct, Plato's grasp of the universal framework would be a confused one insofar as it shifts between treating one and the same principle both as ultimate subject of inherence (a sort of prime matter) and as the space or place of everything. I doubt whether any interpretation of the Receptacle can absolve him of this confusion; however, a good interpretation will be one in which it does not greatly matter.

[107] Johansen, 2004, ch. 6, esp. 118–23.

6.7 The Receptacle fulfils a cosmological requirement

turns into a mass of air) by going out of the Receptacle to some other location (rather as the souls in the myth of Er come into this world from the other world and depart from it to the other world[108]). For the corporeal elements, that would be locomotion from somewhere to somewhere else, with the subject existing throughout. Thus Johansen does not suggest (what would be highly implausible) that Plato confuses the coming to be and perishing of e.g. fire with the locomotion of fire from a sort of limbo to the Receptacle and vice versa; nor (equally implausible) that he deliberately reduces these events to locomotions between the Receptacle and a limbo-place. The suggestion is, rather, that Plato in the *Timaeus* understands coming to be, and likewise perishing, as 'a sort of spatial movement' that involves in each case just *one* place or space: that which the body enters through coming to be (up to which moment it has not existed at all), and that where it exits through perishing (from which moment it has ceased to exist).[109] Consequently, according to this interpretation, Plato is committed to postulating space, i.e. the Receptacle, as that which makes coming into being and perishing possible. It makes them possible by being or providing the place (or places) in terms of which coming to be and perishing are conceived.

It is perfectly true that Plato speaks of the coming and ceasing to be of fire etc. as their entering and leaving the Receptacle. But the question is whether in this he is motivated by a prior understanding of elemental genesis and perishing as a matter of entering and leaving a place or space, the place being conceived of as metaphysically prior to all its occupants. For only then could one claim that the reason for postulating the Receptacle is that without it Plato cannot make sense of elemental genesis. To me, however, it seems that the reverse is the case. Simply (from scratch) to conceive of the coming to be of parcels of fire etc. as their entering a place that is prior to all of them would be very peculiar. On the other hand, to depict the matter in this way when one has already (for whatever reason) postulated the Receptacle, is quite natural.

Johansen also argues that in the geometrical account re-assemblage of the triangles of one sort of particle to compose another sort of particle is locomotion of these triangles. He concludes from this that since the

---

[108] *Republic* x, 614b–621b.
[109] *eisienai* is used of the chorus or characters coming on to the stage; see LSJ s.v. *eiseimi* II. This may help illustrate the notion of a sort of 'entering' that involves just *one* place, since arguably Clytaemnestra (in a given performance) 'comes to be' when and only when Clytaemnestra first appears on the scene; the person who was waiting in the wings was not Clytaemnestra but the male actor assigned the part. *eiseimi* is also used of incoming magistrates or rulers (ibid. III. 4); again, 'the incoming president' does not refer to a *president* who was first somewhere else and has now arrived here.

226 *The genesis of the four elements*

Receptacle as space is necessary for all locomotion, it is necessary for elemental transformation.[110] However, if Plato saw this as a reason for introducing the Receptacle, that entity would surely have appeared loud and clear in the geometrical account of elemental transformation; whereas in fact it goes unmentioned there.

6.7.2 A different proposal

I turn now to the interpretation which I propose. Let us start by taking stock of the properties of the four elements which any acceptable account must allow for, or better still explain. These include their clearly observable qualities such as heat, cold, hardness, liquidity, and so on; they also for the present purpose include any properties which Plato makes Timaeus mention as clearly observable today, such as the inter-transformations. Clearly observable too are the regional movements whereby the four tend to disperse according to their kinds thereby forming separate large-scale homogeneous masses. When the cosmos has been fashioned, these masses show up as distinct parts of the cosmic body. There are also the less observable even if rationally imaginable relations in which small portions of the four often through mutual compounding come to constitute organic parts of mortal creatures.

Plato's *pièce de résistance*, the geometrical account, brilliantly lives up to Timaeus's general insistence on the beauty and excellence of nature. It does so through its starting point in four perfect polyhedra constructed from triangles. In three of the cases the construction provides a perfect explanation of how such polyhedra can metamorphose into one another. A less thorough and precise explanation at this stage might have left it obscure exactly how any of them converts into any others, thereby allowing for the impression that each converts to some other without difficulty. Instead, the mathematical finesse of the actual explanation requires that the cube (the shape of the earth-particle) be dumped in a category on its own as defying transformation (except into different 'isotopes' of itself).[111] This must have seemed a price worth paying. Moreover, by allowing for particles of different sizes the geometry helps explain the conditions that precipitate transformation (56e7–57b7). The geometrical properties are also

---

[110] Johansen, 2004, 124–7..
[111] Plato does not stop to worry that this result might make us rub our eyes and wonder whether their evidence was unreliable for all the supposed transformations.

6.7 The Receptacle fulfils a cosmological requirement

at moments called in to explain the sensible qualities of the four elements (e.g. 61d5–62a5). And these familiar sensible qualities (hardness, heat, the 'cutting' feel of fire, etc.) help provide a picture of how various organic tissues were constituted by means of the elementary materials, and how various physiological processes work (bone-marrow, 73b5–c3; bone, e1–5; flesh 74c5–d2; contributions of fire and air to 'irrigation', respiration, and nutrition, 78a1–79e9; 80d1–7).

But the shapes of the particles, the natures and numbers of triangles from which they were constructed, supply no basis for explaining the large-scale elemental movements. Of course, in the case of inter-transformation and the generation of isotopes the geometry only explains exactly how and why these results arise when they do arise: the actual occurrences depend on non-geometrical contingent facts about contact between parcels of the different elements (56c8–d5). But there is no such geometrical explanation for the separative movements as and when they occur. In fact, the theory's fruitfulness in explaining what it does explain highlights its barrenness from the point of view of someone who wonders about the separative movements.

So if there is some sort of principle that explains these, it is quite unlike anything to be found in the geometric account. Such, of course, is the principle supplied in the passage that is tucked away – rather oddly, we might think – between the end of the discursive passage and the start of the geometrical account. Here (52d4–53a7) the Receptacle is shown swaying all over and thereby shaking the contents in a way that gets them separated out from each other, like a winnowing basket being shaken to separate chaff from grain.

It is worth pausing for a moment over the way in which the Receptacle is shown to be the source of movement. In fact, the ultimate source of movement turns out to be the Receptacle's contents.[112] When portions of different kinds are jumbled together, they are in a state of disequilibrium with one another, i.e. there is a tendency to go in different directions, like the two pans of a scale with unequal weights. The Receptacle, as it were, picks up these myriad local instabilities and identifies itself through and through with all of them so that they somehow amplify into a grand disequilibrium of the Receptacle itself, whereby it sways and thereby shakes the contents apart. This is how things were 'even before the *ouranos* had its genesis' (52d4):

The nurse of becoming, being made liquid and made fiery and receiving the shapes of earth and fire and undergoing all the other affections that accompany these, had

---

[112] Cf. Johansen, 2004, 129–31. For an important detailed discussion see Mohr, 2005, 121–45, esp. 124–32.

an appearance utterly various to behold, and because of being filled with powers lacking similarity and equilibrium it was nowhere in equilibrium, but swayed unevenly all over, being itself shaken by them and shaking them in turn by its motion. And the different <contents> were always being carried in different directions and becoming separated, like the stuff that is shaken and winnowed by baskets and other instruments for husking grain, with the dense and heavy carried one way and the loose and light settling in a different location [*hedran*]. It was in this way that the four kinds then [*tote*], being shaken by their recipient which is itself in motion like an instrument for shaking things, divided off from themselves at furthest remove the ones that were most unlike and pushed into closest convergence together those that were most like. That was why one came to occupy one place [*chôran*], another another, even before the order of the All was constituted from them. (52d4–53a7)

And, as we have seen, the Receptacle's separative action still continues and always will (58c1–4), although on a lesser scale. In the pre-cosmic situation it ensured the large-scale separation of elements into the great tracts which we see today. Such mega-separation is no longer necessary. But, since elemental transformations are always happening, it will always be the case that amounts of one or another element get generated at a distance from the bulk of their kind, and then through the action of the Receptacle they move to join it.

Before analysing more closely the precise relation between the shaking Receptacle and its shaken contents, let us note the cosmological importance of the separative movements. Some degree of spatial sorting out is necessary if (a) the elements are to manifest the distinctive phenomenal properties such as heat and hardness which the geometrical account will later help to explain: these qualities emerge when enough of one kind of individually imperceptible geometrical particles come together. Sorting is necessary too if (b) sufficiently pure samples of the materials are to be available for mixture in due proportion for fashioning organic tissues (73b1–c1; e1–5; 74c5–d2). And it is also necessary if (c) large tracts of the elements are to constitute distinctive environments for the different types of mortal animals (39e10–40a2; cf. 91d6–92c1).

So it is beyond question that the separation is cosmologically necessary; but one might wonder at its rather complicated explanation. Timaeus mainly depicts the pre-cosmic effects (in the passage last quoted), but presumably the causal details carry over to the cosmic era even if on a less dramatic scale. Scattered and jumbled pieces of different materials, through their dissimilarity and mutual lack of 'equilibrium',[113] infect the Receptacle

---

[113] Cf. 57e1–58a2 on the non-uniformity and inequality of the materials as the general cause of the separative movement (whether in the pre-cosmic or cosmic era). See 52e1–5 on the pre-cosmic case.

6.7 The Receptacle fulfils a cosmological requirement

with a disequilibrium that ensures their dispersal like to like. The materials jointly somehow affect the Receptacle so that it shakes them apart; i.e. they do something to it which makes it do something back to them. But why not simplify the account by cutting out the Receptacle, and straightforwardly assigning to the elements, rather as Aristotle does, distinct natural tendencies to be in (or to constitute) distinct regions? It might be replied: the geometrical account which is waiting in the wings cannot explain these movements; but there must be something to explain them. But why must there be? What is absurd about the idea that the separation is simply a basic fact about the four? Or what would be wrong with taking the weaker view that it is basic as far as we currently know, whatever the future may bring to light that might help explain it? Timaeus is surely not committed to providing an immediate position on every question his cosmology may generate. The query 'Why not simplify by cutting out the Receptacle?' might also be met with the reply: 'Well, Plato already has the Receptacle on hand for another purpose, so he turns it to use for the present one of explaining the regional movements.' But this fails to get to the essentials of the situation.

If the regional movements are simply basic attributes of the four elements, then the latter are self-sufficient as regards these movements. For Plato, it would follow that they are not inanimate. (See 46d4–e2, where their inanimacy and status as secondary causes are closely connected with their belonging to the category of 'moved movers', in Aristotle's phrase.[114]) But could Plato (in something like the framework of the *Timaeus*) have treated the elements as ensouled, without absurdity?[115] Could this be combined with reducing them to geometrical particles? That would presumably entail ascribing souls to the particles of each type, whether four types of souls corresponding to the four shapes, or one type whose general propensity is to move its particle towards others of the same kind. The oddity, if not ludicrousness, of endowing individual particles with incorporeal souls would surely push anyone considering this hypothesis into one or another of two less far-fetched (if only because familiar from earlier cosmologies) directions. One of them leads to something like a Democritean alternative: soul in general *just is* atomic particles of a certain kind, and living creatures live because of the presence of these inside the organism.[116] The other

---

[114] Their inanimate status explains why they lack intelligence: 46d4–6; cf. 30b3–5 and 37c3–5.
[115] My pursuing this question is not based on any assumption that Plato seriously considered the option of animating the elements. The purpose is simply to show how much is at stake.
[116] Fire atoms, according to Democritus: see Aristotle *On the Soul* I, 403b31–404a9; 406b20–22.

alternative is to abandon the advantages of the geometrical account, and treat the elements as homogeneous masses. For it is somehow much easier to conceive of such a thing as alive with its own kind of formless life than it is to suppose animate individual particles. So then we may be moving back to a theory like that of the four 'roots' of Empedocles – Empedocles who gave the four elements the names of gods (B6).[117] And when straying into the vicinity of that territory, we are bound to be reminded that Empedocles explained the separative movements as the work of cosmic Strife (B17, 8 and 19; B21, 7; B35, 8–9).[118] Strife as a fundamental cosmic power cannot be countenanced in the Platonic universe; but it would not be so easy to reject Strife out of hand if one lacked a more congenial explanation of the separative movements.[119]

We have just looked at what, from Plato's point of view, would have been some unattractive options.[120] Can we cleanly escape from them by postulating *inanimate* particles and assigning to the Demiurge, or to some kindred rational and mathematically oriented principle, the function of so to speak ferrying them in their different directions? That would be more economical than postulating a distinct cause, the Receptacle; but it would introduce jarring anomaly into Timaeus's narrative. I say this because elsewhere in the account (a) demiurgic and kindred divinely rational

---

[117] Empedocles recognised that his four roots (*rhizômata*) could occur in minute portions, but these were not indivisible particles; cf. Aristotle *On the Heaven* III, 305a3–4. The terms 'roots' suggests animacy. On this and the roots as moving of themselves, cf. Hershbell, 1974, 152.

[118] For qualifications on the point about the movements, see Hershbell, 1974, 155.

[119] Plato takes several measures to exclude Empedoclean Strife. He does so by having the Demiurge enclose the cosmic body within the cosmic soul, 34a8–b4 and 36d8–e5, on which see O'Brien, 1969, 22–3 and 144–5, and 2003. And further back, at 31b4–32c4, the Demiurge makes the cosmic body by binding fire and earth together through intermediates air and water in a continued geometrical proportion; in this way the body was endowed with internal concord and Love (*philia*) rendering it indissoluble except by him who bound it together (32b8–c4). (Plato does not state what the quantities standing in these proportions are quantities of; cf. Cornford, 1935, 51.) This passage simultaneously (a) explains why there are four elements instead of one or two (there must be fire and earth for sight and touch to be possible, and continued proportion between two 'solid numbers' requires two intermediates), and (as if anticipating comparison with the four roots of Empedocles) (b) excludes Strife from the system (Taylor, 1928, 94 and 98–100, and Cornford, 1935, 44, note 4). However, 31b4–32c4 says nothing about elemental movement, hence does nothing to allay any particular anxiety about the explanation of that.

[120] Another difficulty with assigning individual souls to the particles: transformation in that case means that the particles are *mortal animals*, subject to birth and death. But mortals come into Timaeus's account only when the demiurgic ancillaries begin to construct their bodies – *out of* materials consisting of masses of particles. The principal Demiurge cannot make anything that is mortal; and presumably the same would hold of the divine formative principle that prepared the materials (geometrising the traces) for cosmos-forming demiurgy. The only way to segregate this divinity from any commerce with mortals and mortality is by having inanimate particles. (Don't even ask whether, if the particles had souls, these souls would be mortal or immortal.)

6.7 *The Receptacle fulfils a cosmological requirement* 231

causation is responsible for organic or mathematically analysable *formations*. Moreover, (b) the divine agencies are almost always shown making their respective contributions once and for all. Whether the narrative is meant to be taken 'literally' in this respect is a question I leave aside until the next chapter. The point for now is that elsewhere *in the narrative* demiurgic and similar causation is shown carrying out its task once upon a time, so to speak.[121] By contrast, the separative movements of the elements have been going on since before the fashioning of the cosmos, and still go on today.

It will be clear with regard to the separative movements that the Receptacle-account is preferable to any of the above alternatives. This is more because of their various failings than for positive features of its own; but the Platonic cosmologist would perhaps be well satisfied with a postulate whose sole merit is that of keeping intolerable alternatives at bay. How much is at stake we shall soon see more clearly. (One could say too that the *sole* value of Atlas is that he prevents the heavens and the earth from collapsing in on each other, thereby destroying the whole world-order.)

The characteristic movement of a thing is essential to its nature. That gives us easy passage to the thought that the fundamental principle of the elements' separative movements is also nothing other than the fundamental principle of their being – their being what they are at all. So if they were wholly self-sufficient for their movement, they would be self-sufficient for their being, and conversely. If, on the other hand, their movements must depend on an ulterior principle of some kind, so too must their very existence; and this latter dependency – existential dependency on the Receptacle – is what Plato has chosen to exhibit first.

Let us consider the possibility that the four elements are existentially self-sufficient. Plato through a mixture of quasi-logic and imaginative drama may have hustled us into accepting that since (as we are also to accept) they turn into each other, they can be no more than mere *suches* requiring a distinct *this* in which to be. But the inference is faulty. It may be that if one pictures the elements as individually everlasting masses one will be less open to the suggestion that they need something Receptacle-like *in* which to exist. Even so, holding that they (everlastingly) turn into each other does not logically commit one to accepting the latter. One could view them as collectively self-sufficient. The nature of each stage of the cycle[122] would

---

[121] Imperfects, perfects, and aorists are used throughout of divine formation, except (as far as I have been able to see) at 46c8 and 69c3, which are in the present; but at 69c5 the second main verb reverts to the aorist.

[122] If they are not particulate (because of the difficulty of making that cohere with the notion of their being alive and self-moving), there is no reason to exclude earth from the cycle.

make essential reference to adjacent stages simply through being what has come to be from one and what will turn into another. It is true that each of them has to be 'in' something, namely 'in' the cycle; but this is not the way of being 'in' whereby the Receptacle's contents are 'in' the Receptacle, i.e. in it in a sense implying existential dependence on it as prior principle. For nothing has been said to suggest that the cycle is prior to its stages. On this way of looking at things, the cycle exists because and only because the stages exist as mutually referential stages: it is understood simply as the series of them and their transformations. So if, as is possible, the cycle simply takes place – takes place, but not in anything Receptacle-like – then its stages can be said to be in *it*, but not in a sense implying that they, individually or collectively (collectively, they are the cycle), depend for their existence on something Receptacle-like. The reason for pinning this point down is that in the discussion in the next paragraph I want to prescind from any particular theory of the elements either as constituting a transformational cycle or as individually everlasting. I shall also prescind from the question whether they are animate or inanimate.

So how would things be if the elements, individually or collectively as a cycle, were existentially self-sufficient? This would mean not merely that they were there (as the story tells us they were) before the formation of the cosmos, but that they were there in complete independence from anything. And now the question arises: how, if that is so, can it be taken for granted that they would lend themselves to the purposes of the Demiurge and his ancillaries? If they were not only more ancient than the cosmos[123] but also wholly autonomous, how can Plato make it persuasive and imaginatively natural that the Demiurge simply 'took them over', i.e. took charge of them and built from them the perfect body of an immortal cosmos that was to be completed with mortal animals whose bodies too would be built from them? Plato could have stipulated that this was the case, by authorial fiat. But such a move would have been clumsy and, I think, ineffectual: clumsy because no ground would have been prepared for it anywhere in the narrative, and ineffectual because its *ad hoc* character, hard to hide, would have drawn attention to precisely the question it was intended to smother: why should it be taken for granted that the elements really *are* co-operative causes?

---

[123] At 34b10–c5, while labouring over the order of genesis of the cosmic soul and the cosmic body, Timaeus states that God would not have allowed the older to be ruled by the younger. Perhaps we are meant to wonder later on about the nature of the dispensation whereby the elements come to be subordinated to, and so in a sense 'ruled by', the organised cosmos which is their junior.

6.7 The Receptacle fulfils a cosmological requirement

Let us go back to where this idea was introduced:

Well, all these [referring to fire and its contribution to vision] are amongst the auxiliary causes which God uses to subserve him in completing the form of that which is as superlatively good as possible. (46c7–d1)

Timaeus then emphasised the mistakenness of supposing that what are only auxiliary causes are the principal ones of what they help to explain (46d1–e2), and went on to declare the principal benefit of vision. At the time, this warning not to let mere auxiliaries usurp the place of *principal* causes may have prevented us from glimpsing the possibility of a real question about how the elements have even the status of *auxiliaries*. This is not the question discussed in section 6.1 above of whether they are *causes* (albeit only auxiliary) as distinct from mere *sine quibus non* or enablers: it is the question of how they are *auxiliary* causes of the cosmos as distinct from being causally indifferent or even hostile to its construction and continuance. If my interpretation in the present section is on target thus far, we should look back at 46c7 ff. with that possibility in mind. If, after all, one needs to be truly 'passionate about intelligence and knowledge' (*ton nou kai epistêmês erastên*, 46d7) if one is to avoid the common and presumably easy mistake of treating mere co-causes for principal ones, then how come it's open to the Platonic cosmologist just *easily* or simply by his say-so to construct an account that convincingly portrays the supposed subservients as just that: subservient? Postulating the Receptacle is Plato's alternative to the easy say-so; the elaborate vision of the Receptacle is the vision of its contents as in themselves existentially and kinetically passive. The fact that Plato sees himself obliged to present this vision so painstakingly in all its all but incredible (*mogis piston*, 52b2) strangeness shows a powerful sense that the mere say-so could not be enough.

Let us also go back to where Timaeus said:

With Intelligence ruling over Necessity by persuading [*tô(i) peithein*] it to bring towards the best most of what was coming into being, in this way and on these terms, through Necessity's yielding to wise persuasion [*peithous emphronos*], this All came to be constituted. (48a2–5)

We are now asking: why should it be assumed that Necessity (i.e. the elements and their immediate effects) *would* 'yield' to Intelligence's 'persuasion'?[124] The problem is not that Necessity lacks soul (46d4–7), hence

---

[124] This yielding represents the transition from the unordered materials to their being ordered as the cosmos. Plato also in one place applies 'Necessity yields to persuasion' to the transition from rudiments to geometrised materials (56c5–7).

cannot be literally persuaded. Its being persuaded is a metaphor for amenability.[125] It is essentially amenable to being used as the Demiurge wishes. Composing the cosmos and the mortal animals is not an outcome to which Necessity could ever have found its way on its own, but this is nonetheless a *natural* outcome for it. But why should one be allowed to assume this? It would be a patently arbitrary assumption if fire, earth, water, and air, or the cycle of these, were openly granted existential and kinetic self-sufficiency. And a reasonably penetrating critic might be unwilling to grant the assumption if the question of their self-sufficiency were left in limbo. Yet without this assumption the account of the formation of the cosmos and mortal animals is without firm foundation. So the existential and kinetic self-sufficiency of the elements is not one of those questions that can be shelved while we continue working on currently more tractable problems. The only way forward is to make it absolutely clear *now* not only that the elements are not the principal causes in the fashioning of this beautiful rational cosmos, but also that they *are* amenable to contributing to the project. And for this reason we have the Receptacle. It not only accounts for the being and the movements of the physical elements, but it does so as a Mother in closest co-operation with the formal Father-principle.[126] And whatever the precise ontological relationship of the latter to the Demiurge, we know (what is far more important for cosmology) that they are on the same side.

Without the co-operative Receptacle, i.e. *with* self-sufficient corporeal elements, there is no basis for confidence that nature is not only an orderly system now but also immortally so. If the elements are wholly in charge of themselves, then given that they cannot of themselves aim at cosmic and intra-cosmic order, it is only by luck that we have the order we have today. At best we could ascribe this order to some sort of uneasy truce between Necessity and demiurgic Intelligence; but there could be no inherent reason why the truce should last, let alone for ever. The Receptacle is Plato's device for putting such fears at rest. He draws on it to uphold the foundational principle that this cosmos is as perfect as any physical thing could be.

It is worth noting that the position that there *are* intelligible Forms of fire etc. is unique in the *Timaeus* for the sheer amount of persuasive force that

---

[125] Cf. the language of 'willingness' at 57b2 and e3 (= natural tendency), and 75b4 (= natural possibility).
[126] For the benign character of the Receptacle see in particular 88d6–89a1, where the separative movement is held up as a model for physical exercise: bodily health depends on our constantly agitating the body so that like materials within it congregate with like; if we do this we are imitating 'the fosterer, the nurse of the All' (cf. 81e6–82a7).

6.7 The Receptacle fulfils a cosmological requirement

Plato lavishes on securing it.[127] First we have (a) a series of dogmatic and imagistic presentations, introducing the elements first in relation to the Receptacle and then in relation also to Forms (49a4–51a3); then (b) a multi-step argument (against the dismissal of Forms) that derives metaphysical distinctions from epistemic ones with a sort of textbook show of method (51b7–e6); then (c) a dialectical trouncing of the dictum that everything real is in a place and in space, etc. (51e6–52d1). No other single Timaean conclusion receives anything like this multiple, sustained, defence. Why is the position so important to Plato? We have, I think, left behind any temptation to be satisfied with ruminations such as 'Well, Plato was a Platonist, so of course he wanted to have a full range of Forms.' Even if such a generalisation is not completely useless as an explanation, it fails to account for the extraordinary importance of securing the Forms of the four elements. In fact, any idea that Plato here is motivated to extend the domain of Forms by a kind of open-ended imperialistic Platonism seems to me positively misleading, because it distracts us from attending to what, specifically, he *precludes* by securing those particular Forms, namely the unbridled autonomy of substances that are meant to be the materials of the ordered cosmos.

If perceptible fire and the others were wholly autonomous, they could not collectively have come to be,[128] hence could not have been developed from rudiments by the introduction of divine geometry. Their natures would have owed nothing to any source of intelligibility, and would have been just what the senses perceive (51c1–3). Of course a geometrical tale might still be told showing how certain regular polyhedra can turn into each other, etc. But that tale would be saying nothing about the physics of *this* cosmos, our actual one. It could give us physics only on the already secured presupposition that the actual elements have fundamental natures which the senses cannot access, but which intellect has some hope of being able to capture. And since the geometrical tale (involving certain triangles as distinct from other geometrically possible ones for constructing the polyhedra) is not dictated by pure geometry either,[129] working it out without hope of application would be a futile exercise, not part of any genuine branch of learning. So the geometrical account of matter, one of the most important

---

[127] Zeyl, 2000, lxiv: 'The present passage in the *Timaeus* [he is referring to 51b6–52d4] appears to be the only one in the Platonic corpus which purports to be an argument for the existence of Forms.' Scholars who accept interpretation A of the Receptacle-postulate are under some pressure to play down the degree to which the passage really intends such an argument, since A views the existence of Forms as premiss, not conclusion; see e.g. Lee, 1966, 348, n. 16.
[128] They might still have constituted a transformatory cycle. [129] See Chapter 3, n. 27.

parts of the *Timaeus* cosmology, stands and falls with the Receptacle-postulate. This, I think, is why Plato keeps the geometrical account up his sleeve until he has finished presenting the Receptacle. He could, after all, have included a brief forward reference to the geometry near the moment when Timaeus begins to enquire about fire, water, air, and earth. But unless the Receptacle is in place taking care of elemental movement, elemental geometry will cut no cosmological ice. However, I have also argued for a larger thesis: that with the Receptacle-postulate stands and falls not only the geometrical account of matter, but the entire Timaean project of explaining the cosmos by reference to cosmic perfection.[130]

I shall conclude this section by applying a lesson which has already been used to good purpose in Chapter 2: that the *eikotes logoi* of the *Timaeus* are not individual propositions but sections of argument or exposition. It follows that, although *eikotes logoi* are as such refutable in principle, an *eikôs logos* may (indeed, probably must) contain or presuppose non-negotiable principles that might be phrased as single propositions. This means that there is no tension between (1) the overarching importance which I have claimed for the Receptacle-postulate and (2) the fact that just before announcing the three-fold nature of the second beginning Plato has Timaeus invoke again the standard of the *eikos*:

Keeping intact <the rule> announced at the beginning, namely that our competence is for likely accounts, I shall try to give one that has no less likelihood than anyone else's – instead, more – on each topic and on everything together [*peri hekastôn kai sumpantôn*], even as before from the beginning. (48d1–4)

The Receptacle-postulate is foundational to the cosmology because it shows (through a detour into the trans-natural ontology of the 'third kind') how the separative movement of the corporeal elements is compatible with their capacity for constituting stable organised structures. This is relevant to a very wide range of subject-matters in natural science. In the passage just quoted, Timaeus alludes to his own theories and to rival ones. Presumably all theories from whatever school presuppose the elemental susceptibility to

---

[130] Suppose for a moment that the purpose of establishing intelligible Forms for the four elements (thereby motivating their analysis as geometrical particles) had been simply to bring the elements into the domain of what is scientifically explicable. Carrying out this purpose, important though it is, would have been optional in relation to the main cosmological project *if* that project could have independently relied on the amenability of the elements. If that condition were satisfied, Plato would still have had quite a lot to say about the divine crafting of organisms from elements described only in terms of phenomenal qualities. For example, instead of saying that God made bone-marrow starting from particularly 'undistorted and smooth triangles' (73b5–c3), he could have said that the process started from particularly pure samples of the elements.

organisation. As we have seen, a theory is broken-backed unless it can reconcile this phenomenon with the separative movement. Any theory therefore needs a component that, for this purpose, would be functionally equivalent to Plato's Receptacle-postulate. Theories without such a component are indubitably less *eikotes* than the Timaean ones on the same subjects.

We might think that since the reconciliation just mentioned is a problem of natural science, postulating a trans-natural principle such as the Receptacle is not an acceptable solution. At most, we might want to say, Plato's postulate draws attention to the problem.[131] Some different conception might be discovered that would side-step the problem or meet it at less metaphysical expense.[132] But meanwhile, Timaeus is committed to the Receptacle. His tone in the discursive passage from 51d3 to the end is one of flat *refusal* to entertain any doubt or alternative. The conclusion expressed when he does 'cast his vote' (52d2) of course lacks the epistemic authority of a conclusion reached by irrefutable demonstration. But it is every bit as final as a demonstrated conclusion. One takes note of both sides of a question; and when there is no more to say about it, one votes; and the vote once cast cannot be taken back.

6.8 SUMMARY

The main aim of this chapter has been to understand the point of the Receptacle-postulate. For this is one of the most philosophically puzzling questions thrown out by the *Timaeus*.[133] However, a good deal of preparation was called for.[134]

The first task was to home in on the Receptacle-passage via the nested contexts with which it is prefaced and in some of which it is embedded (sections 6.1 and 6.2). This involved fixing first the outermost context, which is about constructing the bodies of mortal animals from the four elements. This theme led to the distinctions between the two great factors of the cosmos, Intelligence and Necessity, and the prioritising of their causal roles: Intelligence is the primary cause, Necessity and its effects are only co-operative causes. 'Necessity and its effects' is a label for the four

---

[131] It is surely a problem even for theories not committed to the assumption that this universe is the most excellent possible physical system.
[132] For a glance at Aristotle in this connection see the concluding remarks of this book.
[133] Cf. Gregory, 2008, in Waterfield, 2008, xlix.
[134] Broadie, 2003, proposed rather the same interpretation but in simpler form (less burdened by preparation).

elements and their properties. These, even though causally subordinate, are immensely important for the science of mortal animals. To see their independent contribution we must study them in abstraction from their place in those constructions: which is to say that we must study them as they were before the cosmos itself was fashioned.

They are also called 'the wandering cause'. This means not that they are a wholly irregular chaos, but that by themselves they would not stay on a steady track of development leading to the production of organisms (and indeed of the body of the cosmos itself). To understand how such developments reliably take place, we must see the wandering cause as subservient to directive Intelligence. But subservience cannot involve compelling the wandering cause against its nature: Intelligence is effective as primary cause only by 'persuading' Necessity.

Having introduced this cluster of ideas, Timaeus announces that the cosmology is to start over from a new beginning. We might momentarily expect to be launched straight into a study of the independent natures and properties of the four elements: this subject is important enough to warrant treating it as a major new chapter of the cosmology. But Timaeus instead approaches somewhat obliquely: the new study will not simply consider the elements *as they were* before the cosmos was fashioned: it will trace *how they came to be* before the cosmos was fashioned. Evidently the correct understanding of how they were, i.e. of their distinctive contributions to the fashioned cosmos, is to rest on understanding their genesis.

We then confronted the fact that Timaeus provides two accounts of the genesis of the four materials: one in which the Receptacle is presented as the 'third kind' along with the two metaphysical kinds familiar from the first beginning; and one in which God constructs the elements geometrically. I summarised and compared the two accounts (sections 6.3 and 6.4). They have several similar features: most notably, perhaps, they both take off from elemental inter-transformation. Even so, each provides something which the other does not. For example, the Receptacle takes care of the separative movement of the elements, which has no ready explanation in the geometrical account.

Against this background I discussed the influential view that the Receptacle is posited in order to solve a supposed problem of general Platonic metaphysics, as distinct from some problem of Timaean cosmology. The supposed metaphysical problem is this: how do sense-perceptible objects manage to *be* at all as images of Forms, since images of Forms is all that they are? Answer: they get such existence as they have by being in the Receptacle. In section 6.5 I laid out this interpretation, and put forward two objections: first, if it is correct, the Receptacle-passage is in the wrong place in Timaeus's account: it should have been placed at the first beginning; and second it ignores the fact that the Receptacle is in some way involved with the four elements specifically, whereas the supposed metaphysical problem is general. In section 6.6 I scanned the 'discursive' portion of the Receptacle-account for evidence supporting the general-metaphysical interpretation. I reached the conclusion that the problematic in this passage moves in the opposite direction. The aim is not (A) to show that because sensibles are frail images of Forms they must have the Receptacle in which to exist. Rather, it is (B) to maintain that indeed there *are* Forms of fire, etc. (sensible fire, etc., are only images of Forms), and to adduce as evidence the inability of fire, etc., to exist otherwise than in the cradle of the Receptacle.[135]

This result leaves us without an explanation of why Plato conceives of fire, etc., as having to exist in the Receptacle. The answer to this question begins to appear when one looks at the undesirable alternative which the second problematic aims to exclude. Whereas problematic A seeks to rule out a scenario in which sensibles do not get to exist at all since only intelligibles exist, in B the excluded alternative is that fire, water, etc., are not images of Forms, but are complete realities, sufficient for their own existence and natures. Before spelling out the cosmological implications of this, I looked at some cosmological interpretations of the Receptacle which turned out not to be compelling (section 6.7.1). Then (6.7.2) I proposed an interpretation whose crucial premiss is this: if the four elements were wholly self-sufficient for their existence and for their characteristic separative movements (aspects that go very closely together), there could be no reasoned assurance (but only a flimsy authorial say-so) that they reliably and everlastingly subserve Intelligence and its purposes. Plato's carefully crafted picture of their dependence on a maternal principle utterly different from themselves, a principle whose paternal counterpart turns out to be nothing other than the formal source of their own nature, provides that reasoned assurance. What it provides is not a new-found proof that the cosmos is everlastingly and securely harmonious and beautiful, but a defence of this article of faith against doubts which a shallower account of the elements

---

[135] The fact that the aim is B and not A does not tell against Silverman's interpretation, I think. Silverman, 2002, treats the Receptacle-postulate as part of the basis for explaining the being of particulars. In my view, this question, as a question of pure ontology, was not on Plato's agenda in the *Timaeus*. However, Silverman's purpose may be to show how the Platonic assumption that sensibles are images of Forms sets a problem about the ontology of particulars, to which the Receptacle is (in part) the solution. Perhaps this problem and its solution should be judged as belonging to a sort of timeless Platonism.

might have provoked and could not have allayed. The assurance is 'reasoned' because reason has invented a way of picturing the elements that does justice to their gigantic cosmic contribution without imperilling the axiom that Intelligence is in charge.

Earlier in the cosmology and on its margins, Plato has scattered glimpses of the elements as savage and hostile to human life and rationality.[136] We are meant, perhaps, to see the task of bringing them into the fold of a cosmology based on beauty and goodness as a daunting one, so that the triumph of achieving it would be correspondingly great. (Perhaps we are meant to wonder momentarily whether the Demiurge might have had to face a battle, Olympus *versus* the Titans as in Hesiod, when taking up his task.) Plato starts his study with a mighty 'problem': the problem of elemental transformation. We are meant to *accept* that this is a genuine phenomenon: it is something we 'see'. Initially, the problem is 'How are we to speak of fire, water, and the others?', and the solution is to translate these nouns into adjectives. We now begin to see (this time with the eye of reason) that the four empirically mighty elements are metaphysically broken-backed. They exist only in dependence on something totally unlike themselves.

That is one great meaning of elemental transformation in the *Timaeus*. But Plato kills two birds with one stone. Scientific theorising about any subject-matter has to begin from a problem. There can be no start without a direction, and direction comes from a question seeking an answer or a phenomenon demanding to be explained. Elemental transformation is also the *explanandum* that launches the geometric particle account. The formal elegance of this theory, its success for three of the four cases, its suggestiveness as a tool for further analysis of the physics and chemistry of matter, give concrete reassurance to Platonists that inanimate fire and water, etc., no less than organic structures, have come into being in accordance with intelligible Forms. Thus the overall problem of bringing the four into the fold of rational cosmology has been solved – almost. For there is an inescapable datum: the separative movements. The particle-theory has no means of explaining this. And the separative movements, as movements, offer no purchase for mathematical analysis into finely structured cycles, phases, or rhythms in which symmetry and proportion hold sway.

---

[136] Cataclysmic flood (22a7); recurrent huge disasters involving water and fire (22c1–d3); recurrent great rains (23a7–8; cf. c4); earthquakes, floods, and marine upheavals (25c7–d6; *Critias* 111a6 ff.; 112a1–4); the newly embodied immortal soul struggles in the body as in a mighty river (43a6–b6); it is battered by sense-perceptions of the external elements (43b6–c7).

6.8 Summary

Imagine approaching the science of the elements with only the geometric particle-theory in hand. The separative movement sticks out like a sore thumb. The difficulty is not just the inadequacy of the attractive geometrical theory to explain all the phenomena. Scientists have to live with that sort of situation much of the time, shelving questions for which they do not yet see answers. The difficulty with this particular theoretical shortfall is much worse. In the first place, leaving it unaddressed undermines the particle-theory. If something as undeniable as elemental movement cannot be made intelligible to mathematicising intellect, why should one go on preferring to believe that the elemental bodies have geometrical structure at all? For movement and body are both essential to the elements. If the whole reality of the movements is just what we perceive through the senses (51c1–4), then the same may be true of their corporeal nature. Moreover, the possibility that their reality is entirely open to sense-perception, is the possibility that they were not made in accordance with intelligible Forms. And this in the Timaean context is equivalent to the possibility that they were not made at all; in which case they have always been around as a matter of brute fact. They depend on nothing and are in complete charge of themselves. As we have seen, countenancing *this* possibility puts the whole cosmological project at risk, not just the geometrical theory of the elements. If their non-self-dependence is an open question, it is an open question whether Intelligence can rely on their subservience. The solution lies in the fact that their whole reality, including that of their movements, is *not* just what the senses perceive; for it is grounded in their non-empirical relation to the non-empirical Receptacle.

In my view, the single greatest impediment to grasping the point of the Receptacle-postulate was thrown into the midst by Plato himself: on seeing the chance of a swift and brilliant triumph over the *endoxon* 'Everything real must be somewhere', he allowed himself to identify the Receptacle with *chôra*, that in virtue of which things are somewhere. This has had two effects. First, many interpreters have been encouraged to assume that the Receptacle-passage is intended or largely intended to present a conception of space or some sort of locational framework as such. And second, since everything sense-perceptible is equally in space and located, attention has been distracted from the special link between the Receptacle and the elements. This has fostered ontological explanations according to which the Receptacle is Plato's solution to some supposed problem, perfectly general in scope, about the relation of sense-perceptibles as such to intelligibles as such.

Notoriously, the Receptacle-passage provides no single clear picture of the relation in which the Receptacle stands to its contents. Is it an underlying subject in which they inhere as qualities? Is it a material of which they are made? Is it a medium in which they subsist? Is it a sort of absolute space? Different passages can be quoted in favour of each of these disparate understandings. There is similar ambiguity about the precise ontological nature of the contents, the copies of the Forms, that appear in it and disappear from it. Are these contents particular masses with their own qualities? Are they subjectless bundles of qualities? Are the copies not particulars at all, but recurrent characteristics, self-identical through different exits and entrances? The interpretation offered in this chapter provides a simple explanation for all these indeterminacies. It is that Plato is not interested in placing the Receptacle or its contents in any of the categories distinguished. His one concern is to show the contents wholly dependent on the Receptacle for their existence and their regional movements. So long as any gesture at any of the categories helps illustrate this point, categorial differences are insignificant. The Receptacle and its contents are whatever they need to be, in order to ensure that the elements are free of any metaphysically primordial self-sufficient agenda that could interfere with their subservience to the Intelligence that made the cosmos.

Some may find it disappointing that Plato's concern is conceptually primitive and unsophisticated by comparison with concerns that might have motivated a more controlled and incisive categorial selection. It is not at all obvious, however, in what way greater perspicuity on that front would have advanced the great project of the *Timaeus*, which is to explain nature while thoroughly respecting the basic principle that the cosmos is as superlatively beautiful and excellent, and therefore as stable and harmonious, as anything in the world of becoming can be.[137] On the present interpretation the Receptacle-postulate is the simple safeguard of that principle. It enables Plato to mark the elements' huge empirical contribution while denying them any semblance of an autonomy that would render incredible their status as auxiliaries.

---

[137] Compare the *Timaeus*'s lack of interest in the great metaphysical question of whether the cosmic paradigm is or is not prior to the Demiurge's intellect (even though Plato had raised something like this question at *Parmenides* 132b3–c11). Again, it makes no cosmological difference. For another example, see Chapter 7, n. 4.

CHAPTER 7

Divine and natural causation

7.1 IN THE BEGINNING?

In several places in the *Timaeus–Critias* Timaeus clearly speaks as if the Demiurge made this cosmos 'once upon a time'. That phrase may not be quite right, since chronological – i.e. measurable – time (*chronos*) is itself an intended feature of the universe that was constructed. *Chronos* came into being only when the visible system of circulating celestial bodies was created (37c6–40d5). Even so, the story that unfolds from Timaeus's first beginning clearly shows a succession of constructive phases, starting with the Demiurge's 'taking over' the pre-cosmic matter (30a3–6; 68e1–4); while in the story that unfolds from the second beginning there is at least one point of demarcation between a phase when the four materials were given their geometric structure, and a phase when the Demiurge proceeded to form them into the cosmos (69b3–c3). And in more than one place Timaeus says simply that the cosmos will come to be or has come to be, as if its not being and its being are related as before and after (34a8–b1; *Critias* 106a3–4).[1] The picture, then, is of a proto-historical inauguration.

The debate, almost as old as the *Timaeus* itself, on whether Plato means this 'literally' has been governed by its connection with the question of the sempiternity of the world (i.e. its everlastingness in both temporal directions).[2] The view that the cosmos is sempiternal had many adherents from the

---

[1] Clay in Cooper, 1997, 1293, mistranslates these lines as: 'I offer my prayer to that god [i.e. the cosmos] who had existed long before in reality, but who has now been created in my words'; likewise Apelt, 1919, 189 and Lee, 1971, 129. The Greek says: 'I offer my prayer to the god who has come into being (a) long ago in reality and (b) just now in my words.' *tô(i) ... theô(i) gegonoti* is equally qualified by *prin men palai pot' ergô(i)* and by *nun de logois arti*.

[2] 'Sempiternalism' in the context of this chapter will refer not to the view that nature has always existed and will always exist in one or another shape or form, but rather to the view that the cosmos in the form it is in today is everlasting in both temporal directions. For a survey of the exegetical debate in antiquity and discussion of the textual evidence in the *Timaeus–Critias*, with references to modern scholarship, see Sorabji, 1983, 268–76; also Sedley, 2007, 98–107. For a useful discussion see Gregory, 2007, 147–51.

early Academy onwards, and the Platonists among them – Xenocrates is named in this connection – reconciled their commitments by supposing that the *Timaeus* account is couched as a proto-historical narrative because the author thought it was easier to teach cosmology that way (*didaskalias charin*; Aristotle, *On the Heaven* I. 10, 280a1[3]). This sort of interpretation implies that the proto-historicity is nothing but a presentational device, so that recasting the work in sempiternalist form should leave all its serious content unaffected.

Postulating a beginning opens the gate to more than one charge of arbitrariness, and arbitrariness about a fundamental fact of the cosmos seems at odds with the principle that the cosmos is as perfect as possible. There is the well-known objection: if God brought order to matter when previously it was disordered, why did God not do this before?[4] There is also the fact that the Timaean story implies that for some finite number n the finished cosmos is currently n years old. Since the value of n must be some number rather than another, even if we cannot know which, the supposed fact of the matter on any given number of years belongs amongst things that are arbitrary and unbeautiful. Why n rather than n plus 1 or n minus 10,000?[5] Further: the Timaean time-system is supposed to be the crowning glory of the immortal, age-free, cosmic god, rendering its life as like as possible to the true eternity of the now without 'was' and 'will be' (37c6–38a2); but can that make sense if time's actual effect is to maintain the cosmos at an ever-changing interval from its birthday?[6] Why (we ourselves may wonder) would any rationalist

---

[3] On the attribution to Xenocrates, see Vlastos, 1939, in Allen, 1965, 383, n. 1. Aristotle does not state that these Platonists were interpreting the *Timaeus* (as distinct from some separate account of their own), but scholars seem to be united in inferring a reference to that work. The evidence is discussed by Cherniss, 1944, 421–3 and Baltes, 1976–8, vol. I, 18–22.

[4] The seed of this argument is in Parmenides B8, 9–10; cf. Aristotle, *On the Heaven* I, 283a11. As Tarán, 1971, 379, and Sedley, 2007, 105; 144–6, point out, in antiquity this type of objection survived the riposte that until God ordered matter, there was no 'before' in terms of chronological or measurable time. But as a matter of fact this particular objection does not cast doubt on the perfection of the cosmos so much as on the perfection of its maker (or the act of his making), and it casts doubt here in so far as the maker is supposed to be divine, the thought being that a god is too perfect to jump into action. In other words, this is a strictly *theological rather than cosmological* objection to the idea of a cosmic beginning. How far it is relevant to the *Timaeus* account may depend on whether we read this primarily as cosmology or as the lead-in to a theology and metaphysics of the incorporeal (cf. Chapter 3 above).

[5] This difficulty arises not precisely from the assumption that God started to make the cosmos, but rather from the assumption of a proto-historical moment when the making was complete. If, as in contemporary cosmology, we hold that the cosmos is still undergoing physical development (e.g. expansion) there is nothing arbitrary about calculating a beginning as many years ago as necessary for the cosmos to have reached the present stage.

[6] But this particular ever-changing interval seems to be exactly what Timaeus does assign to the cosmos when he says at 38a3–4 that it does not belong to intelligible reality to become either older or younger than itself through time, as if this contrasts intelligible reality with the cosmos. As X lives on, it

7.1 In the beginning? 245

philosopher seriously take on such a commitment unless under pressure, as Plato was not, from Judaeo-Christian scriptural revelation? If we assume that the cosmic beginning in the *Timaeus* is not meant literally, these awkward questions disappear.

On the other hand, sempiternalist interpreters face a major question for which there is no satisfactory answer. If the proto-historicism of Timaeus's account is only a device of presentation, why does Plato not make Timaeus explain this to the listeners? It would have been an easy thing to do. A few words to this effect could easily have been added to Timaeus's general remarks about the epistemic character and possible failings of his discourse at 29c1–d3, especially c4 ff. where he asks to be excused if his *logoi* are not 'completely consistent with each other and exact'. Throughout the dialogues Plato, it seems to me, is in general anxious – indeed sometimes laboriously so – to explain where explanation is both necessary and possible.[7]

One might also point out that we are not in a position to take it for granted that Plato could have counted on the immediate recipients of the *Timaeus* to understand its proto-historicism as a mere device of presentation. The fact that some in the early Academy did understand it in that way is not particularly strong evidence that Plato would have reckoned, when writing the work, that such an essential point could need no explanation at all on his part. Aristotle, who interprets the Timaean beginning literally (*On the Heaven* I 280a28–32; III 300b17–18), states that 'everyone' (*hapantes*) up to his time of writing holds that the *ouranos* (i.e. the astronomical system or world system as it is today) had a beginning (279b12). Even if one allows for a degree of exaggeration by Aristotle here regarding the pre-Platonic systems,[8] his statement indicates that the intellectual context in which the *Timaeus* was composed was one in which it would have seemed natural and unexceptionable to understand the present cosmos as having once begun.[9] Since Plato knew that context at least as well as Aristotle did, we have all the more reason to be puzzled by his failure to indicate his real view, if his real view was that there was no beginning. At that time the theory of

---

becomes older than it was at some previous time *t*, which makes it the case that *X* was younger at *t* than it is now; cf. *Parmenides* 151e3–152e10; 141a5–d3. But this is possible only if *X* at each moment has lived a finite time.

[7] At 29b4–5 Timaeus refers to discourses, his own included, as *exêgetai* ('revealers', 'expounders') of their subject-matters. Expounders are surely not supposed to speak in riddles themselves. For discussion of the word *ad loc.*, see Burnyeat, 2005, and Betegh, 2010.

[8] At any rate Cherniss, 1944, 415, does not dispute this statement of Aristotle's.

[9] Thus Aristotle goes to considerable trouble in many places to maintain the contrary view: *Physics* VIII. 1; *On the Heaven* I, 270a12–b25; I. 10–12; II. 1; *Metaphysics* XII. 6.

sempiternity was the new kid on the block; so if Plato in fact endorsed it when writing the *Timaeus* one would have expected him to show this by some clear sign even if he chose to narrate the cosmology in proto-historical style.[10] Plato could easily have made Timaeus say something like: 'But since, Socrates, it is an old tradition among the Greeks, and perhaps among all who enquire about such things, to speak of this cosmos as having come to be, I too in the account I am about to give shall often fall in with this familiar way of speaking, even though doing so might seem rather childish – because it is hard for mortals through a long stretch of discourse on the one hand to express thoughts, and on the other hand to receive them, in terms which, though accurate, are strange and unaccustomed.' But Plato has done nothing of the sort.[11]

It would be unreasonable for a modern scholar to argue that if we today should be swayed by this evidence against a sempiternalist reading, the same evidence ought to have stifled the sempiternalist reading of Xenocrates – which it manifestly failed to do. Xenocrates was a Platonist who evidently was convinced, by Aristotle's arguments or by other arguments, that *the truth* about this cosmos is that it is sempiternal. He therefore had a motive, and from his own point of view a good reason, to see sempiternalism in the *Timaeus*. But this is not a motive or reason that should guide the modern interpreter of Plato.[12]

I cannot help thinking that modern sempiternalist interpreters may to some extent be inspired by one or both of two things: first, the desire to put Plato in the same camp as some of the greatest and most sophisticated Platonists of antiquity, especially Plotinus and Proclus; and secondly, a related sense that it would have been naïve and crude of Plato to be serious about the idea that the cosmos had a beginning.[13] The crucial question,

---

[10] It is also possible that sempiternalism did not arrive on the block until after Plato had brought out the *Timaeus*.

[11] It is not that he is generally reticent about themes being unaccustomed; see 48d5 on the Receptacle and 53c1–2 on the particle-geometry. Aristotle is often castigated for uncharitableness because he sticks to a literal reading whereby order replaced pre-cosmic disorder, instead of understanding the disorder counterfactually as the way things would have been without the Demiurge (*On the Heaven* III, 300b17–18). But the reproach is deserved only if it was unreasonable or disingenuous of Aristotle to expect Plato to have planted a clear warning that the 'before and after' were not to be taken seriously, if that was the intention. If I am right, such an expectation on Aristotle's part would have been perfectly reasonable and fair. This case is quite different from that of the Athens–Atlantis story, which Plato's immediate recipients would have known straight off was fictional (see Chapter 5, section 5.3).

[12] On Xenocrates and his philosophy, see Dillon, 2003b, ch. 3, especially 89–136.

[13] This despite the considerable roll-call of literalist interpreters in antiquity; see Sedley, 2007, 107, n. 30. Anti-literalist interpreters are also, of course, inspired by discrepancies between the surface account in the *Timaeus*, especially what it says about the creation of soul, and accounts in the *Phaedrus* and the *Laws*; cf. Cherniss, 1944, 427–30. Since I am focusing only on the *Timaeus* in this book, I shall not

however, is whether the proto-historical picture does philosophical work for Plato which cannot be done (or could not have been done by him) using a sempiternalist account. If the answer is 'Yes', the proto-historicism is more than a presentational device. One can equally ask whether the proto-historical picture and the sempiternalist one are substantially equivalent. If they are not, then either Plato is gravely conflicted or confused, as well as misleading (he means to present sempiternalism but does so under the guise of a substantially different account as if there were no significant difference), or he is serious about the proto-historicism and we need to understand why.

At the beginning of this section I spoke of the 'literalness' (or not) of the proto-historicism, since this is how the question is often phrased. Just now, however, I have slipped into speaking of Plato's 'seriousness' in this connection, although the terms are certainly not synonymous. In fact, it is not easy to find the right terms for stating the issue. Perhaps the best way to do it is by distinguishing the content of the Timaean cosmology from Plato's presentation of the content. Obviously, to insist in a general way on separating content from presentation would be a very bad rule to bring to the writings of Plato, of all philosophers. Even so, this distinction seems to me to provide a useful tool for the limited purpose of formulating the question of how to understand Timaeus's proto-historicism. It is no good putting this in terms of Plato's 'seriousness', since the fact that something is solely an aspect of presentation would not undermine its seriousness: for example, even if the proto-historicism is only a didactic device, it has the serious purpose of communicating more effectively.

In order to explain why 'literalness' too is not fully adequate, let me return to Aristotle. When he asserts in *On the Heaven* I. 10 that Plato in the *Timaeus* says that the cosmos had a beginning but will have no end, Aristotle is not primarily engaging in Plato-exegesis; he is addressing the first-order question whether the world could have had a beginning but no end. He does not ask himself *why* Plato has Timaeus present the cosmos in this way. Aristotle is only interested in (a) whether this represents Plato's actual view in the *Timaeus*, and (b) whether the view can be true. And he is only interested in question (a) because the answer to it forms part of the dialectical context in which he develops his own answer to question (b): Plato is one of the predecessors whose views he surveys before starting his own positive

---

discuss these arguments. A satisfactory literalist exegesis would, in my view, be one that attributes to Plato a serious *cosmological* reason for the proto-historicism. Thus consistency with dialogues that are not primarily cosmological may not be a crucial consideration. In any case, taking the cosmic beginning non-literally leaves untouched some of the difficulties of reconciling the *Timaeus* with other dialogues; see Vlastos, 1964, 414–17; Sedley, 2007, 104, n. 23.

discussion. One reason for surveying contrary views, Aristotle says, is that ignoring them could undermine the credibility of his own sempiternalist position: it might seem to have been reached by default (*On the Heaven* I, 279b4–12). Now, he could incur the same charge of not taking contrary views seriously if he were to accept too easily the claim put about by some of the Platonists that the Timaean 'beginning' is only a matter of presentation. Aristotle makes it clear that he *would* be accepting this too easily if he accepted their attempt to justify their claim: for their justification fails, as he explains at *On the Heaven* I, 279b33–280a10.[14] Giving this explanation leaves Aristotle free to pursue his own first-order enquiry, citing the *Timaeus* as a contrary view which his method requires him to confront openly.

The point of these remarks is to bring out the business-like first-order nature of Aristotle's interest. His question is simply whether or not it is true, or even possible, that the cosmos had a beginning but will have no end. That being so, if one looks at Timaeus's proto-historicism from Aristotle's corner, so to speak, the matter presents itself in the flattest and baldest terms: the Timaean account is interesting only because, in Aristotle's view, it denies the sempiternalism that for him is the true theory. It is reasonable to call this a 'literal' interpretation of the proto-historicism. However, for us – whose chief concern is not with the actual temporal structure of the physical world, but with Plato's meaning – the flat and literal interpretation is surely disappointing and unacceptable. Plato could not have meant to be simply telling his readers: 'The cosmos has not always existed; for one or another number *n*, it has fully existed for only *n* years.' If we find this an unsatisfying interpretation of what Plato is about, it may seem that the only remedy is to maintain that, despite appearances, the position of the *Timaeus* is a sempiternalist one after all. It may seem as if the only way to escape the flatness of literalism is to suppose that Plato in the *Timaeus* is a secret sempiternalist. But these are not the only options. There is also the possibility that Timaean proto-historicism is in a genuine sense emblematic and indeed mythic, but stands for something important *about the cosmos*

---

[14] They had argued that the proto-historicism should be taken no more seriously than the 'first this, then that' of a geometrical construction; e.g. 'First extend to D the side AB of the triangle ABC, then intersect AD at B with a line parallel to AC.' The proof (that the internal angles are equal to two right angles) depends on the simultaneity (or timelessness) of the relationships. Aristotle points out that the cases are not parallel: the original triangle ABC is still present when the new lines are drawn. They are an addition, not a replacement (otherwise there would be no proof). By contrast, the pre-cosmic disorder of the *Timaeus* cannot be simultaneous with the order caused by the Demiurge, because order and disorder are contraries. The others might have replied that the disorder is really only counterfactual, but presumably they failed to make this point (the example of geometrical construction is irrelevant to it), and there is no reason why Aristotle should have made it on their behalf.

7.2 Proto-historical structures (i)

that cannot, or cannot at all easily, be signified in a more direct way. If this is the case, then the proto-historicism cannot be brushed aside to reveal an underlying sempiternalist cosmology. In short, we need to allow for the possible combination 'not just flatly literal, nor just presentational, but an intrinsic aspect of the *content* being presented'.

The possibility of this third option invites an investigation along the following lines: first, we try to identify any important lesson conveyed by casting the cosmology in its actual proto-historical form, and then, if such a lesson emerges, we consider whether it would still be preserved in a sempiternalist cosmology (even if such a framework would make the message more difficult to read). If the answer is that such a lesson or lessons would be preserved, then the proto-historicism is optional, and we are free to think of it as a pedagogical device: sempiternalist interpreters of the *Timaeus* would not be missing anything philosophically significant. If, on the other hand, the lesson would not be preserved, the proto-historicism is intrinsic to what is being presented. If this were the result, we should have to respect it even if doing so meant tolerating some incoherence in Timaeus's narrative. The reason for mentioning incoherence here is that some interpreters uphold the sempiternalist reading on the ground that adopting it eliminates various incoherences thrown up by the proto-historical appearances of the actual discourse.[15] But we are only entitled to prefer sempiternalism for this sort of reason after we have checked to see that the proto-historical aspects are not doing important philosophical work that could not be done without them. The interpreter would have to weigh the value of the philosophical work in question against the disvalue of the incoherences, such as they are.

I shall take up the task of identifying the lesson of Timaeus's proto-historicism in section 7.4 below. First, however, we must look more closely at the different proto-historical structures appearing in his narrative.

7.2 PROTO-HISTORICAL STRUCTURES (I)

It will be useful to distinguish different ways in which Timaeus's account shows a proto-historical 'before and after'. There are at least three kinds of proto-historical feature, and they should be considered separately.

(PH1) There is the way in which a divine agent is shown introducing order into something previously unordered. Thus we are told more than

---

[15] Classic discussions of some sempiternalist arguments of this kind are Vlastos, 1939 and 1964. See also n. 21 for some references to arguments based on the 'cosmic soul before cosmic body' order of creation.

once that the fashioning of the cosmos began when the Demiurge 'took over' the pre-cosmic materials, as if they are already there before he comes on the scene to make the cosmos (30a4; 68e3). We are also shown a divine agency introducing, at a prior pre-cosmic stage, geometric order into unordered and rudimentary versions of the four elements (53a8–b5; 69b3–4; c1).

(PH2) There is the way in which the work of making the cosmos, body and soul, and mortal animals, is shown proceeding in successive stages. We could also think of the pre-cosmic geometrisation (our second PH1 example) as the first stage in the making of the cosmos itself. It is perhaps arbitrary whether a building project starts when construction begins or when the materials are prepared. Note that a literal reading of PH1 examples does not commit one to a literal reading of PH2. It is possible to conceive of a moment when lack of order was made to give way to complete or finished order without necessarily supposing that the transition occurred in a plurality of successive stages.[16]

(PH3) There is the way in which the completion of the cosmos, mortal animals and all, is shown as having taken place at a moment long ago from *now*: a moment that marks the beginning of the history of the world stretching from its inception to the present day. In the *Timaeus–Critias* we first encounter the PH3 structure as encompassing the dramatic 'today' when the characters Socrates, Timaeus, Critias, and Hermocrates are assembled against the background sweep of a past stretching away from their present, through their 'yesterday', back to the cosmic beginning which Timaeus expounds 'today'. However, when recipients of Plato take a view for or against interpreting the Timaean system as covertly sempiternalist, they are obviously considering the matter from their own real-world temporal perspective; and they are equally obviously considering whether Plato means (or 'literally' means) to convey that the physical world in which he and they live or lived was divinely fashioned *once long ago* in relation to Plato and themselves.[17]

---

[16] (i) Cf. Harte, 2002, 215, n. 99; she attributes the point to Burnyeat (conversation).
(ii) PH2 does seem to assume some kind of beginning to the stage-by-stage process. This is because a point comes when the work done in stages is complete, and it is hard to conceive, or anyway to imagine, how a purposeful series of stages would reach completion unless it had started. However, the beginning of a stage-by-stage process need not be understood in PH1 terms, i.e. as the transition from a situation in which matter pre-existed in an unordered state. One can conceive that God created the world both *ex nihilo* and by stages. Thus PH1 and PH2 are logically independent of each other.

[17] Compare attitudes to Timaeus's discourse and Critias's account. It is taken for granted that the former's subject is something real, namely the cosmos, and then there is dispute about the fictitiousness of the proto-historical presentation. With the latter, by contrast, while moderns may dispute the fictitiousness of the subject ('Has Atlantis and its civilisation ever really existed?'), they assume that, purely fabulous or not, it *is* located in the past: i.e. that evidence about *the past* is what tells for or

The PH3 structure is distinct from PH1 and PH2 in that neither separately nor together do the latter entail PH3. This is because features 1 and 2 merely order things in a narrative, whereas feature 3 locates things in the past relative to the thinker's *now*. One could construct a 'cosmogonic' story with features 1 and 2, and simply leave the matter at that. One might have shown how a cosmos as perfect as possible would come to be if such a thing did or were to come to be. Relations of succession depicted in such an account would be internal to a suppositional cosmogony left unconnected with our world today. (The logical point is the same whether that phrase 'our world today', or its Timaean synonym 'this All', is being used referringly by Timaeus and co. in the dialogue-world, or by Plato and his recipients and other inhabitants of the real world.) It seems clear, moreover, that engaging in a *scientific* cosmogonic account (as opposed to a merely suppositional similar narrative) involves deploying 'our world' or 'this All' to refer to the cosmogonic subject.[18] Thus doing scientific cosmogony – whether Timaeus is doing it or Plato via Timaeus – means using PH3 and not just PH 1 and 2.[19]

At any rate, features PH1 – 3 in combination give the full Timaean proto-historicist picture: the picture of the cosmos brought into being from unordered matter; brought into being by stages; and, long ago completed, being lived in now by us. Our main question is whether Timaean proto-historicism is merely presentational. I shall now discuss each of the three PH features from the point of view of this question.

I shall begin with PH2, the stage-by-stage mode of cosmopoiesis. Then, still in this section, I shall turn to PH1. PH3 will need most attention, and will be the main topic of the next section.

I believe that the PH2 feature can be treated as presentational without loss of philosophical content. As has often been noted, the different stages in the text are distinguished and arranged on systematic principles, in terms of

---

against the truth of the story. However, Neoplatonist interpreters expounded Critias's story (at least so far as it occurs in the *Timaeus*) in sempiternalist fashion, seeing in it an allegory for the timeless or sempiternal play of metaphysical principles.

[18] The point is a truism, yet it gives depth to the repeated demonstratives in Timaeus's culminating statement: 'Finally let us state that our discourse about the All is now complete [*telos echein*]. Having thus received its full complement [*labôn kai sumplêrôtheis*] of mortal and immortal animals, *this cosmos* [*hode ho kosmos*] – visible animal containing <whatever is> visible, sense-perceptible god that images the intelligible – greatest and best, fairest and most perfect [*teleôtatos*], *this cosmic system* [*ouranos hode*] has come to be, one and unique of its kind' (92c4–9).

[19] For a particularly interesting untypical example of a PH3-type construction, see 41d8–42d5. Here the relation between the cosmic beginning and human beings embedded in subsequent history is viewed *ex parte ante*, when the Demiurge instructs the immortal souls about the demands of mortal life. He is looking ahead not, as it might be in a PH2 passage, to the next stage of world-production, but to the future of the having-been-produced human race in the having-been-produced world.

logical, causal, or explanatory order. For example, the two accounts of the pre-cosmic genesis of the materials (the Receptacle and the particle geometry) are presented after the genesis of the living cosmos itself. The reason is that intelligent demiurgy must be established first in the account because it is the principal cause of the cosmos and the mortal animals; the materials are only contributory causes. Another example: in the detailed construction of the mortal animal Timaeus begins with the non-rational aspects of soul. This is because rendering them more controllable is the main reason for major features of the anatomy (69d6–73a8). Another stretch of anatomical construction begins with the bone-marrow because it is through this that soul is united to body in mortals. Then come bones because in them marrow is encased, and the skeleton is the central infrastructure. We may see this order of presentation as reflecting a choice by Plato to expound the anatomy by starting with what is innermost and moving outwards (73b1–76e6). The anatomy culminates with sections on the organs and processes of nutrition, 'irrigation',[20] and respiration; and here we see the body itself working in the opposite direction, i.e. taking in materials from outside and using them in various ways deeper within (77c6–81b4). Depicting all this as a series of divine makings adds clarity by dividing the topics and indicating various relations of dependence; it does not add substance.

In some places serial depiction serves the more rhetorical purpose of emphasis. There is the moment when, after fashioning the cosmic body and soul, the Demiurge rejoiced and was prompted to make this living being 'still more similar to the paradigm' by adding the visible astronomical system, thereby rendering the world subject to chronological time (37c6 ff.). The reason, surely, for marking this part of the work by a new intake of breath, so to speak, is to jerk us into a special act of attention to the magnificence of the system and the purpose behind it. Part of the purpose is to create a lien, the first one mentioned in the whole account, between the immortal cosmos and the rational souls of mortals. Things are designed so that the intellectual motions of the cosmic god, although silent (37b5–6), are not its privileged secrets (like the thoughts of humans when not put into words); instead, they are all the time communicated visually to us so that we may 'come to share in number' (39b5–c1; cf. 46e7–47b2). Then there is the great hinge-point of the whole cosmology where it begins to swing from immortals to the mortals, with the drama of the Demiurge's mission to the other gods, his turning back to the mixing bowl to create the new immortal souls, his investing these with the knowledge they will need, and his

---

[20] That is, the vascular system.

7.2 Proto-historical structures (1)

withdrawal thereupon into his 'own characteristic attitude' as the others begin their work (41a7–42e6). This stage-by-stage account captures various logical and explanatory dependencies, but it also brings out the momentousness of the turn from the genesis of gods to the genesis of mortals by, as it were, showing the transition in slow motion.

There is also the notorious passage where Timaeus speaks of the construction of the cosmic body and the cosmic soul in that order, and then breaks off to say that in fact they were made in the reverse order: '[God] constructed the soul to be prior in genesis and in excellence and <to be> older than the body' (34a8–35a1, especially 34c4–5). But according to some scholars the reverse order cannot be coherently specified.[21] This is because Timaeus characterises certain of the soul's ingredients by reference to 'bodies' (35a1–6). (His picture is that the soul is constituted so as to be cognizant of both the eternal and the sensible, 37a5–c3.) Hence body as such is not straightforwardly posterior to the soul. This is supposed to make it glaringly self-contradictory to speak of the soul as made before the body – even though Timaeus says that that would have been the 'correct' narrative order. The scholars in question infer from all this that Plato is deliberately signalling that *no* time-like order of the events is to be taken literally. I do not accept this inference.[22] But at the same time I see no difficulty in conceding that it is for reasons of presentation, not content, that Plato puts these and the other stages of world-making in time-like relations of before and after. It would be a mistake, however, to conclude from this survey of PH2 examples (successive stages of world-making) that there is only presentational significance in proto-historical features 1 and 3.

I turn now to PH1, the way in which a divine agent is shown putting precosmic disorder into order. Since the disorder is shown as 'there already', PH1 compels us to picture the origin of the cosmos as involving the bringing to an end of a previous situation.

David Sedley has argued that the analogy between human and divine craftsmanship is what leads Plato to presuppose a 'genetic' (i.e. protohistorical) origin: '... the premise that the world had a genetic origin is needed by Timaeus to ground his conception of divine craftsmanship'.[23] The

---

[21] Cherniss, 1944, 424–5; Tarán, 1971, 374–5; Dillon, 1997, 39–40.
[22] The conclusion does not follow, because there is no contradiction. (a) 'Bodies' at 35a1–6 could refer to the corporeal materials of the cosmos, which pre-date the formation of the soul. (b) There need be no contradiction in explaining the nature of *A* by reference to *B* (so that *B* is conceptually prior to *A*) while claiming that *B* comes into being after *A*: more than one kind of priority–posteriority relation is in play.
[23] Sedley, 2007, 106.

aspect of this that I would emphasise has to do with the incorporeal nature of the cosmos-forming intelligence. Human craftsmen make things out of pre-existing materials because they reasonably assume that the materials left to themselves are not going to turn into or otherwise produce the desired objects. Ask one why he assumes it, and the sensible answer would be: 'Well, here is the stuff – it has been here all this while – and the object you are talking about hasn't yet come into being.' In other words, to think of the matter of the cosmos as having been there pre-cosmically is to be thinking of it as something that by itself could never have turned into or generated this world. One extrapolates from how the matter was before the separate incorporeal intelligence intervened to how it would have been if this had not occurred, and one thereby attributes the ordering to the separate intelligence.

Now, the question of whether Plato means the reader or audience to understand that time-like transition to be an aspect of the actual genesis of the cosmos or instead to understand it as a mere presentational device, depends on whether he employs it as a *premiss he needs in order to make it convincing* that the intelligence responsible for this cosmos is incorporeal. We must remember that Plato in the cosmology is aiming to produce *pistis*, assurance or conviction (29c3). Does he need to get his audience to accept the assumption that disorderly matter pre-existed because (he thinks) only in that way can he secure in them the conviction that the divine principle responsible for order is incorporeal, transcends nature? Or can he count on them to be possessed of that tenet already? The answer is surely going to vary for different recipients. For example, let us grant that Plato could count on some of his associates, suppose Xenocrates, to be in a state of solid assurance that cosmic order has an incorporeal source even while also holding that the order has always prevailed.[24] It seems unrealistic, however, to assume that everyone whom Plato was trying to reach with the *Timaeus* fell into this camp. Suppose that with some recipients he is trying to make the position convincing for the first time. (Suppose even that he is trying to make it as convincing as possible to himself.) Of course he will not establish the point about the incorporeity of intelligence with an audience not disposed to be sympathetic to his ideas in a general way. But why should we assume that being thus generally sympathetic automatically carries with it a firm and clear pre-existing acceptance of the tenet that the intelligence

---

[24] According to Dillon's reconstruction, Xenocrates held that the transcendent source is an intelligible paradigm (or, perhaps, paradigms) received by the cosmic soul from prior divine principles (i.e. the *Nous*-Monad and the Indefinite Dyad), and projected by that soul 'onto the physical plane' (Dillon, 2003b, 107).

7.2 Proto-historical structures (i)

responsible for the cosmos is incorporeal? I am arguing, in short, that it would undermine Plato's case in some quarters if he began by stating that a separate divine intelligence is the source of order in the universe, while simultaneously saying: 'Actually, of course, there never was any pre-existing matter; the only correct way to think about unordered matter all by itself is to think: "That is how things *would have been* in the absence of the incorporeal intelligence".' Some of the recipients in this situation might think or say: 'But if the formed matter has always been there, how can it be rational for us to be convinced that the matter itself, corporeal matter, is not in its own way alive and purposeful, so as to have formed itself into the cosmos – something which perhaps it has been doing from everlasting? For this possibility is not excluded by the picture you present.'

No doubt some thinkers near Plato, e.g. Xenocrates, could afford to react to the picture of pre-cosmic matter as if it were meant only to make the point about the separate world-making intelligence more vivid to the childish imagination (as distinct from making it convincing to the rational intellect). And Plato could afford to let such thinkers react in that way. But it seems to me that we simply do not know enough to be able to claim that such thinkers were typical members of the audience whom Plato hoped to reach. That is, we do not know that the intended audience was limited to those who (a) were already committed, clear-headed, incorporealists about the world-making intelligence, and (b) saw no difficulty in combining this tenet with the sempiternity of the cosmos. It may be true that, in the eyes of much subsequent tradition, Xenocrates 'established himself as the official interpreter of Plato',[25] but why should we think that Xenocrates was representative of all those who *Plato* hoped would give serious attention to the cosmology?[26] Only if we had good reason to claim this would we have good reason to claim that the Timaean transition from disorder to order (PH1) is philosophically dispensable.

So far what has emerged is that the dispensability of the PH1 feature would have depended in part on the pre-existing mind-sets of the envisaged audience. Since these may well have been heterogeneous, and perhaps so in respects relevant to acceptance of the incorporeal status of intelligence, we cannot on this basis reach one determinate answer to the question whether PH1 is serious support for the cosmology or is only a dispensable aid to the imagination.

---

[25] Tarán, 1971, 390.
[26] In fact, the *Timaeus* itself suggests that the qualifications for giving it serious attention included only: strong interest in natural science, fairly advanced mathematical training, and some sympathy (at least) for a starting point that asserts the maximal excellence of this cosmos.

7.3 PROTO-HISTORICAL STRUCTURES (II)

Our inconclusive discussion of PH1 (transition from disorder to order) may have left us thinking that Plato might himself have believed *in foro interno* that the cosmos is without beginning, but still expressed himself in a contrary way just to make sure that everyone got the point about the incorporeity of world-making Intelligence. In that case, it might be said, although he was certainly serious about driving home that point, he himself did not seriously view the cosmos as having a proto-historical origin – but the latter is the issue we are discussing. In the present section, however, through examining the meaning and implications of PH3, I shall give a reason for thinking that the *Timaeus* is committed to such an origin.

PH3 is the structure whereby our present-day cosmos is seen as the very same one that was once completely brought into being 'long ago'. Its life began through demiurgic creation, and it has endured since then (and, according to Timaeus, will endure for ever). Now, the main question of this section is the philosophical significance of PH3, but before taking this up let me briefly consider two other questions. These are: (a) the relation of PH3 to PH1 and PH2, and (b) any implications of PH3 concerning the pastwards duration of the cosmos.

(a) I pointed out in the last section that PH1 and PH2 do not entail PH3, either separately or together. What about entailments in the reverse direction? Well, what is essential to PH3 is the idea that once the cosmos had been fully created, a new phase set in, namely its post-creation existence: the existence of that which the act or acts of creation were for. This is the literally temporal existence that is or constitutes the duration of the world. PH3 implies only that the creating has been completed and the creatum has continued in existence. Logically, then, it does not matter whether or not the activity of creating went through successive stages (PH2); nor does it matter whether or not it involved a transition from pre-cosmic disorder (PH1). So PH3 is neither entailed by nor entails PH1 and 2.

(b) At first sight it seems clear that PH3 is compatible with the view that the cosmos has existed from everlasting, i.e. that any given stretch of past time was preceded by an equal stretch of past time (belonging, of course, to the same temporal series). This is because we can think in a purely aspectual way of the cosmos's status as divine creatum. The thought is that at any given moment of its temporal existence the cosmos is a having-been-created thing, and the truth of this leaves it open whether or not there was a first moment of time, or whether or not there is a pastwards limit L, finitely remote from the present, such that every moment of past time lies between

7.3 Proto-historical structures (ii)

the present and L. So PH3 seems to allow for the theory that the cosmos is everlasting in both temporal directions (since the futurewards case is not in doubt in the Timaean context). And this appearance is reasonable as long as we consider the PH3 structure in an abstract and schematic way. But, as we shall see presently, the case changes once PH3 is more concretely understood as applying to a cosmos that fits the Timaean specifications.

Let me now turn to the main question. What is the point of the PH3 structure in the *Timaeus* cosmology? I have already mentioned that it is a way of underlining the identity of the god-created cosmos with this world that is going on round us today. Coming at the point from a slightly different angle, we can further describe the PH3 structure as Plato's way of showing how the divinely originated cosmos is also a *natural* world that proceeds in accordance with natural processes and natural causal connections. The reason for the emphasis is to bring out the fact that the natural workings are not themselves the actions or activities of originating gods. PH3 puts nature (including ourselves) in the foreground and transcendent divine origination firmly in the background, keeping them both separate and connected. It is not clear that there is any better device for this purpose than PH3.

We from our perspective may well find it *prima facie* easier (whatever we ultimately believe) to make sense of or imaginatively realise the natural world's separateness from, rather than its closeness to, a divine origin. This is surely due to the fact that we are so used to thinking of God as incorporeal and transcendent. To us the separateness is so obvious that the problem is in how to connect nature with the divine origin at all. But Plato cannot so easily take for granted the separateness of the two, because divinity and corporeity are not mutually exclusive for him. The Timaean cosmos is itself a sense-perceptible god full of visible astral gods. The outlook that makes this a possible view belongs to the same culture that made possible previous philosophies such as those of Empedocles and Diogenes according to which the corporeal materials of the world, or natural forces operating in matter, are divine and intelligent and are working their regular purposes out through the patterns of nature all around us. Plato's cosmic god is a new scion of the same teleological stock as these older divine principles, and the latter are culturally real enough to Plato to give him the task of deliberately excluding them from his system. The exclusion begins with his thorough 'de-divinification' of the four corporeal elements.[27] It is consolidated by his

---

[27] See Chapter 6, esp. sections 6.7.2 and 6.8.

endorsement of the PH3 structure, which (a) shows the incorporeal origin of nature as always already *having* played its part, and thereby (b) foregrounds *what* was originated, namely the ordinary course of nature itself.

Let us now look more closely at the 'ordinary course of nature' side of the PH3 picture, starting with the cosmic animal itself. Its soul and body were designed and constructed by the supreme and invisible Demiurge, but the motions of the visible celestial system belong to the stars that constitute that system, and their astronomical movements manifest the activity of the cosmic soul itself. The cosmic animal is a *natural* being – one that has the status of a great god because its life is intelligent, immortal, completely self-sufficient, and all-containing, but nonetheless natural because once it has been made by the Demiurge, being assigned its proper motion by him (34a1–5), it works on its own physical and psychological principles.[28] With the mortal animals it is even clearer that they have been constructed to live their own lives in accordance with their own natures and that of the environment. The ancillary gods fashioned their complex respiratory and metabolic systems, but it is clearly the mortal animals *themselves* that will be breathing in and out and undergoing the stages of the metabolic cycle. The gods fashioned the organs of vision, hearing, and speech, but it is of course for the animals to engage in these activities *themselves*. Similarly, the gods designed and constructed the original organs of animal reproduction, but again it is the mortal animals *themselves*, male and female, that are to play their respective roles of insemination, conception, gestation of the foetus. In short, the animals will be living their own lives.[29] Plato's detailed treatments of the structure, materials, and physical workings of various animal organs proclaim the wisdom of divine craftsmanship, but also the mundane biological reality of the natural systems themselves.[30]

---

[28] *Pace* Tarán, 1971, 376–8, Vlastos, 1964, was correct in arguing that there is no contradiction in holding that souls are both self-moving and brought into being by the Demiurge. They are self-moving in that once in existence they essentially move of themselves. But this does not mean that they are self-moving in the sense of being wholly responsible for the fact that they move at all. They owe this fact in part, of course, to their own nature, but also to whatever made them, given that they were made. The anxiety about the corporeal elements discussed in Chapter 6, sections 6.7.2 and 6.8, was lest it turned out that they were self-moving in the stronger sense, i.e. wholly and from always responsible for their own movement and existence.

[29] At 41d1–3 the Demiurge hands over to his ancillaries with the words: '... for the rest, do you, weaving mortal to immortal, bring to completion living creatures: bring them to birth, give them nourishment and make them grow, and as they perish receive them back again.' 'Bring them to birth' means in part: 'Give them the wherewithal for reproduction' just as 'give them nourishment' means 'provide them with food and the wherewithal for nutrition'.

[30] This chapter follows the *Timaeus* in focusing so exclusively on mortal animals as distinct from plants, on which see Chapter 4, n. 21.

7.3 Proto-historical structures (ii)

How is it to be shown that the mundane biological reality of mortal animals has a source that is not merely divine (ageless, immortal, prior to perishable things), but transcendently so? The obvious way to do it is in terms of the PH3 structure. For the present purpose, however, the *Timaeus* gives this structure a particular form which we have not yet discussed. So far, we have said only that PH3 in the *Timaeus* shows the present-day cosmos as having been divinely originated long ago. As long as we consider only the immortal cosmos and the astral gods, it seems clear that 'having been divinely originated' can be understood as purely aspectual,[31] and that 'long ago' can be interpreted as 'infinitely long ago', i.e. so as not to rule it out that the world has existed from everlasting. But when it comes to mortal animals, the *Timaeus* gives us a version of PH3 in which (a) there is a *first* or *prototype* generation directly minted by divine demiurgy, and (b) this gives rise to subsequent generations by natural reproduction.[32] The prototypes belong with, because they head the series of, the post-origin generations, and they do so through natural reproduction. But their primacy connects them equally with the transcendent source. They were divinely made in immediate accordance with the transcendent intelligible paradigm, and through them, because of natural reproduction, the paradigm is somehow reflected in their wholly natural descendants.

What about the immortal parts of nature: the cosmic god and the astral gods? Being immortal they neither beget nor are biologically begotten; hence the notion of a divinely crafted ancestral prototype cannot apply to them. But the world they constitute is incomplete without the mortal kinds. Once those cosmic and celestial gods have been brought into being the mortal prototypes must be brought into being forthwith. The lives of the cosmic and celestial gods cannot have run from everlasting if the series of mortal generations has not run from everlasting. And as far as I can see the latter is ruled out by the assumption of mortal *prototypes*. Perhaps it is possible to conceive of the prototypes as standing at the head of an infinite number of generational removes from their biological descendants, so that the ancestry stretches back through endless time. But in the absence of any obvious model showing how this is possible, it seems clear that the *Timaeus* story as actually presented implies a finite number of generations between now and the prototypes for any given mortal kind, and thereby implies that

---

[31] The use of 'aspectual' in this exposition is meant to convey a conceptual structure. It does not depend on the textual claim that *Timaeus* verb-formations representing divine demiurgic action encode perfective aspect.

[32] I am leaving aside the complication that female humans and brutes are reincarnations of ethically inferior members of the first generation: 42b5–c4; 90e6–91a1; 91d5–92c3.

for some unknowable finite number n the cosmos is now in its nth year. And I do not see clearly how the story is not thereby committed to PH1, the proto-historical transition from the pre-cosmos to the cosmos. Can we think (1) that, for some finite n, the cosmos is now in its nth year, without being committed to the thought (2) that we are now in the nth year measured from a past-wards limit on the series of moments at which it was true to say 'The cosmos (complete with the chronological system) is having-been-originated' (this being understood aspectually, as above)? And can we be confident that Plato and those around him would have been able to think (1) and (2) without also thinking (3) that there was a *when*[33] when the cosmos had not yet come to be, so that it came to be having not been? But any ancient Greek who thinks (3) will surely also think (4) that *when* the cosmos had not yet come to be, there nevertheless existed the materials out of which it was made; since there would be no question of supposing that it came to be but not out of anything.

I have argued that Plato's reason or motive for picturing the cosmos and the systems within it in terms of the general structure PH3 is to mark vividly the difference between, on the one hand, the moment of divine origination and, on the other hand, the natural workings of the order that was originated, while at the same time making it intelligible that they are linked. I then argued that realising the PH3 structure for mortal animals in terms of prototypes makes it difficult if not impossible for him to escape the implication that the world has existed for an unspecifiable finite time. Even if this implication is unsettling,[34] the strangeness has to be balanced against the importance of what is achieved by securing that connection between a natural order and a divine origin.

There may have been a difference, of course, between the way in which Plato thought he needed to present this idea to others, and some more sophisticated grasp of it which he kept to himself. However, before turning to this possibility we must note that the PH3 picture is out of kilter with a vital element of the account, namely the Receptacle-concept. The Receptacle clearly plays its kinetic role *vis-à-vis* the four materials even in the world today. It is natural to suppose that its role of existential substrate should follow suit. But the Receptacle as existential substrate is half of a

---

[33] They need not and should not think of this *when* as in the time series of measurable periods: cf. Vlastos, 1939.

[34] It is unsettling because of the lack of transparency. Compare this case with (a) the biblical account which is designed to enable us to calculate the world's finite age from the ages of known persons in the human generations from Adam, and (b) contemporary cosmology which has various ways of calculating the current age of the universe.

relationship of which the other half is the Forms of the materials. So their part too in the genesis of the materials would be on-going, not played out 'once upon a time'. The transcendent cause, here identified simply with the Forms of fire etc., would be equally causally relevant at every point in the history of the universe.

The discrepancy between this 'continual' formation of the materials and the 'once upon a time' demiurgic fashioning of animals may be one of those 'glaring inconsistencies' which some scholars think Plato has scattered in the *Timaeus* to indicate (as if he had no other way of doing so) that the 'once upon a time' demiurgy is a façade that fronts a sempiternalist position. Whether this is a reasonable hypothesis depends on whether Plato could in his own mind have combined a thoroughgoing sempiternalism with the philosophical point which (I have argued) the PH3 picture is meant to convey. If this point would have been very hard or impossible to preserve in sempiternalist terms, then we are on weak ground for concluding that Plato was 'really' a sempiternalist throughout the *Timaeus* or that the internal discrepancies show anything more than human failure to gain complete control over all parts of a huge and difficult subject-matter.

So the question now is whether it is reasonable to suppose that a sempiternalist Plato could have maintained a clear connection between nature and its divine origin while at the same time marking the clear difference between the two. Sempiternalism entails that if there is a transcendent origin, no generation of mortals is more closely related to it than any other. Consequently, sempiternalists who want to keep the connection with the transcendent origin are committed, I think, to regarding divine demiurgy in the light of the paradigm as equally operative in the coming to be of mortal animals at every stage. And how, if one holds this, can one also coherently hold that mortals in each generation are also genuinely natural causes of their own offspring? Perhaps a reconciliation can be effected, but our question should be whether *Plato* in his place in history could have effected it.

The difficulty of doing so will become clearer if we locate the *Timaeus* in a larger philosophical context. The *once and for all* picture of divine origination can be conveniently labelled 'deism'.[35] Timaean deism has the Demiurge making the cosmic animal which then exists under its own

---

[35] This is the label of contemporary philosophers of theology for the view that once God made the world, the world continued to exist without being constantly created, or recreated, or conserved, or sustained in being by God. More commonly, 'deism' is used of the view that the existence of God can be established without special revelation; also of the view that God created but is not providential.

steam and by the laws of its own nature. The living activity of the cosmic soul in this account seems a good illustration of 'under its own steam'. The Demiurge is said to delight when he observes his product 'in motion and alive' (37c6), i.e. living its own life and, since its life is its existence, exercising its own existence now from itself. The passage may hint that the Demiurge is pleased not only by its excellence but also because it is, as it was meant to be, independent (except for the fact that it exists at his pleasure; he could destroy it if he wished [41a7–b2]). Another very obvious deistic touch: once the Demiurge has set up the immortal souls of mortals and commissioned his ancillaries to construct the mortal bodies, he is depicted as withdrawing (42e5–7).[36] Presumably the account allows us to imagine the ancillaries as likewise withdrawing when the immortal souls start to live in and through the bodies constructed for them.[37]

Now, how easy is it to replace this deistic sort of account with one that understands divine origination as 'never over', but even so preserves the distinction as well as the connection between nature and its divine origin, coherently allowing that natural things in the world today operate by their own powers and activities? The history of Western philosophy shows that this is no mean challenge.[38] The pressure towards asserting that divine origination is immediately necessary to retain the creaturely world in being at every moment of its history, so that all stages, early or late historically speaking, equally radiate from the same transcendent source, can easily end in a vision of nature as an attribute or offshoot or phase of the divine, or in an occasionalism that altogether denies causal powers to natural beings.[39] Obviously there have been philosophers more than happy to surrender to one or another of these resulting visions. However, our concern at the moment is with the difficulty of resisting them if what one wants is to maintain a clear distinction between the operation of nature and the operation of the divine cause of nature. Even today, philosophers of theology are not agreed on exactly how to understand the lien between

---

[36] But Cornford, 1935, 147, n. 1, is right to warn against seeing here the 'rest' (*katapausis*) of Genesis 2:1.
[37] Divine withdrawal makes it easier to declare divine non-responsibility for human depravity (42d2–4; e3–4).
[38] The technicality, sophistication, and ingenuity of recent responses, informed by the subtle and vigorous mediaeval and sixteenth- and seventeenth-century debates, are on display in Freddoso, 1991, McCann and Kvanvig, 1991, and Kvanvig, 2007. See also Oakes, 1977 and Quinn, 1979. On some related discussions in late antiquity and mediaeval Islamic philosophy, see Sorabji 1983, Part IV; for the ancient sources see Sorabji 2004, vol. 2, chs. 8–9. On continuous creation in Neoplatonism, see Phillips, 1997. On the debates from the mediaeval to the early modern period, see Lee, 2008.
[39] We may view Aristotle's rejection of the early Platonistic view on the role of the Idea of Man in human genesis as the ancestor of later defences of 'second causes' as against occasionalism.

7.3 Proto-historical structures (ii)

the world and God in a way that avoids deism (and in general any position that makes God seem causally too remote from the operations of creatures) while at the same time avoiding pantheism or occasionalism; nor is there even agreement on whether a coherent position on the matter is even possible.[40]

One prop for the view that Plato in the *Timaeus* is a crypto-sempiternalist has been the assumption that he could easily have replaced the deistic or PH3 parts of the actual text with sempiternalist versions, but chose not to do so for purely didactic reasons. Although this assumption deserves to be examined critically, it tends to be taken for granted by its adherents. One cannot help suspecting circular reasoning. If some interpreters do not bother to look and see whether the proto-historicism, or some form of it, carries an irreplaceable meaning for the *content* of the cosmology, this is probably because they are already from the outset convinced that the proto-historicism is a childish surface-phenomenon. From their standpoint it is settled and obvious (a) that the account as actually given can be exchanged for an 'adult' sempiternalist version without loss or distortion of content; and (b) that it would have been feasible for Plato *first* to formulate for himself the grown-up sempiternalist doctrine, and *then* to trick it out in proto-historicist clothing. But if instead one scours the different proto-historical features for philosophical meaning, between them they yield the idea that nature has a divine origin, yet is not itself part of or an attribute of or consubstantial with or a phase of the divine origin, any more than the divine origin is part of nature. The question then becomes: could *this* idea, content unchanged, be presented in terms both sempiternalist and coherently available to Plato? The considerations brought forward from the later history of philosophy show that it hardly could. Someone may suggest that Plato was an *in*coherent crypto-sempiternalist. But why is this kinder than allowing that his non-sempiternalist deism, shown in his reliance on the PH3 structure, is serious and sincere? I conclude that Xenocrates's anti-literalist interpretation did the author of the *Timaeus* no favours, and that

---

[40] See the last paragraph of Kvanvig, 2007, for a marked lack of complacency on this score. In outline, a solution, if there is one, will probably turn on a distinction of roles according to which God's task is to be constantly or in a single act creating the entire universe anew by his will alone *ex nihilo*, whereas the task of every finite natural substance is to engage in an existence defined by exercises of powers of a totally different metaphysical order. If the kinds of task are different enough, the reality and powers of finite substances would not seem to compete with, nor therefore to be inconsistent with, the total immediate dependence of everything in nature on the infinite God. Such a highly developed theological perspective, in which divinity is understood as the power of creating *ex nihilo*, was nowhere near being available to Plato.

Aristotle's literalism was not only not uncharitable, but literally correct (even though hermeneutically inadequate in its literalism).[41]

Assigning to the divine world-maker continuous engagement with the world may be conceptually easier in some sectors than in others. For example, it may be relatively easy to assert that divine providence, in the sense of concern about the ethical faring of mortals, never sleeps and is interested down to the last detail.[42] But this in itself has little to do with cosmology or cosmogony. It may also be comparatively easy to hold that the world-maker is the constantly operative cause of celestial motion. Then if one sees the incessant movement of the heavens not as an adjunct to their created being but as of its essence, it is easy to move to the anti-deistic conclusion that a distinct divine power is constantly maintaining them in existence even today. I do not mean to assert that Plato could not or did not have such thoughts about the heavens.[43] But try extending this picture to the detail of the mortal realm, so that a divinity crafts each animal as it comes into existence. The result is absurd if it implies, as it certainly seems to, that intra-mundane causation, i.e. parental procreation, is not responsible for the process. And the very hard work of showing how to avoid this implication still lay in the future. Thus notwithstanding passages in Plato that may suggest the idea of continuous divine creation, there is good reason to accept that when his focus is on the divine origination of mortals, or on this as much as on the divine origination of the heavens, he relies, not merely seems to rely, on a proto-historical (namely, PH3) way of thinking.[44]

---

[41] With Xenocrates there are different possibilities. He may simply have missed the philosophical point of the Timaean PH3 structure. Or he may have seen and sympathised with this point (strict separation of nature's divine origin from its everyday natural workings) but underestimated the difficulty of combining it with his own Platonistic sempiternalism. Or he may not have cared about maintaining the strict separation. Xenocrates wrote separate works on physics and on metaphysical subjects, but we cannot infer from this that he cared about an ontological separation of natural operations from divine ones.

[42] Cf. *Laws* x, 902b ff. The phrase *eis merismon ton eschaton telos apeirgasmenoi*, 903b9, is translated by Saunders in Cooper, 1997, as 'that have perfected the minutest constituents of the universe'; but it means, I think, 'that have accomplished their [sc. own] charge down to the finest differentiation', i.e. have become overseers of every detail (cf. LSJ s.v. *telos* 2–3 and 5).

[43] E.g. at *Laws* x, 896e8–899b9, the Athenian argues that the major processes of the universe are going on under the guidance of perfectly virtuous souls, i.e. gods.

[44] *Sophist* 265c1–e6 may seem to tell in favour of continuous divine production of creatures that 'grow from seeds and roots' and of inanimate formations: see the continuous *dēmiourgountos* at c4 (but see also the perfect participle at 266b4). In fact, the Visitor is making a weaker point: '[Those things are formed] with ratiocination and divine knowledge that comes about from god' (c8–9; cf. d3, 'in accordance with god'); i.e. it is as if the things under formation somehow embody a divine knowledge whereby they are formed. The main claim, which comes at e3 (cf. c7–8), is that ultimately God, not blind nature, is responsible for how growth works. This is consistent with a *Timaeus*-style deism of prototypes. In fact, the parallel at 265e4 ff. between divine and human craft-objects and craft-activities may suggest a deistic conception of the divine ones.

7.4 PROPAGATION OF ANIMALS IN THE *TIMAEUS*

We must look more closely at the causation of mortal animals in the *Timaeus*. This is a perplexing matter. According to the account, demiurgic gods create the first mortal animals, and then it is for the animals themselves to engage in their biological functions. It is they that eat, breathe, and so forth. In a similar way, as we noted, the supreme god creates the celestial system which then runs by its own natural powers stemming from the power of the cosmic soul. Now in these examples so far, what the created being itself naturally does is quite different from what the divine demiurgic agency is said to do. The Demiurge fashions the cosmic soul and the heavens, but the cosmic soul and the heavenly bodies give rise to and exhibit circular motion (33b–39d). Divine agents fashion lungs, stomach, intestines, and vascular system, but the resulting mortal animals use these organs to breathe, digest, and so on (69c–73a; 77c–81e). In these cases there is a clear division of labour between what the divine originators do and what the created beings do once originated. This division reinforces the crucial assumption that nature both depends on a transcendent origin and constitutes an order unto itself. That assumption is correspondingly weakened by any violation of the principle of division of labour.

It is on this score that the generation of mortals in the *Timaeus* presents a problem. The first male and female animals themselves, or physical subsystems within them, can and must (if the world is to continue complete) do what the crafting gods first did: form the bodies of a new generation of mortal animals. Compare this with respiration and metabolism. That an animal breathes and digests does not by itself result in a new such animal capable of breathing and digestion. Hence the fact that it breathes and digests does not logically raise the possibility that its organs of respiration and nutrition came about simply through the breathing and digestion of another like itself. By contrast, the fact that an animal generates offspring of the same kind does raise the lively possibility that it too was generated by an animal of its own kind; and so on back through the generations sempiternally. And if in every case an animal was formed by another such animal, we not only need not, but also logically cannot, invoke divine demiurgy to explain a supposed prototype animal, as there was no first generation and therefore no prototype.

Thus the Timaean account faces embarrassment from the likeness between what the mortal animals do, and what divine demiurgy does, when *what the mortal animals do* is identified specifically as: *production of animals of their kind*. It faces the question why divine demiurgy needs to be invoked to explain the formation from matter of any set of mortal animals. But (according to the argument of the previous section), abandoning the animal prototypes means abandoning the picture whereby each race of animals is both the effect of a transcendent divine cause and (after the first generation containing males and females)[45] a series of natural generations. In that picture, the race as a whole connects with the divine through and only through the prototype generation, with subsequent generations inheriting from it a formation originally divine.[46]

We can cast the problem the other way round. We can ask: how, if divine demiurgy was necessary for the formation of *any* mortal animals from inanimate materials, was it ever subsequently possible for mere mortal animals to bring to formation from similar materials any offspring of their own? The puzzle now is how this happens in any generation otherwise than by the immediate operation of an extra-mundane intelligent principle. Yet if we make that the cause of the genesis of each new mortal individual, we are installing incorporeal powers in place of natural powers, turning natural parents into occasionalist ciphers with no progenerative force of their own but controlled from beyond nature.[47]

One could retort that the appearance of difficulty here is rhetorical, artificial, and exaggerated. What is so paradoxical about holding *both* that divine demiurgy was necessary to produce the first mortals, *and* that from then on mortals produced mortals by natural processes? It is only paradoxical on the assumption that for offspring to come into being by natural processes is as surprising and inexplicable as it would be if the first animals had come into being spontaneously, whether from inanimate matter on its own or even *ex nihilo*, but at any rate not by immediate divine causation. But (the retort continues) natural birth is not in the least surprising or inexplicable. Once animals of a given kind exist – and this includes even the divinely crafted first ones – they produce others of their kind *because it is their nature so to do*. Even if a supra-natural divine act must be postulated to explain why such things exist in the first place, no special principle, and certainly not that kind of principle, is needed to explain why once they exist they reproduce. In this way one might defend proto-historicism concerning the genesis of mortal animals.

---

[45] Timaeus only discusses sexual reproduction.
[46] I have discussed the difficulty of making sense of this more fully in Broadie, 2007.
[47] Cf. the view of the sixth-century Zacharias: 'God is the cause of existence, while fathers are only the instruments (*organa*)', reported by Sorabji, 1983, 306.

7.4 Propagation of animals in the Timaeus

However, we are concerned with the *Timaeus*, a work that does more than tell a divine-creation story about this world and its significant contents. For instance, it does more than tell a straightforwardly religious story like the creation accounts in Genesis 1–2, which are perhaps meant above all to show God's benevolent sovereignty over the world that began when he created its various parts. Timaeus's account has religious significance, but his descriptions of proto-historical divine production are *also* scientific explanations and analyses of what the products are and how they work. Plato is as entitled as anyone else to accept that mortal animals reproduce *because it is their nature to do so*. But since he is offering a comprehensive cosmology, he has the responsibility of showing how this reproductive activity is theoretically possible. Even if he cannot explain it in detail, he should at least be able to show how it fits in with the general project of explaining the world as joint product of Intelligence and Necessity. But his effort in this direction is a conspicuous failure, or so I shall argue. The purely natural generation of animals is unintelligible in his framework. Thus keeping his framework opens the way to theories that postulate a perpetually operative transcendent cause.

The verdict of failure is based on comparison. If Plato's account of reproduction is noticeably inferior, this is because his accounts of the other major biological processes show a high level of precise and detailed analysis. 'Irrigation', respiration, and nutrition are explained at length in terms of (a) the relevant parts of divinely constructed anatomy, and (b) the natural behaviour of elemental matter within the confines of the anatomical structures (77c6–81b4). These are mechanistic explanations, but since the anatomy is designed with a view to these effects and their benefits they are teleological too.[48] For example, the first stage of nutrition is said to be due to the action of fire, which by its natural sharpness chops food into blood and by an oscillation takes this from demiurgically constructed belly into demiurgically constructed veins. The next stage is due to the tendency of the elements in the blood (following the law that prevails in the universe at large) to cluster kind to kind. The nutritive oscillation of fire is due to the in-and-out of air in respiration, which in turn is due to the impossibility of a vacuum together with the natural tendencies and forces of hot and cold air in a confined space. This theory of nutrition is worked out with a wealth of ingenious empirical detail sharply drawn. The theories of 'irrigation' and respiration are equally elaborate or more so. In illustrating the co-operation of divine Intelligence and material Necessity these accounts teach *our*

---

[48] The same is true of the treatment of vision, 45b2–46a2.

intelligences to identify and follow the distinct contributions of each of the two great principles.[49]

The treatment of reproduction (91a1–d5) is quite different. This is made less noticeable by the fact that the topic is not presented alongside the other processes but placed at the end of the cosmology, after the discussions of ageing, death, physical and mental diseases, physical regimen, and the care of the soul.[50] It is as if reproduction, to Plato here, belongs with the negative aspects of mortality. Because we are mortal we age, die, are subject to illness (and therefore have to take steps to care for ourselves): and it is because we are going to die that there has to be the reproduction of mortals for the sake of cosmic completeness. It is true that there has earlier been a hint at the more positive cosmic and metaphysical significance of reproduction. This more positive note is sounded by Plato's theory of semen. Semen is marrow from the head (of the same material as the brain) passed down through the spinal column, and the head is the seat of immortal reason (73b5–e1; 91a4–b4). The semen effects, through successive generations, the immortality of the species, thereby answering on one level to the longing for immortality and divine happiness which at the level of the individual can only be fulfilled through the life of reason.[51] On the empirical plane, however, little more is offered than a dramatic description of familiar facts, with no attempt to theorise about how the processes actually work. Plato neither shows nor invites curiosity as to how, physically, the semen's task is accomplished. He has Timaeus portray the male and female reproductive organs as quasi-autonomous living beings; he calls them 'animals', *zô(i)a* 91a2–3; b6; c2. Timaeus says:

---

[49] Cf. Mourelatos, 1991, 12: '... within the limits set by the teleology, the system involves only two factors, geometrical structure and motion'.

[50] Cf. 90e1–3: 'So now the task assigned us at the beginning of accounting for the universe down to the genesis of the human race seems almost accomplished. For mention should be brief on how the other animals have come to be, since it is a matter on which there is no need to speak at length.' They come into being, starting with human females, as degenerate forms, and only with the mention of women does Timaeus begin to speak of reproduction. This topic occupies 26 lines by contrast with 136 lines on the interconnected theories of 'irrigation', respiration, and nutrition, 77c6–81a4. (This passage does, however, include a discussion of medical cupping, acoustic harmonies, and projectiles, which confirms the account of respiration by explaining additional phenomena on the same principles.)

[51] Here I am following the interpretation of Cornford, 1935, 291–3; 355–6. Cornford shows how the arrangement of topics aptly places the theme of the immortality of the species next to that of individual assimilation to God through proper care of the soul, 89d2–90d7; on biological reproduction and immortality cf. *Symposium* 206e; 207 a and d; *Laws* IV, 721b–c. Although, as I argue, the Timaean treatment of reproduction fails as science by the standard of the rest of the mortal zoology (although even here Timaeus can perhaps claim that his account is no less *eikôs* than anyone else's), even so it, like the account of vision with which the mortal zoology began, helps to tie together the immortal and mortal aspects of the cosmos (cf. Chapter 6, section 6.1, on the greatest good of vision).

Appetite [*epithumia*] and longing [*erôs*] on each side bring them together, and – as if plucking fruit from the tree – seed the womb like a fertile field with animals invisibly small and unformed [*adiaplasta*]; and then after differentiating their parts [*diakrinantes*] nurture them within until they grow large instead; and after that lead them into the light, thereby bringing to completion the generating of animals. (91c7–d5)

And that is the extent of the embryology. There is no attempt to analyse the process of gestation, or to imagine in detail any more basic processes by which the offspring come to be differentiated and to take nourishment and grow within the womb. That Plato speaks of the reproductive organs as themselves *animals* indicates that mechanistic analysis has thrown in the towel. For what the mechanistic analyses sought to explain in terms of more basic principles is, precisely, the workings of animals.

It may seem ungenerous to harp on this failure. On the point that reproduction is treated with less scientific virtuosity than the other processes, it may be thought that we should admire virtuosity when present but not make an issue when not, especially in a particularly inaccessible area of biology. There is, however, a deeper reason not to acquiesce in the Timaean account of reproduction: the general framework of the cosmology leaves no room for effective theorising on the subject.

The problem is this: (1) the *Timaeus* seems undeniably committed to a naturalistic treatment of animal reproduction; (2) such a conception, given the fundamentals of the cosmology, ought to be explicable in terms of the two and only two Timaean world-making principles, divine Intelligence and material Necessity; but (3) it cannot be explicated in those terms.

By a 'naturalistic' treatment of reproduction I mean one that aims to deal with that phenomenon as it occurs in the world today, and to describe and explain it in terms of natural objects and natural agencies. Whatever has been the role of transcendent Intelligence in instituting a world with these arrangements, once instituted the creatures belong to nature. This is so even with the prototype animals. They were made by the gods to be real mortal animals, not glove-puppets of gods.

A further look at the text confirms that the account of reproduction involves the PH3 structure (i.e. the feature that displays the present world of nature as the result of divine world-making considered as complete and over). The male and female systems were divinely crafted, and now operate autonomously. The gods devised the generic phenomenon of sexual desire and constructed[52] the physical systems (spoken of as 'animals', as we saw).

---

[52] Cf. *sunetrêsan*, 'they bored a connecting channel', 91a6.

The build-up towards coition is then described naturalistically (91b2–c7). On the male side, the ensouled marrow from the spinal column seizes the chance of an outlet through the male organ, where it implants an appetite (*epithumia*) for emission and a longing (*erôs*) for procreation. The male organ becomes 'unruly and imperious' (*apeithes te kai autokrates*); while on the female side the womb, described as an 'internal living creature desirous of child-making', is in agony if left long unseeded; to the point where the appetite and longing on each side:

> bring them together, and ... seed the womb ... with animals invisibly small and unformed; and then after differentiating their parts nurture them within until they grow large instead; and after that lead them into the light etc. (91c7–d5)

The point of quoting this passage again is to bring out the fact that the subject of the plural verbs is 'appetite and longing'. Thus the picture is of a single process: the same appetite and longing for procreation first arouse each side, then bring them together, then are jointly active within the female right through until birth.

The activity is said to be a *forming of the unformed*, and herein lies the philosophical problem. There is no place for this sort of mindless formation in the great dualistic scheme of Intelligence and Necessity. The domain of Necessity can only submit to formation of the organic structures, not initiate or guide it. And Intelligence goes to work through *intellectual* activity such as the divine demiurgic thinking that gives itself a goal reflectively, works out ways to meet it, takes note (a kind of reflection) of the beauty of the product, makes reasoned decisions prioritising one value such as intelligence in mortals over another such as longevity; or such as the thinking of the cosmic soul that continuously articulates relations of sameness and difference so as to produce in itself understanding (*nous*), knowledge, and firm and true beliefs and convictions; or such as the thinking of mortals, whose intelligence too is intended for truth about identities and differences, but which keeps staggering into confusion through interference by alien impulses, until rescue comes via the deliberate self-care of a *learning*-regime focused on the 'harmonies and revolutions of the All'. Moreover, all intelligence is immortal. The point of mentioning these features of Timaean intelligence in different examples is to bring out the fact that in all these ways the forces that supposedly shape the embryo could hardly be more different. They are mortal psycho-physical forces crafted by the secondary demiurges. So far as animals are subject to these forces they are not reflective; they do not deliberate; their operation is not spelt out by reference to truth, knowledge, or learning; their fulfilment is defined not as

7.4 Propagation of animals in the Timaeus

self-perfecting assimilation to the cosmic harmonies and revolutions of the unique and everlasting cosmos, but as the successful procreation of mortal by mortal. Yet in carrying out their work these forces presumably do what so far only divine demiurgy guided by the extra-mundane paradigm has been shown as able to do, namely persuade material Necessity to contribute to their project.

Notice the absence of even a hand-wave towards a mechanistic account of gestation. If Plato had imagined embryological development on the model of his accounts of 'irrigation', respiration, and nutrition, he would have gestured at a possible analysis in terms of some kind of internal female structure built from corporeal materials and activated by the injection of other corporeal materials on coition. Instead, his chosen agent of formation is the very same combined appetite and longing from each side that initiated the whole process, the male and female cravings working together and both continuing to operate within the womb. Longing and appetite officially fall on the 'soul' side of the soul–body contrast (69c7 ff.; 70d7–8); but here that contrast melts away, since the language at 91b2–4 actually identifies the male appetite with the male sex-organ itself.[53] It is striking that Plato assigns to procreative *erôs* the task of actually developing the foetus, for this makes *erôs* into something very different from the passion as we experience it. This embryological *erôs* can act completely unbeknownst to the subject, and its operation is a marvel of controlled complexity, very different from the dizzy rush of the felt impulse.[54] It seems that with this highly theorised *erôs* Plato is on the way to admitting a third sort of principle into his cosmology, something that is neither Intelligence nor material Necessity nor the combined effect of the two of them. Even though it is a product of divine demiurgy, this *erôs* is a principle because its mode of causation is *sui generis*.

The cosmology began from the axiom that this cosmos is as beautiful and excellent as any generated thing can be. From this it was deduced that its maker (since the cosmos is generated) must have been a good god looking to an intelligible ungenerated paradigm. From these foundations and within this framework numerous accounts were developed of specific aspects of the universe. Narratives of the divine making were at the same time studies of the materials, structures, and workings of the objects made. So that the

---

[53] 'This marrow, being instinct with life (*empsuchos*) and finding a vent, implanted in the part where the venting occurs a lively desire for egress, and so brought it [sc. that part] to completion as an Eros of begetting' (Cornford's translation with slight changes; see Cornford, 1935, 357, note 1).

[54] This is a throwback to Empedocles's Cypris; cf. B98. The sexual *erôs* of *Timaeus* 91c–d passes seamlessly from being the felt passion (before and at copulation) to being an intra-uterine formative agency; i.e. in Cartesian terms it passes from being something 'mental' to being something 'physical'.

contrast, no less than the connection, between originative divinity and originated nature would be clear, i.e. so as to guard against the easy (for fourth-century Greeks) conflation of nature and divinity, the account showed the natural world of today with its divine origination firmly behind it, finished and over. It showed this by showing the divine originative principle making a world not yet made. Thus it was a proto-historical picture. It had to be completed with an account of mortals, including the processes that define mortality: sense-perception, nutrition and respiration, and reproduction. But in a natural world of which the divine origination is over, formative origination in general cannot be over, as mortals must be produced in each generation. Divine origination has to be superseded by a natural power instantiated in a series of mortal individuals to form and give birth to beings like themselves. So even if the world is as excellent and beautiful as anything generated could be, it must contain beings whose excellence of form is due to nature, not to anything transcendent, and due to an aspect of nature that cannot be analysed as the joint product of Intelligence and inanimate Necessity. If *sui generis* biological nature can achieve so much in any given generation, there is no need to postulate divinely minted prototypes to account for excellent biological form. (That made sense only when it seemed that the alternative was the impossible one of making basic matter the principal cause.) But if mortals come to be only through generation from mortals, the series of mortal generations stretches back forever. So, therefore, does the cosmic system within which they live.

In the early Academy thinkers as different as Aristotle and Xenocrates were united in embracing sempiternalism. The arguments in Aristotle for this world-view do not mention a special weakness in the *Timaeus* account of mortal coming to be. Even so, it is interesting to compare the sempiternalisms of Aristotle and Xenocrates in the light of what has emerged in this section. We can see their stances as each representing one of the two elements unstably held together in the Timaean PH3 picture. The picture tries to integrate origination in accordance with the transcendent paradigm with thoroughgoing naturalism about the world thus made. Once prototype mortals become part of the picture we have to accept the asymmetry of a world that began and will not end, and the arbitrariness of its being n years old now, for some indeterminable n. I am not convinced that Plato would have minded those implications. In themselves they do not undermine what the picture was meant to achieve. What makes the structure unstable is the parity (in terms of *what* they produce) of divine and mortal causal powers. For parity of product suggests parity of modes of origin; so if divine origination of mortals is ever necessary or ever dispensable, how is it not

7.4 Propagation of animals in the Timaeus

equally necessary or dispensable for every generation? Either way, prototypes disappear. If each stage has a naturalistic origin, none can be the first; and if each has a transcendent origin, none can be non-arbitrarily first. The structure falls apart into rival monodic sempiternalisms. The version of Xenocrates accepts the Timaean legacy of explaining mortal genesis at every stage in terms of Necessity and transcendent intelligible Forms (like the Idea of Man rejected in Aristotle's *Metaphysics*[55]). The other version, Aristotle's, is based on a new conception of the nutritive and reproductive soul as a non-intelligent formative power. This too is pre-figured in the *Timaeus*, in the procreative mortal *erôs* that appears only at the very end.

When sempiternalism took over amongst Plato's younger associates, he was probably still a working philosopher and in a position to interact with its proponents. This may well have been so when Xenocrates put forth the statement that the proto-historicism of the *Timaeus* was only a pedagogical device. So why did no one manage to get from Plato an answer on whether the Timaean cosmology was really sempiternalist? For it is hard to believe that there would have been no record of the answer had he given one. Thus we have to suppose that if Plato was active during those developments he chose not to discuss the question.[56] Now, if the others were debating on whether to understand the *Timaeus* in a flatly literalist way (i.e. the salient question being whether the Timaean cosmos has a temporal beginning and no temporal end), Plato may have had reason to feel that he should not take sides on this. That would be so, if, as I have argued, he had adopted the PH3 structure to express something serious that had nothing directly to do with theories about the temporal profile of the cosmos. There is also the real possibility that the PH3 structure was his best or even his only tool for expressing the intended relation between nature and its divine origin. Centuries of discussion of the nature of such a relation and its problematic demands of connection and distinctness have brought us terms which Plato did not have, such as 'transcendent' and 'naturalistic'. Thus we can explain the conceptual aim of the Timaean PH3 structure in more abstract terms, and we can try to implement that aim in ways that do not depend on the structure. But with Plato perhaps the situation was this: he could not endorse the anti-literalist interpretation of Xenocrates since this would have entailed abandoning what the PH3 structure stands for; nor, however,

---

[55] E.g. 'Evidently then there is no necessity, on this ground at least, for the existence of the Ideas. For man is begotten by man, each individual by an individual', XII, 1070a26–28, tr. Ross.

[56] Dillon, 1989, 72: 'What is disturbingly plain ... is that the Master himself managed to avoid giving any definitive account of what he meant to his immediate followers. How he managed to avoid this, I do not know, but I see no other explanation of the phenomena.'

could he endorse Aristotle's literalism since this by itself misses the point of PH3. If this was so, Plato's rational course was silence.

7.5 SUMMARY

This chapter has centred on two main questions. What is Plato aiming at in presenting the Timaean cosmology in proto-historical terms? And is he successful?

In answer to the first, I have argued that with the proto-historicism (or at least one form of it) Plato is making a point of considerable philosophical significance. This point has to do with his subject-matter, the cosmos; it is not a manner or mode of presentation that could be replaced while leaving philosophical and cosmological content the same. Therefore the proto-historicism is not solely the pedagogical device that so many interpreters have claimed it to be. For something cannot be 'only a pedagogical device' unless eliminating it would leave the content unchanged in important respects.

However, what counts as 'important respects' is not something on which everyone can be expected to agree. Interpreters would be less disposed to see the proto-historical framework as contributing anything significant to the content to the extent that, for whatever reason, they have invested heavily in the sempiternalist interpretation of the *Timaeus*. This would have been the situation of any ancient thinkers who (i) thought that they had good independent grounds (cosmological, theological, metaphysical, logical) for affirming the sempiternity of the universe, and (ii) regarded Plato as the voice of truth in metaphysics and cosmology. It would also be the situation of any modern interpreters who (whatever their own first-order views about the universe) (i) believe that according to 'real Platonism' the cosmos proceeds timelessly from its transcendent origin, and therefore is sempiternal, and (ii) believe that the author of the *Timaeus* was a 'real Platonist'. Such interpreters have to decide whether the reasonableness of this pair of commitments outweighs the arguments in this chapter.

In section 7.1, I asked why, if the proto-historicism is only presentational, Plato does not make Timaeus drop a hint, or more than a hint, to this effect. I then pointed out that on Aristotle's evidence it would have been perfectly natural for Plato to write his cosmology in proto-historical terms. This naturalness is of course consistent with holding that the system is really a sempiternalist one, but it does underline the oddity of Plato's having given no sign that this is so, if it is so. I also argued in section 7.1 that taking the proto-historicism to be saying something important about the cosmos is not the same as taking it 'literally' if 'taking it literally' means seeing it as first and foremost a flat denial of the proposition that the cosmos has always existed. It is understandable that this aspect should have been uppermost to Aristotle, because his interest in what the *Timaeus* says springs from his interest in cosmology. But his specific focus should not control the shape of the exegetical question for us, who are interested in the *Timaeus* as a creation of the human intellect.

In section 7.2, I distinguished three kinds of proto-historical features in the account, and said that each must be examined on its own merits. The conclusion that any given one does or does not introduce philosophically important content cannot be carried over to the others. I accepted that nothing philosophically significant is lost if PH2, the way in which the cosmopoiesis goes through successive stages, is understood as merely presentational. It was not so easy to arrive at a single conclusion about PH1, the way in which the origination of the cosmos is shown as a transition from pre-cosmic disorder. I argued that the image of pre-cosmic disorder terminated by an intervening separate Demiurge may well be designed to establish the incorporeity of the world-making intelligence: the image puts it beyond doubt that matter by itself could not generate or turn into (and this includes 'timelessly generate' and 'timelessly turn into') the cosmos. Even if some in Plato's early audience did not need the image in order to be certain of the point about incorporeity, this may not have been true of all; and we have no good reason to assume that he was really only speaking to the former from a shared sempiternalism that would have used the image merely as a sort of dressing.

In section 7.3 I discussed PH3, whereby the divinely made cosmos is the world in which we live today. I argued that this structure is meant to exhibit the world both as divinely originated and as a natural system working naturally. By deistically putting the transcendent origination back at the beginning of things, so that ever since it is only in the background, Plato distances himself very clearly from the Empedoclean or Diogenean kind of system, where the corporeal matter of the contemporary cosmos (or some force invested in matter) is the divine crafting Intelligence. I argued that in order to fit PH3 to the fact that the complete cosmos involves generations of mortal animals, Plato had to assume a first or prototype generation, the immediate work of divine demiurgy. The subsequent generations then come to be in the ordinary biological course of things. But a first generation (anyway in the absence of a special explanation to the contrary) inevitably seems to imply a finite time between now and when the cosmos was first complete.

Despite possibly unwanted implications, the main point conveyed by the PH3 structure is of great philosophical importance, in my view. The next question was whether this point could survive replacement of the deistic PH3 picture by one in which divine origination is never over. Still in section 7.3, I argued that the later history of philosophy shows that it is in fact conceptually very difficult, even if possible, to posit constant or continual divine origination without sliding into an occasionalism in which 'second' causes are not really causes at all, so that what we think of as 'nature' is, as it were, an immediate manifestation of divine activity. I inferred that the deistic picture would have been Plato's only way to convey the thought that the world is both divinely originated and a domain of natural beings working in natural ways. Since this is substantial philosophy it follows that PH3 is not a merely presentational feature of the *Timaeus*.

Throughout this discussion I worked from the assumption that if any proto-historical feature turns out to carry a philosophical point which Plato could not have expressed in a non-historical way, this undermines the common anti-literalist claim that incoherences arising from the proto-historicism are evidence that it is to be taken as only presentational. Perhaps there are incoherences in the *Timaeus* account which could be ironed out by eliminating proto-historical elements, but we cannot assume that Plato would have sanctioned getting rid of them in this way if it meant also getting rid of a philosophically important message. Here let me add that the readiness of some interpreters to seize on incoherences as immediately tending to support a sempiternalist reading manifests, in my view, a predisposition not to look for anything philosophically substantial in any of the proto-historical features.

In section 7.4 I argued that the conception of prototype mortals reproducing the species by natural means is unstable. Any account in which the biology of mortal animals produces the same kind of result that divine demiurgy was postulated to explain in the first place raises a double question: is the divine demiurgy ever necessary if sometimes it is not, and is it ever dispensable if sometimes it is not? On this basis we can see the *Timaeus* account as naturally giving way to theories in which each generation is caused in the same way; thus there is no room for prototypes, and sempiternalism becomes the order of the day. I further argued that Plato's account of reproduction fails to make sense within the dualistic framework of Intelligence and Necessity. In effect, Plato treats the mortal reproductive system (shared between both parents) as a distinct third type of principle. Like Intelligence it is formative of matter, but it is mortal and non-intellectual. We can see this as the precursor of Aristotle's nutritive-reproductive soul, just as we can see the motif of the eternal, intelligible, paradigm as hallmark of the tradition commonly known as 'Platonism'. The brand-name reflects the fact that in the *Timaeus* Plato embraces the paradigmatism wholeheartedly, whereas he admits the non-intellectual formative principle only (I think) *malgré soi* and perhaps without properly realising what he was doing.

Having begun this chapter by asking why, if the proto-historicism is only presentational, Plato did not say as much, even within the *Timaeus* itself, I ended section 7.4 with a related question which has puzzled scholars: if we assume that he knew that his associates disagreed with each other on whether to take the account 'literally', why did he not enlighten them one way or the other? The discussion in the chapter suggests answers to both questions. The answer to the first would be that the proto-historicism is not just presentational. The answer to the second may be that, even so, Plato did not want to stamp the Timaean account with the literalism ascribed to it by Aristotle. Such literalism overlooks the point of the PH3 motif as I have interpreted it. Nor could Plato have explained what the point is that Aristotle's literalism misses if using PH3 was his only way of expressing that point.

It may also be that he came to see the conceptual difficulties besetting the Timaean account of the genesis, divine and natural, of mortal animals, and also to realise that some of these difficulties stem straight from PH3. Even so he may have found it impossible to give up the philosophical insight conveyed by PH3. He may have remained convinced that in some way the insight had to be valid, even though, as the history of philosophy suggests, a satisfactory solution to the problem of combining it with sempiternalism was beyond his reach. In the conflicted situation just described, he might have thought that the best thing was to move ahead with other studies (such as the *Laws*) without giving the world his own retrospective take on whether he had been right or wrong to postulate a cosmic beginning in the *Timaeus*. If the honest answer would, as I suspect, have been 'right *and* wrong', yet he lacked the conceptual apparatus to show how this is not inconsistent – then letting it out might have undermined his Timaean brainchild's chance of being taken on as a serious sparring-partner for other philosophers embarking on their own investigations of nature and divinity.[57]

---

[57] Relevant too are the observations of Dillon, 1997, 42, and 2003b, 16, on Plato's legacy (in the early Academy) of free enquiry as distinct from 'a fixed body of doctrine'.

In conclusion

While the chapters of this book are interconnected in various ways, I shall end by retracing aspects of one recurrent theme in particular: namely Plato's concern to repudiate and build bulwarks – mythic but also conceptual bulwarks – against the kind of materialism exemplified by Empedocles and Diogenes of Apollonia. This type of materialism, unlike that of the fifth-century atomists, sees intelligence and purpose as fundamental causes of order in nature, and sites this intelligence and purpose in corporeal matter. Timaeus's speech is crafted for people who share this bent for thinking in terms of cosmic Intelligence, but it provides them with a 'better way' of realising this type of world-view than the way of the earlier teleological materialism.[1]

The figure of the separate and transcendent Demiurge replaces the notion of one or more material principles immediately invested with soul, mind, intelligence, purpose.[2] The figure is inspired, of course, by that of the human craftsman who brings skill to bear on separate materials, 'persuading' them to fall in with his purpose – this being a purpose they could not

---

[1] (i) This is not to imply that the *Timaeus* cosmology does not also target fifth-century atomism, for which soul and intelligence are derivative phenomena, *explananda* rather than first causes. But it has been beyond my scope to discuss Plato's response to the atomists.
(ii) The emphasis of the present book is in line with Menn's 1995 study, which understands the *Timaeus* as a critical effort to improve on earlier systems in which some kind of divine Intelligence is first principle and source of cosmic order. This aspect of various earlier systems has recently been exhibited in detail by Sedley, 2007. See also Gregory, 2000, chs. 1 and 10, and 2007, chs. 5, 6, 8, and 9, for complex and nuanced discussions of teleology in Plato and his predecessors. However, scholars sometimes write as if the teleological approach as such is what mainly differentiates the Timaean cosmology from earlier systems; e.g. Steel, 2001, 105–6.

[2] There is plentiful use of analogies from human artifice in the cosmological thought of some of Plato's predecessors; see Solmsen, 1963; Lloyd, 1966, 272–6. It is not always clear whether reference to an artefact is simply meant to illustrate (1) the principles of working of some natural structure, or whether it additionally implies (2) that the natural structure was brought into being for a purpose. The great Timaean innovation is the interpretation of (2) in terms of a divine source of shaping that is separate from the matter shaped.

possibly have set for themselves. For better or worse, this new model of world-making gives *carte blanche* for infusing cosmology with the most refined *human* values of formal beauty and intellectual fitness. It frees the teleological approach to roam well beyond its starting point of data consisting in patterns and functional arrangements that are obvious in the world of our experience. Such familiar natural structures may be seen as clear evidence of a superhuman intelligence at work in the natural world, and they may elicit from theorists enormously ingenious attempts to explain the mechanisms by which the structures are realised. But they suggest no clear paths of extrapolation to more recondite cosmic values such as the invisible mathematical beauties of Timaeus's particles and the series of ratios by which the Demiurge defines, in parallel, the cosmic soul and our rational souls, thereby also laying the trail for human intellectual salvation. By, in effect, placing *us* in the world-making perspective, the figure of the separate Demiurge encourages us not to hold back in envisaging a cosmos framed to satisfy our own *a priori* criteria of fitness and perfection, which may be as esoteric in their rigour and sophistication as our intellectual powers and education can encompass.

So the separate-Demiurge model is in this way a liberating one for the cosmological imagination. Whether that ultimately makes it a 'better way' is beyond my present remit to consider. We may find embarrassing the ease with which, in Plato's hands, it generates claims whose verifiability is entirely a matter of their appeal to a sense of mathematical aesthetics. Or we may see here seeds of the later victory of the mathematical approach to science.[3] But such a discussion would take us too far afield, especially as the mathematical approach has outgrown any initial foundation in the figure of a human-like separate Demiurge. Our question for now is whether this figure, given other elements of the Timaean mythic construction, offers a better way than the teleological materialism of Plato's predecessors.

I argued in Chapters 1 and 4 that Plato needs the separate Demiurge in order to accommodate in the new context of cosmology what has been presupposed in the ethical and political dialogues: namely, that reason in us is an individualised source of responsibility. Interpreters who in the interest of theoretical economy eliminate the separate Demiurge and give over his function to the cosmic soul, have economised too far, in my view. In effect they try to return the *Timaeus* to a vague pantheism that fudges the difference between human and cosmic reason, failing both to delineate individual human autonomy and to mark off the ethical and cultural sphere from the

---

[3] For a brief and clear discussion of these major issues see Brisson 2006.

domain of natural science. I argued that the *Timaus* preserves and highlights those differences by postulating, in the form of the separate Demiurge, a distinct source for the human rational soul.

It is worth noting that this ring-fencing of human rationality does not result in a chasm of disconnection between human reason and the natural world. This is so because the separate Demiurge is also, by a distinct and prior operation, the source of the rational cosmic soul, which is an intrinsic aspect of the divine cosmos. The cosmic soul is as it were the elder and superior sister of human reason, being made first by the same god and from similar but not identical incorporeal materials. One great task of abstract theology is to make sense of the relations between God the creator or maker of the natural world; the natural world itself; and us. On this front, Timaeus's carefully delimited or partial pantheism, whereby the created system of nature is itself a god within which we live our distinct lives while it exclusively enjoys a life that is just its own, has something to offer that is not so easily available from the austere monotheism whose only god is the transcendent and wholly incorporeal one who created the world. For that kind of monotheistic framework rules out representing the difference between nature and human individuality as based on the difference between a fully immortal cosmic (and therefore physical) divinity and a mortal-immortal intra-cosmic being; hence in seeking to conceptualise what sets us apart from nature it understandably draws on the theme of a direct and special relation between the human individual (or community) and the one creator god who is beyond the world of nature. On the basis of this special human–divine relationship, the human rational and spiritual core can easily seem to stand over against nature, having nothing in common with it. By contrast, in the Timaean scheme nature itself in the form of the cosmic god is the ideal version of a type of which we are imperfect versions.

As well as the separate Demiurge, there is the Receptacle. No interpreter, as far as I know, has maintained that Plato 'does not really mean' the Receptacle in the way it has been maintained that he does not really mean the separateness of the Demiurge or the proto-historical beginning. The problem has always been to understand just what it is that he does mean by the Receptacle. I have argued in Chapter 6 that this figure is introduced to underwrite the basic cosmological requirement that the corporeal materials of the cosmos be amenable to demiurgic organisation.

Their amenability would not, I think, be nearly so problematic if the basic source of cosmic organisation had been the cosmic soul itself. It would surely have been easy for Plato's audience to accept that the cosmic soul *just is* in control of the materials that constitute its body. For this is part of what it is for a soul to animate its body: it maintains organisation of the materials constituting the body. But here are some further consequences of settling for that position: an animating soul cannot intervene wholly *de novo* to take over its corporeal materials; if it animates, it must always have been possessed of some sort of body or other. Well, can one conceive it as fashioning its already possessed body into a more developed form, or as regulating the growth of its body by taking over more and more material from outside? Such possibilities of a developing cosmic body would put in jeopardy Timaeus's basic assumption, intrinsic to his cosmological method, that the cosmos as we have it today is completely perfect, since this implies 'completely finished'. The second possibility above also has the consequence that the growing cosmic body would be at the mercy of collisions with external materials: what if it were damaged before achieving maturity? It seems that the only way to preserve the assumption of the present-day perfection of the cosmos while doing without the separate, i.e. wholly bodiless, Demiurge, is to postulate a cosmos free of any sort of proto-historical nascence or development. Then we should have sempiternity of the perfect cosmos; but with it we should have no clear marker of a distinct source, over and above the cosmic soul, to account for the rational souls of humans.

By separating the Demiurge who accounts for these lesser rational souls while setting him up as also the cause of the cosmic divinity, soul and body, Plato puts him in charge of the materials for that body: but as user, not as animator. The price of this conceptual and mythic development is loss of automatic right to assume that the materials would simply co-operate with their demiurgic organiser – a right that would have been secure if the organising cause were their animator. The Receptacle is Plato's answer to this problem. As metaphysical matrix of the corporeal masses, it serves up fire, water, air, and earth to the Demiurge in all the amenability needed for him to carry out the project for which they are necessary.

If this account is on the right lines, with the separate Demiurge giving rise to the cosmological necessity of the Receptacle, interpretations that see fit, on whatever grounds, to eliminate the separate Demiurge are almost certain to misunderstand the role of the Receptacle. Amongst possible misunderstandings a leading example is the casting of the Receptacle as solution to the purely ontological (supposed) 'problem of participation' inherited from dialogues such as the *Phaedo* and the *Republic*. Some interpreters, I believe, have unconsciously exaggerated the difficulty of this problem precisely in order to make sense of its receiving such a massive 'solution' as the Receptacle.

On the picture so far, the separate Demiurge, which necessitates the Receptacle, is in the system to safeguard, above all, the individuality of human reason. But I also argued in Chapter 1 that if we hold that Plato did not mean the separate Demiurge except as a presentational device we are committed to taking the same line about the proto-historical beginning. If that is correct, then if Plato is likely to have had a good philosophical reason for casting his account proto-historically, that too was a reason for him to accept the separate Demiurge. In Chapter 7 I argued that at least one sort of proto-historical structure was necessary for combining the idea that the cosmos has a trans-natural origin with the idea of it as a world of things working according to their own natures, their operations being theirs and not the ongoing activity of an incorporeal source. Of course, some of the most important natures constituting this world are in fact divine: see the great cosmic god and the astral gods. But this does not affect the point. Considered as working in accordance with their own natures, Timaeus's celestial gods are as natural as the mortal animals.

Insofar, then, as the figure of the separate Demiurge is bound up with the proto-historical structure just mentioned, the Demiurge stands for the synthesis of two disparate things: the status of nature as nature and its status as an expression of trans-natural Intelligence. Separating the Demiurge from the materials of the cosmos ensured that his authorship of the finished product was authorship of something separate from himself (Chapter 1). So too, placing his authorial action at the beginning of history ensures that this history is the distinct career of the cosmos itself and its inhabitants, as opposed to being a phase in the life of the divine source. And even if such a scheme seems unsatisfactory in the light of one or another more streamlined theology, we cannot complain that it leaves us in a world bereft of divinity, because the great cosmic god and the astral gods will always be present.

However, as emerged in Chapter 7, the proto-historical scheme breaks down when we try to apply it to the genesis of mortal animals: transcendent Intelligence is needed to craft the physique of the prototypes, but they by their own unintelligent formative power must, and therefore can, reproduce its work in the subsequent generations. The conceptual instability of this construction topples it over into one or another form of sempiternalism in which the origination of mortals is the same in every generation.

I shall conclude with a brief coda on Aristotle's version of this type of theory. The king-pin of Aristotle's sempiternalism (so far as it applies to the sublunary world) is his concept of the nutritive soul – backed, of course, by his polemic against Platonistic Ideas as causes of natural genesis. Each individual mortal creature is biologically formed by its own nutritive soul, which is a non-intelligent principle of life that regulates nutrition and growth, and reproduction in kinds that self-propagate (*On the Soul* II, 413a20–33; 415a14–b7). Thus the nutritive soul (1) takes over from Plato's divine demiurges the work of producing mortal organisms and their parts. And (2) because the nutritive soul immediately animates the body it shapes, it, unlike Plato's separate Demiurge, needs no Receptacle-principle to ensure amenability in the corporeal materials making up the organism. In another way too (3) the nutritive soul puts paid to Plato's Receptacle. As I argued in Chapter 6, the Receptacle is postulated as somehow explaining the unforced local movements of the inanimate elements. This was because for Plato the alternative – local movement of fire, air, earth, and water in virtue of their own natures – would have meant that they are invested with lives and purposes of their own, owing nothing to the Demiurge or any formative principle, and raising yet again the problem of amenability. It was to exorcise this bugbear that Plato devised the concept of the Receptacle. Aristotle recognises the same four elements. He, however, defines sublunary life in terms of the nutritive soul: an intricate plexus of form-producing and form-preserving functions notably absent from the careers of fire, air, earth, and water. This frees Aristotle to treat the elements as unequivocally lifeless while at the same time straightforwardly granting them their own internal principles of movement and rest (*Physics* II, 192b8–15; *On the Heaven* I, 268b26–29). The fact that they move of themselves to their respective regions carries no presumption of self-assertive vitality, since they plainly lack the form-producing, form-preserving, functions that indicate nutritive soul (*On the Soul* II, 416a9–18). Under this new dispensation there is nothing for Plato's trans-natural Nurse of Becoming to take care of, and accordingly she has vanished without trace.[4]

Such are the consequences of Aristotle's idea of nutritive soul, which operates single-handed in several directions to displace foundational elements of the Timaean system. It says much for that system's concentrated unity that Aristotle's new conception could affect it so pervasively all at once.

---

[4] Aristotle himself seems unaware that his theory of the nutritive soul makes the Nurse obsolete in this particular way; presumably this is because he identifies her with matter and substratum (*On the Heaven* III, 306b16–19; *On Generation and Corruption* II, 329a13–24; cf. *Physics* IV, 209b10–13; 210a1–2) and does not attend to her kinetic role.

Appendix on 'parts of the paradigm'

In Chapter 3, section 3.4, I used the phrase 'a part of the paradigm' (referring to the Demiurge's paradigm). The phrase is a term of art, and I used it first in connection with (1) an intelligible content such that divine demiurgy produces a generated object that accords with it. Then later in the section I used it in connection with (2) an intelligible content that depends on human activity for implementation in the realm of genesis, but which is present to the Demiurge in that his world-making deliberately allows for such human implementations. Thus in terms of (2) an intelligible I is 'part of' the paradigm without being such that divine demiurgy produces objects that accord with I. Now, there is, presumably, a further way in which some intelligibles are 'parts of' or 'in' the cosmic paradigm without being such that divine demiurgy produces objects that accord with them. This would be (3) the way in which Forms of the materials used by the Demiurge to construct the cosmos are 'in' the cosmic paradigm. For the materials are not part of what *he produces*, yet he obviously produces with an eye to their Forms, these being the intelligible natures of the materials used. Similarly, formulae of the ingredients for a stew are 'in' the stew-recipe, but not in such a way as to be sub-recipes for producing parts of the whole that the stew-recipe is a recipe for. For example, a formula for flour is 'in' the recipe for beef and dumpling stew but not in it as a sub-recipe; an example of the latter would be the recipe for the dumplings. So the recipe for beef and dumpling stew, a practical quiddity (cf. Chapter 3, section 3.2) (a) tells us what to make if making that type of dish, (b) features (or presupposes) a formula for flour, but (c) does not tell us what to make if someone wanted to make flour. Now, returning to the Demiurge, the phrase 'intelligible world', with which Chapter 3 opened, can generate confusion. Commentators who speak of Plato's 'two-worlds' metaphysics, especially in the context of the central books of the *Republic* and *Parmenides* Part I, sometimes use 'intelligible world' to mean the whole gamut of intelligibles, this being contrasted with the totality of sensibles. In this sense, it is a tautology that all intelligibles are members of the intelligible world and members of it in the same way, since all that this means is that it is true of each of them that it is an intelligible and not a sensible object. But moving to the *Timaeus*, one can, unfortunately, confuse 'intelligible world' in this sense with the Demiurge's paradigm. (For just as we might call the Form of human being 'intelligible Human Being', so we might call the Form or intelligible paradigm of the [demiurgically organised] world [i.e. the *kosmos*] 'intelligible World'.) It can then seem as if the Demiurge's paradigm contains or features every intelligible (or every cosmological one) in the same way; i.e. it is as if the difference between (1) and (3) above has disappeared. It can then seem as if Plato is committed to the doctrine that demiurgic implementation of the world-paradigm consists in the production, in the sphere of genesis, of the organised cosmos *and* its materials. (Thus the Demiurge does not in fact 'take over' materials that were already around, as said at 30a4; cf. 68e3.) This wholesale way of looking at the transition from eternal-intelligible to generated-sensible, obliterates any difference – crystal clear in the text – between Plato's first and second cosmological beginnings, i.e. between (i) the transition from unformed pre-existing materials to the organised cosmos, and (ii) the prior genesis of those materials themselves. (In one of the two accounts of the genesis of the materials, God is involved, but in this role he is not called 'Demiurge', since demiurgy as such is responsible for the transition from materials to cosmos.) It is now as if there is only one beginning, at which all cosmological Forms without distinction are relevant all at once, so to speak. Erasure of the difference between the two beginnings (or claiming that it is merely presentational) is a feature of the sempiternalist interpretation discussed in Chapter 7. It is also a feature of the ontological interpretation of the Receptacle: see Chapter 6, especially section 6.5. There may be secure reasons for preferring either or both of these interpretations, but the glide of thought just outlined is surely not one of them.

References

Algra, K. (1995) *Concepts of Space in Greek Thought*, Leiden
Allen, R. E. ed. (1965) *Studies in Plato's Metaphysics*, London
Apelt, O. (1919) *Platons Dialoge* Timaios *und* Kritias *übersetzt und erläutert*, Leipzig
Archer-Hind, R. D. (1888) *The* Timaeus *of Plato*, London; repr. Salem, NH, 1988
Artmann, B. and Schäfer L. (1993) 'On Plato's "Fairest Triangles" (*Timaeus* 54a)', *Historia Mathematica* 20, 255–64
Baltes, M. (1976–8) *Die Weltentstehung des Platonischen Timaios nach den antiken Interpreten*, Leiden
Baltzly, D. (2010) 'Is Plato's Timaeus Pantheistic?', *Sophia* 49, 193–215
Barnes, J. ed. (1984) *The Complete Works of Aristotle, the Revised Oxford Translation*, Princeton
Berti, E. (1997) 'L'oggetto dell' *eikôs muthos* nel *Timeo* di Platone', in Calvo and Brisson, eds., 119–32
Betegh, G. (2010) 'What Makes a Myth *eikôs?*' in *One Book, The Whole Universe*, ed. R. Mohr and B. Sattler, Las Vegas, 213–24
Brague, R. (1982) *Du temps chez Platon et Aristote*, Paris
Brisson, L. (1992) *Timée/Critias, traduction*, Paris
  (1998a) *Le Même et l'Autre dans la Structure Ontologique du* Timée *de Platon* (2nd edn.), Sankt Augustin
  (1998b) *Plato the Myth-Maker*, translated, edited, and with introduction by G. Naddaf, Chicago; originally appeared as *Platon: les mots et les mythes*, Paris, 1994
  (2006) 'Plato's Natural Philosophy and Metaphysics', in *A Companion to Ancient Philosophy*, ed. M. L. Gill and P. Pellegrin, Chichester, 212–31
Broadie [Waterlow], S. (1982) 'The Third Man's Contribution to Plato's Paradigmatism', *Mind* 91, 339–57
  (2001) 'Theodicy and Pseudo-history in the *Timaeus*', *Oxford Studies in Ancient Philosophy* 21, 1–28
  (2003) 'The Contents of the Receptacle', *The Modern Schoolman* 80, 171–89
  (2004) 'Plato's Intelligible World?', *Proceedings of the Aristotelian Society*, Supplementary Volume 78, 65–79
  (2007) 'Why no Platonistic Ideas of Artefacts?', in *Maieusis: Essays in Ancient Philosophy in Honour of Myles Burnyeat*, ed. D. Scott, Oxford, 232–53

(2008) 'Theological Sidelights from Plato's *Timaeus*', *Proceedings of the Aristotelian Society*, Supplementary Volume 82, 1–17
(2009) '*Metaphysics* B. 4, 999a24–b24: *Aporia 8*', in *Aristotle, Metaphysics Beta*, ed. M. Crubellier and A. Laks, Oxford, 135–50
(2010) 'Divine and Natural Causation in the *Timaeus*: The Case of Mortal Animals', in *La Scienza e le Cause a partire dalla* Metafisica *di Aristotele*, a cura di F. Fronterotta, Bibliopolis (C. N. R., Istituto per il Lessico Intellettuale Europeo e Storia delle Idee), 73–92
(forthcoming) 'Fifth-century Bugbears in the *Timaeus*', in *Presocratics and Plato: A Festschrift in Honor of Charles Kahn*, ed. A. Hermann, V. Karismanis, and R. Patterson, Las Vegas
Bryan, J. (forthcoming) *Likeness and Likelihood in the Presocratics and Plato*, Cambridge
Burnet, J. ed. (1902) *Platonis Opera Tomus IV, Clitopho, Res Publica, Timaeus, Critias*, Oxford
(1924) *Plato's* Euthyphro, Apology of Socrates, *and* Crito, Oxford
Burnyeat, M. F. (1992) 'Utopia and Fantasy: The Practicability of Plato's Ideally Just City', in *Psychoanalysis, Mind and Art*, ed. J. Hopkins and A. Savile, Oxford, 175–87; reprinted in *Plato 2*, ed. G. Fine, Oxford, 1999, 297–308
(2005) 'EIKÔS MYTHOS', *Rhizai* 2, 143–65
Bury, R. G. (1929) *Plato:* Timaeus, Critias, Cleitophon, Menexenus, Epistles, *with an English translation*, Cambridge, MA.
Calvo, T. and Brisson, L. eds. (1997) *Interpreting the* Timaeus–Critias, *Proceedings of the IV Symposium Platonicum*, Sankt Augustin
Carone, G. R. (1997) 'The Ethical Function of Astronomy in Plato's *Timaeus*', in Calvo and Brisson, eds., 341–50
(2005) *Plato's Cosmology and its Ethical Dimensions*, Cambridge
Carpenter, A. D. (2010) 'Embodied Intelligent (?) Souls: Plants in Plato's *Timaeus*', *Phronesis* 55, 281–303
Cherniss, H. (1944) *Aristotle's Criticisms of Plato and the Academy*, Baltimore; repr. New York, 1962
(1945) *The Riddle of the Early Academy*, Berkeley
(1956) '*Timaeus* 52c2–5', in *Selected Papers of Harold Cherniss*, ed. L. Tarán, Leiden, 1977, 364–75
Code, A. (2010) 'Aristotle on Plato on Weight', in Mohr and Sattler, eds., 201–11
Cooper, J. ed. (1997) *Plato, Complete Works*, Indianapolis
Cornford, F. M. (1935) *Plato's Cosmology: The* Timaeus *of Plato*; repr. Indianapolis, 1997
Coxon, A. (2009) *The Fragments of Parmenides*, 2nd edn., Las Vegas
Cristiani, M. (2003) 'L'ordine delle generazioni e la generazione del tempo nel *Timeo*', in Natali and Maso, eds., 259–74
Crombie, I. M. (1963) *An Examination of Plato's Doctrines*, vol. II, London
Crubellier, M. and Laks, A. eds. (2009) *Aristotle's* Metaphysics Beta, Oxford, 2009
Diehl, E. ed. (1904) *Proclus Diadochus in Platonis Timaeum commentaria*, Leipzig
Diels, H. and Kranz, W. eds. (1964) *Die Fragmente der Vorsokratiker*, Zürich/Berlin

Dillon, J. (1989) 'Tampering with the *Timaeus*: Ideological Emendations in Plato', *American Journal of Philology* 110, 50–72
  (1993) *Alcinous: The Handbook of Platonism, Translated with an Introduction and Commentary*, Oxford
  (1997) 'The Riddle of the *Timaeus*: Is Plato Sowing Clues?', in *Studies in Plato and the Platonic Tradition*, ed. M. Joyal, Aldershot, 25–42
  (2003a) 'The *Timaeus* in the Old Academy', in Reydam-Schils, ed., 80–94
  (2003b) *The Heirs of Plato: A Study of the Old Academy*, Oxford
Festugière, A. -J. (1966–8) *Commentaire sur le Timée /Proclus; traduction et notes*, Paris
Freddoso, A. (1991) 'God's General Concurrence with Secondary Causes: Why Conservation is not Enough', *Philosophical Perspectives* 5, 553–85
Frede, D. (1996) 'The Philosophical Economy of Plato's Psychology: Rationality and Common Concepts in the Timaeus', in *Rationality in Greek Thought*, ed. M. Frede and G. Striker, Oxford, 29–58
Fronterotta, F. (2001) ΜΕΘΕΞΙΣ: *la teoria platonica delle idee*, Pisa
  (2006) *Platone*, Timeo: *Introduzione, traduzione e note*, Milan
Gadamer, H. -G. (1980) *Dialogue and Dialectic, Eight Hermeneutical Studies on Plato*, trans. by P. Christopher Smith, New Haven
Gerson, L. (1990) *God and Greek Philosophy*, London
Gill, C. (1977) 'The Genre of the Atlantis Story', *Classical Philology* 72, 287–304
  (1979) 'Plato's Atlantis Story and the Birth of Fiction', *Philosophy and Literature* 3, 64–78
  (1980) *Plato: The Atlantis Story*, Bristol
  (1993) 'Plato on Falsehood – Not Fiction', in *Lies and Fiction in the Ancient World*, ed. C. Gill and T. P. Wiseman, Exeter, 38–87
Gregory, A. (2000) *Plato's Philosophy of Science*, London
  (2007) *Ancient Greek Cosmology*, London
  (2008) 'Introduction' to Waterfield, ix–lvii
Hackforth, R. D. (1936) 'Plato's Theism', in Allen, ed., 439–47
Harte, V. (2002) *Plato on Parts and Wholes*, Oxford
  (2010) 'The Receptacle and the Primary Bodies', in Mohr and Sattler, eds., 131–40
Hasker, W. (1998) 'Creation and Conservation, Religious Doctrine of', *Routledge Encyclopedia of Philosophy*, ed. E. Craig (on-line resource)
Hershbell, J. (1974) 'Empedoclean Influences on the *Timaeus*', *Phoenix* 28, 145–66
Jackson, H. (1884) 'Plato's Later Theory of Ideas III' [the *Timaeus*], *Journal of Philosophy* 13
Johansen, T. K. (2004) *Plato's Natural Philosophy*, Cambridge
  (2009) 'From Plato's *Timaeus* to Aristotle's *De Caelo*', in *New Perspectives on Aristotle's* De caelo, ed. A. C. Bowen and C. Wildberg, Leiden, 9–28
Kahn, C. (2007) 'Why is the *Sophist* a Sequel to the *Theaetetus*?', *Phronesis* 52, 33–57
Kvanvig, J. (2007) 'Creation and Conservation', *Stanford Encyclopedia of Philosophy*, http://plato.stanford.edu/entries/creation-conservation/
Lampert, L. and Planeaux, C. (1998) 'Who's Who in Plato's *Timaeus-Critias* and Why', *Review of Metaphysics* 52, 87–125
Lang, H. and Macro, A. eds. (2001) *On the Eternity of the World, Proclus*, Greek Text with Introduction, Translation, and Commentary, Berkeley

Lee, E. N. (1966) 'On the Metaphysics of the Image in Plato's *Timaeus*', *Monist* 50, 341–68
Lee, H. D. P. (1971) *Plato, Timaeus and Critias, translated with an introduction and appendix on Atlantis*, Harmondsworth
Lee, S. (2008) 'Occasionalism', *Stanford Encyclopedia of Philosophy*, http://plato.stanford.edu/entries/occasionalism/
Lloyd, G. E. R. (1966) *Polarity and Analogy*, Cambridge
 (1968) 'Plato as a Natural Scientist', *Journal of Hellenic Studies* **88**: 78–92
 (1975) 'Greek Cosmologies', in *Methods and Problems in Greek Science*, 139–63; repr. Cambridge, 1991
 (1983) 'Plato on Mathematics and Nature, Myth and Science', in *Methods and Problems in Greek Science*, 333–51; repr. Cambridge, 1991
Loraux, N. (1986) *The Invention of Athens: The Funeral Oration in the Classical City*, trans. A. Sheridan from *L'invention d'Athènes: histoire de l'oraison funèbre dans la "cité classique"*, Paris, 1981
Marg, W. ed. (1972) *Timaeus Locrus, De natura mundi et animae*, Leiden
Martin, Th. H. (1841) *Études sur le Timée de Platon*, Paris
Mason, A. (2006) 'Plato on Necessity and Chaos', *Philosophical Studies* **127**, 283–98
McCann, H. and Kvanvig, J. (1991) 'The Occasionalist Proselytizer: A Modified Catechism', *Philosophical Perspectives* **5**, 587–615
McKirahan, R. (1994) *Philosophy Before Socrates*, Indianapolis
Menn, S. (1995) *Plato on God as Nous*, Carbondale
Miller, D. (2003) *The Third Kind in Plato's* Timaeus, Göttingen
Miller, M. (2003) 'The *Timaeus* and the "Longer Way"', in Reydam-Schils, ed., 17–59
Mohr, R. (2005) *God and Forms in Plato*, Las Vegas (revised and expanded version of *The Platonic Cosmology*, 1985, Leiden)
Mohr, R. and Sattler, B. eds. (2010) *One Book, The Whole Universe, Plato's* Timaeus *Today*, Las Vegas
Morgan, K. (1998) 'Designer History: Plato's Atlantis Story and Fourth-Century Ideology', *Journal of Hellenic Studies* **118**, 101–18
Morison, B. (2002) *On Location: Aristotle's Concept of Place*, Oxford
Morrow, G. (1950) 'Necessity and Persuasion in Plato's *Timaeus*', *Philosophical Review* **59**, 147–63, reprinted in Allen, ed., 421–38
Mourelatos, A. P. D. (1991) 'Plato's Science – His View and Ours of His', in *Science and Philosophy in Classical Greece*, ed. A. C. Bowen, New York, 11–30
 (2010) 'The Epistemological Section (29b–d) of the Proem in Timaeus' Speech: M. F. Burnyeat on *eikôs mythos*, and comparison with Xenophanes B34 and B35', in Mohr and Sattler, eds., 225–47
Naddaf, G. (1998) 'Introduction' to Brisson, 1998b
Nails, D. (2002) *The People of Plato: Prosopography of Plato and the other Socratics*, Indianapolis
Natali, C. and Maso, S. eds. (2003) *Plato Physicus: cosmologia e antropologia nel Timeo*, Amsterdam
Nesselrath, H.-G. (2006) *Platon Kritias, Übersetzung und Kommentar*, Göttingen

Nightingale, A. W. (1995) *Genres in Dialogue: Plato and the Construct of Philosophy*, Cambridge
Oakes, R. (1977) 'Classical Theism and Pantheism: A Victory for Process Theism?', *Religious Studies* 13, 167–73
O'Brien, D. (1969) *Empedocles' Cosmic Cycle*, Cambridge
 (1984) *Theories of Weight in the Ancient World*, vol. II, Paris and Leiden
 (2003) 'Space and Movement: Two Anomalies in the Text of the *Timaeus*', in Natali and Maso, eds., 121–48
Opsomer, J. (2000) 'Proclus on Demiurgy and Procession in the *Timaeus*', in Wright, ed., 2000a, 113–43
Osborne, C. (1996) 'Creative Discourse in the *Timaeus*', in *Form and Argument in Late Plato*, ed. C. Gill and M. M. McCabe, Oxford, 179–211
Patterson, R. (1981) 'The Unique Worlds of the *Timaeus*', *Phoenix* 35, 105–19
 (1985) *Image and Reality in Plato's Metaphysics*, Indianapolis
Pender, E. E. (2000) *Images of Persons Unseen: Plato's Metaphors for the Gods and the Soul*, Sankt Augustin
Phillips, J. F. (1997) 'Neoplatonic Exegeses of Plato's Cosmogony (*Timaeus* 27C–28C)', *Journal of the History of Ideas* 35, 173–97
Platt, A. (1927) *Nine Essays*, Cambridge
Pradeau, J.-F. (1995) 'Être quelque part, occuper une place: ΤΟΠΟΣ et ΧΩΡΑ dans le *Timée*', *Les Études philosophiques* 3, 375–99
 (1997) *Le monde de la politique*, Sankt Augustin
Quinn, P. (1979) 'Divine Conservation and Spinozistic Pantheism', *Religious Studies* 15, 289–302
Rabe, H. ed. (1899) *Philoponus de Aeternitate Mundi contra Proclum*, Leipzig
Reydam-Schils, G. ed. (2003) *Plato's* Timaeus *as Cultural Icon*, Notre Dame
Reynolds, J. (2008) 'How is the Third Kind in Plato's *Timaeus* a Receptacle?', *Ancient Philosophy* 28, 87–104
Rivaud, A. (1925) *Platon, Oeuvres Complètes, X, texte établit et traduit*, Paris
Robinson, T. M. (1986) 'Understanding the *Timaeus*', in Robinson 2004, 7–22
 (1992) 'The Relative Dating of the *Timaeus* and *Phaedrus*', in Robinson 2004, 33–42
 (1993) 'The World as Art-Object: Science and the Real in Plato's *Timaeus*', in Robinson 2004, 43–64
 (2004) *Cosmos as Art Object: Studies in Plato's* Timaeus *and Other Dialogues*, Binghamton
Rosenmeyer, T. G. (1956) 'Plato's Atlantis Myth: "Timaeus" or "Critias"?', *Phoenix* 10, 163–72
Ross, W. D. (1960) *Aristotle's* Physics: *A Revised Text with Introduction and Commentary*, Oxford
Rowe, C. (1986) *Plato: Phaedrus*, translation and commentary, Warminster
 (1999) 'Myth, History, and Dialectic in Plato's *Republic* and *Timaeus-Critias*', in *From Myth to Reason? Studies in the Development of Greek Thought*, ed. R. Buxton, Oxford, 263–76
 (2002) *Aristotle,* Nicomachean Ethics, trans. C. Rowe, introduction and commentary by S. Broadie, Oxford

Runia, D. (1997) 'The Literary and Philosophical Status of Timaeus' *Prooemium*', in Calvo and Brisson, eds., 101–18
Rutherford, R. B. (1995) *The Art of Plato*, London
Sallis, J. (1999) *Chorology*, Bloomington
Sattler, B. (2010) 'A Time for Learning and for Counting: Egyptians, Greeks, and Empirical Processes in Plato's *Timaeus*', in Mohr and Sattler, eds., 249–66
Sayre, K. (1983) *Plato's Late Ontology*, Princeton
  (2003) 'The Multilayered Incoherence of Timaeus' Receptacle', in Reydam-Schils, ed., 60–79
Sedley, D. (1999) 'The Ideal of Godlikeness', in *Plato 2*, ed. G. Fine, Oxford, 309–28
  (2002) 'The Origins of Stoic God', in *Traditions of Theology*, ed. D. Frede and A. Laks, Leiden, 41–83
  (2007) *Creationism and its Critics in Antiquity*, Berkeley
Shorey, P. (1888) 'Recent Platonism in England', *American Journal of Philology* 9, 274–309
  (1889) 'The *Timaeus* of Plato', *American Journal of Philology* 10, 45–78
Silverman, A. (2002) *The Dialectic of Essence*, Princeton
Siorvanes, L. (1996) *Proclus: Neo-Platonic Philosophy and Science*, Edinburgh
Solmsen, F. (1942) *Plato's Theology*, Ithaca
  (1963) 'Nature as Craftsman in Greek Thought', *Journal of the History of Ideas* 24, 473–96
Sorabji, R. (1983) *Time, Creation and the Continuum: Theories in Antiquity and the Early Middle Ages*, London
  (2004) *The Philosophy of the Commentators 200–600 AD*, London
Steel, C. (2001) 'The Moral Purpose of the Human Body: A Reading of *Timaeus* 69–72', *Phronesis* 46, 105–28
  ed. (2008) *Procli in Platonis Parmenidem commentaria*, vol. II, Oxford
Strange, S. (1985) 'The Double Explanation in the *Timaeus*', *Ancient Philosophy* 5, 25–39, reprinted in *Plato 1*, ed. G. Fine, Oxford, 1999, 397–415
Tarán, L. (1971) 'The Creation Myth in Plato's *Timaeus*', in *Essays in Ancient Greek Philosophy*, ed. J. Anton and G. Kustas, Albany, 372–407
Tarrant, H. (2007) *Commentary on Plato's* Timaeus, *vol. 1, Book 1, Proclus on the Socratic State and Atlantis*, translated with introduction and notes, and with a general introduction by D. Baltzly and H. Tarrant, Cambridge
Taylor, A. E. (1928) *A Commentary on Plato's* Timaeus, Oxford
Thein, K. (2008) 'War, Gods and Mankind in the *Timaeus-Critias*', *Rhizai* 5, 49–108
Vidal-Naquet, P. (1986) 'Athens and Atlantis: Structure and Signification of a Platonic Myth', in *The Black Hunter: Forms of Thought and Forms of Society in the Greek World*, trans. A. Szegedy-Mascak, Baltimore, 263–84; based on 'Athènes et l'Atlantide: structure et signification d'un mythe platonicien', *Revue des etudes grec* 77, 1964, 420–44
  (2007) *The Atlantis Story: A Short History of Plato's Myth*, trans. J. Lloyd, Exeter; first published as *L'Atlantide: petite histoire d'un mythe platonicien*, Paris, 2005

Vlastos, G. (1939) 'The Disorderly Motion in the *Timaeus*, in Allen, ed., 379–99
  (1964) 'Creation in the *Timaeus*: Is it a Fiction?', in Allen, ed., 401–19
  (1969) 'Reasons and Causes in the *Phaedo*', *Philosophical Review* 78, 291–325, reprinted in G. Vlastos, *Platonic Studies*, Princeton, 1981, 76–110
Waterfield, R. (2008) *Plato:* Timaeus *and* Critias, *a new translation, with an introduction and notes by A. Gregory*, Oxford
Whittaker, J. (1969) '*Timaeus* 27d5 ff.', *Phoenix* 23, 181–5
  (1973) 'Textual Comments on *Timaeus* 27c-d', *Phoenix* 27, 347–91
Wright, C. (1992) *Truth and Objectivity*, Cambridge, MA.
Wright, M. R. ed. (2000a) *Reason and Necessity*, London and Swansea
  (2000b) 'Myth, Science and Reason in the *Timaeus*', in M. R. Wright, ed. (2000a), 1–22
Zeyl, D. (2000) *Plato,* Timaeus, *translated with introduction*, Indianapolis
  (2009) 'Plato's *Timaeus*', *Stanford Encyclopedia of Philosophy*, under 'Plato', http://plato.stanford.edu/entries/plato-timaeus/
  (2010) 'Visualising Platonic Space', in Mohr and Sattler, eds., 117–30

General index

(Note: except where a different reference is specified, 'Critias' and 'Socrates' refer to the *Timaeus–Critias* characters.)

Abrahamic theism 11–12, 20
anamnêsis (recollection) 171–2
anatomy, benevolent design of 89
  see also vision
Anaxagoras 17, 21, 175
animation *vs* use of matter 280–1
Aristotle 15, 53, 68, 198, 245
  literalism 246–7, 263–4, 274
  sempiternalism 245, 272, 273
  theory of nutritive soul 276–7, 282–3
assurance (*pistis*) 36–7, 254
Athena 156, 157, 159–60, 164
Athenian empire 132, 135, 140
Athens–Atlantis story
  compared with Timaeus's monologue 169–70
  fictional status of 119, 127, 145–6
  transmission of 127–30, 166
atomism 278
  see also Democritus

beginning, second 181, 183

causes
  vs enabling conditions 175, 176
  one–one *vs* one–many 17–18, 21, 23, 109–10
  primary *vs* auxiliary 174, 178–9, 181–2
Charmides 155
charter-myth 141–3
chôra (space) 190, 203, 212, 214–15, 216, 219–22, 225, 241
corporeal elements
  amenability of 195, 234
  as auxiliary causes 232–3
  disorderly motion of 182
  genesis of 184, 193–4
  geometry of 191–2, 226–7
  non-intelligent, inanimate 9, 25–6, 174, 178–80, 182, 229, 230

  pre-cosmic nature of 182
  rudiments of, 191–2, 194, 197, 235
  separative movements of 190, 227, 228
  transmutation of 187, 191–2, 193, 231–2
  see also Forms of
cosmic soul 15–16, 17–19
  construction of 92
  kinship with human reason 14, 19–20, 21, 95, 280
  parallels with cosmic body 94
  see also pantheism; reason
    in mortals
cosmology
  as Platonic genre 47, 50–1, 52
  vs ethics 123
  vs metaphysics 60, 62, 65, 66, 73, 75
  possibility of 29, 31, 33
  sections of 47, 48–50
cosmos
  beginning of 23–4, 39, 243, 245, 282
  body of 90–91
  completeness of 19, 89, 122–3
  divinity of 12–15
  excellence of 9, 18, 24, 105–6, 234, 239, 242, 281
  and possibility of sense-perception 91
  uniqueness of 16–17, 18–19, 72
craftsmanship, human and divine 29, 37–8, 108–9, 112, 253–4, 278–9
creation *ex nihilo* 10–12, 263
Critias
  identity of 133–4, 153
  polymorphy of 116–17, 147–8, 171
  and Socrates 169
  and Timaeus 168–9
Critias of the Thirty 134, 135, 153–5, 157
  in the *Charmides* 155
Critias, unfinishedness of 118

293

deism 261–2, 263
demiurgic ancillaries 22, 89
Democritus 20, 229
Diogenes of Apollonia 10, 20, 25, 257, 278

eikos (likely), the 184
  as epistemic standard 35–6, 39, 185
  levels of 47
  pun with *eikôn* (likeness) 33, 34
  and refutability 38–9, 43
  see also cosmology, sections of
Empedocles 10, 25, 230, 257, 271, 278
entering and exiting 224–5
Eros 86, 271, 273

females 86, 268
formation 265, 266, 270–1, 272, 282
Forms 189, 190, 205, 209–10
  of the corporeal elements 193, 197, 207–9, 210–12, 213, 215, 216, 217, 222–3, 234–5, 261
  see also images, metaphysical; realism, Platonic; quiddities

Good, Form of the 44, 81

heaviness and lightness 193
Heraclitus 10
Hermocrates of Syracuse 133, 135–6, 140
history 146–7, 148–9, 150, 151–2, 171
  see also memory; records

images, metaphysical 198, 203–4, 212, 213, 217, 218–19, 221
  see also Forms; participation; Third Man regress
immortality, arguments for 97–9
individuality 21, 84, 95–7, 99, 102, 104, 279, 282
  see also responsibility
Intelligence (cosmic)
  and Necessity 174, 181, 234, 267–8, 269, 270, 271, 272
  and persuasion 183, 233–4
'intelligible world', ambiguity of 60, 284–5
intelligibles, thick 71, 74–5, 80
  see also realism
Isocrates 45

luck 156, 157, 159, 160, 234

Marathon, battle of 130, 132, 135, 136, 137, 138, 139–40, 144, 145
mathematics 44, 55
  and metaphysical first principles 78
  and physics 55–6, 78

pure *vs* applied 76
memory 146–7, 160–1, 171
  see also anamnêsis
monotheism 22, 280

naming problems 193, 197
natural disasters 135, 156
nature 258, 269
  vs culture 106, 124, 152, 279–80
  vs the ethical 105–6
  vs transcendent origin 8, 257–8, 259, 260, 265, 269, 271–2, 282
non-negotiable positions 52–3, 158, 236
nutrition etc., mechanistic explanation of 267

occasionalism 262–3, 266
One and Indefinite Dyad 44, 78

pantheism 21, 100, 262–3, 279
paradigm, changeless *vs* generated 27, 66–7
  see also cosmology, possibility of; Socrates, method of
paradigm (cosmic), parts of 82, 123, 284–5
participation 200
Peloponnesian war 133, 135, 140
Phaedrus myth of descent 103–104
plants 91–92
prayer 14, 39–40
pre-cosmic disorder 253–5
pre-cosmic transitions 191
Proclus 61, 71, 93
Prometheus 101, 112
proto-historical structures 249–51, 282
prototypes of mortals 259–60, 265–6
providence 264

quiddities 68, 70, 73, 80

realism, Platonic 63, 80–1
reason in mortals
  distinct from cosmic soul 94
  and embodiment 107
  pre-carnate preparation of 88
  see also cosmic soul
Receptacle, the 186, 188, 189–90, 260–1, 280, 281
  and contents, metaphysics of 197–8, 241–2
  as cosmological postulate 223–37
  and general ontology 198–200, 201–4, 281
  kinetic function of 190, 195, 200, 219, 227–9, 231
  as Mother 189, 194–5, 205, 234
  see also Forms
records 130, 156, 157, 159–60
reincarnation 91, 95–6, 110
reproduction 268–70

responsibility 19, 95, 101–2
  see also individuality
return-feast symbolism 42–3, 118–19, 120, 123, 127, 128, 151–2, 167

self-knowledge 155
semen 268
sempiternalist interpretation 243–4, 245–7, 263
Sicilian expedition 133, 140
Socrates 121–2
  civic ideal of 144–5, 146, 148, 158
  method of 148, 149–50, 159, 162
  see also anamnêsis
Socrates in the *Parmenides* 51
  in the *Phaedo* 45, 120, 126–7, 136, 174–6, 177
Solon 130, 155, 156–46, 156, 164, 165
soul, care of 14
Speusippus 55
stages of world-making 251–3
story-telling 40–2, 47, 136–7, 138, 139, 146–7, 153, 165–6
Strife 230

third kind 186
Third Man regress 70, 74–5, 200
this All 3, 8, 30, 92
this and *such* 187, 188, 189, 204, 205, 206, 216, 218, 231
Timaeus–Critias, dramatic date of 131, 132–3

ungrudgingness 13, 14–15

vision
  chief benefit of 174, 177–8
  nocturnal 180–1
vitality and bone-marrow 110–11

wonder 172

Xenocrates 55, 244, 246, 254, 255, 263, 264, 272, 273
Xenophanes 37

Zacharias 266

Index locorum

AESCHINES
Against Timarchus 173 154

AESCHYLUS
Agamemnon 160–2 14

ALCINOUS
Didaskalikos, 8–10 202

ANAXAGORAS
B12 17

ARISTOTLE
Eudemian Ethics
VII, 1237b33 169
VII, 1238a16 169

Metaphysics
I, 982b9–10 15
I, 982b19–20 172
I, 982b31–983b10 15
I, 983a12–19 172
I, 990a5–8 71
I, 992a32–b1 55
VI, 1026a16 185
VII, 1037a15 185
XII, 1070a26–28 273
XII.6, 245
XII, 1072b13–26 15

Nicomachean Ethics
VI, 1140a1–23 112
VIII, 1159b31 169
IX, 1168b8 169
X, 1177b31–4 15
X, 1178b7–32 15
X, 1179a22–30 15
X, 1181a12–b2 68

On Generation and Corruption
I, 7 15
II, 329a13–24 283

On the Heaven
I, 268b26–29 283
I, 270a12–b25 245
I, 278b18–21 182
I. 10–12 245
I, 279b4–12 248
I, 279b12 245
I, 279b33–280a10 248
I, 280a1 244
I, 280a28–32 245
I, 283a11 244
II.1, 245
III, 300b17–18 245, 246
III, 305a3–4 230
III, 306b16–19 283

On the Soul
I, 403a29–b2 175
I, 403b31–404a9 229
I, 406b20–22 229
II, 413a20–33 283
II, 415a14–b7 283
II, 416a9–18 283

Physics
II, 192b8–15 283
III 202a9–12 15
III, 202a32 15
III, 202b2–3 15
IV, 208a27–29 220
IV, 208a29–31 215, 222
IV, 208b29–209a1 221
IV, 209a23–5 221
IV, 209a24–5 215
IV, 209b10–13 283
IV, 209b11–17 220
IV, 210a1–2 283
IV, 210b21 ff. 215
IV, 212b28–9 215
VIII.1, 245

296

Index locorum

Politics
VII, 1323b39 50

DIOGENES OF APOLLONIA
(Diels–Kranz)
B5 20

EMPEDOCLES (Diels–Kranz)
B6 230
B17, 8 230
B17, 19 230
B17, 20–1 180
B21, 7 230
B35, 8–9 230
B98 271

GORGIAS (Diels–Kranz)
B3 215

HERACLITUS (Diels–Kranz)
B62 87

HESIOD
Theogony 120 86

ISOCRATES
Antidosis
82–3 68
268 45

PARMENIDES (Diels–Kranz)
B8, 9–10 244
B8, 60–1 35
B10 86
B12 86
B13 86

PHILIP OF OPUS
Epinomis 988a5–b7 15

PHILOPONUS
De Aeternitate Mundi, contra Proclum,
 24–6 70

PLATO
Apology
20d–23b 177
30d–e 177
32c4–d8 153
36d1–37a1 136
37e–38a 177

Charmides
155a 130
157d3–5 155

164c5–165b4 155

Cratylus
389b1–3 68

Critias
106a1–b6 14
106a3–4 243
106a3–b7 39–40
106b6–8 114
106b8–108a4 43, 148
108a5–b3 42
108b3–5 42, 129
108b4 43
108b4–5 135
108d1–4 146
108d6 129, 135
108e1 146
108e1–121c5 118
108e4–5 130
109a2–4 118
109b1 ff. 118
109b1–c1 152
109b1–d2 134
109c6–9 116
109c6–d2 159
109c7 120
109d1–2 125
109d2–110a7 146
109d2–110b2 146
110b1–2 146
110e3–111c8 166
111a6 ff. 240
111e3 125
112a1–4 240
112c3–4 125
112e4–5 125
112e4–6 156
112e8 146
112e9–10 169
113a3–b4 130
113b2–4 161
113c2 ff. 116
115b5–6 172
117a6 172
119c1–d2 116
119c6–d1 146
119e2–4 146
120c3–4 146
120d8 150
120e1–121c2 125
121a8–b1 166
121b7 85
121c5 42
121c6 84

Crito
44c–54c 177
51a7–c3 121

Euthyphro
6b7–c7 22

Gorgias
523e1–6 180

Laws
III, 698a9–699d2 141
IV, 721b–c 268
VII, 820c8–9 50
X, 896e6–899b9 264
X, 902b ff. 264
X, 902b5–6 41
X, 903b9 264

Parmenides
130b1–3 200
130c1–d5 51
130c2–4 209
132a1–b2 70, 200
132b3–c11 242
132c12–133a4 70
132c12–133a7 200
133b4–134e8 200
138a2–b6 222
141a5–d5 245
151e3–152e10 245

Phaedo
70c–72d 98
72e–77a 98
73a–76c 171
78b–80b 98
79a6–c1 180
79b7–11 180
80d5–7 180
81e2 111
82d9 ff. 111
83d1 111
85e3 ff. 16
96a–99e 45
96a5–100a3 120
98b7–99b6 175
98e1–99a4 175
99a1 175
99a6–b3 175
99b2–6 175
99c6–8 177
99c8 ff. 177
99c9–d1 126
102b–107a 98

108c5–113c9 126
109a9–b3 33
118a16–17 136

Phaedrus
245c–e 98
246a3–249b5 103–4
246a6–7 103
248a6–b3 104
248c6–7 104
249e4–250c8 74

Philebus
12c1 14
28c6–8 170
29a6–30d8 100
29a9–30d8 100

Protagoras
320c8–322a2 101
321c5–6 101
326c8 69

Republic
II, 378b8–e3 22
III, 414b–415d 143
IV, 424a1–2 169
IV, 441d5–e2 99
IV, 442d7–9 99
IV, 451c ff. 86
V, 475e3–480a13 33
VI, 489d–495b 135
VI, 499c7–d1 121
VI, 506c5–VII, 517c5 33
VI, 508c4–d10 78
VI, 509d4–6 78
VI, 510b4–9 62
VI, 510d5–511a1 76
VI, 511b3–c2 61–2
VII, 514a1–520d4 78
VII, 519c8–520d4 78
VII, 522e5–525c6 78
VII 523a1–524d5 209
VII, 532a1–d1 78
X, 596e5–597e5 28
X, 608e–611a 98–9
X, 614b ff. 96
X, 614b–621b 225
X, 617c5 122
X, 617d6–e5 19
X, 617e3–4 121

Sophist
216a1–2 115
240a7–c5 199

265c1–e6 264
266b4 264

Symposium
206e 268
207a 268
207d 268
210a1–212a5 74

Theaetetus
155d2–5 172
174e5–175b4 86
175b9–d7 78
176e3–177a8 166
210d3–4 115

Timaeus
17a2–3 42, 119
17b1–4 142
17b2–4 42
17b5–7 146
17b5–19b2 161
17c1–3 158
18a5 120
18c1–4 86
18c6–d6 166
18c7 146
18d6–8 146
18e4 146
19a7–b2 127
19b3–c1 119
19b3–c8 117
19c2–3 120
19c2–8 120, 150
19c7 136
19c8–d3 120
19e5 120
19e5–20a1 147
19e8–20c3 142
20a1–2 133
20a1–5 134, 147
20a2 165
20a4 120
20a6–7 147
20a7–b1 147
20b7–c1 117
20b7–c3 42, 119
20c4–6 142
20c4–d1 117
20c5 150
20c6–d1 130, 158
20c7 134
20d7–8 131, 138, 142
20d7–21a3 135
20d7–21d8 117

20d8–1 170
20d8–e1 156, 165
20d8–e4 130
20e1–2 130
20e4 146
20e4–6 128
20e5 172
21a1 130, 146
21a2 106, 131, 133
21a7–b1 130
21b1 157
21b2 134
21b4–d3 130
21b6–d3 165
21b7 134
21c1 156, 159
21c3 146
21c4–d3 165
21c5–d1 130
21d1–3 146
21d4–5 122, 128, 142, 157
21d4–8 156
22a1–b8 146
22a2–4 155
22a5–b3 155
22a7 240
22b4–c2 155
22b6–8 157
22c1–d3 240
22c1–23d1 156
22e4–5 146
23a1–b6 146
23a7–8 240
23b3–d1 155–6
23b4–5 157
23b6–7 128
23b7 125
23c2–3 146
23c3 157
23c3 ff. 61
23c4 240
23c5–d1 125, 128
23c6 165
23d1 156
23d2 172
23d4–e5 106
23d6 ff. 159
23d6–e2 116
23d7 130
23e2–4 130
23e3–4 146
23e5–6 128
24a2–c5 157
24b7–d6 125
24c4–d3 134, 152

24c4–e1 156
24c4–25d6 117
24c5–6 128
24c5–d3 160
24c7 160
24c7–d2 164
24d1 120
24d4 165
24d6 160
24d6–e1 122, 146
24d7 172
25a6 172
25b5–6 122, 128
25b5–7 125
25b7–c8 130
25c6–d3 135, 156
25c7–d8 240
25d7 130, 161
25e2–4 130, 146
25e2–5 159
25e2–26a2 135
25e4–5 131
26a1–2 146
26a1–b2 161
26a4 161
26a7–b1 130
26b1–2 130
26b1–7 146
26b2–c3 161
26b4–7 133
26c2–3 146
26c3–4 130
26c5–7 117, 118
26c7–d3 138
26c7–d5 118, 161
26d1–5 142
26d5–6 142
26d6 118
26e2–27a1 124, 162
26e3 106, 131, 133
26e4–5 42, 142
26e5–27a1 118
26e7–27a2 119
27a–b6 158
27a2 ff. 114
27a2–3 42
27a2–5 39
27a2–7 124
27a2–b6 118, 142
27a2–b8 42
27a3–5 2
27a4 30
27a5–6 61
27a7–b6 61, 141
27a8 160

27b1–4 160
27b4 146
27b7–8 42, 119
27b7–9 124
27c1–29d3 184
27c1–d1 184
27c4 2, 30
27c6–d1 14
27d2–29b2 199
27d5–28a3 128
27d5–28a4 186
27d5–28a6 12
27d5–29b1 193
27d5–29d3 27, 52
27d6–28e4 36
28a1 36
28a2–3 35, 208
28a4–5 52
28a6–29a6 139
28a6–8 52
28a6–b2 13, 27–8, 149
28b2–4 14
28b2–7 33
28b2–c2 12
28b6–c3 8
28b7–8 32
28b7–c2 36, 203
28c1 35, 36, 208
28c2–3 52
28c3 109
28c3–4 18, 85
28c3–29a2 66
28c3–29b1 28
28c4 3, 30
28c5–29a2 63
28c5–29a5 13
28c6 28
28e5–29b2 186
29a1–3 28
29a3–4 47
29a4 9
29a6 92
29b1 52
29b1–d3 34–5
29b2 31
29b3–c3 49, 54, 128
29b4 52, 245
29b5–c1 77
29b8 34
29c1–2 37, 71
29c1–d3 245
29c2 33, 37
29c2–3 162
29c3 254
29c4–5 41, 194

Index locorum

29c4–7 181
29c4–d3 39
29c5 30
29c6 48
29c7–8 43, 47
29c7–d1 45
29c7–d3 181, 184
29d1 129
29d2 23, 33
29d5 184
29d7 3
29e1–3 13, 14–15
30a2–6 8, 182
30a3–5, 29
30a3–6 243
30a4 182, 194, 250, 285
30b1–5 13
30b1–c1 90
30b3–5 229
30b4–5 13
30b5 2
30b7 46
30c2–31a1 90
30c2–31b3 18, 72
30c3–31b1
30c7–8 18
30c7–31a1 30
30c8 3
31a2–b3 7, 29, 30, 90
31a3–b3 3
31a4–32c4 93
31a8–b3 19
31b4 ff. 32
31b4–32c4 76, 93, 230
31b4–34a7 93
31b4–34b3 15
31b4–8 91
31b8–32c4 91
31c1–3 111
31e2–3 161
32b7 111
32b8–c4 230
32c3–4 111
32c5–33a6 93–4
32c5–33b1 7, 17
32c5–b1 29
33b–39d 265
33b1–34a7 90, 93
33c1– 34a7 94
33c1–3 91, 94
34a1–5 94, 107, 258
34a1–8 94
34a8 13
34a8–35a1 253
34a8–b1 194, 243

34a8–b4 230
34a8–b9 41
34b2 17
34b3–36d7 15
34b5–8 17
34b5–9 100
34b10 ff. 18
34b10–c5 232
35a1 ff. 84
35a1–6 95, 253
35a1–36e1 92
35a7 93
35a7–8 183
35b–36c 1, 2
35b2 93
36b4–6 93
35b4–36b5 76
36b7 93
36c2–d7 94
36d8–e5 230
36e2–37c3 22
36e3–5 15
37a5 94
37a5–c3 253
37a6–40d5 243
37b5–6 252
37c–38c 2
37c3–5 229
37c6 262
37c6 ff. 252
37c6–7 73–4
37c6–d1 39, 124
37c6–38a2 244
37c7 18, 109
37c8 73
37d1–38c3 72
37d2–7 73
37d5–7 220
37d5–e7 106
37e3–38a5 72
38a3 244
38a7 73
38b8–9 13, 73
38e2–3 50
39b5–c1 252
39b10 194
39e3–40a1 85
39e3–40a2 51
39e7 ff. 19
39e10–40a2 228
40a7–b6 86
40b8–c3 86
40d3–5 41
40d4 194
40d6–41a3 84

Index locorum

41a3–43a6 84–7
41a3–7 194
41a5 3
41a6 85
41a6–7 41
41a7 18, 85, 109
41a7 ff. 51
41a7–b2 262
41a7–b6 16
41a7–42e6 253
41b7–c2 19
41c3 3
41c8 88, 89, 100
41d1–2 87, 103, 173
41d1–3 258
41d2–3 88
41d4–42d2 101
41d4–42d4 38
41d4–7 20
41d4–8 88, 95
41d5–6 92
41d6–7 103
41d8 104
41d8–42d5 251
41d8–42e4 88
41e1–2 88
41e2–4 102
41e3–4 84, 103
42a1 41, 152
42a3–4 102
42a4–5 86
42a7
42b1–2 112
42b2 87, 100
42b3–5 13
42b3–c4 103
42b4 102
42b5–c4 259
42c1–4 91
42d2–4 102, 123, 262
42d2–e4 19
42e3–4 262
42e5–6 23
42e5–7 262
42e6 ff. 173
42e6–7 103
42e6–43a1 182
42e7 87, 109
42e8–43a1 95
42e8–43a6 111
43a4–44b7 173
43a5 110
43a5–6 107
43a6–44b1 89
43a6–b6 240

43a6–c5 107
43b4–e4 17
43b6–c5 17
43b7–c7 32
43d3–6 107
43d4–7 95
43d4–8 95
44b1 110
44b8–c4 173
44c7–d1 46
44d5 110
45a3–b2 179
45b2 ff. 173
45b2–46a2 267
45b3–4 173
45b4 111
45b4 174
45b4–d7 180
45b7–d6 32
46c7 ff. 233
46c7–d1 233
46c7–e5 177
46c7–e6 174
46c7–e6 174
46c7–e7 53
46c7–47c4 174
46c7–47e1 178
46d1 174
46d1–e2 233
46d4–6 229
46d4–7 13, 179, 182, 233
46d4–e4 229
46d4–e6 178
46d7–e2 st 176
46e3 52
46e6 174
46e6–c4 20
46e7 ff. 178
46e7–47b2 252
46e7–47c4 177
47a1–e2 89, 90
47a3 2
47a4–b2 45
47a7–8 85
47b1 120
47b4 120
47b6–e2 173
47c4–e2 174
47d4–7 53
47e3–48a5 53
47e3–48a7 181
47e3–48e1 181–5
47e6–7 46
48a2–5 53, 183, 233
48a2–52d4 53

Index locorum

48a5–7 182
48a7–b3 48, 79
48a7–b5 183
48b3–5 182
48b3–d1 79
48b5–c2 184
48b7 184
48b8 2
48c2 ff. 185
48c2–d1 61, 185
48d1–2 46, 48
48d1–4 48, 184, 236
48d2 48
48d2–3 79
48d3 48, 184
48d3–e3 79
48d4–e1 14, 48, 184
48d5 246
48d6 46
48e1 79
48e2 2
48e2 ff. 80
48e2–49a4 198, 220
48e2–49e7 187
48e2–52d4 199, 200, 201
48e3–49a4 186
48e4 52
48e4–5 202
48e4–49a1 128
48e6 205
49a2 202
49a3–4 186
49a4–51a3 235
49a5–6 202, 205
49b1–50a2 193
49b2–50a2 187
49b2–50a4 204
49b7–c4 205
49b7–c5 205
49b7–c7 190
49b8–c1 187
49c1 187
49c7–d1 187
49d4 187
49e7 202
49e7–8 188
49e7–50a4 188
50a2–3 189
50a2–4 202
50a4–5 205
50a5–e10 188–9
50a6 196
50b1 196
50b6 205
50b6–8 202

50c 189
50c1–5 224
50c2 202, 205
50c3 188
50c4–5 205
50c4–52a7 51
50c5 73
50c7–d2 198
50c7–d4 205
50d1 73
50d1–2 189
50d2–3 194
50d5–51b6 205–6
50e1 224
50e2–4 189
50e5 202
50e6 200
51a1 189, 205
51a1–2 73, 202
51a1–3 189
51a4–5 205
51a4–8 189
51a6 189
51a7 189, 202, 220
51a7–b1 206
51a7–b2 186, 189
51b4–6 189
51b6 204, 205
51b6–7 206
51b6–52d1 206
51b6–52d4 190, 235
51b7–8 217, 222
51b7–c5 207, 215
51b7–e6 235
51b8 211
51b8 ff. 222
51c1–3 235
51c2 208
51c4–5 211
51d2 208
51d3 237
51d3–52a7 128
51d3–7 208, 216
51d3–e8 211
51d7 208
51e1–6 208, 212
51e6 212, 216–17
51e6–52b1 198
51e6–52b2 213–14
51e6–52d1 199
51e6–52e1 235
52a1–b2 212
52a5 73
52a5 ff. 222
52a7 36, 208

52a8 219
52a8–d3 203
52b1 202
52b2 186, 233
52b3–5 203, 221
52b3–d1 214–15
52b4–5 219
52b6–c5 218
52c2–3 73
52c2–5 203
52c4–5 214
52d2 237
52d2–4 216
52d3 219
52d3–4 198
52d3–53a7 190
52d4–53a7 190, 200, 227–8
52d5 189
52e1–5 228
53a5–b5 250
53a7–8 191
53a7–b1 2
53a7–b5 196
53a7–b7 190–1
53a8 197
53b1–3 174
53b4–7 194
53b5 192
53c1–2 246
53c1–3 76–7
53c4–54a7
53c4–55c4 76
53c4–6 193
53d4–6 76, 192
53d4–7 79, 185
53d5–6 46
54a4–b2 40, 50
54b5–8 196
54b5–d3 192
54d3–55c4 192
55c7–d6 3, 30
55d6–56b6 76, 192
55d8–56a3 193
55d8–56b3 195
56a1–b6 46
56b7–c3 192
56b7–c7 b 180
56c3–7 192
56c3–8 194
56c5–6 183
56c5–7 233
56c8–d1 46
56c8–d5 227
56e7–57b7 226
57a7–c6 190

57b2 234
57b7–c6 195
57c7–d5 192
57c8–d5 46
57d5–7 46
57e1–58a2 228
58a2–4 195
58a2–c4 190
58c1–4 228
59c5–d2 44, 45
58c5–e2 192
59c6 48
60b6–61c2 51
61d5–62a5 227
64a2–68d6 32
64a2–68d7 180
64a7–c3 193
64e4–5 193
65b7–c3 45
65d2 193
66a4–5 193
67c4 ff. 181
67c7 193
67d1 46
67d3 193
68c6–7 174
68d2 46
68e1–3 194
68e1–4 182, 243
68e1–69a4 176
68e1–69c6 181
68e2 174
68e3 8, 250, 285
69c7 86
69a5–b2 181–2
69b2–c3 194, 196
69b2–c7 191
69b3–4 250
69b3–c3 243
69b6–8 193
69c–73a 265
69c1 250
69c3–4 194
69c5–6 182
69c7 ff. 271
69c7–d6 108
69c7–72d3 104
69c8 86
69d5 86
69d6–73b1 252
69d7–70a7 89
70a7–c1 89
70c1–d6 89
70d7–8 271
70d7–71a3 89

Index locorum

71a3–b1 22
71a3–d4 89
72a4–6 155
72c1–d3 89
72d4–8 55
72d7–8 46
72e3–73a8 89
73b1–c1 228
73b1–e1 111
73b3–4 110
73b3–76e6 252
73b5–c3 227, 236
73b5–e1 268
73b8 ff. 22
73c3 110
73d5–6 110
73e1–5 227, 228
74c5–d4 227
74d6 ff. 22
74d7 111
74e10–75c7 176
75b2–c7 89
75b4 234
75b7–d2 ff. 22
75c5 89
75d1–5 89
75d7 89
76b1–d3 51
76c6 89
76d8–e6 91
76e1 89
76e7–77c5 91
77c–81e 265
77c6–81a4 268
77c6–81b4 267
77c8–81b4
78a1–79e9 227
80d1–7 227
81e6–82a7 234
86b1–87b9 105
87a7–b6 18
87b4–6 105
88c1 120
88d6 202
88d6–89a1 234
89d2–90d7 268
90a2–d7 14, 20
90c6–d5 173
90e1–3 268
90e2 2
90e3–92c3 103
90e6–91a1 259
90e8 46

91a1–d5 268
91a2–3 268
91a4–b4 268
91a6 269
91b2 268
91b2–4 271
91b2–c7 270
91c2 268
91c7–d5 269, 270
91d5–92c3 259
91d6–92c1 228
91d6–92c3 91
91e3 120
92a5–9, 13
92c4 2
92c4–9 41, 251
92c6 3
92c6–9 13
92c7 73
92c8–9 3

PROCLUS
de Aeternitate Mundi
  Argument 2 70
in Parmenidem IV, 888.29–890.11 75
in Parmenidem IV, 911.27–913.11
  75
in Timaeum I, 1A; 4A; 4F 61
in Timaeum V, 316A 93
in Timaeum III, 140A; 144C 90

SAPPHO
Fr. 118 157

THUCYDIDES
II. 37.1 148
II. 43.2 156
VI. 33.5 140
VI.76.4 140

XENOPHANES (Diels–Kranz)
B23 37

XENOPHON
Memorabilia
I. ii. 12 154
I. ii. 14 154
I. ii. 29–31 153
I. ii. 31 ff. 153
I. iv. 8 20, 100

ZENO OF ELEA (Diels–Kranz)
A24 215

Lightning Source UK Ltd.
Milton Keynes UK
UKOW03f2258100714

234893UK00001B/85/P